Controlling the Dangerous Classes

A Critical Introduction to the History of Criminal Justice

Randall G. Shelden

University of Nevada-Las Vegas

Allyn and Bacon

Boston • London • Toronto • Sydney • Tokyo • Singapore

Editor-in-chief, social science: Karen Hanson
Series editorial assistant: Karen Corday
Composition and prepress buyer: Linda Cox
Manufacturing byer: Megan Cochran
Cover administrator: Brian Gogolin
Editorial-production service: Modern Graphics, Inc.
Electronic composition: Modern Graphics, Inc.

Copyright © 2001 by Allyn & Bacon
A Pearson Education Company
Needham Heights, Massachusetts 02494

Internet: www.abacon.com

Library of Congress Cataloging-in-Publication Data
Shelden, Randall G., 1943-
   Controlling the dangerous classes : a critical introduction to the history of
criminal justice / Randall G. Shelden.
      p. cm.
   Includes bibliographical references and index.
   ISBN 0-205-31889-4 (pbk.)
      1. Criminal justice, Administration of—United States—History. 2.
Crime—Government policy—United States. 3. Prisons—United States—
History. 4. Juvenile justice, Administration of—United States—History. I.
Title.

HV9950 .S54 2000
364.973—dc21
                                                            00-040133
Printed in the United States of America.

10 9 8 7 6 5 4 3 2 1   05 04 03 02 01 00

Contents

Foreword

Documented and interpreted in this book is the rise of the modern phenomenon of criminal justice. We move from the making of criminal law to the enforcement and administration of the law to the punishment and confinement of the offenders of the law—and, finally, to the new millennium and its industry of crime control. In the larger perspective, *Controlling the Dangerous Classes* is part of the long tradition of bearing witness to the important events of the times. Randall Shelden, as author, is bearing witness in a comprehensive and critical analysis of the development and practice of what has become known as *criminal justice.* In a fundamental and essential way, this book is the bearing of witness to the *injustices* of the criminal justice system. This is accomplished through a deep sense of what transcends criminal justice—social justice.

As criminologists, we are witnesses to the various forms of violence, to the atrocities, and to the sufferings of many people. As with journalists, photographers, peace workers, and fellow social scientists, we witness and report the sufferings throughout the world. Observations and reports are made of the Holocaust, the ethnic wars, illness and starvation, sexual abuse, and the many other sufferings of being human in the modern world.

The witness obviously is not a neutral observer that a simplistic dichotomy of active agent and passive observer might suggest. The witness is certain to be in the right place at the right time—and, once being there, is moved by conscience to actively observe and report what is being witnessed. If actions more physical in nature follow, they follow because first there has been the witnessing. Without prior witnessing, there will be no subsequent action that is wise and appropriate. Witnesses act with clarity and purpose because they have the awareness and conscience of a witness. Ready and with open mind, the witness truly sees what is happening, and knows what further action is to be taken. Without witnessing, any action is unfocused, confused, and little more than chasing the wind.

There is plenty for the criminologist to witness. Make your own list of what we as criminologists should be witnessing. My own current witnessing is to the kinds of suffering and violence that are a systematic and structured part of contemporary existence. In fact, the largest portion of violence is structured and is generated by or committed by governments, corporations, the military, and agents of the law.

The war at home is against the poor. It is a war that is waged to maintain inequality so that the rich can maintain their position. Whole populations are being held hostage in poverty, sickness, addiction, and brutality against one another—remaining unemployed, underemployed, and uneducated. Prisons are overflowing, and prison construction and operation are growing industries. The rich not only create the war to secure their position but also profit from the war. In our own nonviolent actions and protests, founded on witnessing, we take our stand. "Which side are you on?" is still the relevant question.

Directly associated with the war on the poor—the war to keep a minority of the population rich—is capital punishment. The death penalty—state-sponsored murder—is the final resort of a violent and greedy minority. That so many (the majority of the population when polled) support the practice of capital punishment is all the more reason that criminologists as witnesses are needed to expose, to analyze, and to protest. Someday, I am certain, historians will note that the United States was one of the last nations to continue to violate the most basic of human rights: the right to life. It was one of the last nations to systematically violate the rights of its own citizens.

Everything we do as criminologists is grounded in a moral philosophy. Whatever we think and do, our criminology is the advancement of one moral philosophy or another. And each moral philosophy generates its own kind of witnessing—in the events to be witnessed and in the form of the witnessing. The work in criminology that is historically important is the work that is informed by a moral philosophy. As witnesses, we are on the side of life; a reverence for all life. Such is the way of peace.

Richard Quinney

Preface

This book was many years in the making. I recall writing significant portions of Chapter 1 (on the historical development of the law) back in 1977, when I was a "rookie" in the academic field. I had just accepted a position as Assistant Professor at the University of Nevada-Las Vegas in the Department of Criminal Justice. One of the classes I was going to teach was "Introduction to Criminal Justice." In the summer of 1977, I began to review introductory criminal justice textbooks in order to decide which book to assign to students in my class. I was rather shocked to find literally no book that I thought did a decent job of not only describing how this system worked (I mean *really* worked) but also why. I recall thinking that I should try to write my own. So I began doing just that, starting with what is now Chapter 1 of the present book. As it turned out, I did write an introduction to criminal justice, and a large part of Chapter 2 of that book was the historical development of criminal law. There were several chapters in that book devoted to the history of different components of the criminal justice system (besides the law, separate chapters were devoted to histories of the police, prisons, and juvenile justice—something totally unheard of then and now, as far as introductory criminal justice texts are concerned) (Shelden, 1982).[1]

I had developed an avid interest in history throughout my graduate-school years, which continued after I became a college professor. In fact, my dissertation was on the emergence of juvenile justice in Memphis, Tennessee (Shelden, 1976). Shortly after the publication of my textbook, I began to think about writing a more complete book on the history of the criminal justice system. My original goal was to compile a reader on the subject. I even had a rough outline of the readings that would be included. In time, other matters began to interfere—as they often do in academia—and I eventually put this project on the shelf. But I never completely forgot about it; it remained something I longed to do.

About two years ago, I began to work on a revised edition of that original introduction to criminal justice textbook. While working on that revision (which has yet to be completed), I began to update some of the original historical material. It finally dawned on me that I was actually writing not one but *two* books and that the historical material was enough for a totally separate book. An old dream was resurrected, and so I decided to write that history book after all. The result is the book you have before you.

This project involves a passion I have had since my graduate-school days; namely, the subject of history. I recall becoming fascinated by the history of the criminal justice system. While working on my dissertation, I would spend several hours in the library, not in the sociology or criminology section, but in the history section. I suppose what fascinated me most was the persistent fact that in so many ways history keeps repeating itself and that we somehow never seem to learn from it. But what I learned most of all is this: Because we often repeat history (as the philosopher Santayana once said, those who fail to study history are doomed to repeat it), it occurred to me that *things don't just happen by accident* and that if history does in fact repeat itself, then there is a reason for the persistence of some social phenomena. If we examine something happening today and then go back in history and find that it has occurred not once or twice but *repeatedly*, then the problem is much deeper than we imagined. As sociologists, we are supposed to look for *patterns* of human interaction and social processes. At least, that is what some of the leading figures in sociology have suggested (e.g., Marx, Durkheim, Weber, and especially C. Wright Mills). If something persists, there must be an important reason. If someone begins to look at the conditions within many juvenile "correctional" institutions and finds that they are often appalling and, in some cases, a violation of human rights, there is the tendency to believe that this is just a product of some current and unusual situation. But if we look deeper, and look at it historically, we quickly learn that this is a *pattern* that can be traced back at least as far as the houses of refuge in the early nineteenth century. In doing so, we will realize that this current "appalling" situation is not some aberration but rather part of a long tradition. We may realize that this is so because *this is how we have always treated those without much power and influence in society*. We then know what we are up against if we are going to make changes.

This realization is what has guided me in the writing of this book. Looking at the past is important because it takes us to the present and then into the future. Some who read these passages will recognize the influence of one of my favorite historians, Howard Zinn, who has influenced me more than any other historian. It was his book, *The Politics of History* (first published in 1970 and revised in 1990), that had a profound influence on me during my graduate-school days in the early 1970s. I have never forgotten some of the lessons learned from reading that book, as well as his *A People's History of the United States* (1995).

I have also learned much from someone who technically is not a true historian (to call someone *technically* not a *true* historian seems rather crude as I write these lines because it suggests that the only people who can possibly be real historians are those with the proper credentials—namely, having a degree in the subject—which is obviously not the case): Noam

Chomsky. Something he wrote in one of his books struck me as being extremely significant and insightful—significant in the sense that he simply asked what should be a rather common-sense question having to do with history. In his book *Year 501: The Conquest Continues*, Chomsky was writing about the bombing of Pearl Harbor, the "date which will live in infamy," as Franklin D. Roosevelt put it. In typically Chomskian language, he remarks that in all the talk about Japanese aggression, one important question is omitted: "How did we happen to have a military base at Pearl Harbor, or to hold our Hawaiian colony altogether?" In other words, what were we doing there in the first place? The answer is: We "stole Hawaii from its inhabitants, by force and guile, just half a century before the infamous date, in part so as to gain the Pearl Harbor naval base" (Chomsky, 1993: 243). A tough question, to be sure, but the kind that is rarely asked. Such are the kinds of questions I try to raise in this book.

This book is about asking critical questions such as "What is a crime?" and "What is law?" and "Whose interests are served by the law and the criminal justice system?" and "What are the patterns that are constantly repeated?" and "How does such a system relate to larger issues such as social inequality, social class, race, and gender—especially social class?"

One final comment is in order so there will be no confusion about my own perspective, which guides the direction and content of this book. I do not subscribe to some simple, easy-to-state "theory" of the law and the criminal justice system. I do not classify myself as an avowed supporter of one theory or another. My general orientation (as will soon be obvious) is quite critical, even Marxist in many ways. I am not going to argue that there is some vast conspiracy among the "ruling class" (there is in fact a ruling class and they do in fact rule, but their rule is not monolithic; see Domhoff, 1998) to use the law and the legal system to trample on the rights of ordinary citizens, especially the poor. Nor am I going to argue that every law is a mere reflection of the interest of this class—or any class, for that matter. What I will argue is that, when looking at the *results* of the law in general and the daily operations of the criminal justice system—that is, the outcomes of legal decision—the entire system *generally* comes down hardest on those with the least amount of power and influence, and *generally* comes down in the most lenient fashion on those with the most power and influence. I am not going to try to advance a new theory of lawmaking; that I leave to others. My purpose here is to show the inherent bias in the American system of law and justice—a bias generally based on social class, but also on race, gender, and age—and to show how it is grounded in the historical development of the law and the criminal justice system.

This book is not meant to provide an encyclopedic coverage of the history of criminal justice in America. Books by others provide a great deal of detail that is omitted here. Rather, this book is an introductory overview—a *primer* if you will—of the subject. Literally thousands of articles and several recent books can be consulted if you are interested in probing deeper into this subject (see the references at the end of this book).

As in any scholarly endeavor, many people need to be thanked for their assistance. The author wishes to extend his personal thanks to a most helpful critic, Robert Weiss, for some very insightful comments on earlier drafts of this book. Thanks also to Nicole Rafter for her comments on an earlier draft. My thanks to a true friend, Bud Brown (to call him just a colleague would not do justice), for his support (not only sharing ideas about crime and criminal justice but also about life in general) over the years and his contribution to Chapter 3. To Richard Quinney, deep gratitude is extended, not only for writing the foreword to this book but also for his inspiration throughout my thirty-year career as an academic criminologist. Richard, your words so long ago have remained with me all these years as an inspiration—and your words today in another way also inspire. Thanks also to Noam Chomsky for his encouragement in developing some of my own critical insights concerning the nature of our society and the distribution of power (from not only many of his books but also from the innumerable conversations in person and via e-mail). Thanks also to Howard Zinn, for some encouraging words via his books, recorded speeches, and e-mails. To Allyn and Bacon editor Karen Hanson, thanks for your tremendous support—extending a contract for this book was a real confidence-builder.

As always, for standing beside me with patience and love, thanks are extended to my wife Virginia. Once again, she had to tolerate a major project of mine. I promise to skip a few months between the end of this project and the next one!

Note

1. In case anyone is interested, this book was originally published by a small company called Winthrop Publishing. Shortly after the first printing of this book (Fall 1981), the company was purchased by Little, Brown.

Introduction

The History of Criminal Justice from a Critical Perspective

One of the twentieth century's most eminent historians, Howard Zinn, once wrote that "history is written from records left by the privileged" (Zinn, 1990: 102). By this he merely meant that historical writings tend to be biased and written from the point of view of those in power. Similarly, the history of criminal justice is written largely from the point of view of those in power. In this case, we see a history that, among other things, takes the law for granted and too often treats the criminal justice system in a social, political, and economic vacuum. Such standard histories also largely ignore critical issues such as class, race, and gender in the analysis. Moreover, the effect of the development of capitalism is rarely discussed. Issues such as racism, inequality, poverty, and class conflict are rarely raised. If they are, it is usually merely in passing, as if they were aberrations in an otherwise ideal system.

A typical example comes from one of the most popular histories of criminal justice, written by Samuel Walker. At one point he discusses the issue of "vigilantism" in the 1700s and correctly notes that it was one method among many of the elite to control the "dangerous classes." However, he then notes that this phenomenon "formed a violent and ugly scar on the history of criminal justice" (Walker, 1980: 32–33).[1] But was this merely a "scar" or was it part of a much larger pattern that has repeated itself throughout our history? A more careful look at history reveals that such scars have continued to appear, over and over again, well into the present era. (Need we look any farther than the beating of Rodney King or the systematic incarceration of millions of African Americans throughout the 1980s and 1990s?)[2]

Zinn also noted that in writing history, the historian cannot be neutral, because "he writes on a moving train." Thus, your history is naturally

1

biased—but so are all the other histories. Zinn notes that "our work is value-laden whether we choose or not" (Zinn, 1990: 35–36.) Therefore, I would like to state categorically that this book is in this sense "biased." It takes a critical approach to the subject matter. And what do I mean by a "critical approach"? By taking a critical approach, which implies a conscious and deliberate inquiry of the criminal justice system, students are encouraged to search for obscure assumptions, identify various facets, unravel different strands, and evaluate what is most significant. A critical approach necessitates the use of our imaginations, and requires us to look at things from perspectives other than our own and to consider the *consequences* of each perspective.

A critical perspective also utilizes what C. Wright Mills called the *sociological imagination*. By this Mills meant that the best way to understand the world around us is to "grasp history and biography and the relations between the two within society." More specifically, he wrote that through the use of this method, "the individual can understand his own experience and gauge his own fate only by locating himself within his period [of history]. . . ." Using the sociological imagination causes us to distinguish between what Mills called *personal troubles of milieu* and *public issues of social structure*. By *personal troubles*, Mills referred to those very personal, private matters that "occur within the character of the individual and within the range of his immediate relations with others." A problem becomes a *public issue of social structure* when the issue has to do with "matters that transcend those local environments of the individual" and when "some value cherished by publics is felt to be threatened" (Mills, 1959: 5–8).

Critical thinking includes, among other things, attempting to transcend the current social order and institutional arrangements. Through this process we no longer merely accept "what is"; rather, we attempt to visualize "what could be." Paraphrasing the late Senator Robert Kennedy, some may think about what is and ask why, while others (i.e., critical thinkers) think about what could be and ask why not. Quinney has suggested that critical thinking means developing the ability to "think negatively, through oppositions." Such a method of thinking allows us "to entertain alternatives" and to move to "reconstruct our lives" while breaking free of the current ideology (Quinney and Wildeman, 1991: 37). Michalowski suggests that critical thinking involves exercising "careful judgment or judicious evaluation" and, with respect to the critical study of crime, that such a perspective "demands that we examine not only what the law says is crime but also *why* the law says it is so. To do this we must dig beneath the everyday assumptions and unquestioned 'truths' about crime and examine the social, economic, political, and historical roots of both crime and the ideas about it that are taken for granted" (Michalowksi, 1985: 14).

A critical historical perspective can help us address the question of "why not" because, in looking back, we might be able to see with greater

clarity what "could have been." Zinn has argued for wh
history." By this he means a "value-laden historiograph,
puts it, you "can't be neutral on a moving train."[3] He suggests,
tory can be useful from this perspective: (1) "We can intensify,
sharpen our perception of how bad things are, for the victims of the wor.
(2) "We can expose the pretensions of government to either neutrality or
beneficence"; (3) "We can expose the ideology that pervades our culture—
using *ideology* in Mannheim's sense: rationale for the going order"; (4) "We
can recapture those few moments in the past that show the possibility of a
better way of life than that which has dominated the earth thus far"; and (5)
"We can show how good social movements can go wrong, how leaders can
betray their followers, how rebels can become bureaucrats, how ideals can
become frozen and reified" (Zinn, 1990: 36–55). Admittedly, this is quite a
task, and in this book I will try to accomplish at least some of what Zinn has
suggested.

Part of what Zinn is suggesting is that a critical perspective (or in his
words, *radical history*) seeks to achieve what critical criminologists call *social
justice*. By this term I mean a form of justice that "is appropriate for a society
based on cooperative social relations" rather than relations based on human
exploitation and greed (Quinney and Wildeman, 1991: 15). Unfortunately,
our modern system of justice takes place within a society that is highly stratified by race, class, and gender. It is my contention that *equal justice cannot be
achieved in an unequal society.* The justice system in American merely rein-
forces these inequalities. Social justice, in contrast, seeks to eliminate such
systemic problems as poverty, racism, sexism, and class inequality that generate most of the crime we experience.

Social class is of crucial importance in the shape of many patterns of
social life, as a multitude of studies have demonstrated (Domhoff, 1998;
Gilbert, 1998; Rothman, 1998). However, there are important interconnec-
tions between race, gender, and class that always need to be considered.[4]
When viewing the history of criminal justice, all three are quite important in
that class, race, and gender bias is systemic in American society, which has
serious consequences for the criminal justice system, as well as all other
major institutions. It will be shown throughout this book that all three variables have been important in terms of the passage of criminal laws and their
enforcement; that is, class, race, and gender bias are operating at every
stage. Yet, while not downplaying the importance of race and gender, I will
treat class as the most important variable. The reasons should become
apparent to the reader; however, some preliminary remarks about the
importance of class are in order at this time.

As the title of a recent book suggests, "class counts" (Wright, 1998). As
far as the criminal justice system is concerned, social-class position determines in large part the following: (1) which behaviors come to be defined as
"criminal" and thus subject to their enforcement; (2) *who* is defined as "crim-

al"; (3) how far into the criminal justice system a particular case is processed; and (4) the final sentence of a criminal case. Class is also related to whether one can make bail and whether one has an attorney, and even the quality of the representation (Cole, 1999; Reiman, 1998).

A critical perspective also challenges the conventional wisdom about the nature of our criminal justice system by arguing that the system not only fails in its duty to protect us from crime and make us feel safe, but also that it is actually *designed to fail*. In making this argument, I am borrowing the ideas of Jeffrey Reiman, who calls this way of looking at criminal justice the *Pyrrhic defeat theory*. In military terminology, a *Pyrrhic victory* is when a particular battle is won but the costs in terms of troops lost amount to a defeat. Reiman suggests that "the failure of the criminal justice system yields such benefits to those in positions of power that it amounts to success" (Reiman, 1998: 5). Such "success" comes in the following forms: (1) by focusing primarily on the crimes of the poor and racial minorities, it distorts the crime picture by deflecting the discontents and anger of middle-class Americans toward the poor and racial minorities, rather than toward those in positions of power above them; (2) the American criminal justice system, in its "war on crime," makes it look as if the most serious threat comes from the crimes of the poor and racial minorities, when in fact the greatest harms—both in terms of life and property—come from the crimes of the very rich; (3) by focusing on *crime control* and the punishment of *individual offenders*, the system fails to address some of the major causes of crime. This is what Reiman calls the *ideological* functions of the criminal justice system. By focusing exclusively on the individual offender, writes Reiman, *"it diverts our attention away from our institutions, away from consideration of whether our institutions themselves are wrong or unjust or indeed criminal' "* (Reiman, 1998: 156).

Reiman illustrates this by quoting from Debra Seagal, who wrote about a prime-time television "real crime" show based on videotapes of actual police arrests. In her article, Seagal discusses how focusing on individual criminals diverts our attention from the social context of crime and, indeed, communicates the idea that these offenders exist in a social vacuum. Seagal writes as follows:

> By the time our nine million viewers flip on their tubes, we've reduced fifty or sixty hours of mundane and compromising video into short, action-packed segments of tantalizing, crack-filled, dope-dealing, junkie-busting cop culture. How easily we downplay the pathos of the suspect; how cleverly we breeze past the complexities that cast doubt on the very system that has produced the criminal activity in the first place. (Seagal, 1993, quoted in Reiman, 1998: 157)

In a similar vein, one writer has noted that the big hoopla about "family values" by Dan Quayle over both the riots in Los Angeles following the Rodney King verdict and an episode in the television series *Murphy Brown* (the main character is a single woman who decides to have her baby out of wedlock and raise it herself) completely ignored the "social context" of the lives of most women and most inner-city African Americans. She noted that:

> . . . the erasure of the L.A. uprising in the *Murphy Brown* incident moved the debate away from issues of race, from the condition of inner cities, and from the deteriorating economic base in the United States to a much safer, symbolic ground. By shifting the debate from the material conditions of inner cities to the discursive field of "family values," both parties occupied a much more comfortable terrain for debate. (Stabile, 1993: 289)

This is an example of what is known as *symbolic politics* (e.g., Gordon, 1994: 4). Similarly, television crime shows constantly inform the public about the dangerous criminals in our midst without any attempt to explain why. The viewer is left with the impression that these criminals come out of nowhere. Reiman concludes by saying that:

> To look only at individual criminality is to close one's eyes to social injustice and to close one's ears to the question of whether our social institutions have exploited or violated the individual. *Justice is a two-way street—but criminal justice is a one-way street.* Individuals owe obligations to their fellow citizens because their fellow citizens owe obligations to them. Criminal justice focuses on the first and looks away from the second. *Thus, by focusing on individual responsibility for crime, the criminal justice system literally acquits the existing social order of any charge of injustice.* (Reiman, 1998: 157)

Indeed, while the property crimes reported to the FBI cost the American people an estimated $3 billion to $4 billion per year, the most recent estimate of the annual costs of corporate and "white-collar" crime is in excess of $200 billion, or five hundred times the estimated cost of property crimes (Mokhiber, 1996: 61; Clinard, Quinney, and Wildeman, 1994: 192). The list of specific crimes seems endless, and includes bribery of government officials, defense-contract fraud, health-care–provider fraud, and corporate tax evasion. Moreover, the corporate share of the tax burden has declined from approximately 25 percent in the 1950s to less than 10 percent today (Friedrichs, 1996: 85). The list of corporate and white-collar crimes also includes price-fixing (costing consumers more than $100 million each year), price-gouging ("systematic overcharging" with markups as high as a phenomenal 7,000 percent), false advertising and product misrepresentation, corporate stealing from employees (e.g., cheating workers out of overtime pay and violations of minimum-wage laws), unfair labor practices, surveillance of employees, theft of trade secrets, monopolistic practices, defrauding investors (e.g., the Equity Funding case, which inflated stock prices by claiming $200 million in nonexistent assets), and many more (Mokhiber, 1996: 87; Friedrichs, 1996: 83–93). And all of this does not even include various forms of what is referred to as *occupational crime*, such as retail fraud on the part of small businesses, service-business fraud (especially prevalent in the car-repair industry), and various forms of medical crime, especially Medicaid and Medicare fraud, which is estimated to be as high as $25 billion per year (Friedrichs, 1996: 104).

Reiman notes that the "decisions as to what to label and treat as crime are not compelled by objective dangers" (Reiman, 1998: 60). Statistically speaking, the gravest threats to us are not from robbers, burglars, rapists, and the like; rather, they are from those who wear a suit and tie to work, or a white medical coat, or who occupy plush offices in corporate headquarters or powerful positions within the government. Their weapons are ballpoint pens, scalpels, computers, or their voices (as when they decide to go to war). Numerous studies have documented the real dangers from corporate and state crime.[5]

The case cannot be overstated that, in general, *the criminal justice system focuses primarily on those crimes that have the highest probabilities of being committed by the poorest segments of our society and almost virtually ignores those crimes committed by the richest segments of our society, crimes that actually harm us the most.* This is one of the main themes of Reiman's book, aptly titled *The Rich Get Richer and the Poor Get Prison* (Reiman, 1998). In this book, it will be demonstrated that this tendency has a strong historical basis and has been in fact a constant theme from the very beginning of American history, if not earlier.

Before moving ahead, it is necessary to take a critical view of what is the basic foundation of the criminal justice system, the *criminal law*. Without the criminal law there is, technically, no "crime." But this is more than an academic exercise, for to examine this idea is to begin to expose the law and legal system as an important aspect of social life. More than this, however, these perspectives also apply more generally to the *entire criminal justice system*, not just the criminal law per se. The last perspective to be discussed, the *critical* perspective, will serve as a general theoretical framework for the entire book.

Perspectives on Criminal Law

Why are some behaviors prohibited by law while others are not? It doesn't take much analysis to figure out that some very harmful behaviors are perfectly legal—such as the possession and consumption of cigarettes and alcohol, not to mention addictive prescription drugs. However, drugs such as marijuana, heroin, and cocaine are illegal, yet not nearly as harmful as cigarettes and alcohol.

Also, while there is a law that prohibits the killing of another human being (called *homicide* or just plain *murder*), in some contexts the taking of a human life can be perfectly legal, such as a police officer killing a citizen who threatens his life, the application of the death penalty, killing in the time of war and, more recently, the controversial actions of Dr. Jack Kevorkian, the so-called "suicide doctor."

Moreover, even if there is clear evidence that one probably took another person's life or committed some other crime, there may be different *interpretations* of whether a law was in fact violated. These interpretations may come from a variety of criminal justice "actors," such as the police (who may "look the other way" at certain violations) and district attorneys who decide that this wasn't "really" a crime (Sudnow, 1965).

Finally, we have behaviors that do tremendous harm to mostly women; namely, rape and battering. Theoretically, rape is supposed to be universally condemned, yet numerous studies have documented how in many instances men accused of rape are not arrested, or not prosecuted if arrested, or if prosecuted are acquitted—often because certain key actors in the criminal justice system decided that "she deserved it" or "she led him on." Similar conclusions have been reached with regard to battering.[6]

Thus, we can conclude that the law is more than words on paper. It has a dynamic quality of its own, for it does not exist in a vacuum. Rather, it is a reflection of a particular society at a particular point in time. As Quinney writes, the law "is also a method or *process* of doing something. As a process, law is a dynamic force that is continually being *created and* interpreted. Thus, law in action involves the making of specialized (legal) decisions by various *authorized agents*" (Quinney, 1970: 37). Law is a creation of specific people holding positions of authority; it is not the creation of a divine authority, as was once believed.

The law, because it is a *social* product, must be viewed *sociologically*, for the law is first and foremost a social institution, complete with a system of roles and status positions (i.e., lawyers, judges, legislators, and police officers). Also, it contains an ideology; that is, a set of values supportive of the legal system and the existing social order (Quinney, 1974). The law, moreover, is a *social process* with many different people interpreting and applying it in various social contexts. How the law is interpreted and applied depends, as we shall see, on many extralegal factors, such as class and race.

A question that has concerned scholars for many years is that of the origins and functions of criminal law. Through the years, scholars have offered a variety of different perspectives of the law with various names, including *consensus, societal needs, pluralist, interactionist, interest group, conflict, elite theory, ruling-class theory, critical, Marxist,* and many more. For purposes of simplification, all of these perspectives will be reduced to the following three main views: (1) the *consensus/pluralist*, (2) the *interest group/conflict,* and (3) the *critical/Marxist.*[7] Each perspective is reviewed in the following sections.

Consensus/Pluralist Model

The *consensus/pluralist* model of law contends that legal norms are a reflection of the values held in common by the majority of the population. In other words, legal norms reflect the "will of the people." This is perhaps the oldest and most articulated perspective on criminal law. A variation of this view is that criminal law merely makes official what are common norms or rules of everyday behavior. In other words, what has been custom (e.g., rules followed because everybody has always followed them) eventually becomes the law. From this perspective, the criminal law reflects the *social consciousness of a society* and the kind of behavior a community universally condemns. Thus, the criminal law (and law in general) represents a synthesis of the most deeply held moral values and beliefs of a people or society. The violation of such laws serves, in effect, to establish the "moral boundaries" of a community or society, according to nineteenth-century sociologist Emile Durkheim (Durkheim, 1947).

Another variation of this view is that the law functions to achieve *social equilibrium* or to maintain *order*. The law is an instrument used to resolve conflicting interests in a society. Roscoe Pound, one of the most famous legal philosophers, believed that the law was a specialized organization of social control, as well as a form of *social engineering* in a "civilized" society. Without organized social control, said Pound, man's aggressive self-assertions would prevail over his cooperative social tendency, and civilization would come to an end. Hence, criminal law serves as a sort of social "glue." Pound also suggested that the law adjusts social relationships in order to meet prevailing ideas of fair play (Pound, 1922 and 1942; see also Geis, 1964; Quinney, 1970: 33).

Another way of expressing the consensus view is the common phrase "there ought to be a law," meaning that people should "rise up" and demand that a certain form of behavior be outlawed. This model is based on the assumption that there is a consensus by the majority of the people in a society about what is good and proper conduct—an assumption which is highly suspect.

This model, thus, argues three main points. First, law helps to maintain *social order* and it is the *best* way to do so—in other words, the only way to maintain *order* in society is through the law or, as commonly phrased, the "rule of law." Second, law reflects a more or less universal consensus on what is or is not "proper" behavior. Third, law and the criminal justice system protects public, not private, interests. In other words, the law is neutral and helps to resolve conflicts between competing interest groups (and it follows that those who uphold and interpret the law—police, courts—are neutral as well).

This view also argues that a society needs not only law but also a strong centralized state to prevent people from becoming barbarians and engaging in what eighteenth-century philosopher Thomas Hobbes (1947) described as a "war of all against all." Such a view assumes that once upon a time, humans were simply "mean and nasty" to one another, thinking only of themselves in a selfish way, and that there was constant civil strife and war. This, we are told, is just human nature. Yet such a view is contradicted by years of anthropological and historical research, which has proved that prior to our modern era, thousands of human societies existed (beginning 40,000 to 50,000 years ago) in small, economically cooperative groups. This research shows us that state-created law is not the only way to maintain order and peace. But in modern capitalist societies, based as they are on competitive social relations and class (as well as racial and gender) inequalities, the view of human nature as self-centered and in need of control becomes a rationalization for a capitalist order and leads inevitably to the idea that we *need* law in order to *restrain* people's "naturally wicked" ways (Michalowski, 1985: 47–48).

Interest Group/Conflict Model

The consensus/pluralist model assumes that law is a reflection of societal needs. This leads us to ask, "Whose needs?" The term *society* is far too general and vague. Such a view assumes that what is good for one group or segment is good for all segments. In a society segmented along class, racial, and gender lines, this is clearly not an appropriate view. The *interest group/conflict* model of law attempts to answer some of these questions. This view begins with the basic fact of modern industrialized societies, which are highly stratified and unequal in terms of the distribution of power and life chances. Using this base, conflict theorists contend that the law reflects the interests of some groups at the expense of others. One of Quinney's earlier works, *The Social Reality of Crime*, perhaps best exemplifies this approach. He states that society is characterized by diversity, coercion, change, and conflict. Law is a *result* of the operation of *interests*. More specifically, "law incorporates the interests of specific persons and groups. . . . Law is made by men, representing special interests, who have the power to translate their interests into public policy" (Quinney, 1970: 35).

Quinney's theory of the *social reality of crime* was organized around the following six interrelated propositions (Quinney, 1970: 15–25):

1. Crime is a definition of human conduct that is created by authorized agents in a politically organized society.
2. Criminal definitions describe behaviors that conflict with the interests of the segments of society that have the power to shape public policy.
3. Criminal definitions are applied by the segments of society that have the power to shape the enforcement and administration of criminal law.

4. Behavior patterns are structured in a segmentally organized society in relation to criminal definitions, and within this context persons engage in actions that have relative probabilities of being defined as criminal.

5. Conceptions of crime are constructed and diffused in the segments of society by various means of communication.

6. The social reality of crime is constructed by the formulation and application of criminal definitions, the development of behavior patterns related to criminal definitions, and the construction of criminal conceptions.

An important component of Quinney's theory is four interrelated concepts, including (1) process, (2) conflict, (3) power, and (4) action. By *process*, Quinney is referring to the fact that "all social phenomena . . . have duration and undergo change." The *conflict* view of society and the law is that in any society "conflicts between persons, social units, or cultural elements are inevitable, the normal consequences of social life." Further, society "is held together by force and constraint and is characterized by ubiquitous conflicts that result in continuous change." *Power* is an elementary force in our society. Power, says Quinney, "is the ability of persons and groups to determine the conduct of other persons and groups. It is utilized not for its own sake, but is the vehicle for the enforcement of scarce values in society, whether the values are material, moral, or otherwise." Power is important if we are to understand public policy. Public policy, including crime-control policies, is shaped by groups with special interests. In a class society, some groups have more power than others and, therefore, are able to have their interests represented in policy decisions, often at the expense of less powerful groups. Thus, for instance, white, upper class males have more power and their interests are more likely to be represented than those of working- or lower-class minorities and women. Finally, by *social action*, Quinney is referring to the fact that human beings engage in voluntary behavior, which is not completely determined by forces outside their control. From this perspective, human beings are "able to reason and choose courses of action" and are "changing and becoming, rather than merely being." It is true that humans are in fact shaped by their physical, social, and cultural experiences, but they also have the capacity to change and achieve maximum potential and fulfillment (Quinney, 1970: 8–15).

Quinney's model is based on a conception of society as segmental rather than singular. In a singular society there is a common value system to which all persons conform. The law reflects these common values (this is what the consensus/pluralist model supports). In a segmental society there are numerous segments, each having its own values and interests. Thus, "some values of a segment may be incorporated into some of the criminal laws." Moreover, many segments are in conflict with one another; some segments have values and interests that conflict with other segments. The passage of laws, therefore, is primarily the outgrowth of these conflicting interests. These laws are the product of interest groups who are aware of what their true interests are and organize to promote these interests. The important point here is that the *interest structure* in modern American society is characterized by an unequal distribution of *power and economic resources,* and those who have the greatest amount are most able to have their interests represented by the law. Indeed, those groups that have little or no power will have little or no opportunity to have their interests represented in the law and in public policies in general. Thus, powerless groups such as women, minorities, youth, and poor people are rarely represented (Quinney, 1970: 39–41). Quite often, laws are passed after vigorous campaigning on the part of various interest groups (or perhaps even one group), or what one writer has called *moral entrepreneurs* (Becker, 1963). Thus, this group (or groups) lobbies Congress, writes letters to newspapers, and engages in other activities in order to get a piece of legislation written into law. Such groups do not necessarily represent "the people"; more often than not they represent themselves or some other small but powerful group.

A Critical/Marxist Model

The *critical/Marxist* model of law, which derives largely from the theories of Karl Marx and modern-day Marxist writings, resembles the interest group/conflict model in that it focuses on group conflict and power as important variables, but it also differs in many important ways. A critical perspective challenges us to view the law and the legal order in a specific social and historical context. Such a view argues that the law—and in fact the entire the legal system—is one of many institutions that are part of what Marx called the *superstructure* of society. Therefore, it operates to help support and perpetuate the *substructure* or economic base—namely, a capitalist economic and social system.

Although there are several variations of the critical perspective on the law, they can be categorized by two major approaches: (1) the *instrumentalist* perspective, and (2) the *structuralist* perspective.

The Instrumentalist Perspective. This is essentially the classical position taken by Marx himself when he asserted that the law and the legal order (and the *state* itself) serves mostly as an "instrument" or tool through which the ruling class (i.e., that relatively small group that owns and controls most of the wealth in society—or what Marx called the *means of production*) dominates the society. Marx and Engels summarized this position in *The Communist Manifesto* when they wrote that "the executive of the modern state is but a committee for managing the common affairs of the whole bourgeoisie" (Marx and Engels, 1955: 11–12).

One of the best illustrations of the instrumentalist position in recent years was postulated by Quinney in *Critique of Legal Order: Crime Control in Capitalist Society*, in which he asserted that "Criminal law is used by the state and the ruling class to secure the survival of the capitalist system and, as capitalist society is further threatened by its own contradictions, criminal law will be increasingly used in the attempt to maintain domestic order" (Quinney, 1974: 16). The legal order, in short, is used to help keep the ruling class in power. The legal order is also used to keep the subordinate classes "in their place" (i.e., perpetuate a social-class system) by defining some of their behaviors as "criminal," while ignoring similar or identical behaviors among members of the ruling class or other powerful individuals.

Critics of this position maintain that it is too extreme, that it exaggerates the cohesiveness of the ruling class and its use of the legal order. Not every law is passed to preserve the current social order, nor is every law passed solely to represent the interests of the ruling class; clearly, some legislation favors groups other than the dominant class. Often even subordinate classes are represented in legislation, although it can be said that much of this legislation nevertheless does not threaten the basic social order and the class that rules that order. The instrumentalist position also ignores the many occasions when even members within the ruling class have conflicting interests and thus not all of their interests are reflected in law. It may be true that the instrumentalist position is most helpful for analyzing the relationship between social class and law in the earlier eras of American development, but as "the relationship between law and the state changes over time," other perspectives need to be considered. In short, say critics, the law does not always support economic interests alone (Lynch and Groves, 1989: 23–24).

The Structuralist Perspective. This perspective suggests that law is the result of various *contradictions* inherent within the capitalist system, which in turn create various problems that even the ruling class cannot easily manipulate. Thus, the nature of the capitalist economic system is that law might sometimes operate against the short-term interests of the ruling class but in favor of the long-term interests of the capitalist system as a whole. Classic examples include the passage of Anti-trust laws in the early 1900s, laws against discrimination in employment, minimum-wage laws, consumer-protection laws, and laws supporting labor unions (Chambliss and Seidman, 1982; Greenberg, 1991; O'Connor, 1973). In other words, the ruling class does not always get its way.[8]

Those supporting this position also maintain that the state often acts independently of the ruling class, rather than being a mere "instrument" of that class. To be sure, the law can and will be used when the capitalist system appears to be threatened. However, in day-to-day affairs, the various parts of the "superstructure" (e.g., law, ideology, politics, education, media) have a lot of autonomy. Thus, not every political decision, not everything taught in school, and not every law is a reflection of the narrow interests of capitalists. Chambliss makes the following cogent point on this issue when he notes that every year there are literally thousands of laws passed by various legislators, some local, some national. He then notes that:

> Some laws are clearly passed for the specific interest of an individual; others emerge out of lobbying by groups representing substantial portions of the population; yet others, perhaps the majority, are no more than an expression of the views and interests of legislative committees. (Chambliss, 1993: 30)

Having said this, how can we summarize what a critical/Marxist perspective of the law and legal order has to say? The position of the author is that the law is not some mystical force beyond the comprehension and control of human beings. Too often the law is thought of as a cure-all for societal ills. Also, it has been said that society is ruled by law, not by men. On the contrary, it will be argued that society is ruled by men (and not women, it should be noted) and that the law serves to legitimate and sometimes obscure this rule. The Watergate scandal during the Nixon Administration and, more recently, the impeachment of President Bill Clinton demonstrated for all that very powerful men run the country, not some abstraction called "The Law." Moreover, it has been commonly believed that the law serves as a protective device that shields the victim and punishes the offender; is capable of righting wrongs; and is impartial, incorruptible, and equitably applied, providing equal justice for all. In the coming chapters, however, examples will be cited in which this has not been the case. In short, it will be shown that this belief is largely a fiction.

I am not going to claim that the law reflects the wishes or interests of the ruling class—or any other class—at all times, it would be absurd to make such a claim. Quite often, no doubt, members of the ruling class (or the ruling class *as a class*) could not care less about the daily operations of the legal system. Where the law and legal order do reflect the interests of the ruling class is mainly through the dominant definitions and popular conceptions of *crime* and *criminals*. As discussed previously, these popular conceptions serve the interests of the rich in the sense that they deflect attention from the crimes committed by their own class. In fact, for all practical purposes, the criminal justice system ignores the crimes of the very wealthy and the crimes committed by the state itself.

It also needs to be pointed out that this society is characterized by a tremendous amount of inequality and that a very small proportion of the population do in fact own the "means of production." The share of the total wealth going to the top wealth-holders has increased, with the top 5 percent getting 61 percent of all household wealth in 1997, up from 56 percent in 1983. During this same period, all other households received proportion-ately less (Sklar, 1998). Overall inequality, measured by what is known as the *Gini Index of Inequality* (a scale on which zero means everyone earns the same amount and 1 means one person earns all), has gone up since the late 1960s. Whereas in 1970 the index for the United States was 0.353, in 1996 it was at 0.425, larger than any other industrialized nation (Miringoff and Miringoff, 1999: 105).

During this same period, the proportion of total income received by the top 5 percent of households went from 16.6 to 20 percent. The "super-rich" reaped the most benefits from "trickle-down economics" of the 1980s, as the wealthiest 10 percent of the population received 85 percent of the stock-market gains between 1989 and 1997. According to *Business Week's* annual survey of executive salaries, the average Chief Executive Officer (CEO) earned 419 times the pay of the average worker in 1998, up from a ratio of forty-two to one in 1980. Indeed, the rich are getting richer and practically everyone else is getting poorer (Sklar, 1999; see also the following studies for further confirmation of increased inequality: Wolff, 1995; Phillips, 1990; Domhoff, 1998). Most of the increase has been the result of the tax reforms of the Reagan-Bush years in the 1980s, resulting in an estimated one trillion dollars going to the very rich (Bartlett and Steele, 1992).[9] One study found that between 1977 and 1994, the share of after-tax income of the top 1 percent of all families increased by 72 percent, compared to a decrease of 16 percent by the bottom 20 percent of all families (Shapiro and Greenstein, 1997).

In terms of net worth, although the top 1 percent of households held about 20 percent of all the net worth in the late 1970s, by the end of the 1980s their share had risen to more than 35 percent. Also, whereas the mean family income of the top 5 percent was eleven times greater than the bottom 20 percent of the population in 1978, by 1994 it was 19 times greater (Gilbert, 1998: 107). As of 1993, 42 percent of all households had a net worth of less than $25,000, while 25 percent had a net worth of less than $5,000 (11.5 percent had a net worth of either negative or zero). About 10 percent had a net worth in excess of $250,000—and this latter segment of the population held two thirds of all the wealth in the country (including more than 90 percent of the value of all bonds, about 86 percent of all stocks, more than 80 percent of all non-home real estate, more than 90 percent of the total business equity, and 88 percent of the value of all trusts).

Given this amount of wealth and the power that comes with it, it logically follows that the legal order, in the final analysis, will ultimately be controlled by this small proportion of the population because of the simple fact that it owns and controls most of the assets of this country (for documentation about a "ruling class" and the extent to which it does in fact rule, see Domhoff, 1979 and 1998).

It really doesn't matter that the law does not always side with these rulers, for it doesn't have to, as long as profits can be made and the capitalist system survives. And it is not as if no one else but this small group of capitalists receives the benefits of capitalism, for a lot of other people do as well. Historian Howard Zinn illustrates this in his analysis of the passage of the U.S. Constitution. He notes that the Constitution and the Bill of Rights were passed primarily to protect private property; so many at that time did own property, so it was in the interests of many people to have property protected. But while many people owned property, most owned only a little; a small group owned a lot of property (and they still do today). Zinn notes:

> The Constitution, then, illustrates the complexity of the American system: that it serves the interests of a wealthy elite, but also does enough for small property owners, for middle-income mechanics and farmers, to build a broad base of support. The slightly prosperous people who make up this base of support are buffers against the blacks, the Indians, the very poor whites. They enable the elite to keep control with a minimum of coercion, a maximum of law—all made palatable by the fanfare of patriotism and unity. (Zinn, 1995: 98–99)

The Bill of Rights gave just enough liberties to the masses to build support for the ruling class of the period and the government. But, as Zinn notes, what was never made very clear "was the shakiness of anyone's liberty when entrusted to a government of the rich and the powerful." This was shown, for instance, when Congress passed a law that essentially abridged freedom of speech guaranteed by the First Amendment: the Sedition Act of 1798 (Zinn, 1995: 99).[10]

Thus, the law and the legal order especially favor the very wealthy, but they favor enough of the rest of the population to appear to be equal. Yet the law clearly has never done a good job supporting the most marginalized sectors of the population: the poor in general, and African Americans, Native Americans, and other minorities. Lawrence Friedman, notable historian of law and criminal justice, had this to say:

> Law is a fabric of norms and practices in a particular society; the norms and practices are social judgments made concrete: the living, breathing embodiment of society's attitudes, prejudices, and values. Inevitably, and invariably, these are slanted in favor of the haves; the top-riders, the comfortable, respectable, well-to-do people. After all, articulate, powerful people *make* the laws; and even with the best will in the world, they do not feel moved to give themselves disadvantage.
>
> Rules thus tend to favor people who own property, entrepreneurs, people with good position in society. The lash of criminal justice, conversely, tends to fall on the poor, the badly dressed, the maladroit, the deviant, the misunderstood, the shiftless, the unpopular. (Friedman, 1993: 101)

The "Dangerous Classes"

Many of the daily activities of the American criminal justice system have revolved around controlling, regulating, containing or in some way "keeping tabs" on those groups deemed "dangerous." The term *dangerous classes* was apparently first used by Charles Loring Brace in his book of 1872 called *The Dangerous Classes of New York* (Brace, 1872).

However, there is some indication that the term, as used by Brace, was synonymous with what Marx called the *lumpenproletariat*, first used in his famous work with Engles, *The Communist Manifesto*, originally published in 1848. In the various English translations since then, the term *dangerous class* has been used instead of *lumpenproletariat*. In its original usage, Marx and Engels referred to this segment of society as "the social scum, that passively rotting mass thrown off by the lowest layers of old society" (Eastman, 1959: 332). Although this original definition does not include criminal behavior as part of the meaning of the term, Anthony Giddens nevertheless quotes the following passage from a collection of writings by Marx and Engels, where the authors include under the heading of *lumpenproletariat*, "thieves and criminals of all kinds, living on the crumbs of society, people without a definite trade, vagabonds, people without a hearth or home." The key idea conveyed is that this special segment of society was inevitable under capitalism in that it is "not wholly integrated into the division of labor" (Giddens, 1971: 38). For Marx and Engels, this was more a *moral* evaluation of a certain segment of society.

A closely related term is what Marx referred to as the *relative surplus population* or *reserve army*, which refers to a more or less chronically unemployed segment of the population, primarily because of mechanization that renders them redundant and hence superfluous as far as producing profits is concerned. This segment helps keep wages down and is absorbed back into the general working population when labor is scarce. This group is also a "lever of capitalistic accumulation" and in fact is "a condition of existence of the capitalist mode of production" (Giddens, 1971: 57). This "surplus" population should be seen as a much larger category of people than the *lumpenproletariat*, the latter of which comes closest to what I refer to as the *dangerous classes*.

This population has shown remarkable growth during the last couple of decades of the twentieth century, especially when we consider the global scale. Weiss (1999b: 468) suggests that there are three parts to this surplus population, as follows: (1) the "officially" unemployed who are actively seeking work; (2) a group of completely discouraged workers at the bottom of the social order; and (3) those who are "invisible" because they are not actively seeking work by reporting to state employment offices (those defined as *unemployed* are registered with the state).

There is a dual character to the dangerous classes or surplus population. As Spitzer noted, the surplus population at times has been viewed by those in power as a "threat"—social "junk" or "dynamite" (as was the case with almost the entire working class in the early years of the labor movement during the last half of the nineteenth century) or as a possible resource (e.g., a form of cheap labor or a group to exploit to keep wage levels down) (Spitzer, 1975). Moreover, the exact nature of this class has changed over the years, ranging from the working class in general in the nineteenth and early part of the twentieth centuries, to very specific categories in more recent years, such as racial minorities, the "underclass," and "gangs."

The term *dangerous classes* has become quite popular and is commonly used in many discussions of the history of crime and criminal justice in this country. It was used by Eric Monkkonen in his historical study of crime and criminal justice in Columbus, Ohio (Monkkonen, 1975) and also more recently by Dianna Gordon in her study of drug laws and the "war on drugs" (Gordon, 1994).

Many other writers have echoed the same themes, while using different words. Thus, for example, John Irwin's excellent study maintains the view that jails function to manage the "rabble" or "underclass" in society, rather than focus on serious crime per se (Irwin, 1985). He notes that many studies have referred to such terms as *social trash, social refuse, social junk, riffraff, dregs,* and the like (ask any police officer and terms such as *asshole,* or *dirt balls,* or *scum bag* will be frequently used). By *rabble,* Irwin means the "disorganized" and "disorderly" and the "lowest class of people." They are people who have been regarded as "disreputable" and "detached" from mainstream society. Just like social welfare has been used to regulate the poor, jails have been used for a similar purpose (Irwin, 1985: 2; see also Piven and Cloward, 1972). In this book it will be argued that the entire legal system—from the making of the laws to their enforcement—functions like Irwin's jail: to regulate, manage, and control the dangerous classes. We could easily substitute *rabble* or other terms; the meaning is essentially the same. Historically, the terms *crime* and *poverty* (or the old eighteenth-century term *pauperism*) have been used interchangeably. Even the term *delinquency,* as will be shown in Chapter 5, was practically synonymous with the word *pauper* or poor person.

This theme is echoed not only by Irwin, but also by Noam Chomsky in several of his writings (Chomsky, 1994, 1996a, and 1996b) and Jonathan Simon in his historical study of the parole system (1993). Simon is quite explicit about one of the main functions of the parole system, in that it has become part of one of the main functions of the modern criminal justice system: namely, in his words, to "secure" the underclass. He argues that in modern times in the middle of "declining public spending on most forms of social support for the poor, criminal justice is one of the few programs left that takes tax dollars from relatively better-off communities and their governments, and spends them on relatively poorer communities and their governments (*even if only to lock them up*)." However, continues Simon, what is happening is that such resources are not used so much to control crime as to *contain* crime "in the underclass" (Simon, 1993: 258).

What is even more important is Simon's characterization of what is occurring in what he calls "waste management." He argues that since many of the young males caught up in the criminal justice system may likely become "lifetime clients" of this system, it behooves governments to figure out methods of *maintaining* this population "at the lowest possible cost." This, says Simon, means that we may have to rethink our reliance on an increasingly costly penal system; hence, an expansion of parole. Simon was predicting this in a book published in 1993; since that time, the prison system has expanded to reach an all-time high although, to be sure, the number of those on probation and parole has also expanded at about the same rate.

One of the central arguments in this book is that the management of the dangerous classes is not a recent phenomenon. On the contrary, it will be noted throughout that this has always been one, if not the major, function of the criminal justice system. This argument is based on a Marxian interpretation of one of the negative aspects of capitalism; namely, that it produces very distinct *social classes* with significant differences in the benefits resulting from the huge profits from capitalist enterprises. The very nature of capitalism itself produces periodic economic fluctuations, one result of which is the constant creation of large segments of the population that become superfluous (i.e., not needed to produce profits), which in turn often become labeled as "dangerous" to the more privileged groups. Because we are too civilized to murder or torture this group (as more totalitarian dictatorships do) and we can no longer transport it to another country, it must be in some way "managed" and "controlled." Using the various components of the criminal justice system is one method among many.[11]

One result of social inequality is vast differences in the probabilities of having one's behaviors labeled "criminal." Evidence for this is found throughout the social science literature during the last half century or more.[12] Therefore, the legal system responds accordingly and, more often than not, tends to focus its attention on those from the less privileged sectors of society: the poor, racial, and ethnic minorities and women (especially women of color, who more often than not are also poor, which provides an excellent illustration of the interplay of race, class, and gender) (Messerschmidt, 1997).

I do not intend in this book to offer a precise definition of the term *dangerous classes*. I am not certain it can be done; perhaps it should not be done. I think that, historically, different groups have been so labeled at different points in time. An example cited many times throughout the course of this book might better clarify the changing nature of the "dangerous classes"; I am referring to various attempts to control the use of drugs. As will be discussed in more detail in Chapter 1, the groups targeted by these drug laws include (1) the Chinese and opium laws around the late nineteenth and early twentieth centuries; (2) marijuana legislation, which targeted mostly Hispanics and African Americans during the 1930s; (3) heroin laws, targeting especially African Americans in the 1950s; (4) various psychoactive drugs (e.g., LSD) used by mostly white "hippies" and anti-war activists—the dangerous classes of the 1960s; and (5) "crack" cocaine used mostly by African American inner-city youth, along with women (especially minority women) in the 1980s.

Prohibition laws throughout the nineteenth and well into the twentieth century focused mostly on lower-class immigrants, starting with the Irish in the mid-nineteenth century. Most of those in the forefront of the Temperance Movement were middle- and upper-class people who associated most of the problems of urban America with the consumption of alcohol. Corporate leaders argued that drinking (especially in working-class saloons) would interfere with productivity and profit. It was no accident that saloons were often the location of much labor organizing, and most of the organizers and union members were immigrants. So, for the dominant classes, "clamping down on drinking and saloons was part of a much broader strategy of social control. . . ." In fact, the passage of the eighteenth Amendment to the Constitution was considered a "blow against Bolshevism and anarchy. . . ."(Reinarman and Levine, 1997: 5–6).

Outline for the Book

Throughout this book there is one overriding theme, which can be stated as follows: *the making of laws and the interpretation and application of these laws throughout the criminal justice system historically has been class, gender, and racially biased.* More to the point, as Cole noted, there are really two systems of justice: "one for the privileged and another for the less privileged" (Cole, 1999: 9). Moreover, one of the major functions of the criminal justice system has been largely to control and/or manage those from the most disadvantaged sectors of the population; that is, the "dangerous classes." This theme prevails in each chapter of this book, from the development of the criminal law, through the development of the police institution and the juvenile justice system, to our treatment of women and the prison system. Succinctly, the entire legal system has been and continues to be controlled and dominated by those in power at any given historical period and thus favors those with the most resources at their disposal. Those receiving the brunt of the full enforcement of the law have been predominantly those who comprise the "dangerous classes."

One way to make this perspective clearer is to consider the phrase "the golden rule," which usually refers to the old biblical sentiment of "do under others as you would have them to do unto you." However, there is another meaning attached to this phrase—one that most people would probably feel uneasy about, although they might agree: "those who have the gold make the rules."

To admit the truth in this statement is not easy in a country known as a "democracy." After all, this is supposed to be a government "of the people, by the people, and for the people." Moreover, we are supposed to live under the "rule of law," not of men.

Most citizens have the sense that a few rich people control things, that "money talks," and that if you have money and power, you can get away with almost anything, even murder. Yet the word *class* (and words like *class conflict* and *class oppression*) is not often used in everyday discourse. But it is obvious that the average citizen is aware of it—and aware of some of the gross inequalities that exist, even though the media and most politicians avoid referring to them. A recent poll found that more than 80 percent of the public feel that the current economic system is "inherently unfair," and more than 70 percent believe that business "has gained too much power over too many aspects of American life" (Chomsky, 1996c: 417).

Classes and class differences are realities in modern American society, and have been since the start of the republic. Perhaps nowhere is this better illustrated on a daily basis—sometimes for all to see—than in our system of justice. Because those who create laws and those who interpret laws are drawn largely from the wealthiest class, it comes as no surprise that those brought into the criminal justice system will be those drawn largely from the lowest social classes. On any given day, in courtrooms all over the country, we have essentially one class passing judgment on another class. Our system is fundamentally a system of class justice.

Notes

1. In the second edition of this book (Walker, 1998), Walker rewrote this section and instead of referring to such incidents as "scars," he suggests that "vigilantism represented the worst aspect of popular justice" (p. 37). Curiously, he notes that the "lawlessness" [his quotes] was what he called a "paradox," in that "most organized episodes were led by the wealthy leaders of the community who sought to impose law and order."

2. In a book filled with documented evidence, David Cole (1999) demonstrates the class and racial bias that he argues is *built into* the modern criminal justice system, a bias that is constantly reinforced daily by criminal justice decision-makers and backed up by Supreme Court decisions. My argument in this book is that what Cole documents for the last half of the twentieth century has been a persistent feature of the American criminal justice system from the beginning.

3. Part of this phrase originally came from his book *The Politics of History*, (2nd ed.) Urbana: University of Chicago Press, 1990 (first edition was in 1970), p. 35. But it is the title of his own personal biography (Zinn, 1994).

4. The subtitle of one popular text ("Class, Race, and Gender") illustrates this importance (Rossides, 1997).

5. Space does not permit a complete review of these studies. For further documentation, refer to studies already cited plus the following: Geis (1996), Calavita and Pontell (1994), and Poveda (1994).

6. The research on this topic is far too numerous to cite here, but for a good summary, see Belknap (1996) and Swisher, Wekesser, and Barbour (1994).

7. See the following for extended discussions of these theories: Chambliss (1993), Quinney (1970, 1974, 1980), Michalowski (1985), Lynch and Groves (1989), Whitt (1993), and Weiss (1983).

8. A variation of this view is called the *class-dialectical model,* which argues that to understand the functions of the law, one must understand the institutional structure of society and the different social classes that comprise a society. True, dominant classes try to preserve those institutions that best add to their hegemony (e.g., economic and political institutions). However, "power is potentially available to the subordinate classes if they become sufficiently class-conscious and politically organized to wrest control or to challenge the control of the means of production. Thus, the power of the dominant class is not absolute." (Whitt, 1993: 266)

9. Bartlett and Steele note that as a result of the 1986 "Tax Reform Act," the average 1989 tax savings for those earning $1 million or more came to $281,033 (a tax cut of 31 percent), compared to $37 for those earning less than $10,000 (11 percent tax cut). They also found that during the 1980s, the increase in salaries of people earning more than $1 million per year came to 2,184 percent.

10. One of our "founding fathers," James Madison, said that the primary role of the government is "to protect the minority of the opulent against the majority." His colleague, John Jay, flatly stated that "The people who own the country ought to govern it" (quoted in Chomsky, 1998: 7).

11. Similarly, social welfare functions in this way. See, for instance, Piven and Cloward, 1972; see also Chomsky (1994, 1996a) for a similar line of argument.

12. Numerous citations could be listed here, but only the following will be noted: Quinney (1970), Cole (1999), Currie (1998), Walker, Spohn, and DeLone (1996, 2000), and Hawkins (1995). For a good treatment of gender bias, see Chesney-Lind and Shelden (1998) and Chesney-Lind (1997).

1

Perpetuating the Class System

The Development of Criminal Law

Introduction: Nature and Functions
of Criminal Law

The foundation of the modern criminal justice system is the criminal law. After all, technically speaking, there is no "crime" without "criminal law." Criminal law is the body of laws that justifies the existence of a criminal justice system. Without criminal law there would be no purpose for a criminal justice system. The U.S. Constitution provides for the creation of laws by state legislatures and Congress. In essence, "Law is the formal statement of authority that is exercised by the state" (Zalman and Siegel, 1994: 13). Executive-branch officials and the courts are given authority, through provisions in the U.S. Constitution, to enforce these laws. The criminal justice system is the *instrument* designated by executive-branch officials to enforce laws that pertain to criminal behavior.

The basis of the American criminal justice system is found within the three branches of our government: legislative, executive, and judicial. The "legal authority" to establish an official response to crime comes from this structural arrangement. "Legal authority, like other forms of authority, may be enforced by threatening or physically coercing people to comply or by economic rewards" (Terkel, 1996: 200). The legislative branch defines which behaviors are to be prohibited by the criminal law and how the violations are to be punished; the judicial branch (e.g., the courts) interprets these laws and determines whether they are constitutionally valid; and the executive branch creates the official response in terms of agencies, personnel, and the like.

The legislative branch is the most important of the three branches because these individuals define the behavior the violation of which constitutes "crime." Of particular importance are legislatures at the state and local levels because the bulk of "criminal acts" are violations of state and local laws. In fact, the state and federal legislatures have created, in effect, the two major criminal justice systems: state and federal. Thus, we have state and federal law-enforcement systems, state and federal courts, and state and federal prison systems. The reader should be aware of who the individuals are who constitute the legislature, at both the state and local and at the federal level. These groups do not necessarily represent all of the population, because the majority of those who occupy legislative seats (especially at the federal level in the Congress and the Senate) have been predominantly white males from upper-class backgrounds (Domhoff, 1998, 1990, 1979; Bennett, 1994: 439-442).

The most primitive method of settling disputes has been when the powerful overpower the less powerful by force or intimidation. The "civilized" method, however, is to let a third party handle the matter. The problem, of course, lies in the objective and/or neutral nature of the third party, who may be called the *judge* or the *court*. Is this third party objective or neutral, and is the judge or the court beyond the control of the powerful? If the answer to either question is "no," then the civilized method is simply an impersonation of the primitive method, which is masked to conceal the real identity of the judge or the court agents of the powerful. Through a survey of the history of criminal law, it will be demonstrated that the powerful, often at the expense of the powerless, have always maintained control of the law. Interestingly, those who have had the most influence in legislating and enforcing law have done so in a way that masks their intentions.

Exploring the emergence of modern criminal law is a long journey far back in time to ancient civilizations. Thus, this chapter necessarily begins with a look at how criminal law developed in early societies such as Athens and Rome.

Criminal Law in Ancient Times

The roots of our modern criminal justice system go back to at least ancient times—in Biblical Israel, classical Athens, and in Rome—back as far as 1200 B.C. The law and legal system reflected the type of society that existed. In this case, we are talking about a highly stratified society, where slaves did most of the work, especially in Athens and Rome. Each of these societies displayed different forms of economic development, which in turn shaped their definitions of and responses to offending behaviors.

Israel was moving from a mostly nomadic existence based on the herding of sheep and goats to an established agricultural society located in the "promised land." Not surprisingly, in Israel the law and criminal justice system reflected deep religious influences. Wrongful conduct was an offense that threatened the close bonds of society, and a wrong committed by any member of God's chosen people could bring divine wrath down upon the entire nation (Johnson and Wolfe, 1996: 19–32).

Athens during its classical period (594–404 B.C.) was based on the commercial activity of the Mediterranean. Rome, a republic, was a constitutional state ruled by aristocrats. Rome was very dependent on trade and employed a vast army of foreign slaves for its farms, manufactories, and households.

A common theme within these societies was that a harm was essentially a harm against an individual or a family, rather than a harm against the state. In fact, the initiation of a criminal case depended on the initiative of the person wronged or, if he had been killed, by his family or kinfolk. Thus, criminal procedure perpetuated the primitive system of revenge. The state did not act as a *prosecutor*, as we understand the term today, but rather as a weigher of evidence and the dispenser of punishment.

Depending on the offense, the punishment often literally "fit the crime," but not always. In the case of homicide, the law in Israel stipulated that whoever killed would be put to death; however, in Athens, the punishment was expulsion from Athens and the surrounding countryside. Different punishments were administered depending on whether the killing was intentional. If unintentional, sometimes the families of the victim received some sort of compensation—known as *blood money.*

In all three societies, the harshest sanctions were against intentional killers, with lesser penalties for unintentional killers. In general, sex offenses were dealt with less severely. Theft was almost always dealt with through some form of compensation. In each system, the victim or victim's family or kin was responsible for bringing the offender to justice, and justice was administered by local officials. Most importantly, in the local courts it was common to rely on *group decisions* as superior to the judgment of an individual.

Emergence of Criminal Law in Athens

Criminal law, as we understand the term today, developed only when the idea of "private vengeance" was replaced by the notion that the entire community also was victimized. This idea in turn evolved into the notion that the "state," which theoretically came to represent the entire community or "the people," also was harmed and became authorized to take action. Criminal law, and hence criminal justice, is based on three key ideas (Quinney, 1970: 44):

1. An offense against an individual is also an offense against the "public order" and the "state."

2. The methods of punishment are administered by the state and not solely by the victim.

3. The protection the law provides theoretically should apply to all citizens, not just particular groups.

In Athens, the criminal law emerged during the sixth century B.C. At that time, Athens was ruled by a small aristocracy that controlled a very large citizenry—the peasant proprietors, the artisans, a lower class of "freemen," and an even lower class of slaves. The discontent this situation produced led the rulers to compromise (they were legitimately afraid of a revolution). The rulers essentially created a system of "popular courts" and provided for appeals and granted certain rights to every citizen, with the right of all citizens to initiate prosecutions (Quinney, 1970: 46).

Criminal Law in Rome

Until the middle of the fifth century B.C., the law in Rome was devoted mostly to private matters. The *Law of the Twelve Tables,* the codification of Roman "customary law," was essentially a "private criminal law" in the sense that it was based on the notion that a victim could seek private vengeance against an offender. This collection of laws was compiled around 450 B.C. As noted by Tigar and Levy, these tables "outlined only the simplest of legal principles . . ." and they were characterized "by reliance upon magic and ritual as integral parts of legal procedure and as means for the creation of obligations." This law guaranteed certain rights, but mostly "to the members of the clans that had founded the Roman Republic"; that is, the ruling class (Tigar and Levy, 1977: 11).

However, as Rome grew from a rural agricultural community to a mighty city-state, the existing law under the *Twelve Tables* proved to be inadequate. Indeed, this legal system was inadequate to handle the growing conflicts between an urban proletariat and slave population and a powerful yet small ruling class. Between the third and second century B.C., the state began to use the criminal law to protect the interests of the ruling class by passing laws such as treason, arson, violence (except violence committed by the state itself), and theft of state property (Tigar and Levy, 1977: 47). Indeed, the existing laws did not provide much protection to the growing number of merchants, "whose wealth was increasing at the expense of small peasants and artisans." The emerging society was dominated by traders, bankers, landowners, and the military that protected their interests. The existing labor force of the time was either slave or half-free, mostly conquered and colonized people. The ruling class clearly shaped the law in their favor, yet claimed that this law and legal system was *jus gentium,* or a natural law or law that protected all the people. The adoption of the *jus gentium* "reflected the conquest by the new Roman ruling class of its foreign and domestic enemies" (Tigar and Levy, 1977: 14).

Acephelous or "Non-State" Societies and Law

Prior to the Norman Invasion of England in 1066, most societies had not been under what we call today the "rule of law." Rather, many societies were under the "rule of custom" (Diamond, 1974). As noted by Michalowski, many of these earlier societies were what he termed "non-state" or *acephelous* societies, which means "without a head"; that is, with no identifiable ruler. Such a society had no centralized state or government nor any written law. What is important, however, is that most of these societies (and there were literally thousands of them) were "characterized more by order and cooperation than by chaos and competition" (Michalowksi, 1985: 45–46). What is significant about these societies is not that they were free from any sort of deviance or what we would call "crime," but rather how the people handled such problems without some sort of centralized authority or state. In these societies, deviances were handled informally, because they were essentially *disputes between individuals or families.*

Acephelous societies are obviously quite different from modern, highly complex, capitalist societies. In the former, human relations are more apt to be based on personal relationships, that in turn are based on mutual obligations and respect. In modern societies, with personal relatedness missing, legal rules are established, which are backed by the threat of punishment. Conformity to such rules too often depends on the state's ability or even willingness to enforce them or an individual's own commitment to obey them (Michalowski, 1985: 53).

In these non-state societies, deviance was handled usually through one of four ways: (1) blood revenge (usually in cases of homicide where the victim's kin kills the murderer); (2) retribution (typically the victim or the family returns the harm done with something similar); (3) ritual satisfaction (typically involves some form of "symbolic" demonstration of the offender's guilt, such as suffering public ridicule); or (4) restitution (involving some payment to the victim for the harm done). The last type was the most common, revealing the extent to which the victim is directly involved in the response to the offense—in other words, the focus is more on the victim than the offender, unlike our modern court system (Michalowski, 1985: 62–63). Such a response assumed some form of continuing relationship between the victim and the offender, or at least between the two families—something obviously missing in today's society (Chambliss and Seidman, 1982; Hoebel, 1973).

Criminal Law in Medieval Times

The fall of the Roman Empire was one of the most important events of early history, a process that took several centuries to unfold. When the final fall came in 426 A.D., criminal law and criminal justice understandably changed. The "Dark Ages" soon began, so-called because of the confusion and illiteracy that developed. Christianity became one of the few unifying characteristics of the period, with the Roman Catholic Church a central authority figure and one of the last vestiges of the Roman Empire. Political authority increasingly fell into the hands of local kings and landlords. In the age of feudalism that followed, poor farmers and merchants began to associate themselves with a powerful lord, who provided security to them in return for either services or taxes. The control of crime became based on kinship groups. Johnson and Wolfe describe the situation at that time as the beginning of the modern "nation states":

a slow accretion of power in the hands of noble families, based upon dynastic alliances and also upon their standing among peoples of similar language, culture, and traditions. As territorial magnates consolidated control, their people found new cohesion in their differences from neighboring states and nations; the result was the rapid decline of a pan-European culture that had once been based upon Roman culture and the Christian church and its teachings. The other consequence was the rise of a new view of man based upon his individual importance as a member of a kindred group, a clan and a society. . . . This new view of man was founded less upon religion or political philosophy and more upon the necessities of a more primitive and violent world. (Johnson and Wolfe, 1996: 36)

A new kind of relationship was formed, one based on reciprocal rights and duties between the lord and the workers. But there was no unifying legal order, as local customs prevailed throughout Europe, although many were based in part on Roman law. Tigar and Levy make a similar point that "the need for survival and military defense, the lack of a Roman governmental presence and of the Roman legions, made possible and necessary a manorial system in which one finds the origin of what later writers were to term *feudalism*" (Tigar and Levy, 1977: 23).

The term *feudalism* can be described as a system whereby land is held by a *landlord* who grants individuals (*peasants*) the right to live and work the land as tenants and sometimes perform military service. It is a system based on the agricultural mode of production with a caste or slave type of social order (Chambliss and Ryther, 1975: 132). Feudalism was legitimated by the institution of *serfdom*, whereby peasants were "legally unfree" and "were deprived of property rights, though they had rights of use" (Bottomore et al., 1983: 166).

The feudal system emerged mostly as a result of the uncertainties of the Dark Ages. Millions of small farmers and artisans were forced into this system because of the need for protection or by direct force. Europe was indeed a dangerous place to live during this period because there were invasions from all directions, from the Hungarians to the east to the Moors from the south and the Scandinavians from the north. Feudalism represented a sort of "retreat into the manor and village of a ruling class deprived of protection by a decayed and dying imperial government." In other areas, it was a shift from a pastoral nomadic existence to a more stable agricultural life. The ultimate source of the feudal system was "the act of homage" between two men, one the stronger (the *lord*) and the other the weaker (the *vassal*). The vassal tilled the land owned by the lord in an "oath-bound relation of dominance and subordination" that lasted the lifetime of the vassal and extended to his heirs. This manoral society predominated throughout Europe until around the eleventh century. The manor was self-sufficient, with little trade outside its boundaries, not unlike the slave system in the southern United States (Tigar and Levy, 1977: 23–25). (A variation of this form of society still existed in the United States during and immediately after slavery, known as *sharecropping*.)

While most people were accustomed to Roman law, each group had its own customary law as well. Eventually most legal principles of Roman law were replaced by local customary laws within the manors. By the end of this period (approximately the eleventh and twelfth centuries), Western Europe was "under the rule of a patchwork system of local customs, influenced in varying degrees by Roman law." Germany, the Low Countries, and what is now the northern part of France were under their own customary laws. Thus, after the Norman Invasion in 1066, English law came under the influence of not Roman law but Norman law (Tigar and Levy, 1977: 26–27; Johnson and Wolfe, 1996: 36–37).

By the tenth century, England was divided into about eight large kingdoms, each with some form of centralized authority—namely, *tribal chiefs*. In time, they were replaced by kings who became both landlords and military leaders of their *kingdoms*. Compensation for offenses became the responsibility of the king, lord, or bishop rather than the kinship group (Quinney, 1970: 46). This was the kind of society that existed around the time William the Conqueror became King of England in 1066, following the Norman Invasion.

Emergence of Criminal Law in England

American criminal law is largely an outgrowth of the Norman Conquest and the reigns of William the Conqueror (1066–1087) and Henry II (1157–1189). When William became the King of England in 1066, the country consisted of many different groups with different lifestyles and customs. Each group had its own leader and there was no centralized authority or "state." The only unifying characteristic was the existence of Christianity. In fact, the major landowner at that time was the church. One of William's first acts was to unify this diverse land and to declare himself the supreme "landlord" of the country. Thus, the land that formerly belonged to the several groups or tribes and then different landlords now belonged to the king.

William began his takeover by separating the lay and ecclesiastical (i.e., church) courts and sending his own judges into the different sections of the country to enforce the "King's peace." Understandably, this move resulted in a great deal of conflict between the church and the state, a conflict that did not subside until the reign of Henry II. In the end, however, the king won. One result was that personal transgressions, formerly handled locally and according to the customs of the people, became defined as *crimes* or harms against the state. It became the state's prerogative to punish transgressors and, in many cases, to collect fines (which, in addition to the levy of taxes, no doubt added significantly to the king's coffers). The new centralized government was stronger and more efficient than before. Cheyney describes some of these changes as follows:

A body of trained, skillful government officials now existed, who were able to carry out the wishes of the king, collect his revenues, administer justice, gather armies, and in other ways make his rule effective to an extent unknown in the preceding period. The sheriffs, who had already existed as royal representatives in the shires in Anglo-Saxon times, now possessed far more extensive powers, and came up to Westminster to report and to present their financial accounts to the royal exchequer twice a year. Royal officials acting as judges not only settled an increasingly large number of cases that were brought before them at the king's court, but also traveled through the country, trying suits and punishing criminals in the different shires. The king's income was vastly larger than that of the Anglo-Saxon monarchs had been. (Cheyney, 1913: 17–18)

This is an important development and should not be passed over lightly. What occurred was that the order of custom (i.e., handling disputes locally and according to the customs of the people) became the "rule of law." As Diamond observed, "Law arises in the breach of a prior customary order and increases in force with the conflicts that divide political societies internally and among themselves. Law and order is the historical illusion; law *versus* order is the historical reality" (Diamond, 1974: 49). Hence, William the Conqueror enlarged his control of the nation through the coercive power of a state apparatus, an apparatus that stood above the people and represented the interests of the king. By making personal transgressions "crimes," the people could be more easily controlled. In short, criminal law served the function of exercising state (i.e., the king's) power.

However, as Weber noted, no political authority can rule through raw force alone (Weber, 1946). Rather, it must rule through a consensus of the governed. Hence, rulers must legitimize their rule; that is, their domination must be seen as legitimate by the people. The ruling class of England began a series of "reforms" that solidified its rule and helped legitimate it in the eyes of the people. For instance, the state began to use an ostensibly independent and unbiased set of bureaucratic government officials to handle disputes, known as *justices of the peace*. The ruling class also separated judicial and legislative functions. Rules of evidence, due process, the use of writs, rights of appeal, and other rules were established. In addition to these procedures, the use of *peers* (i.e., jurors) to decide guilt or innocence helped legitimize the king's rule. In a sense, it was good logic because, in the minds of the people, if a person was found guilty, it was the fault of his or her peers rather than of the king or his representatives.

The king and other members of the ruling class used additional measures to legitimize their rule. One method was to foster the view of the king as sovereign. The Christian religion lent spiritual support to the king and the state and, therefore, the legal system as well. In short, the king could do no wrong; he was answerable only to God. To question the king (or the state or the law) was to question God. The king's law stood as the ultimate morality. The criminal law became, in time, more than mere descriptions of crimes and their punishments. The criminal law—indeed, the formal law and legal order itself—became a powerful *ideological* force that justified the rule by a few. The way this was accomplished in England is shown through a study by Douglas Hay, which is discussed in the next section.

Criminal Law as an Ideological System of "Legitimate" Control

The thesis that criminal law adds to the hegemony[1] of a ruling class has been given factual support in an historical account of changes in England's legal order during the eighteenth century. In the opening chapter of *Albion's Fatal Tree: Crime and Society in 18th Century England*, Hay argues that during this period criminal law functioned as an *ideological* system of control that served to *legitimate* and add to the *hegemony* of the English ruling class. Criminal law—in particular, its enforcement—reinforced the belief that the ruling class was fit to rule and that it served the interests of all the people. There were three aspects of the law as an ideological system: *majesty, justice,* and *mercy* (Hay, 1975).[2]

The *majesty* of the law was emphasized by the excessive formality of the legal system. This formality could be seen in the pomp and ceremony displayed in courtroom activities and when justices visited country villages. It also could be seen when judges used their courts as platforms to address the multitude by making rhetorical statements about the virtues of authority and obedience, the fitness of the social order, and the inculcation of dominant values supportive of that order, such as respect for the law, the king, and God.

The idea of *justice,* especially "equal justice for all," was displayed by the hanging of a man of wealth following judgment by a jury of his peers, even though this was indeed a rare occurrence. More importantly, the myriad procedural rules enabled some accused persons, even poor people, to be set free on a technicality. As Hay stated:

> The punctilious attention to forms, the dispassionate and legalistic exchanges between counsel and judges, argued that those administering and using the laws submitted to its rules. The law thereby became something more than the creature of a ruling class—it became a power with its own claims, higher than those of prosecutor, lawyers, and even the great scarlet-robed assize judge himself. To them, too, of course, the law was The Law. The fact that they deified it, that they shut their eyes to its daily enactment in Parliament by men of their own class, heightened the illusion. When the ruling class acquitted men on technicalities, they helped instill a belief in the disembodied justice of the law in the minds of all who watched. In short, its very inefficiency, its absurd formalism, was part of its strength as ideology. (Hay, 1975: 33)

In other words, the law was made to appear as if it had divine origins and that it was above class interests and control. The law's strength as an ideological force lay in the belief that the nation was under the rule of law rather than the rule of wealthy men. The myth of the rule of law remains to the present day.

The *mercy* of the law was shown through the extensive use of pardons of condemned men and the fact that the number of executions remained fairly stable, while offenses punishable by death increased in the eighteenth century. What appeared was a form of what Weber called *khadi justice*, in which there was much formalism in the administration of the law, but in which the law "was nevertheless based on ethical or practical judgments rather than on a fixed, 'rational' set of rules" (Hay, 1975: 40). In other words, justice was administered in a very informal, almost *ad hoc*, manner with few formal procedural rules. Such mercy reinforced the benign paternalism of the ruling class, especially on the numerous occasions when even the poor were granted reprieves. Hay provides the following conclusion:

> Here was the peculiar genius of the law. It allowed the rulers of England to make the courts a selective instrument of class justice, yet simultaneously to proclaim the law's incorruptible impartiality, and absolute determinacy. . . .it allowed the class that passed one of the bloodiest penal codes in Europe to congratulate itself on its humanity. It encouraged loyalty to the king and the state. (Hay, 1975: 48–49):

Emergence of the Concept of "Crime"

The emergence of criminal law (and hence the notion of crime) in England did not occur in a vacuum. Rather, it emerged in the context of larger structural changes in economic and political institutions. As has already been suggested, it reflected a shift from feudalism to nationalism (before this time there was no concept of "England," "nation," or "country") and the replacement of blood ties as a basis of social order to ties based on land ownership (i.e., private property). Moreover, the notion of crime carried with it the notion of sin. Furthermore, the concept of *mens rea* (i.e., guilty mind) also emerged during this time. Jeffery comments as follows:

> The concept of *mens rea* was derived from the Christian view of sins of the mind. Sins can be punished individually, not collectively, so that the individual and not the clan or family is responsible. Only individuals have souls that can be saved; social groups do not possess souls, and for that reason tribal responsibility gave way to the Christian notion of individual responsibility. (Jeffery, 1969: 30)

In short, a new legal system emerged along with changes in th〔 structure. Criminal law and the notion of crime emerged from the tra〔 ⌐⌐⌐⌐ from tribal to state law. The differences between these two legal systems is summarized as follows (Jeffery, 1969: 31):

Tribal Law	State Law
Blood tie	Territorial tie
Collective responsibility	Individual responsibility
Family as unit of justice and order	State as unit of justice
Feud or compensation	Punishment

The social structure of tribal society was held together through clans of or not of families, offenses were the responsibility of the collectivity, and it was their duty to settle offenses through either feud or compensation. Under state law (as in today's society), the social structure was held together through private property, the individual was solely responsible for his or her actions, and the state stepped in to administer justice through a system of punishment.

There was, however, a much larger change occurring, that of the emergence of capitalism as a dominant economic form and, with it, the coming of what is known as the *state*.[3] This is a society based on the "centralization of power under some ruler or government with the authority to issue directives and commands binding upon all members of the society" (Michalowski, 1985: 69). As state societies emerge, there also emerges a system whereby the victim of an offense begins to take a back seat in the proceedings, as the state takes over handling disputes. As suggested in the previous chart, the individual is gradually substituted for the family or kinfolk as the offended party. Eventually, it is the *state itself that is the offended party* and, therefore, is supposed to act as a sort of "representative" of the victim, rather than the victim's kin.

In time, what occurred was the development of a technology capable of producing a *surplus* of goods and a complex *division of labor*, along with a system of stratification and a very *politicized economy*. What eventually happened was that a centralized power base arose that began to compel or coerce a surplus from the workforce. This eventually led to inequality among different groups, with one group—the group that rises to power and has control over the means of production—controlling most of the surplus and therefore wealth. Once this occurs, the threat of trouble comes in the form of "revolutions, peasant and slave uprisings, labor strife, and common crimes as groups or individuals seek to effect either a personal or more general redistribution of wealth and power." Thus, there arises the need for a formal system of "law" to respond to such threats to the prevailing order (Michalowski, 1985: 74–75). Therefore, it is not surprising to find the general conclusion among many scholars to the effect that formal law came about only with the rise of *private property*. As Bentham wrote, "Property and law are born together and die together" (quoted in Michalowski, 1985: 75). This is exactly what occurred, beginning during the period between the eighth and eleventh centuries. Several case studies of these changes and how the legal system changed are available, two of which are discussed in the next section. What these two cases show is that the law and the new legal order placed primary importance on the protection of private property and the social inequalities that the emerging system of capitalism produced (Tigar and Levy, 1977).

Two Case Studies: The Law of Theft and the Law of Vagrancy

Two studies of the origins of two specific criminal laws in early English society provide evidence that the law often reflects the interests of the rich and the powerful, and tends to punish mainly the poor and the powerless: studies of the law of theft (Hall, 1969) and the law of vagrancy (Chambliss, 1975a).[4]

The law of theft dates from the fifteenth century in the famous Carrier case of 1473, which resulted in a totally new view of the concept of theft. In this case, the defendant, who was hired to carry bales of merchandise to Southampton, opened the bales and absconded with the contents. He was arrested and charged with a felony.

Prior to this case, the necessary element of theft was *trespass*. The property had to be literally removed from the premises before larceny could legally have occurred. But the accused in this case already had possession of the bales; therefore, technically, he could neither have committed trespass nor be charged with theft. The judges broke precedence and ruled that breaking into the bales and removing the contents constituted trespass, because possession of the bales did not mean possession of the contents (today this would probably be considered *embezzlement*).

The Carrier case must be understood in the economic and political context within which it occurred. When this case was decided, England was in the middle of a commercial revolution. With the onset of industrialism and early forms of capitalist development, there came a dependence on foreign trade. King Richard III, a merchant himself, had provided protection to foreign merchants that guaranteed safe passage for their goods. It was in the interests of the commercial class to ensure favorable relations with foreign merchants (the complainant in this case was an Italian merchant), and because the courts were subservient to the crown, they too had to protect the interests of the merchants.

During the fifteenth century, the number of merchants greatly increased and Southampton became the leading port of trade. Furthermore, the contents of the bales in this case consisted either of wool or cloth or both, which, coincidentally, were the leading products of the time. Therefore, Hall concludes that "the interests of the most important industry in England were involved in the case" (Hall, 1969: 50). Criminal law, specifically the law of theft, lagged behind the needs of the times (i.e., the needs of the rising merchant class) and was changed to meet those new needs through the Carrier case.

One more important point must be mentioned in this regard. During this period, feudalism was disappearing and the Black Death in 1348 (plus various enclosure movements) forced millions of peasants off the land and killed many more. Economic changes brought about by the declining feudal economic system created a new class of vagabonds and beggars, who were cut adrift from the mainstream of the newly emerging economic system known as *capitalism.* In short, there were simply not enough jobs to go around and this new class had to develop alternative methods of making a living. One method was stealing. Inciardi made the following summation of this process:

> As trade and commerce developed in seaports and interior cities assuring landowners a ready market for foodstuffs, land became valuable and many peasants were forced from their land. The decreasing yield from the soil, however, led to the initiation of the three-field system, thus forcing additional serfs from the land that had to remain fallow. In England specifically, the economic changes during this period were closely associated with the rise of the rogue and vagabond class. Ownership of land became individual rather than communal. Serfs had attempted to improve their conditions by severing themselves from the soil and accepting wages, but this alternative led to a more intense state of destitution. As sheep farming increased, the enclosure acts, which began in the twelfth century, more drastically affected the peasants, for their lands, as well as waste lands, suddenly became usable as pasture. (Inciardi, 1975: 7)

Understandably, merchants and landowners wanted to protect themselves from these hordes of peasants who, within a few centuries, would earn the label of "dangerous classes."

Before capitalism, it was customary for villagers and farmers to freely take wood from the forests (as well as wild game, fruit, and even the contents of wrecked ships) because it was considered "common land." After capitalism emerged, these activities were defined by the state as crimes. Thus, criminal law helped to create *private property* by defining *common rights* (e.g., taking of wood) as crimes.[5]

The emergence of the law of vagrancy, and the different uses of this law throughout history, gives evidence that the profit-making classes use the law to control and/or regulate the labor force and groups who are perceived as a threat to their dominance. Chambliss's analysis provides us with this illustration (Chambliss, 1975).

t vagrancy statute was enacted in 1349 in England. The origi-
lated that it was a crime to give alms to any person of sound
dy who was unemployed. In actual fact, the law was passed to
provide a steady supply of cheap labor to landowners and to regulate the
labor force. The prime force behind this law was the famous Black Death of
1348–1349, the pestilence that reduced the population in England by about
one half. Among the results of this wave of pestilence was the reduction in
the size of the labor force and the corresponding reduction in the profits
of the lords of the manors and other employers. Cheyney describes it as
follows:

> After the Black Death the same demesne lands were to be cultivated, and in
> most cases the larger holdings remained or descended or were regranted to
> those who would expect to continue their cultivation. Thus, the demand for
> laborers remained approximately as great as it had before. The number of
> laborers, on the other hand, was vastly diminished. They were, therefore,
> eagerly sought for by employers. Naturally, they took advantage of their posi-
> tion to demand higher wages, and in many cases combined to work at the old
> accustomed rates. (Cheney, 1913: 104–105)

This period witnessed a significant change in social-class relations and
in the composition of the workforce. What the new laws indicated was that
more people were beginning to make their living by working for a wage,
whereas before they had not (they worked the land as serfs). Workers were
becoming more mobile, searching for the best jobs at the highest wages. In
short, it was the beginning of a capitalist economic system (Huberman,
1963). This system became a constant battleground between owners and
workers (still going on today). The conflict is at the heart of the capitalist
social order: it is the inherent contradiction within a capitalist system,
whereby the process of producing commodities is essentially a *public*
process involving many different people, while the results of such production (in this case the *profits)* are *privately* owned.[6]

In response to this significant change, the landowning class passed a
series of laws known as the Statutes of Laborers in 1349. The new law stipulated that every man "when offered service at these wages must accept it
. . . if any laborers, men or women, bond or free, should refuse to accept such
an offer of work, they were to be imprisoned. . . ." (Cheyney, 1913: 107).

This was an obvious attempt to respond to the growing poverty and
the concomitant threat to social order. It was a period when "bread riots
were common and landless farmers poured into English cities" and
vagrants were perceived as being a challenge to "social order" (Adler, 1989a:
213). The vagrancy laws passed at this time were consciously designed to
control the mobility of the laboring classes and to protect mostly the interests of the landowners. The laws were designed "to curtail the mobility of
laborers in such a way that labor would not become a commodity for which

the landowners would have to compete" (Chambliss, 1975: cation of such laws was widespread, focusing not only o also "rogues" and thieves, along with "gypsies, Irishmen, ̤. university scholars found begging without permission, and peau. (Adler, 1989a: 213).

In time, the law was altered to adapt to changing social and economic conditions. In 1530, the law was reactivated (after being dormant for several years) as a result of a shift in focal concern from the idle and those refusing to work to such criminal types as rogues and vagabonds, plus others who developed criminal careers because of their marginal positions in society and the shortage of employment opportunities. Indeed, the merchants and other capitalist entrepreneurs needed protection from those whose life conditions forced them to steal in order to survive.

It would be a mistake to conclude that it was simply the narrow interests of the capitalist class at work here. Obviously, ordinary citizens were concerned about the threats posed by rogues and vagabonds of an earlier era and common criminals throughout nineteenth- and twentieth-century American society. Vagrancy statutes continued to be used to cover a wide variety of social problems. In fact, as Adler correctly points out, vagrancy codes throughout the nineteenth century defined *vagrant* in such broad terms that "anyone who threatened social order" could be arrested. On numerous occasions, they were used to arrest labor organizers and rebellious workers, "tramps" and "beggars," and a whole host of other "undesirables" (Adler, 1989a: 214–215). A study of the use of vagrancy laws in early nineteenth-century St. Louis shows quite clearly that local merchants and capitalists, as well as most ordinary citizens, wanted protection from "outsiders" such as "wanderers" and "paupers" (poor people). After all, their presence was a threat to social order and the creation and maintenance of a stable business climate, the profits of which accrued mostly to the wealthy. However, enough profits "trickled down" to enough people to mean that many ordinary citizens would naturally perceive threats from rogues, vagabonds, wanderers and a host of other undesirables. The laws reflected the interests of the capitalist class of St. Louis—and a number of others as well (Adler, 1986). However, the social conditions that created a class of vagabonds, wanderers, petty thieves, and paupers were the result of an expansive capitalist system that allowed great fortunes to be amassed by a relatively small group of capitalists throughout the nineteenth century, while creating hordes of poverty-stricken people left completely out of the emerging "American Dream."[7]

From this review, we can concur with Adler who appears to be challenging the Marxist interpretation of vagrancy laws, yet his comments seem to support my own interpretation that such laws, like laws in general, do in fact reflect the interests of the dominant classes and seem to concentrate on those deemed "undesirable" or perhaps even "dangerous," while simultaneously being supported by other classes (who are usually the most directly victimized). Thus, the use of the criminal law (in this case, vagrancy laws) has been an excellent illustration of "controlling the dangerous classes."

The use of criminal law to protect the interests of the dominant classes, its use as an ideological system of control, and its use to secure and protect the foundations of a particular economic system continued as colonists began to settle in America. The American legal system, with a few modifications, was simply an adaptation of English criminal law.

Emergence of Criminal Law in America

In Colonial America, many of the laws had religious foundations that were based primarily on maxims from the Old Testament (Erickson, 1966; Haskins, 1960; Powers, 1966; Nelson, 1975). The maxim "eye for an eye" was reflected in some of the punishments. Several capital offenses (i.e., punishable by death) had Biblical foundations, including idolatry, witchcraft, blasphemy, bestiality, sodomy, adultery, and cursing or smiting a parent. The Puritan leaders in the Massachusetts Bay Colony developed a conception of a government that was divinely ruled. The "word of God" served as a basis for the newly established order. The governor and his magistrates "were granted power through divine authority. As 'Gods upon earth,' the leaders must be fully obeyed in order that the covenant be kept." Governor John Winthrop expressed this view when he stated:

> . . . the determination of law belongs properly to God: He is the only lawgiver, but He hath given power and gifts to man to interpret his laws; and this belongs principally to the highest authority in a commonwealth, and subordinately to other magistrates and judges according to their several places. (Quinney, 1970: 61–62)

For Winthrop and other rulers, this was an easy method to secure their own power and legitimacy.

It is clear that the rulers of the Massachusetts Bay Colony used the legal system to secure their conception of "order" in addition to their hegemony. It is also true that the law was used to persecute those who threatened the traditional religious beliefs. Haskins goes so far as to suggest that "the government of Massachusetts was thus a dictatorship of a small minority who were unhesitantly prepared to coerce the unwilling to serve the purposes of society as they conceived it" (Haskins, 1960: 44–45). The majority of the cases handled in the courts were offenses against morality, such as adultery, cohabitation, fornication, indecent exposure, blasphemy, and the like (Nelson, 1975: 37–38). There were even laws specifically against Quakers, who were a serious threat to the religious rulers of the time. For instance, it was a capital offense for a Quaker to return to the colony after banishment. Three Quakers were hanged in Massachusetts because of the violation of this law (Friedman, 1993: 32). Obviously, crime and sin went hand in hand during this time. However, throughout this period, instability was constantly at hand; eventually, a change that threatened the very foundations of Puritan society came during the seventeenth century.

Erickson noted several "crime waves" during the seventeenth century and suggested that these served to help establish the *moral boundaries* of the Puritan settlement. That is, by enforcing various laws that were violated during these crime waves, the *consensus* on what was "good and proper" conduct was "reaffirmed" (Erickson, 1966). Chambliss offers a different interpretation; he suggests that these crime waves were precipitated "by power struggles between those who ruled and those who were ruled" (Chambliss, 1976: 11). The case of Anne Hutchinson is illustrative: she began holding meetings in her home, which included religious discussions that gave an interpretation of the Bible that conflicted with the popular beliefs of others in the Commonwealth. She and her followers were accused of being *antinomians* (a religious sect that opposed the dominant Puritan religion) and subsequently were banished as criminals.

Some twenty years later, the emergence of the Quakers created another conflict. They, too, were punished for their "blasphemy"; in fact, it was a criminal offense to be a Quaker. In the 1670s, in Salem, the outbreak of witchcraft provided the arena for yet another power struggle. This was partly a diversionary tactic used by the rulers at a time when their authority was threatened by England. As Chambliss notes, "the potential diversion of witchcraft served to give at least the appearance of a reaffirmation of authority in the hands of those who ruled" (Chambliss, 1976). Those who were defiant or hostile to the rulers were put to death; those who confessed and generally accepted the legitimacy of those in power were spared the death penalty. A total of nineteen people were executed, mostly women (Friedman, 1993: 46). (See Chapters 3 and 6 for more details on the Salem witch trials.) By labeling others as *criminal, heretic,* or *witch,* the rulers were able to reduce conflict and control the rest of the population.[8]

The most noteworthy changes in American criminal law came on the heels of the American Revolution. The rise of the bourgeois class (primarily planters, merchants, and lawyers) to power brought with it attempts to centralize the powers of a new state and, in effect, to control those who threatened the new social "order" (Takagi, 1975). In other words, criminal law was changed to meet the demands of a changing society. Nelson's study of criminal law in post-Revolutionary America is instructive. He says that the period immediately following the Revolution was a time of great civil strife and disorder (e.g., Shay's Rebellion). The new rulers "feared organized groups of malcontents bent upon the reconstruction of society . . . they feared such political activity because they expected that it would be economically motivated. . . . In short, their fear was that the economically underprivileged would seek material gain by banding together to deprive the more privileged persons of their wealth and standing" (Nelson, 1974: 111). There was a shift in the focal concern of criminal law from enforcing morality to the protection of private property (owned by a very small minority) and social order. Court cases reflect this shift, for the bulk of the cases after the Revolution concerned property and public order offenses, whereas previously most cases involved offenses against morality.

Laws that explicitly protected the political order of Britain were adopted to serve the same purposes in America. For instance, the Sedition Act was passed in 1798 and provided for the punishment of those who made any statements against the newly formed government. "The law, as well as curtailing loyalty to the British, became an instrument of the Federalists in their attempt to suppress the activities (considered pro-French) of the opposition Republican Party." Similarly, the law of treason was used to secure the new order, especially those laws that were "anti-loyalist," for example—those that disfranchised the loyalists (Quinney, 1970: 58).

The period immediately following the war of independence was a period of reform of the criminal law. Ideally, the leaders wanted a legal system that was not monarchic and authoritarian, like it was under British rule. In part, the new legal codes would follow some of Becarria's formulations.[9] The famous Bill of Rights was part of this reform effort and about half of them were directly related to criminal matters. More than anything else, however, such reforms were an effort by those now in power to create an ideology that the new nation was to be one under the rule of law instead of the rule of men. In fact, of course, it was and continues to be a nation under the rule of men—specifically white, upper-class men.[10] The notion of rule of law merely camouflages the nature of power and control in this society.

This period also witnessed many other legal reforms, the most important of which was the abandonment of various public punishments (e.g., whippings and the stocks and the pillory), narrowing the number of crimes punishable by death, the creation of a full-time uniformed police force (see Chapter 2), and the creation of a new prison system (see Chapter 4).

More than anything else, however, the reforms merely made it easier for those in power to create a legal system that help reinforce their rule. It is inherently class-biased, which can be seen in the text of the Constitution, written as it was by men of property and wealth (Beard, 1935). Was it any accident that Native Americans, women, and slaves were systematically excluded from the creation of the new government? In a sense, the newly emerging criminal justice system became, in Friedman's words, "the strong arm of the stratification system" (Friedman, 1993: 84). Nowhere is this better illustrated than with regard to the matter of race.

Racism and the Law

The development of legal institutions in America corresponded to the development of racist ideologies and the oppression of Native Americans, African Americans, and other racial and ethnic minorities. The law, especially during the nineteenth century, was used to regulate and control the labor of minorities. Two groups—Native Americans and black slaves—were especially troublesome (to those in power) by their presence in early American history, and the legal system did its best to keep them in their place.

When Columbus began his explorations into the New World, it marked the beginning of a "confrontation between the conquerors and the conquered on a global scale" (Chomsky, 1993: 3). The Arawaks, the first West Indians Columbus met, were a peaceful group, and they ran out to greet the visitors, bearing gifts, food, and water. Columbus was to write in his log that "With fifty men, we could subjugate them all and make them do whatever we want." However, the traits displayed by the Arawaks were not those that stood out among Europeans, "dominated as it was by the religion of popes, the government of kings, the frenzy for money. . . ." What Columbus wanted more than anything else was gold in order to finance the conquests of Spain, a society where about 2 percent of the population owned 95 percent of the land. He found no gold, but in the process about half of the 250,000 West Indians on Haiti died within two years; by 1515, there were approximately fifty thousand Indians left; and by 1550, there were five hundred; by 1650, *none* of the original Arawaks were left. It has been estimated that more than three million Indians perished in the West Indies between 1492 and 1508, prompting one writer to describe this as "complete genocide" (Zinn, 1995: 1–7).[11]

The law supported the wholesale confiscation of their land throughout the nation and the genocide committed against them. These people were ruled by a foreign law rather than their own customs (in this case, a tribal society ruled by tribal law was overthrown and ruled by a capitalist society and legal system). The peculiar logic of European law maintained that the West Indians had only a "natural" right to the land, but not a "civil right." Obviously, from this point of view, the natural right had no legal standing; that is, "legal" from the point of view of the European conquerors. The entire invasion of North America was based on an ideology born of a civilization based on the relentless drive to amass profits, no matter what the outcome in human terms. It was a civilization based on subjugation that confronted a world based more on egalitarian relations (Zinn, 1995: 13–22).

Many of the broken "treaties" were supported by the American legal system. Native American land was confiscated through trickery and the "white man's law" by the use of the legal term *title*, which was foreign to the native language and was an invention of a capitalist economy (i.e., private property as a new concept). This confiscation, writes Deloria, was supported by the U.S. Supreme Court in a nineteenth-century case known as *Lone Wolf v. Hitchcock*. Deloria notes that the court in this case "laid down the principle that the tribes had no title to the land at all. Rather the land was held by the United States and the tribes had mere occupancy rights" (Deloria, 1969: 46). Burns cites another case (*Johnson v. Macintoch*, 1823) where the court ruled that "discovery gave exclusive title to those who made it," thus upholding the claim that whites "discovered" America (Burns, 1974: 264; Brown, 1971).

In the case of African Americans, the law supported slavery and their kidnapping from Africa. Profits from the slave trade were enormous, as so many have noted—and perfectly legal. Slavery became a form of labor exploitation and a method of controlling the labor market. Numerous laws had to be passed to help perpetuate slavery. Laws were passed in the Carolinas prohibiting free blacks from traveling into Native American country, apparently on the assumption that the two groups might join together. It was common for black and white slaves and servants to run away together, so laws were passed to prohibit this. For example, Virginia passed a law in 1661 prohibiting a white English servant from running away with a black slave. In 1691 it passed another law prohibiting interracial marriages. Many slaveholders felt uneasy keeping so many black slaves without many white servants to help keep "order" on the plantations. So in 1717, Parliament passed laws making transportation a punishment for crime, resulting in "tens of thousands" of convicts being sent to various colonies, especially Maryland and Virginia. By the end of the seventeenth century, laws were passed throughout the southern states that made slavery a perpetual condition for black people. In fact, with the coming of the American Revolution, "freedom" became a reality for whites only. As Burns noted, the Constitution itself guaranteed the continuation of the slave trade, the return of fugitive slaves, and "the counting of black persons as three-fifths human beings for purposes of taxation and representation" (Burns, 1990: 116).

The various slave codes passed throughout The South became a common method of legalizing slavery. Such codes "legislated and regulated in minute detail every aspect of the life of a slave and of black/white interaction; assured white-over-black dominance; and made black people into virtual nonpersons . . ." (Burns, 1990: 117). It was not merely the plantation owners, but rather the entire community that was involved in the legal regulation of slaves. As merely a few examples among hundred, there were many "slave patrols" and the law authorized these men to pick up runaway and "disorderly" slaves and slaves who were found without a pass (Zinn, 1995: 31, 54–56). What the law did was to codify and express "the basic theorem of slave law." It represented the "massive power of masters and mistresses, and the power of their agents and overseers" (Friedman, 1993: 85).

One example of the racist nature of the law in the case of African Americans is demonstrated in a law passed in 1855 in the state of Kansas. The law stipulated that a white man convicted of raping of a white woman could be sentenced to no more than five years in prison. However, the penalty for a black man for the same offense was castration. Wherever such a law was in force, it was reserved almost exclusively for African Americans (or, in some cases, for Native Americans) (Burns, 1990: 115).

Regular courts in The South would deal with the more serious crimes committed by slaves, which, however, were mostly property crimes. In some cases, slaves convicted of violent crimes were hanged; not surprisingly, most of these cases were rape, always involving a white victim. The hangings were well attended and whites made certain that blacks attended, to send a clear message that a black person dare not commit a violent crime against a white person. In these cases, the white owner was compensated for slaves put to death. In Louisiana, for instance, the "public treasury" provided up to $750 per slave; in South Carolina, the value attached was much lower, at $122.45 per slave (Friedman, 1993: 88).

After the Civil War, the legal system worked to keep African Americans in their place, with vaguely worded vagrancy laws (reactivated after being dormant), Black Codes, and the famous Jim Crow laws creating segregation in hotels, restaurants, and other public places (Woodward, 1955; Shelden, 1979). In short, there was a concerted effort to search for any legal means necessary to maintain the status quo. What many of the legal codes did was to keep so-called "free" blacks tied to the land (owned by whites) via the system of *sharecropping* (a throwback to the feudal system and a form of slavery). This became a form of perpetual debt. (The movie *Sounders* dramatically depicts this economic system.) The doctrine of "separate but equal" was upheld by the Supreme Court in *Plessy v. Ferguson* in 1896. In this famous case, a man named Homer Plessy (who was described as not really black but an octoroon) purchased a first-class train ticket and sat in a "white only" section. He was summarily ejected from the train and tossed in jail in New Orleans. He claimed in his defense that this was in violation of the thirteenth and fourteenth amendments. It went all the way to the U.S. Supreme Court where, by an eight to one vote, the court rejected the appeal. Writing for the majority, Chief Justice Henry B. Brown said that the segregation of the races is "natural" and "if one race be inferior to the other socially, the Constitution cannot put them upon the same plane." In a famous dissent, Justice John Marshall Harlan wrote that the "Constitution is color-blind" (Friedman, 1993: 96). Obviously, the Constitution was color-blind in theory only. In fact, there was really never any intention among the framers of this document to include "lesser" people, like slaves, Native Americans, and even women as having "equal rights before the law." In this sense, the Constitution has served as an ideological prop for the capitalist system, claiming that this system is "the best of all possible worlds," at least for the minority who reap the most benefits.

Another method of control involved various voting barriers, which were supported by law throughout The South. An example of such legal practices was the "grandfather clause," a law stipulating that in order for a man to vote, his grandfather had to have been eligible to vote—an obvious impossibility for blacks, for no black man had ever been granted the vote in America. In short, the entire legal system, from the wording of specific laws to the penal system (e.g., with convict leasing), helped maintain white rule in The South after the Civil War (Genovese, 1976; Shelden, 1979; Adamson, 1999; Myers and Massey, 1999). Chapter 4 discusses the convict-lease system, another form of slavery.

Other minority groups have fared little better at the hands of the legal system. These groups were often subjugated by means of criminal law to provide capitalists a steady supply of cheap labor during the nineteenth century and well into the twentieth. The legal system lent support to and made possible capitalist expansion in the nineteenth century. For example, Chinese people were recruited to do the back-breaking work of building the railroads to The West, beginning with the Gold Rush in the 1840s (Dinnerstein and Reimers, 1975: 57). Wu makes the following observation:

> . . . The Chinese were initially brought into the United States to meet the serious labor shortages which then affected economic growth, particularly in California. As a rule, they performed unskilled labor, the kind of strenuous and menial jobs which whites tended to shy away from. For a short while, the Chinese immigrants were generally welcomed; racial prejudice gave way temporarily to economic necessity. The Chinese were admired as "our most orderly and industrious citizens," "the best immigrants in California," "law-abiding," "inoffensive," and "tractable." (Wu, 1972: 2)

However, shortly after the railroads were completed and their labor was no longer in great demand, the Chinese began to be looked upon as "dangerous," "criminal," "deceitful and vicious," and "inferior." In 1882, Congress passed the Exclusion Law, which prohibited Chinese workers from entering the country and denied them citizenship rights. Between 1882 and 1902, Congress passed a total of thirteen discriminatory laws against the Chinese people (Wu, 1972: 5).[12] This was one of the most obvious examples of how criminal law was used to aid the profit-making adventures of nineteenth-century capitalists, often known as the *robber barons*. Josephson noted that two "captains of industry," Leland Stanford (after whom Stanford University was named) and Elsworth Huntington, helped finance the building of railroads to The West with the help of the low wages paid to Chinese workers. In fact, Huntington reportedly paid his Chinese workers $1 per day, about half the wage given to white men (Josephson, 1962: 86). Laws

were passed that restricted Chinese from owning proper
court, and becoming naturalized citizens.[13] Japanese Amer
similar fate, especially during World War II, when many wei
concentration camps. As Burns notes, "The barbed-wire poιιcy ..~
rized by the President, implemented by Congress, and ultimately approved
by the Supreme Court, on the ground of national security" (Burns, 1974:
267). It is interesting and ironic that many were imprisoned or otherwise
hassled by the legal system during the Nixon Administration in the late
1960s and early 1970s for "national security" reasons.

European immigrants were also the subjects of selective laws, once
American capitalists had made full use of their cheap labor. Corporations
(especially railroads) actively recruited European peasants through the
benevolence of state legislatures, which established the legality of having
corporate agents do the recruiting. Although several groups wanted immigration restricted, it was not until the 1920s that Congress enacted laws to
this effect. The Johnson-Reed Immigration Act of 1924 placed quotas on the
number of immigrants allowed to enter the country (Dinnerstein and
Reimers, 1975: 71).

The situation of Mexican Americans was similar to that of those
groups discussed previously. Railroad owners and large southwestern agricultural growers recruited Mexican Americans in large numbers to do the
menial work. Following the passage of the Johnson-Reed Immigration Act,
the agricultural growers in The American Southwest put pressure on
Congress to exempt Mexican Americans from the quota that this act established; Congress acceded to their demands. It was not until the depression
of the 1930s that the border patrol emerged and actively restricted immigration (Dinnerstein and Reimers, 1975: 71, 97).

An Illustrative Case: The Tramp Acts

Another example of legislation aimed at the control of immigrant and other
powerless groups was the passage of the Tramp Acts during the late nineteenth century. As Harring observes:

> The Tramp Acts were part of an increasing tendency of state legislatures to
> expand the criminal law. These laws, adopted in the 1870s and 1880s in a large
> number of states, particularly in The Northeast, outlawed travel without visi-
> ble means of support and subjected a significant proportion of the working
> class to the threat of months in prison at hard labor. (Harring, 1977: 873)

These acts were passed during a period of economic changes, with
various depressions and recessions, during the late nineteenth century. A
new social type was created, the "tramp," as thousands of workers "took to
the rails" in search of jobs. Most of these workers were unemployed immi-

grant males who, rather than accept the low wages (or no jobs at all) in the factories of The Northeast, decided to travel in search of better opportunities. In many ways, this was a classic example of the pioneer spirit so admired within the American ethos. However, this large pool of surplus labor became difficult to control, and capitalists viewed them as a threat because they would not play by their rules (i.e., take the jobs capitalists offered at the prevailing wage). Quite often a linkage was made between tramping and criminal activity, which made it easier for those in power to justify the repression of this group (Harring, 1977: 875).

The Tramp Acts were actually extensions or modifications of vagrancy laws already on the books. Behavior that was previously punished as a misdemeanor was now considered, if committed by a tramp, a felony and punished with three years of hard labor. Thus, rather than the law deriving from the consensus of the majority and seeking to protect all of the people, the Tramp Acts clearly reflected a minority interest, in this case the manufacturers.

It seems obvious that the legal system has time and again supported the rich and powerful above all others. They use the law to help perpetuate their power and control. For instance, according to the Maryland Constitution of 1776, to run for the office of governor one had to own five thousand pounds worth of property and to run for state senator, one thousand pounds. Thus, about 90 percent of the population was automatically excluded. In his classic work *An Economic Interpretation of the Constitution*, Beard found clear evidence that it was the richest people in the colonies who wrote the Constitution and established the government. He made the point that the rich, in order to maintain their power, must either control the government directly, or "control the laws by which government operates" (Beard, 1935, quoted in Zinn, 1995: 89).

Throughout the nineteenth century, various laws were passed that helped create and sustain vast differences in wealth and social standing in American society. The list is almost endless; examples include the following:

- The Homestead Act of 1862, which promised 160 acres to anyone willing to cultivate the land for five years for $1.25 per acre, was beyond the reach of the average person (most could not come up with the required $200), so rich speculators bought up most of the land.
- During the Civil War, Congress gave 100 million acres to railroads and established a national bank, resulting in a partnership between big business and the government, thus guaranteeing huge profits.
- A "Contract Labor Law" passed in 1864 enabled companies to sign "contracts" with foreign workers if they pledged to give back twelve months worth of wages to help pay the cost of immigration. (Zinn, 1995: 233–234)

Controlling the Dangerous Classes: Drug Laws [14]

Perhaps no area of legislation has created more controversy than legislation against the use of certain drugs. The sordid history of anti-drug legislation is filled with emotions and vested interests. To fully understand these laws, we need to examine briefly the history of the use and abuse of drugs.

The use and distribution of opium can be traced at least as far back as the eighth and ninth centuries, when Turkish traders began to seek markets for their homegrown crop. The trade in opium was rather inconsequential until capitalism began to replace feudalism, around the sixteenth century (Chambliss, 1977).

Leaders in the opium market at this time were the Portuguese. Because Europe had little to offer Asia in terms of goods to trade, the Portuguese ships began to raid Asian vessels in search of marketable goods. What they found was opium, which they could readily use in trade for tea, silk, spices, and pottery.

As opium dens began to flourish, European powers—through the British East India Company—gained almost total control. As addiction to opium began to spread throughout China, the Chinese began to make attempts to stem the flow of the plant. Britain fought back, defeating the Manchu Dynasty in the Opium War (1839–1842) and gaining possession of Hong Kong, the major port of the opium trade. One result of the ensuing treaty between China and Britain was that the British were to enforce laws against smuggling. But while the Chinese law forbade smuggling opium, British law did not. Thus, Britain was given complete freedom in the control of the opium trade. After another brief war broke out in 1856, opium was legalized. Hence, the profit for Britain in opium was increased immeasurably. But a tax was imposed by China, and Chinese farmers were given the right to grow the plant.

During the last half of the nineteenth century, European countries almost literally took over as colonies all of Southeast Asia. A famine in China reduced the labor force and caused thousands of Chinese to immigrate. The Chinese went to major cities in Southeast Asia and as far away as the United States. They brought with them the British-encouraged opium habit, which proved to be helpful to colonial governments since those addicted were a compliant workforce. Chambliss comments as follows:

> The opium trade was carefully, albeit corruptly, organized and controlled by an unholy alliance between colonial officials, local governments, and entrepreneurs who were given government franchises to import and sell opium. The profits were substantial. Opium sales provided 40 to 50 percent of the income of colonial governments. Opium profits helped finance the railways,

canals, roads, and government buildings, as well as the comfortable living conditions of colonial bureaucrats. (Chambliss, 1977: 78)

By the 1840s, there were more than 2,500 opium dens in Indochina, providing for about 45 percent of all tax revenues.

During the last half of the nineteenth century, the growing of opium in China increased and began to compete with the demand for Indian- and Turkish-grown opium. Britain and America (who came upon the scene much later) were soon forced to look elsewhere for profits. The major producing monopoly eventually centered on the Golden Triangle (i.e., where Laos, Burma, and Thailand meet). In the meantime, the French began to invest in this trade and eventually took monopolistic control of Indochinese opium. This proved to be a successful weapon against Communist insurgence, as the French were able to pay off hill tribes and local leaders who would support the French in their struggle.

Prior to the twentieth century, the common attitude toward drug use in both the United States, and Britain could be characterized as *laissez-faire*. The use of such highly addictive drugs as opium and cocaine was common and accepted in both countries. A survey of thirty-five Boston drugstores in 1888 discovered that more than three fourths (78 percent) of prescriptions refilled three or more times contained opium (Levinthal, 1996: 154).

The use of various forms of cocaine gained acceptance for both its anesthetic and psychopharmacological properties throughout the late nineteenth century. In fact, by 1883, cocaine was indexed in fifty scientific papers. "Among its uses, cocaine was prevalent as an anesthetic for ophthalmological surgery, and widely prescribed for such respiratory ailments as asthma, whooping cough, and tuberculosis during this time." Even Sigmund Freud supported its use "as an antidote for morphine addiction and alcoholism, as an aphrodisiac and a cure for asthma" (Trueblood, 1999: 4; Musto, 1973; Helmer, 1975).

By 1890, cocaine had become the primary ingredient in many elixirs and other "restoratives" that claimed to relieve a variety of disabilities, such as common colds, asthma, headaches, influenza, and depression. Cocaine was also found in cigars, cigarettes, chewing gum, and various "tonics"—most notably, Coca-Cola (Trueblood, 1999: 4).

The first influx of opium into the United States came with Chinese workers (commonly known as *coolies*) starting in the 1850s. Opium was used to combat the psychological pain of their work and as relief from physical illnesses. From the point of view of employers, it was good business, in terms of both profit and pacifying workers.

Opium came into the United States legally through normal business channels. By the 1880s, however, when mining and railroad building had declined, the United States became concerned with the number of Chinese (and other) immigrants coming into the country. The two countries agreed to stop Chinese immigration in return for a reduction in opium going to China via American shipbuilders. The first anti-opium legislation passed in 1886, making it illegal to trade in opium (Chambliss, 1977: 65).

After the Civil War, attitudes began to change and strong opposition developed toward the smoking of opium; an attitude directed mainly toward Chinese immigrants. Opium smoking—in contrast to opium *drinking* in the form of laudanum and similar legally prescribed products used by middle- and upper-class people—eventually became associated with criminal activity, and demand for the control of opium dens grew. In response, the first recorded drug law in the United States was passed in 1885, an ordinance in San Francisco banning opium dens (Levinthal, 1996: 49, 154–155; U. S. Sentencing Commission, 1995: 112). To quote a newspaper at that time, such an ordinance was passed for fear that "many women and young girls, as well as young men of respectable family, were being induced to visit the dens, where they were ruined morally and otherwise" (Levinthal, 1996: 155).

Then, in 1887, the federal government prohibited the importation of opium by the Chinese, and in 1905 restricted opium-smoking in the Philippines. For several years thereafter, "the United States launched a series of international conventions designed to foster narcotics control activity, including the Shanghai Opium Convention of 1909 and the 1911 International Conference on Opium at The Hague" (Trueblood, 1999: 5).

The regulation of opium-smoking came to epitomize the widespread fear and hostility of Chinese immigrants. It also "became the catalyst for the ensuing wave of reform sentiment that began to sweep the country respecting the use of any narcotics." These fears put extraordinary pressures on policymakers, the result of which was the passage of the Pure Food and Drug Act of 1906. This act required manufacturers to disclose the amounts of alcohol or "habit-forming" drugs (specifically opiates and cocaine) on product labels, although the law did not restrict the sale or use of these substances (Levinthal, 1996: 50).[15]

By the turn of the century, the opium trade had shifted from India to Turkey and then to Southeast Asia, especially the Golden Triangle. Opium dens were run and organized by the governments of China and other Southeast Asian countries, and profits supported both local and colonial governments.

In 1898, Bayer (a German pharmaceutical company) began distributing a product that it claimed was nonaddictive and had the same medical value as opium but without the undesirable side effects. This product was called *heroin*.

Like the attitude toward opium, as the use of cocaine became increasingly associated with minorities and crime, it was no longer perceived as a benign substance. Myths about the invincibility of "crazed" African Americans under the influence of cocaine were created and perpetuated through newspaper headlines such as one in 1913, which read: "Drug-Crazed Negroes Fire at Every One in Sight in Mississippi Town." It was believed that cocaine bestowed such brute strength on these "animals" that they were impervious to any and all efforts at social control—bullets included (Trueblood, 1999: 5; Goldstein, et al., 1997).

By 1914, almost every state in the nation had passed laws regulating the use and distribution of cocaine, all in the name of "crime control" (Trueblood, 1999: 5). In 1914, the United States passed the Harrison Act. This law made it illegal to trade in opium or its derivatives (including heroin) without registering with the federal government and paying taxes. Further interpretations of the act through court rulings (e.g., the Linder case in 1925) made it illegal to sell or possess these drugs (Lindesmith, 1965). The significance of this legislation was that the law, in effect, shifted attention from one class of drug addicts to another. As Duster noted, prior to the passage of the Harrison Act, the average drug addict was of middle to upper-middle class in origin, with the majority being middle-class housewives, mostly white. "Whereas in 1900 the addict population was spread relatively evenly over the social classes (with the higher classes having slightly more), by 1920, medical journals could speak of the 'overwhelming' majority from the 'unrespectable' parts of society" (Duster, 1970: 11). Thus, anti-drug legislation during this era followed previous legislation. In effect, it sought to control the "unrespectable" sector of the population, specifically the "dangerous classes" (especially racial minorities).

This legislation apparently made little difference as far as the drug business was concerned. After World War I, the heroin and opium business became highly competitive, run by local merchants who made special arrangements with merchant seamen and mercantilists. By 1938, the heroin business had grossed an estimated $1 billion annually (Chambliss, 1977: 67).

As the "law and order" crackdown on these drugs continued, Congress became even more punitive. It began enacting a series of laws that placed more restrictions on the use and distribution of illegal drugs. Perhaps more significantly, it created a new bureaucracy to regulate and enforce the new laws, the Federal Bureau of Narcotics, in 1930. This new agency was charged with enforcing drug laws (excluding alcohol), and the nation's first "drug czar," Harry J. Anslinger, was appointed its first commissioner (Trueblood, 1999: 7; U.S. Sentencing Commission, 1995: 133). "Anslinger was a staunchly conservative member of the Treasury Department during the Prohibition Era, who garnered the support of several important conservative U.S. Congressmen during his thirty-two–year tenure—not the least of whom was Senator Joseph R. McCarthy" (Trueblood, 1999: 6; Levinthal, 1996: 51).

The Great Depression and the end of Prohibition placed severe constraints on Congress in the allocation of federal spending in general, and spending for the Bureau of Narcotics. Anslinger, desperate for power and money, seized upon several unsubstantiated rumors in the 1930s concerning so-called "degenerate Spanish-speaking residents" in The Southwest who were going on crime sprees allegedly while smoking marijuana. Anslinger began calling it the "assassin of youth" and identifying it as the next major public menace (Levinthal, 1996: 51). According to law enforcement, this "killer weed," as it began to be referred to, "aroused sexual excitement and led to violent crimes" (Trueblood, 1999: 7; Goldstein et al., 1997). Soon thereafter, the movie *Reefer Madness* was released.

Reefer Madness, which has since become somewhat of a classic illustration of the hysteria surrounding certain drugs, showed the "moral decline of innocent young people unwittingly enticed into a deviant subculture of marijuana-smoking youth" (Trueblood, 1999: 7). This film was partly responsible for the passage of the Marijuana Tax Act of 1937, which regulated and taxed marijuana at the federal level. A series of state laws followed, criminalizing marijuana possession (Becker, 1963).

However, the Marijuana Tax Act and all the state laws passed in its wake predictably failed to reduce drug-consumption patterns of marijuana. The proposed evils of marijuana failed to materialize; eventually, public concern decreased and marijuana was no longer the subject of intense drug legislation.

However, it did not take too long for new drugs to come onto the scene. The 1960s saw a number of amendments to the laws then in effect. In 1961, for example, the United Nations adopted the single convention on narcotic drugs, establishing regulatory schedules of psychotropic substances. In 1962, the Bureau of Narcotics changed its name to the Bureau of Narcotics and Dangerous Drugs. Note the addition of the words *dangerous drugs*, perhaps signifying a shift in policy direction. Also, at the urging of President Kennedy, Anslinger retired (Trueblood, 1999: 7–8; Levinthal, 1996: 51; U.S. Sentencing Commission, 1995: 114).

It is clear that the interests of "the people" have not been represented in drug-control legislation. For the most part, the interests involved have been those of the manufacturers and the federal government, especially the Federal Bureau of Narcotics (now called the Drug Enforcement Administration). Evidence of the latter's influence is seen in the case of the first anti-marijuana legislation, the Marijuana Tax Act. As Becker noted, the Federal Bureau of Narcotics almost singlehandedly (with the help of "expert" testimony from certain manufacturers) outlawed marijuana with the passage of the Marijuana Tax Act of 1937. However, little concern over the evils of marijuana was evident until the 1960s (it had always been used mainly by lower-class people and minority groups), when middle- and upper-class youths began to use it (Becker, 1963).

In the meantime, two legislative acts (i.e., the Boggs Act of 1951 and the Narcotic Drug Control Act of 1956) substantially increased the penalties for possession and sale of drugs tremendously. For instance, in 1956 the penalty for first-offense possession was from two to ten years; for second-offense possession, the penalty was from five to twenty years. Gradually, the use of marijuana spread and so did the number of arrests. Then, during the late 1960s, pressure began to build for the decriminalization of marijuana. One of the prime motivating forces behind the reduction of penalties for possession of marijuana has been the growing number of young people from wealthy and influential families who had been arrested and sentenced to prison. The reform of the marijuana laws in the state of Nebraska is an illustration.

Galliher and Baum evaluated the legislation that resulted in decreased penalties for possession of marijuana in Nebraska in 1969. The bill, which reduced possession to a misdemeanor (a seven-day jail sentence as maximum), was passed without much fanfare. Few notices appeared in the newspapers and there was little debate. In such a conservative state as Nebraska, the authors note, this was quite unusual (Galliher and Baum, 1977).

Further probing found that about six months prior to the bill's introduction, a county attorney's son and the son of a college professor were arrested for possession of marijuana. The district attorney prosecuting the case told the authors that he felt it would be easier to get drug convictions if it was reduced to a misdemeanor. Other district attorneys agreed and said they wanted a law that was enforceable.

The state senator who sponsored the bill promised to make the bill retroactive in order to cover the sons of the college professor and the county attorney. It is apparent that the increasing use of marijuana by middle- and upper-class youth was the prime mover behind this bill. District attorneys, seeking easier convictions (possibly to increase their chances for reelection), were supportive of the bill. The issue of the seriousness of marijuana-possession laws only developed with visible and seemingly widespread use among the sons and daughters of the wealthy. "As long as marijuana use appeared only among the poor, the problem of drug convictions didn't emerge for either conservatives or liberals" (Galliher and Baum, 1977: 81).

One of the most notorious examples of vested interests of manufacturers is seen in the passage of the Comprehensive Drug Abuse and Prevention Act of 1970. This act was the outcome of a bill (S-3246), originally called the Controlled Dangerous Substances Act, introduced in September 1969 (Graham, 1977).

A few basic facts about the manufacture and distribution of drugs may help us understand the significance of this bill. In 1976, drug companies spent around $40 million on magazine advertising and another $97 million on television advertising. Retail sales during 1975 totaled $8,146,000,000 on prescription drugs alone. Obviously, the drug companies had a direct interest in the outcome of this bill.

There were three schedules under the proposed bill, each categorized according to the degree of penalties assessed to violators and the extent of enforcement required. Amphetamines (such as those consumed in the millions by housewives, business executives, truckers, and many other "respectable" people) were placed in Schedule III; "hard drugs," such as LSD, heroin, cocaine, and marijuana, were placed in Schedule I.

The U.S. Senate began to hold hearings in September 1969. Testifying for President Nixon (who was the bill's strongest supporter) was Attorney General John Mitchell. Medical testimony was offered by Dr. Sidney Cohen of the National Institute of Mental Health. He said that "50 percent of the lawfully manufactured pep pills were diverted at some point to illicit channels" (Graham, 1977: 89). Evidence was brought forth that five New York City pharmacies had shortages of from 12 to 50 percent of their stock in Librium and Valium (two of the most widely used Schedule III drugs in America). The Bureau of Narcotics and Dangerous Drugs had evidence that these drugs were connected with thirty-six suicides and 750 attempted suicides. Others testified to the harmful effects of both Librium and Valium. However, these and many other questions were never fully discussed during the hearings. The bill passed the Senate and went before the House of Representatives on January 23, 1970.

In the House hearings, John Ingersoll of the Bureau of Narcotics and Dangerous Drugs testified. Concerning the problem of diversion to illegal sources, he said, "Registration is . . . the most effective and least cumbersome way" to solve this problem. He recommended, among other enforcement efforts, biennial inventories of the stocks of these drugs. Still, there was no guarantee that the drugs would not be diverted into illegal channels.

Dr. Dorothy Dobbs of the Federal Drug Administration testified that amphetamines have limited medical use, that dependency can result, and that they cause "extreme personality changes" with "the most severe manifestation" being psychosis.

Congressman Claude Pepper of Florida led an investigation team that found a great deal of laxness in drug companies. For instance, an agent of the Bureau of Narcotics and Dangerous Drugs said he was able to pass himself off as a doctor and ordered twenty-five thousand units of amphetamines through two mail-order houses in New York.

Several other experts testified to the dangerous effects of amphetamines and other drugs placed in Schedule III. But apparently this testimony was not enough to offset the very favorable testimony given by drug-company representatives, such as those from Hoffman-La Roche Labs (a company that earned a profit in excess of $4 billion on Librium and Valium alone). The bill passed with most of the amphetamines being placed in

Schedule III (with very limited restrictions on their manufacture and distribution) (Graham, 1977: 93–97).

Recent Developments: Crack versus Powder Cocaine

Among the most recent developments in the criminal law, perhaps the most controversial—and one that reflects a theme of this book—is legislation pertaining to cocaine and the obvious differences between the powdered variety and that of "crack." Consistent with previous drug epidemics, the rampant media coverage of crack cocaine during the 1980s created a "moral panic" of unprecedented proportions. The literature regarding drug scares and the creation of moral panics, suggests that these events are independent phenomena, not necessarily related to actual trends or patterns in drug use or trafficking (Brownstein, 1991: 94). Research on illicit drugs often emphasizes the disparity between the perceived threat of that substance and the actual social harm involved (Jenkins, 1994: 12). As Reinarman and Levine argued, the response of the media and the political establishment appears to have been well out of proportion to the actual dimensions and seriousness of the crack problem (Reinarman and Levine, 1997a; Brownstein, 1991; Zimring and Hawkins, 1991). In fact, examination of the National Institute of Drug Abuse (NIDA) Household Survey in 1991—near the peak of the crack epidemic—finds that less than 1 percent of the respondents had used crack during the pervious month, and only 1 to 2 percent had ever used crack in their lives (Belenko, 1993: 13). The emergence of the crack cocaine "epidemic" in this country was unprecedented in its media coverage and the public, political, and legislative response. Like no other drug before it, crack became a symbol for America's fear of crime and public order during the 1980s.[16]

Fueled by sensationalized media accounts and political posturing, crack cocaine became the catalyst for the "war on drugs" (Belenko, 1993; Reinarman and Levine, 1997a). Crack also became the target of a previously unparalleled punitive legislative response, ultimately culminating in the Anti-Drug Abuse Acts of 1986 and 1988. These acts implemented a 100-to-1 quantity crack-to-powder-cocaine ratio for federal sentencing provisions, and criminalized simple possession of as little as 5 grams of crack cocaine, resulting in a mandatory five years in prison, compared to probation for possession of the same amount of powder cocaine. It should come as no surprise that the former drug has been used mostly by poor African Americans and other minorities, while the latter has been used by more affluent whites (U.S. Sentencing Commission, 1995).

The surrounding social and political context of legislation of cocaine was that of the "get tough" approach to crime that emerged in the late 1970s and early 1980s. During that time, racial and class images dominated the discussion, with the image of the "crackhead" being a poor, lower-class African American male.

As the 1980s began, the conservative agenda of the Reagan Administration began to take hold almost immediately. During this time came the reemergence of "determinate sentencing" (U.S. Sentencing Commission, 1995: 115), which came at a time of decreasing public tolerance for crime, a growing skepticism toward rehabilitation, and an increasing acceptance of a more general "get tough" attitude toward crime (Belenko, 1993: 11). The result was the Sentencing Reform Act of 1984, which created the U.S. Sentencing Commission and Determinant Sentencing. Specifically, the act directed the U.S. Sentencing Commission to promulgate "a system of detailed, mandatory sentencing guidelines to assure more uniform federal court sentencing decisions." In addition, the act abolished parole for defendants sentenced under the sentencing guidelines (U.S. Sentencing Commission, 1995: 115).

It was at this time that crack cocaine suddenly appeared on the streets of America. Crack, or "rock" cocaine as it was originally referred to, first began to be reported around November, 1984. The first published report about rock cocaine described it as the "drug of choice" in the ghettos of Los Angeles. This report appeared in the *Los Angeles Times* with the ominous title of "South Central Sales Explode into $25 'Rocks'" (*Los Angeles Times*, 1984; Klein, Maxson, and Cunningham, 1991).

"Within six months, a barrage of almost daily media coverage focused on crack use flooded into American households, catapulting concerns regarding illicit drug use to the forefront of the public agenda" (Trueblood, 1999: 11). On May 18, 1986, the *New York Times* published a front page article entitled "Opium Dens for the Crack Era," which described the "pernicious and addictive qualities" of crack cocaine (Brownstein, 1991: 85).

The media coverage peaked in June and July of 1986 following the death of Len Bias. That same year, Don Rogers of the Cleveland Browns professional football team died from a cocaine overdose. However, the death of Len Bias became the catalyst for subsequent Congressional legislation to enact the strict 100-to-1 ratio for sentencing of crack cocaine. During the Congressional Hearing that was to follow on July 15, 1986, "Bias's death was cited eleven times in connection with crack cocaine" (U.S. Sentencing Commission, 1995: 123).

Bias died of cocaine intoxication the day after he was the second player drafted in the National Basketball Association's College draft in 1986 by the Boston Celtics (the death of "ordinary" African Amercians from similar causes would never cause such publicity; after all, they were not worth millions in profits to the Boston Celtics). Although the method of cocaine ingestion that killed Bias was not known at the time of his death, Bias' death was surrounded by newspaper articles running headlines and stories containing a quote from Dr. Dennis Smyth, Maryland's Assistant Medical Examiner, "Bias probably died of free-basing cocaine." Yet, despite the fact that two other medical examiners in the same office found that Bias' death probably had nothing to do with crack cocaine, Dr. Smyth's assertions received the bulk of the coverage (U.S. Sentencing Commission, 1995: 122).

During July, 1986 alone, there were seventy-four evening-news segments regarding crack cocaine, many of which were reinforced by the erroneous belief that Bias's death was due to a crack cocaine overdose. About a year later, during the trial of Brian Tribble (accused of supplying Bias with cocaine), Terry Long, a University of Maryland basketball player who participated in the cocaine party that led to Bias's death, testified that he, Bias, Tribble, and another player snorted *powder* cocaine over a four-hour period. Tribble's testimony, however, received limited media coverage (U.S. Sentencing Commission, 1995: 123).

In the months leading up to the 1986 elections, more than one thousand stories appeared about crack cocaine in the national press, including five cover stories each in *Time* and *Newsweek*. NBC News ran four hundred separate reports on crack cocaine, fifteen hours of air time. *Time* called crack cocaine the "issue of the year" in its September 22, 1986, issue; *Newsweek* called it the "biggest news story since Vietnam and Watergate" (June 16, 1986). CBS's news program *48 Hours* ran a documentary entitled "48 Hours on Crack Street," which became the most watched documentary in television history (Johnson, Golub, and Fagan, 1995: 275). ABC News termed crack a "plague that was eating away at the fabric of America" (Belenko, 1993: 23; Reinarman and Levine, 1997b: 20–22).

Similar to other moral panics, the creation of the crack epidemic was a product of the media in its relentless drive to "make news" and thus make profits. These types of panics have been described as a "disconnect" between image and reality (Miller, 1996: 155). Although the NIDA annual reports suggest that crack cocaine use was limited to an extremely small drug-user subculture (i.e., 1 to 2 percent of the population), the media's hype regarding the use of this drug became the catalyst for an enormous concern pertaining to its widespread use. This is illustrated by a Gallup Poll showing that respondents described drug abuse as the most important problem facing the country. Trueblood aptly describes this moral panic in the following manner:

> In the midst of this media frenzy, the election campaign of 1986 became a forum for politicians to try to out-platform one another in their efforts to demonstrate their concerns and the need for swift draconian measures of social control with respect to drug abuse. Interestingly, the creation of this particular drug panic allowed the development of a conservative agenda, even during a predominantly liberal Congress. With conservatives and liberals alike quickly acknowledging the newest drug "menace," silence regarding this issue would too readily be interpreted as being "soft" on drugs.
>
> The ensuing reactionary agenda toward drug users and traffickers resulted from social, political, and ideological forces. Emerging during an era of increasing momentum toward strict punishment of drug users and dealers,

and with a presidential administration that had a strong ideological focus toward individual accountability and an aversion for sociological and economic explanations of social problems, the spread of crack cocaine into the inner city provided a convenient scapegoat for diverting attention from pressing social and economic problems and blaming a specific powerless group for social disorder. (Trueblood, 1999: 17)

As the election year progressed, the media, police officials, and politicians provided a continuous barrage of heated rhetoric concerning the alleged widespread use and abuse of crack cocaine (Johnson, Golub, and Fagan, 1995: 276). Some of the assertions made in these reports were not supported by scientific data at the time and, in most cases, turned out to be patently false (U.S. Sentencing Commission, 1995: 122). Indeed, one of the most interesting aspects of the anti-crack crusade was that, unlike previous anti-drug efforts, it occurred during a time when there was plenty of research regarding its psychopharmacological and behavioral effects. But the anti-drug crusaders ignored the research and used purely anecdotal information derived from media and law-enforcement sources to link crack to a wide variety of social problems, including violent crimes, escalation of drug abuse, child abuse and neglect, and prostitution. One of the most common myths was that crack was "instantly addictive" and that "innocent" people were being transformed into "compulsive crack-smokers." Moreover, crack use was "driving" people to commit violent crimes and to drop out of the labor force, and that "crack gangs" were in control (Johnson, Golub, and Fagan, 1995: 276). Most who were in the forefront of developing drug policies knew of some of the research that had been done, which contradicted their views; however, they ignored the research findings. (For more details, see Baum, 1997).

The Anti-Drug Abuse Act of 1986 emphasized the use of punishment and social control to fight drug abuse, despite research that overwhelmingly supported the use of treatment and education (Baum, 1997). The 1986 act also established two tiers of mandatory prison terms for first-time drug traffickers—five- and ten-year minimum sentences. Under the new law, these prison terms are determined solely by the quantity and type of drug involved in the offense (U.S. Sentencing Commission, 1995: 116). The act further expanded funding for police and corrections, adding to an already growing "criminal justice industrial complex," as it authorized $1.7 billion in new money to fight the "war on drugs"—which was in addition to the already authorized $2.2 billion. A mere 14 percent of the funds were allocated for treatment and prevention (Johnson, Golub, and Fagan, 1995: 288; Belenko, 1993: 14).

The act distinguished between two forms of cocaine with identical chemical composition—powder and crack—and isolated crack for more severe punishment. Lesser quantities of crack than powder cocaine would

57

five- and ten-year mandatory minimum penalties applicable to
of cocaine, thereby imposing an inconceivable 100-to-1 quantity
ɔwder to crack cocaine (i.e., it takes one hundred times as much
poɯ   ɔcaine as crack to trigger the mandatory minimum penalties) (U.S.
Sentencing Commission, 1995: iii).

In reviewing the legislative history of this act, Congress's conclusions
respecting the "dangerousness" of crack cocaine relative to powder cocaine
flowed from four assumptions:

> First, crack cocaine was viewed as extraordinarily addictive: both relative to
> powder cocaine and in absolute terms. Second, the correlation between crack
> cocaine use and the commission of other serious crimes was considered greater
> than that with other drugs. Floor statements focused on psychopharmacologi-
> cal driven, economically driven, as well as systemic crime. Third, the physio-
> logical effects of crack cocaine were considered especially perilous, leading to
> psychosis and death. Fourth, members of Congress felt that young people were
> particularly prone to using crack cocaine. Finally, there was great concern that
> crack cocaine's "purity and potency," the cost per dose, the ease with which it is
> manufactured, transported, disposed of, and administered, were all leading to
> widespread use of crack cocaine. (U.S. Sentencing Commission, 1995: 118)

Specifically, the act provided the following penalties for first-offense
cocaine trafficking (Trueblood, 1999: 19):

> 5 *grams* or more of crack cocaine Or *500 grams* or more of powder
> cocaine = five years mandatory minimum penalty
> 50 *grams* or more of crack cocaine Or *5,000 grams* or more of powder
> cocaine = ten years mandatory minimum penalty

The initial set of guidelines became law in November 1987. In January
1989, the Supreme Court upheld the constitutionality of the U.S. Sentencing
Commission and the guidelines in *Mistretta v. United States*, 488 U.S. 361
(1989).

The 1986 act was expedited through Congress, leaving in its wake a
very limited legislative record to which we can refer to explain either the dif-
ferentiation in the sentencing in crack and powder cocaine or the speed
attendant to its enactment. The history of the 100-to-1 quantity ratio that
emerged from this Act, therefore, can only be understood in the context of
the individual members' floor statements pertaining to the act. Senator
Hawkins, for example, spoke in support of the 1986 act in terms of the
urgency of this legislation. As usual, creating *fear* among the public is important, especially when citing "national security" as a reason to be fearful.
Hawkins stated that "drugs pose a clear and present danger to America's
national security."[17] Ironically, this same excuse was used repeatedly during

the Cold War, which justified huge expenditures within the Pentagon system (Chomsky, 1992).

As the 1986 elections grew near, the heightened public concern and the media-driven national sense of urgency surrounding the crack problem created a political context in which Congress was pressured to act quickly, so it dispensed with much of the typical deliberative legislative process including, most importantly, committee hearings. Preliminary versions of this bill proposed various quantity ratios for the sentencing of crack offenders. The original version of the house bill, HR 5484, in fact, contained a quantity ratio of 20-to-1, and was introduced on behalf of the Reagan Administration by Senator Dole. As the 1986 act quickly advanced through the legislative process in late summer and early fall, after consulting with law-enforcement professionals, but without holding hearings, the Senate set specific quantity levels for the entire range of illegal drugs, including powder and crack cocaine, that would trigger the five- and ten-year mandatory minimum penalties. The resulting legislation increased the powder cocaine-to-crack ratio from its original form of 20-to-1 to 100-to-1 (U.S. Sentencing Commission, 1995: 117–120).

Federal circuit courts addressing the constitutionality of crack-cocaine penalties have upheld the current federal sentencing scheme, including the 100-to-1 ratio.[18] The courts have held that the penalty distinction was created out of the legitimate congressional objective of "protecting the public against a new and highly potent addictive narcotic that could be distributed easily and sold cheaply" (U.S. Sentencing Commission, 1995: 118).

It should come as no surprise that the heated media coverage of crack surrounding the elections of 1986 quickly evaporated following the passage of the 1986 act. As media coverage waned, however, so did public concern about drug abuse. A *New York Times*/CBS poll during 1987 indicated that only 3 to 5 percent of the public viewed drugs as the most pressing social problem (Belenko, 1993: 25).

During 1988, however, there was a resurgence in media and political attention toward crack. Fueled by the 1988 presidential election, candidates again attempted to gain attention and to demonstrate their "toughness" against crime and drug use by enacting strict penalties for drug use. Part of this hysteria was caused by George Bush's use of the Willie Horton case (an African American man on furlough who killed someone) (Anderson, 1995; Chambliss, 1999: 13–31). Caught up in the renewed anti-drug fervor, Congress again escalated the war against drugs, culminating in the enactment of the Anti-Drug Abuse Act of 1988.

Despite a continuing dearth of research regarding the effects of crack, two years after the enactment of the Anti-Drug Abuse Act of 1986, Congress decided that it was time to again "get tough" on drugs and drafted the Anti-Drug Abuse Act of 1988. Among other features, the Act established a new cabinet-level White House Office of National Drug Control Policy (a "Drug Czar"), charging its Director, William Bennett, to submit to Congress an annual National Drug Control Strategy (Belenko, 1993: 15; for a good critique of Bennett's views and policies, see Baum, 1997).

With respect to crack, Section 6371 of this act established increased federal penalties for "serious" crack offenses. It made crack cocaine the only drug under the act with a mandatory minimum penalty for a first offense of simple possession (Zimring and Hawkins, 1991: 105). The act made first-time possession of more than 5 grams of a mixture or substance containing cocaine base punishable by at least five years in prison. Second- or third-time offenders were subject to similar penalties for possessing as little as 3 grams or 1 gram, respectively (U.S. Sentencing Commission, 1995: 123).

Not surprisingly, there was little debate on the amendments establishing the mandatory minimum crack-cocaine possession penalties. Senators argued, without factual evidence, that the supply of cocaine was greater than ever before. It was also argued that crack cocaine causes greater physical, emotional, and psychological damage than any other commonly abused drug. (U.S. Sentencing Commission, 1995: 125). The 1988 act passed the Senate by an almost unanimous vote (87–3) on October 14, 1988; shortly thereafter, the House followed suit (by a vote of 346–11).

On September 5, 1989, President Bush took advantage of the media frenzy in a major televised speech about drug abuse, once again bringing crack to the forefront of public concern. In an attempt to illustrate the rampant proliferation of crack, President Bush waved vials of crack in front of the television cameras, claiming that Drug Enforcement Agency (DEA) agents had seized the drugs from a dealer in Lafayette Park, right outside the White House. The shock value was as expected, but it turned out to be a complete fabrication, as it was eventually discovered that the DEA could *not find* any crack dealers in Lafayette Park. Agents had to lure an uncooperative dealer to the park and make the arrest. Because the speech was written prior to the arrest, the DEA was directed to take whatever steps were necessary to provide the appropriate evidence needed by the President to substantiate these claims (*Washington Post*, 1989). This example illustrates the hype and political hyperbole surrounding the crack epidemic during this time (Jenkins, 1994: 12).

Throughout this period, media coverage further intensified fears about crack by focusing on the alleged involvement of gangs (of course, always African American or Hispanic) and the tendency to use random violence, including the claim that crack was spreading into all corners of the nation, including white middle-class suburbs (*Newsweek*, 1988: 65). News articles about gangs and violence invariably quoted local or national law-enforcement officials as the only source of information about gang involvement and their role in the spread of crack.[19] For example, a *Washington Post* article on February 22, 1988, described how the Jamaican posses had introduced crack to Washington D.C., and quoted a narcotics Task Force as stating that "crack is just taking over" (Belenko, 1993: 27). Similarly, one of the major *Time* magazine stories, relying almost exclusively on reports from police, concluded that the crack "war" was being lost to gangs (*Time*, 1988: 21).

These accounts, however, were soon contradicted by research in the area of gangs, violence, and crack. Indeed, despite accounts of nationally syndicated, highly centralized street gangs dominating crack-cocaine distribution, the research supports an alternative view. Specifically, researchers found that street gangs neither played a predominant role nor appeared to have brought much extra violence of organizational character to crack distribution. Rather, it was concluded that crack distribution could be attributed to drug dealers, not street gangs (Klein, Maxson, and Cunningham, 1991: 626).[20]

The media continued to develop this theme, focusing its attention, as always, on the potential vulnerability of the white middle-class (a classic use of fear tactics). For example, the *New York Times* published a full-length editorial called "Crack—A Disaster of Historic Dimensions," in which the author portrays crack as "uniquely destructive" and a threat that has "spread to middle America" (*New York Times*, 1989a). Also, in its Sunday edition, the *Times* began a two-part series with a front-page article entitled "The Spreading Web of Crack," stating that "Crack, which has been devastating entire inner-city neighborhoods, has begun to claim significant numbers of middle- and upper-class addicts, experts have found" (*New York Times*, 1989b). The image of not only crack but also the specter of a growing underclass of mostly African American crack dealers "invading" middle America is evident in these stories.

The research completely contradicts these claims, however. The evidence is quite clear that most drug-related violence is confined to people who live in or near drug communities and neighborhoods. Also, few people are likely to be the stereotypical "innocent bystander" of drug-related violence. In fact, data from the New York City Police Department during the first half of 1990 reveal that *only 1.4 percent of all homicide victims were innocent bystanders* (Brownstein, 1991: 95–96).

Finally, although it appears from the research that drugs and violent crime are clearly related, the extent to which that relationship may be causally related is the subject of much discussion. The research by Goldstein suggests three models of that relationship: psychopharmacological (crimes resulting from behavioral effects of the drug), economically compulsive (crimes committed by people financially driven to support their drug habits), and systemic (crimes related to the market and distribution of a drug). What Goldstein's research found was that contrary to media accounts, violent crime surrounding crack use is primarily confined to the inner cities and is a result of the violence attendant to the marketing and distribution of crack cocaine (Goldstein et al., 1997; Baumer, 1994).

Whose Interest Does the Law Serve?

Given what has been said in the preceding pages, one question might be raised: Do *all* criminal laws operate in the interest of powerful groups? More specifically, does the *passage* of every criminal law serve only these interests? The reader may wonder about such laws as those prohibiting homicide and assault. It would be absurd to suggest that every criminal law on the books was passed solely to preserve the interests of the rich and the powerful—it is more complicated than that.

This issue gets to the heart of the three models of the law discussed in the introduction to this book. From a consensus standpoint, law reflects values held by everyone in a society and does not represent the narrow interests of a ruling class. From the interest groups/conflict perspective, law reflects certain interests as opposed to other interests of various competing "interest groups" in a society. From a critical/Marxist point of view, law mainly reflects the needs and values of a ruling class.

There is no easy answer to this question, but some attempt should be provided. To begin with, upon reviewing the history of criminal law, one has to conclude that law has often reflected the interests of the ruling class. More than that, however, the law has been used to a large extent to enhance the power of a ruling class and/or to control groups in a society perceived as "dangerous"—whether these groups are black slaves, Native Americans, "vagrants," union organizers, lower-class immigrants, or simply the poor.

This is not the same thing as saying that every criminal law represents ruling-class interests only—or the interests of any other group, for that matter. There is also the distinction to be made between the *intent* of a specific law and the *result* in terms of a law's interpretation and enforcement. Returning to Quinney's *Social Reality of Crime* theory, recall that one of his propositions stated that "criminal definitions are applied by the segments of society that have the power to shape the enforcement and administration of criminal law" (Quinney, 1970: 18) And that "behavior patterns are structured in segmentally organized society in relation to criminal definitions, and within this context persons engage in actions that have relative probabilities of being defined as criminal." Thus, it may very well be that although the *intent* of a specific law was not to reflect the sole interests of a ruling class, the *result* has been unmistakable: those who have been arrested and processed through the criminal justice system have consistently been those drawn from the bottom of the social-class structure.

Let's take a specific example, a law that should theoretically reflect the interests of all the people and should show the least amount of bias: laws concerning the crime of homicide. Once upon a time, *homicide* was defined by custom as a tort, but when it became a concern for the state, "restitution was replaced by a "debt to society." The current law against homicide is not as clearly defined as one might expect. Typically, such laws refer to acts such as the willful taking of another person's life (premeditated murder), the accidental yet negligent taking of another life (as in a fight), or the killing of someone while committing another crime (as in robbery). Yet, what is missing from the law of homicide are such cases as (1) the production of goods that can cause harm or even death to consumers (as in the case of the Ford Pinto and numerous other cases); (2) various working conditions that can result in death for many (e.g., black lung disease among miners and the manufacture of the chemical kepone); and (3) the perpetuation of poverty conditions that cause infant mortality and other forms of sickness and death suffered by the poor (Hepburn, 1977; Chambliss, 1993; Breggin and Breggin, 1998).

The real-life circumstances of an offense rarely correspond to abstract statements codified into law. As Chambliss notes, the interpretation of *homicide* varies tremendously. On the one hand, police can shoot "fleeing felons" and executioners can carry out the death penalty, while soldiers kill in war under direct orders. States may engage in mass murder and genocide (including the United States).[21] And, of course, the killing of millions of Jews in Germany was sanctified by German law (and was turned into a "crime" mostly because Germany lost the war) (Chambliss, 1993: 37). An appropriate commentary, although written in 1936, further illustrates this point. In commenting on the fortune of the Astor family, Gustavus Myers wrote in his book *History of the Great American Fortunes*:

> Is it not murder when, compelled by want, people are forced to fester in squalid, germ-filled tenements, where the sunlight never enters and where disease finds a prolific breeding-place? Untold thousands went to their deaths in these unspeakable places. Yet, so far as the Law was concerned, the rents collected by the Astors, as well as by other landlords, were honestly made. The whole institution of Law saw nothing out of the way in these conditions, and very significantly so, because to repeat over and over again, Law did not represent the ethics or ideals of advanced humanity; it exactly reflected, as a pool reflects the sky, the demands and self-interest of the growing propertied classes. . . . (quoted in Zinn, 1995: 233–234)

It would be an exaggeration to suggest that all laws serve the interests of a ruling class or any other particular group. Some laws do serve such interests, as we have seen, and many acts committed by powerful people are not considered criminal. We need only a passing reference to the costs to our society of corporate crime each year. According to Federal Bureau of Investigation (FBI) figures, about two people will be murdered within the next hour (most often by a gun or knife). However, according to one recent study, about fifty-six thousand Americans die on the job every year or from

...seases as black lung, brown lung, asbestosis, and other
various occupations (about six per hour) (Mokhiber, 1996:
...imate puts the number of annual deaths from work-related
...J00, with deaths from job-related diseases ranging from a low
to a high of 390,000. Work-related accidents kill an estimated
1U, ...id result in 1.8 million disabling injuries each year (Friedrichs, 1996:
80). One author estimates that the overall work-related death rate is around
115 per 100,000, compared to a homicide rate of around 8 per 100,000
(Michaloski, 1985: 325–328).

All of these cases are examples of criminal offenses, covered by various criminal laws enacted ostensibly to serve the interests of the general
public. Yet the enforcement is practically nonexistent. Perhaps it is because
these offenders came from the highest echelons of society, were "pillars of
the community." In the minds of most people, they were not really "criminals," or at least they were not perceived as "dangerous," which is in part
due to a massive system of propaganda put forth by this same class
(Chomsky, 1989). Yet collectively these particular offenses cost thousands of
lives and several hundred billion dollars each year. For the most part, they
are indeed *white*-collar crimes, for they are committed overwhelmingly by
wealthy white males. In fact, there is no way anyone can argue that the
worst crimes are committed by racial minorities. Yet within our criminal justice system, racial minorities (and the poor in general) are overwhelmingly
subjected to the actions of the system, filling our jails and prisons. It is a rare
occurrence when a perpetrator of a corporate or state crime goes to prison.

Thus, the most important point is that most laws that are *enforced* the
most vigorously happen to be those most likely to be violated by relatively
powerless groups, especially the poor and racial minorities. It can also be
the case, as illustrated in this chapter, that the legal system is used to oppress
or otherwise control certain groups. The law can indeed be a selective
instrument of class justice, as the critical/Marxist view of the law contends.
Friedman, an expert on the history of American criminal justice (although
not a Marxist historian), makes an appropriate and astute observation about
our laws and legal institutions: "Laws and legal institutions are part of the
system that keeps the structure in place, or allows it to change only in
approved and patterned ways. The criminal justice system maintains the
status quo." Friedman goes on to note that most people want the status quo,
or at least the parts they have (even if it may be little). They obviously do
not want others to harm them or take their property. However, some have a
lot more than others and have a lot more power. Hence, the law "protects
power and property" and keeps the distribution of wealth intact, while
keeping those at the bottom in their place (Friedman, 1993: 830).

Friedman also observes that in the beginning, the American republic
was supposed to be based on "justice, equality, and opportunity—but looking back, we see something quite different. Says Friedman:

> We see a republic created, on the whole, by and for white Protestant men; behind the flag-waving and the Fourth of July parades, we see the hideous grinning faces of inequality, oppression, biases overt and covert, cruelty, lack of understanding, intolerance. This was no pure or ideal democracy; far from it . . . . It was a half democracy, an adolescent democracy, a smug democracy . . . criminal justice followed, as it always did, the pattern of social norms. It fell, as it always has fallen, more heavily on the underclass, on the deviants, on the "outs.". . . Criminal justice was the strong arm of the stratification system. It was part of the process that made subordination real. And subordination was real, most notably, for American blacks; also for members of other minority races; and for the poor, the deviant, the unpopular. (Friedman, 1993: 84)

Finally, Zinn's comments on the notion of the rule of law is appropriate here. He observes that in modern capitalist democracies, abstract rules and a "legal order" have replaced feudal lords and kings. Thus, the law gives the *appearance* of being impersonal. He notes that the law

> . . . is on paper, and who can trace it back to what men? And because it has the look of neutrality, its injustices are made legitimate. It was not easy to hold on to the "divine right" of kings—everyone could see that kings and queens were human beings. A code of law is more easily deified than a flesh-and-blood ruler. (Zinn, 1997: 373)

When we had the "rule of men," those who were oppressive could be readily identified—slaves rebelled against their masters, for example. But in our own era, we have impersonal bureaucracies, large corporations, and laws contained within not easily understood state *penal codes* (e.g., California Penal Code and Nevada Revised Statutes). The law hides unequal wealth and power and theoretically treats everyone the same. Paraphrasing the French philosopher Anatole France, the law prohibits both the rich and the poor from sleeping on park benches and traffic laws treat every driver alike (the driver of a twenty-year-old car and the driver of a limousine are both *equally* subjected to the speed laws). This is the great "equality" of the law in societies beset by huge disparities of wealth (Milovanovic, 1994: 18).

The legal order punishes—very severely in some cases—those who rise up to protest inhumane social conditions, whether we are talking about abolitionists and union organizers in the nineteenth century or civil rights protesters in the 1960s or anti-nuclear protesters in the 1990s. Those who challenge the status quo will often come face to face with the raw power of the state. I would like to close this chapter with another quote from Zinn, who wrote, "What life is best worth living—the life of the proper, obedient, dutiful follower of law and order or the life of the independent thinker, the rebel?" (Zinn, 1997: 402).

Notes

    1. The term *hegemony* refers to the dominance of one group or nation over another, especially its *influence* or *authority*. If, for instance, a king has hegemony over the masses of people within his domain, his values and opinions are generally accepted and are thought to be "proper" or "the way things should be," even though there may be other, more valid opinions and values. Thus, the king (or some other powerful ruler) rules through the "consent of the governed," so that force only needs to be used sparingly. Most ruling classes throughout history, especially in capitalist societies, have had this sort of hegemonic control over the society. In short, rulers maintain their dominance because the majority of the people have been convinced (often through the use of sophisticated forms of propaganda) that such rulers are acting in the best interest of the people, even though they are not always doing so. For further elaboration on the use of propaganda as a means of control in capitalist democracies see, for instance, Chomsky (1989).

    2. For a critique of this book, see Langbein (1983); see also a rebuttal by Linebaugh (1985).

    3. The concept of *state* has been almost impossible to define precisely. One of the best definitions comes from Miliband (1969: 49–54), who writes that "the state" is not a thing as such, but rather it "stands for a number of particular institutions which, together, constitute its reality. . . . " He goes on to note that there is a "state system," which consists of what we normally regard as the "government," including the Congress, the Senate, and other similar institutions (e.g., Parliament in England) along with various administrative units (e.g., regulatory commissions), the military, the police, and the judicial system. One of the keys to understanding the state is that it is related to the "business of rule," as Poggi notes. Poggi defines the state as a "complex set of institutional arrangements for rule operating through the continuous and regulated activities of individuals acting as occupants of offices. The state, as the sum total of such offices, reserves to itself the business of rule over a territorially bounded society. . . ." (Poggi,1978: 1). This definition gets to the heart of the matter since the "state" is involved in *ruling* the society; that is, in some form of *domination* over others. The key question is, "for whose benefit"?

    4 A very serious critique on Chambliss's interpretation of vagrancy laws was done by Adler (1989a), followed in the same issue of this journal by a rebuttal by Chambliss (1989), which in turn was followed by Adler's rebuttal to Chambliss (Adler, 1989b). Reading the dialogue between these two scholars might best be described as an academic version of a "cat fight," which left me concluding that nobody "won" the "contest"; it was more of a "draw" than anything else. Where appropriate, I reference these authors in this section of the chapter.

    5. See the following for discussion of this subject: Marx (1975), Linebaugh (1976), and Ditton (1977). The articles by Linebaugh and Ditton are reproduced in Weiss (1999a).

    6. This relationship forms an important component—perhaps the *most important component*—of Marx's analysis of capitalism. This is spelled out in some detail in Marx's own work, especially the classic *Capital*. The interested reader may find a far more readable summary of these issues in Marx (1988); an insightful analysis of some of these issues can be found in Heilbroner (1985). For a contemporary account of some of the negative aspects of this conflict see Chomsky (1999a).

    7. For a fascinating analysis of the accumulation of wealth by a relatively small group of "robber barons," see Josephson (1962). See also Zinn (1995), especially Chapter 11.

    8. The phenomenon of "witch hunts" was not a new phenomenon, and it certainly did not end with the Salem case. Throughout history, there have been instances where those in power engaged in activities aimed at "ferreting out" those who threatened the status quo. To engage in "witch-hunting" essentially means to look for excuses to control or even get rid of those who threaten the social order, often based on vague definitions of the threatening behavior, which often includes "guilt by association" or "guilt by accusation." The

Inquisition was a classic example. It was also a good example of the process of *scapegoating,* which is part of the witch-hunting phenomenon. Thus, those in power can claim that instead of themselves and their rule, there are others—in this case, "witches"—that are the source of major social problems. And it is no accident that the majority of those accused of witchcraft (and later of being "Communists") have been the poor. The phenomenon of "moral panics" is similar. In every case, the "witch hunt" or the "moral panic" takes place during times of great social conflict, change, and upheaval. In the twentieth century, we have witnessed such "witch hunts" as the "Red Scare" during the late 1910s and early 1920s, the McCarthy communist witch hunt in the early 1950s, the targeting of African American, anti-war, and other activists groups in the 1960s and early 1970s, and the more recent attempts to control minorities via the "war on drugs" and "war on gangs." Some are even suggesting the investigation of President Clinton was a form of "witch hunt" carried out by Independent Counsel Kenneth Starr with support from the Far Right. For further study of this fascinating phenomenon (including moral panics), see the following: Harris (1978), Pfohl (1994), Erikson (1966), Cohen (1972), and Goode and Ben-Yehuda (1994).

   9. This is in reference to the famous book written by an Italian, Cesare Beccaria, originally published in 1774, which set out to establish some consistency in the criminal code. See Beccaria (1963).

   10. Throughout American history, often during times of upheaval and social change, those in power will take a few otherwise isolated cases and reassert the importance of the rule of law, especially during those times when it would appear to any sane observer that the nation is in fact under the rule of men, not of law. The most recent case in point is the investigation of President Clinton. How often have those in Congress, the Senate, and various political "pundits" referred to this case as about the rule of law? Speaker of the House Newt Gingrich flatly denied (despite overwhelming evidence to the contrary) that the "Starr Report" (a report by the Office of Independent Counsel) was not about sex, but about the rule of law (as reported on CNN, September 22, 1998). Similar comments were repeatedly heard during the Watergate hearings in the early 1970s.

   11. Zinn notes that out of an estimated West Indian population of around ten million when Columbus landed, less than a million would eventually survive after the various wars and diseases introduced by Europeans. He cites one tragic example: on Martha's Vineyard in 1642, there were about three thousand Wampanoags; by 1764, there were only 313. On nearby Block Island, they numbered between 1,200 and 1,500, but by 1774 there were only fifty-one (Zinn, 1995: 16).

   12. Examples of these laws included a San Francisco ordinance that made it against the law to operate a laundry except if the building were made of brick or stone. Because no buildings were made of such materials at this time, Chinese owners were in violation of the law. If a white person owned the building, the law was waived (Friedman, 1993: 99).

   13. The following is a statement from a Congressional Senate Report, dated 1876 (ironically, on the first anniversary of the Declaration of Independence, which declared that "all men are created equal"): "The burden of our accusation against them [the Chinese] is that they come in conflict with our labor interests; that they can never assimilate with us; that they are a perpetual, unchanging, and unchangeable alien element that can never become homogeneous; that their civilization is demoralizing and degrading to our people. . . ." Quoted in Leong (1998).

   14. The author is indebted to UNLV graduate student Deena Trueblood for providing some excellent material for the following section, taken from her masters thesis, "Crack Cocaine and Social Control: The History of Cocaine Legislation." Direct quotes will reference Trueblood (1999).

   15. When the United States became involved in the Vietnam War, it too took advantage of the opium trade. The CIA became a major trafficker in this huge industry. Profits from the opium trade resulted in huge financial savings on the part of the Southeast Asian leaders. American planes helped ship the opium to Saigon, where it was processed into

heroin and either sold to American GIs or shipped to the United States, often in the coffins of American soldiers (McCoy, 1973). For a similar account, focusing on the connection between the CIA and the Contras, see Webb (1998).

16. One method by which the dominant classes can more easily control the masses is through scare tactics, whereby you create large-scale fear (even if the fear is totally unjustified, as in this case) and create demand for "law and order." The fear almost always creates simultaneously the need for scapegoats for various social ills, so that close scrutiny of the real sources of the problems—the activities of the dominant classes—is not done. For further discussion of this phenomenon, see Chomsky (1989, 1994). For a more recent discussion of the use of fear, see Glassner, 1999.

17. 132 Congressional Record 24, 436 September 26, 1986.

18. Some examples are *United States v. D'Anjou*, 16 F.3d 604 (4th Cir.), *cert denied*, 114 S. Ct. 2754 (1994) (equal protection); *United States v. Angulo-Lopez*, 7 F.3d 1506 (10th Cir. 1993), *cert denied*, 114 S. Ct. 1563 (1994) (equal protection, cruel and unusual punishment); *United States v. Thurmond*, 7 F.3d 947 (10th Cir., 1993), *cert denied*, 114 S. Ct. 1311 (1994) (equal protection, due process); *United States v. Jackson*, 968 F.2d 158 (2d Cir.), *cert denied*, 113 S. Ct. 664 (1992) (vagueness); *United States v. Simmons*, 964 F.2d 763 (8th Cir.), *cert denied*, 113 S. Ct. 632 (1992) (due process, equal protection, cruel and unusual punishment); *United States v. Levy*, 904 F.2d 1026 (6th Cir. 1990), *cert denied*, 498 U.S. 1091 (1991) (vagueness); *United States v. Cyrus*, 890 F.2d 1245 (D.C. Cir. 1989) (equal protection, cruel and unusual punishment). But see *United States v. Davis*, No. 93-0234 (N.D. Ga. August 26, 1994) (invalidating heightened statutory penalties for cocaine base as impermissibly vague based on lack of scientific distinction between "cocaine" and "cocaine base").

19. The use of "experts" is one of the five main "filters" Herman and Chomsky cite in their "propanganda model" of the news media. Such filters are used to frame issues in a way that distorts reality and serves the interests of the rulers (Herman and Chomsky, 1988).

20. Similar media accounts associating crack and random violence were also a central theme to media stories in 1988 and 1989 (Brownstein, 1991: 85). The CBS network, in an effort to capitalize on the revived crack hysteria, inaugurated its 1989–90 season on *48 Hours* with a three-hour special. "Return to Crack Street" constructed a compelling picture of the realities of drug-related violence that was spreading and becoming random in its selection of victims. This documentary, and other media reports of its time, typified the media's attempt to present crack as being out of control, extending its reach into white middle-class America (Belenko, 1993: 27; Reinarman and Levine, 1997b).

21. There is significant literature documenting the complicity of the U.S. government in killings and torture on a grand scale. These instances are well documented in the following works: Chomsky (1988, 1993); Chomsky and Herman (1979); and Parenti (1995).

2

The Development of the Police Institution

Controlling the Dangerous Classes

The police of today are the most visible representatives of the state. Of all the criminal justice agencies, the police receive the largest share of government funding (Maguire and Pastore, 1995: 4). The police are usually viewed as being in the forefront in the "war on crime" or as representing the "thin blue line" between "civilization" and "anarchy." Yet the police, as an institution of social control and as an occupational subculture, are probably the least understood. To develop an understanding of the police, this chapter will trace the historical development of this unique institution. As we will see, *policing* as an activity of a governmental unit is not new; however, the police *as an institution and distinct bureaucracy,* as we know it today, is a rather recent invention, unique to modern capitalist societies.

Early Police Systems

Police systems have differed over the years depending on the prevailing economic and political systems. Not every type of society has had an organized police system, at least as we know it today. In general, *the more stratified a society, the greater will be the reliance on formal methods of social control—* in this case, organized police forces (Chambliss and Seidman, 1982: 34). As a corollary to this general principle, we might add that police forces in stratified societies have always functioned to help maintain class control and, in effect, help perpetuate the existing stratification system. In so doing, the police as an institution has functioned to serve the interests of dominant groups (Bacon, 1939). Quite often, as we will see, a police system developed as a response to organized threats against the dominance of a small ruling class, especially in nineteenth century American society.

One of the earliest known police systems existed in Babylonia during the years when Hammurabi issued his famous code (2181–2123 B.C.). It appears that the police were under the direct control of monarchs, the ruling class of the period. One police historian stated that "the Babylonian monarchs possessed vast landed estates, the feoffee being bound to come up when summoned and serve as soldier or slave-driver or policeman." Later, in the years before Christ, several societies ruled mostly by kings and monarchs had strong, efficient central governments, with "order" maintained by a *gendarmerie* (i.e., totalitarian police force) as well as standing armies (Reith, 1975: 179).

In early Greece, there existed a law-enforcement system known as the *kin-police* in which, in a sense, all citizens were policemen. In other words, it was a self-sufficient and self-policing community. In time, however, prosperity created greater wealth, concentrated in the hands of a few, and "created social classes and political and other parties in the state, and the need of these to put individual and class interests before the interests of the community as a whole" (Reith, 1975: 191).

During the Roman Empire, policing again took these forms. Rome had many of the characteristics of stratified societies elsewhere. The inequalities that existed created wars, internal strife, and riotous behavior among the masses. Reith states that:

> Successful wars and the loot and wealth with which they provided some Romans in the capital altered and enhanced the status and divisions and power of classes and factions in the Roman community. Abundance and cheapness of slaves enabled the rich to exploit the land, dispossess the older class of peasant farmers, and, in consequence, Rome became crowded with an increasingly large population of aimless, workless, discontented, and often hungry malcontents, for the control of whose power of insurrection there was only the weak machinery of oratory.... Against the activities of swarms of discontented slaves, only repressive measures were possible.... (Reith, 1975: 214)

After many years of civil strife, Augustus (63 B.C.–14 A.D.) took control and maintained "law and order" with an imperial police force known as the *Vigiles*, a combination of police and firemen. Among the expressed goals of this force was that of "arresting thieves and returning fugitive slaves" (Kelly, 1975: 9). Augustus had a police force of ten thousand in a city with a population of about three-quarters of a million, or one policeman for every seventy-five citizens (Reith, 1975: 226). Today, by comparison, we have one police officer for every three hundred to four hundred citizens.

As noted in Chapter 1, as Rome shifted from a mostly rural agricultural society to a rather large city-state, the previous informal social norms (e.g., Twelve Tables) could no longer function effectively, as there were growing conflicts between the rulers and an increasing proletariat and slave population.

One interpretation of the rise of the Roman police is that it resulted from the need to control "crime in the streets," which allegedly was rising quite rapidly (although there is no hard data to confirm this). This view also suggests that among the causes of this "crime wave" were the absence of adequate street lighting, inefficient law enforcement, "minority problems" [whatever this means], and the existence of swamps outside the city which made "a perfect hideaway for the marauders and fugitives who victimized Rome" (Kelly, 1975: 6). This interpretation apparently takes the perspective of those in power because crime in the streets often consisted of riots and rebellions by slaves and other oppressed people. Considering the degree of inequality that existed in Rome, one of the major functions of the police was to protect the property and powerful positions of the rulers.

To use a comparative analogy, we might look briefly at the police system in the southern states of America, especially during the days of slavery. Police forces were established to control the slaves, especially to prevent any protests they might wage (there were many and the potential was always present). Indeed, as one noted historian wrote, these patrols were established to "curb runaways, hold down interplantation theft, and prevent the formation of insurrectionary plots." In many instances, these patrols "whipped and terrorized slaves caught without passes after curfew" (Genovese, 1976: 22, 617). After the Civil War, police forces were increased, but their major function remained the same: control the black population. As in Rome, southern police were enforcing the law, the law of those in power.

Not much is known about the police after the fall of the Roman Empire except that with the coming of feudalism, social control came to be a function of individual kings and nobles and their private armies. *Organized police forces*, as we understand the term, did not exist during this period. This was to change following the Norman Invasion in the eleventh century.

The Emergence of the Police Institution in England

Prior to the development of capitalism, English society was organized around a feudal system of production, with kings, barons, and various landlords constituting the ruling class. As we saw in the previous chapter, William the Conqueror created his own unique legal system, complete with justices of the peace and various kinds of police forces.

Prior to the Norman Invasion, policing was a community responsibility (as it was in all feudal societies). Each village in England was divided into units of ten families, called *tythings*. In each tything, a person known as a *tythingman* was responsible for keeping order in his section of the village (his section being similar to what are called *beats* in modern policing). A system known as the *mutual pledge system* was used whereby small sums of money were awarded to citizens who reported crimes to the tythingman or who responded to the tythingman's "hue and cry" (an announcement that a crime had occurred). In addition to catching thieves, the tythingman also reimbursed those who lost property (Reith, 1975: 26). The mutual pledge system and other forms of citizen participation in crime control were forerunners of the vigilante, the bounty hunter, and similar forms of citizen arrest.

As villages grew, tythings were combined to form *hundreds* (each with ten tythings) that were policed by *constables*. These hundreds were eventually combined to form *shires* (what we would today call counties), which were policed by individuals known as *shire-reeves* or *sheriffs*. Eventually, the Normans established the *vicecomes* to take the place of sheriffs. "The shire court of the vicecomes became, often, merely an instrument for collecting unjust and oppressive fines and taxes." The tythingman later became known as the *chief pledge*. This officer came under the authority of the

Knights of the Shire (under direct authority of kings), who also became known as *justices of the peace*. By the fourteenth century, the chief pledge came to be known as the *petty constable* and, later on, the *parish constable* (Reith, 1975: 28).

The *constabulary system* became the dominant form of policing in England until early in the nineteenth century, and was even copied in America. "The constable did not use his power to discover and punish deviation from the established laws. Rather, he assisted complaining citizens if and when they sought his help" (Parks, 1977: 196). The constable served during the day while at night, citizen volunteers took turns as night watchers. Policing, in other words, became a community responsibility and was under the control of the community. The constable, moreover, was not concerned with preventing crime in the sense that we know it today. That is, he did not spend his time ferreting out potential criminals; this was to change in the nineteenth century.

This form of policing could not survive the growth of population, the rise of the cities and, especially, the emergence of a capitalist economy with the parallel emergence of class divisions. In this new type of society, the *voluntary* observance of the law no longer held the social order together. According to Reith, such a system of social control seems to never survive:

> ... ineffective from the advent of community prosperity, as this brings into being, inevitably, differences in wealth and social status, and creates, on this basis, classes and parties and factions with or without wealth and power and privileges. In the presence of these divisions, community unanimity in voluntary law observance disappears, and some other means of securing law observance and the maintenance of authority and order must be found. (Reith, 1975: 210)

What should be added to this statement is that "authority and order" is defined by those in power, and that typically means keeping the masses under control. The gradual transition to capitalism in the eighteenth century brought with it increased class divisions and a growth of a large propertyless and powerless surplus population. The presence of this mass of humanity posed a definite threat to the prevailing social order and the ruling class, which brought forth demands for a highly organized and centralized police force, primarily to control the "dangerous classes."

The Metropolitan Police of London

Feudal society in England was coming to a close by the fifteenth and sixteenth centuries as capitalism began to take over as the dominant economic form. By the end of the seventeenth century, the enclosure movements and other repressive actions by the emerging bourgeoisie had forced many landless peasants to the cities in search of jobs, a process vividly described by Marx (Marx, 1977: Chapter 27–31). As one might expect, the masses of propertyless peasants began to engage in various forms of revolt and criminal activity in response to their plight. The propertied classes attempted to contain this revolt and discontent and to generally maintain "order." One of the first attempts to maintain order was the organization of the famous Bow Street Runners by Henry Fielding, a famous police reformer of the time (Reith, 1975: 135; Lyman, 1975: 13). This was accomplished during the 1740s, at about the time that new criminal careers were emerging, such as pirating, highway robbery, and begging.

After the formation of the Bow Street Runners, economic conditions began to worsen in England; by 1770, prices were rising faster than wages. One result was the famous Gordon Riots, a revolt by members of the working class against rising prices. Parliament and property owners (often indistinguishable) became alarmed and fearful of the presence of mobs. The police, as usual, were criticized for their general inefficiency and inability to control the riots, and the military had to be called to the scene. The police often agreed with the protesters and often lived in the same neighborhoods and, therefore, were not neutral enough for those in power, whereas the military were (Lyman, 1975; see also Critchley, 1975). Whenever riots threatened the estates of the ruling class, local magistrates called out various associations of the gentry to put down the riots. Sometimes the army or militia was called out, but local magistrates distrusted their loyalty. Even though the local gentry resisted the formation of a full-time police force, the rulers' tendency to call out the army risked further problems. More importantly, from the perspective of the merchants, riots disrupted the marketplace and hurt business (Humphries and Greenberg, 1993).

As the geographical extent of trade expanded, it became more difficult to prevent theft based on the previous methods of informal, almost ad hoc and individualistic methods. In 1798 Patrick Colquhoun, a successful Glasgow businessman (known as the "Father of Glasgow"), wrote a very influential book called *A Treatise on the Police of London* in which he stated: "The sole intention of the author . . . is to secure the inhabitants of the Metropolis against the alarming consequences to be dreaded from the existence of such an atrocious and criminal confederation. . . " (Lyman, 1975: 18). Colquhoun estimated that this "confederation" numbered around 115,000 in a total population of 999,000 (i.e., 11.5 percent). He was apparently most concerned about rioters and other people who made up the "dangerous classes." One model of policing that was present at that time was the Thames River Police, which was originally established as a sort of private police force financed by the West India Company merchants doing business in the port of London (it financed about 80 percent of the force) in order to reduce property losses due to theft and other threats to maritime commerce. Although it was a short-lived enterprise (it was abolished two years later and replaced by the Marine Police Establishment), it served as a forerunner of things to come (Critchley, 1972: 51–54; Spitzer, 1993: 586).

Up until around 1820, there continued to be strong resistance to the formation of an organized, twenty-four–hour police force. There was also a strong tradition in England of handling offenses as private matters. As suggested previously, for a number of years police officers were hired by private individuals to recover their stolen property or to solve whatever crime had been committed. A magistrate in 1821 said that "officers in abundance are loitering about the police offices, in waiting for hire. Protection is reserved for individuals who will individually pay for it" (Richardson, 1974: 7).

In the meantime, economic conditions continued to worsen in England. In 1807, for example, England blockaded French ports, resulting in severe unemployment and a rise in hunger and poverty among workers. A severe winter in 1810 and a harvest failure in 1812 added more problems. The use of machinery by factory owners began to displace workers, who soon became mere appendages to the machines. As expected, the workers began to protest. One of the most famous revolts was the Luddite Riots in late 1811 and early 1812. The workers destroyed machines and generally disrupted the entire factory system, a system that was quite oppressive (i.e., men, women, and children working up to eighteen hours per day under grueling conditions). The government's response was to make the destruction of machines punishable by death!

The War of 1812 resulted in increased profits and temporarily calmed things down as employment rose. But a depression between 1815 an 1822 resulted in widespread unemployment and more unrest. The Corn Laws of 1815 increased the price of bread, which was a mainstay of the poor, thus resulting in increased poverty and rioting. Once again, the government responded with repressive measures by passing the famous Six Acts (known also as the "Riot Acts"), which prohibited unauthorized drilling and authorized the seizure of "seditious and blasphemous literature." (Ironically, the British passed similar laws against American colonists prior to the Revolution.) Events during the 1820s convinced Parliament and other powerful leaders that armed intervention of the military was doing more harm than good (e.g., resulting in a decline of legitimacy toward Parliament and the existing police). The death of eleven and wounding of between five hundred and six hundred citizens who were peacefully attending a lecture (labeled as a "mob" by local magistrates) convinced the majority that an alternative was needed.

The depression temporarily ended around 1822, but a panic in 1825 resulted in the closing of many banks, the lowering of wages, and a rise in unemployment, all of which brought about a new wave of riots and protests by workers. At this time, Sir Robert Peel (known as "Bobby," after whom the London "bobbies" were named) became Home Secretary and for several

, ars worked with other supporters. Finally, after many years of debate, the Metropolitan Police Act was passed in 1829 (Lyman, 1975: 21–28).[1] It was modeled in part after the Thames River Police.

The formation of the Metropolitan Police of London was supported primarily because of a growing concern by those of wealth and power about the presence of mobs. Such a concern is not unique in history, and many a police force has been established for this reason.

Peel was of critical importance in the creation of the first police bureaucracy. He was not only a large landowner, he was also a shrewd politician (a Tory). As the son of a wealthy manufacturer, he was able "to weld the alliance of landowners, manufacturers, and fractions of the petty bourgeoisie that finally succeeded in establishing a bureaucratic police force in England." The establishment of a full-time, salaried *bureaucratic* police system was seen as a more efficient method of social control that represented two new developments in the history of policing: (1) rule through an essentially "impersonal" bureaucracy that seemingly represented the more "general interests" of society as a whole, rather than the ruling class; and (2) "a deeper, more finely tuned penetration of formal control into everyday life" (Humphries and Greenberg, 1993: 481).

The Metropolitan Police Act was passed in 1829 without serious opposition. The passage of this act and the creation of the London police represented the centralization of the state—a definite sign of the times as the capitalist system began to grow rapidly (Lynch and Groves, 1989: 84–85).

Peel sought to legitimate his police force in the eyes of the people by arguing that the police would serve the interests of *all* the people. He stressed that the new role of the police would be the prevention of crime through increased patrols, on the assumption that more police automatically resulted in less crime (a claim that has never been empirically demonstrated). The police would have a civilian character, since they would be recruited from the ranks of the working class. The police, moreover, would be "service-oriented" (Lyman, 1975: 33–36). Silver offered another explanation for the passage of the Metropolitan Police Act; namely, that it would shield the rulers from the masses. He wrote:

> If the power structure armed itself and fought a riot or a rebellious people, this created more trouble and tension than the original problem. But, if one can have an independent police which fights the mob, then antagonism is directed toward the police, not the power structure. A paid professional police force seems to separate "constitutional" authority from social and economical dominance. (Silver, 1967: 11–12)

Hence, there was a shift from control of policing on the community level (as it was with the constable form of policing) to control by the state (which in turn was under the direct control of the rulers).

The idea that the police would prevent crime by patrolling the streets in search of "suspicious" activities and/or persons and identifying "potential troublemakers" was the most important break with the past. The concern over the presence of mobs and radical protests and political parties helps explain the formation of this type of police force. The police could now serve more direct class-control functions (as well as other more routine functions) by patrolling those communities wherein live the poorest and most oppressed people, thereby "keeping tabs" on them or "keeping a lid" on potential disorder. Moreover, because their role shifted to that of the *prevention* of crime, the police eventually became the scapegoats for increasing crime rates. Also, the focus of the police on individual or potential offenders shifted the causes of crime away from social conditions to the individual.

There is much evidence that the wealthy classes and the working classes and the poor shared different views of the police. Richardson notes that a "parliamentary committee of 1834 noted the possibility of abuses of power; still it found the Metropolitan Police 'well calculated to maintain peace and order. . . ' and further found that the police were 'one of the most valuable of modern institutions'." Yet, Richardson continues, the poor and the working classes "considered the police more as an element of control than as a group of protectors. In a sense, the police monitored the behavior of the dangerous classes so that the comfortable and satisfied could sleep more soundly at night or not be annoyed by the sight of public drunkenness" (Richardson, 1975: 14).

The Development of the Police Institution in the United States

Early forms of policing in America were similar to those existing in England prior to the early nineteenth century. We have already referred to the southern police system, where police forces consisted primarily of slave patrols before the Civil War. In the North, especially in such large cities as New York, Boston, and Philadelphia, the rulers hired out their own police to serve as night watchers, some specifically to guard warehouses and homes. At times, the militia was called upon to suppress disorders, which were common during the late eighteenth century. For the most part, however, policing in colonial America was at the community level, with some form of constabulary system dominant (Parks, 1977; Center for Research on Criminal Justice, 1977: 21–22).

Throughout colonial America, the local sheriff and constables were the backbone of law enforcement. The "night watchman" patrolled the streets in larger communities. Constables and night watchmen, incidentally, were ordinary citizens. Eventually, the Dutch introduced a paid watch system in New York (1648) and in Boston a similar system was adopted (1663); both were soon abandoned because they were too expensive. The sheriff was generally appointed by the governor and he became the chief law-enforcement agent in the county, with numerous duties (e.g., jury selection, in charge of local jails). Just like night watchmen and constables, however, the sheriff was often neglectful of his duties and incidences of corruption were common (Friedman, 1993: 28–29).

In New York City, as late as 1845, there were one hundred marshals in addition to a part-time watch of around one thousand men known as *constables*. These police officers were not salaried but were paid fees for recovering stolen property or providing other police services. At night, a group of volunteers served as watches (Richardson, 1975: 22).

Most historians agree that the growth of population, increased immigration, the emergence of class divisions, and resulting urban disorders were the major factors associated with the rise of an organized police force (Bacon, 1939; Lane, 1967; Richardson, 1970; Silver, 1967). Richardson, writing of the New York Police, argues that between 1830 and 1845 there was "a marked upsurge in crime, vice, and disorder" in addition to "rapid population growth with sharp increases in immigration, heightened distinctions between class, ethnic, and religious groups with consequent social strain, and a dizzying economic cycle of boom and bust." He also contends that the city was no longer "a homogeneous community with a common culture and shared system of values and moral standards" (Richardson, 1975: 16). In a similar vein, Lane notes that Boston was plagued with some of the same changes. He notes especially: "Riot, one of the first problems recognized as beyond control, dramatized the need for force. The leaders of government were firmly set against popular violence as a means of political and social protest" (Lane, 1967: 24–25. Ironically, the leaders of the American Revolution supported popular violence as a means of political and social protest. Apparently, these same leaders (and the next generation) did not apply the same logic to the protests of other oppressed groups; both Lane and Richardson fail to point this out.

Most police historians (e.g., Lane and Richardson) claim that these changes inevitably resulted in a breakdown in normal mechanisms of social control and the development of a full-time organized police force. The following statement by Kalmanoff epitomizes this conventional view of the rise of the police in the United States:

> While the need for social control diminishes in the presence of increasing stability, rapid or extensive change will necessitate the development of new or improved mechanisms of maintaining social order. As in England, the Industrial Revolution in the United States was accompanied by profound and rapid social change. Traditional social patterns were disrupted by the migration from rural to urban areas, the inevitable competition for employment, and the pressures of urbanization. The problems of transition were aggravated by

the extremely heterogeneous nature of American society
influx of new immigrants from Europe and other areas. So
nomic development, and a growing class structure in
demonstrated the inadequacy of the prevailing methods of
ticularly in rapidly developing urban areas. (Kalmanoff, 19.

This point of view generally takes the form of the popular consensus argument by suggesting that "the people" were supportive of the newly created police forces in the mid-nineteenth century. In fact, the organization of a full-time organized police force was the result of actions taken by business and political leaders in large cities in the North. In fact, there was a great deal of opposition on the part of the working class. According to one view:

> Workers did not accept such exploitative conditions (i.e., union busting, depressing wages, and other practices on the part of employers) without resistance. This took its most organized form in labor strikes that directly threatened the high profit levels that employers maintained through the exploitation of workers. (Center for Research on Criminal Justice, 1977: 23–24)

In Lynn, Massachusetts, for instance, workers on three occasions organized to defeat shoe-manufacturer mayors; the largest issue was the strike-breaking activities of the police.

Two recent studies, one by Harring and McMullin on the rise of the Buffalo police and one by Harring on the Milwaukee police, challenge some of the conventional interpretations of the rise of the police. It is true, as Harring and McMullin argue, that the rise in disorders required new methods of social control. However, these new methods were perceived as necessary by those in power. Indeed, the business leaders in the major cities of the North felt threatened by the specter of urban disorder, the presence of "mobs," and the "dangerous classes." The attitude toward these groups (and the working class in general) was similar to white attitudes toward blacks in the South: these powerless groups would seize power. The studies by Harring and McMullin and by Harring present evidence that (1) the size of the police force increased more rapidly than both the rise in population and the increase in crime; (2) "crime" was primarily of the "public order" variety, such as disorderly conduct, vagrancy, and the like; and (3) the police were created and under strict control by business and political leaders. Let us pursue this matter further with a closer look at the rise of the police in Buffalo, New York (Harring, 1976, 1978; Harring and McMullen, 1975).

An Illustrative Case: Buffalo, New York

Both Lane and Richardson argue that in New York and Boston the rise of a full-time police force in the 1840s and 1850s followed a rapid increase in

...e and disorder. But there is no evidence that these periods contained more crime and disorder than earlier periods. The period just before the American Revolution and for decades to follow witnessed a great deal of crime and disorder (e.g., Shay's Rebellion). Moreover, the population of eastern cities was not as homogeneous prior to the 1840s as both Lane and Richardson suggest. Rather, these cities were quite heterogeneous with a well-defined class structure, numerous ethnic groups, and the existence of slums (Harring, 1976: 55).

Additional evidence indicates that the rise in police personnel did not correspond to a rise in crime. This is evident in Boston as well as in Buffalo (Ferdinand, 1967). Harring and McMullin show the figures on arrests, population growth, and the changes in police personnel in Buffalo.

Between 1873 and 1880 the police force actually declined, as did total arrests, but population increased by about 32 percent. Between 1880 and 1890, the police force increased by more than 100 percent, while population increased by about 67 percent. Then, between 1890 and 1900, the size of the police force increased by about 80 percent, twice the percentage increase of the population. Hence, the theory that an increase in population causes an increase in the size of the police force fails to explain why the growth of the police was far greater than the increase in population.

At first glance, one might conclude that there is a close relationship between the increase in the size of the police force and crime. But crime, as measured by arrests (as it is here), is open for interpretation. Between 1873 and 1900, total arrests rose by about 125 percent, population increased by about 200 percent, and the police force increased by 259 percent. However, note the percentage of arrests that were of the "public-order" variety, which included at that time such offenses as drunkenness (public), disorderly conduct, vagrancy, and the charge of being a "tramp." It is well known that such charges are usually rather vague and depend solely on police discretion. For each year these offenses constituted the majority of all arrests (ranging from 59 to 74 percent of the total), but between 1885 and 1900 they averaged 70 percent or more of all arrests.

What is also interesting is the fact that the overall *rate* of the police force increased by only 20 percent during the entire period, but actually *decreased* by 28 percent between 1873 and 1880, whereupon it began to increase quite rapidly, going up by two thirds (67.7 percent) between 1880 and 1900. Similarly, the overall arrest rate decreased by about 50 percent between 1873 and 1885, only to be almost exactly reversed between 1885 and 1900, as it went up by almost exactly 50 percent. Similarly, the arrest rate for public order offenses decreased by around one third from 1873 and 1880, only to increase by a phenomenal 469 percent between 1880 and 1900! Meanwhile, the arrest rate for crimes of violence did not show any apparent pattern, going down by 55 percent between 1873 and 1885, then up by 72 percent between 1885 and 1890, then down by 7 percent between 1890 to

1895, then back up again by 21 percent between 1895 and 1900.

It just so happens that this period witnessed the greatest amount of political unrest in Buffalo, as elsewhere in the nation.[2] Moreover, Harring and McMullin found that most of those arrested during periods of political unrest were laborers who were charged with these offenses in the context of social and political struggles (Harring and McMullin, 1975: 12).

It is also interesting that the percentage of arrests that were crimes of violence remained fairly constant throughout this period: ranging from a low of 0.6 percent in 1873 to a high of 1.1 percent in 1880, but averaging less than 1 percent of the total. Hence, "crime in the streets" did not consist of direct personal harm to individuals, but rather it consisted of primarily harm (or political threats) to industrialists as thousands of workers struggled to gain union recognition and a decent standard of living, behavior that was labeled by Buffalo industrialists as "criminal." Clearly, the "rabble" were getting out of line and needed to be "contained." (For a modern variation on this theme, see Chomsky, 1994.)

The conventional analyses of the rise of the police also cite the importance of urban disorders, especially what is commonly referred to as *rioting*. It is true that this was of major concern during these times, just as riots were a major concern during the time of slavery in the South and during the American Revolution. But it was of major concern to those who held positions of economic and political power: in the South, the white plantation owners; in the North, manufacturers; during the Revolution, the British. Indeed, throughout the nineteenth century, there were widespread political turmoil and resistance as workers—in response to gross exploitation by capitalist owners—sought to gain some form of democratic control of their lives, especially the workplace. The owners used various techniques to keep workers in line, such as hiring "scabs" to work while workers were on strike, token advancement of leaders, and, more commonly, the use of both private and public police forces. The police became the tools of the owners in many cases, for they were ordered to break up strikes and arrest workers on vague charges, such as disorderly conduct. Not surprisingly, Harring and McMullin found that arrests for these offenses increased during periods of rioting and declined sharply after the turmoil came to a close.

Not coincidentally, the greatest economic crisis in U.S. history up to that period occurred in 1893, with 642 banks failing and sixteen thousand businesses closed. Unemployment stood at around 20 percent. Labor unions, starting to get a foothold in the country, organized mass protests. In 1892 alone, strikes occurred all over the country, including Buffalo, and they continued for many years thereafter. Only a few years earlier, the infamous Haymarket bombing occurred in Chicago in 1886, as about three thousand workers assembled at Haymarket Square. About 180 policemen were ordered to be present. A bomb exploded, killing seven policemen. Eight so-called "anarchists" were arrested, tried, convicted, and sentenced to death, despite little evidence that they did it; four were hanged, one committed suicide in jail, and three were eventually pardoned by Illinois Governor John Altgeld and sent to prison. To date, no one knows who threw the bomb and serious questions have consistently been raised about the guilt of those arrested. This case drew international attention and would continue to draw protests well into the twentieth century. Subsequent to this event, police continued to be hired by industrialists to quell labor protests, which often led to indiscriminate violence against protestors and arrests and imprisonment on disputed or minor charges (Zinn, 1995: 265–276).

Finally, most historians cite the "inevitable" problems of overcrowding, slums, and the like as causing problems in social control and giving rise to increases in police manpower. But this view overlooks the fact that it was primarily the low wages paid to immigrant workers that created slums, not to mention forced segregation and other forms of discrimination. Harring wrote:

> Industrialization occurred in the context of cut-throat competition among capitalists in which low wage levels were a major source of profits. Skill levels were reduced to facilitate the control of workers and to reduce wages. Frequent depressions further reduced wages and made workers' income highly unstable. (Harring, 1976: 57)

The police throughout this time were under direct control of upperclass business and political leaders, thus lending support to the notion that they were the "tools" of the ruling class. For instance, in Buffalo between 1872 and 1900, there were seventeen police commissioners, of which fourteen were businessmen. There were also nine police superintendents, of which four were businessmen. These businessmen were concerned—first and foremost—with protecting business interests that were usually contrary to the interests of the workers. In Buffalo, labor problems were cited more often than crime as justification for additional police personnel, according to annual police reports. One police report in 1893 reveals that in response to a strike, the entire police force was ordered on duty; many other reports reveal identical responses. Police were also ordered to break up the meetings of workers who were attempting to organize unions. In addition, because Polish immigrants in Buffalo were especially troublesome, the police department set up special Polish precincts to help control them and to aid in their (i.e., Polish) "socialization" (Harring and McMullin, 1975: 10–13).

In Buffalo, New York, Boston, and most other industrial cities, the police were actively recruited from working-class communities. At first, many officers were reluctant to exert the kind of control their superiors (i.e., the upper class) wanted. But the owners often bribed them, such as offering them more pay than given to other workers, hiring police from one immigrant group to control another immigrant group (e.g., Irish police control-ling Italians and Poles), and other measures (Harring and McMullin, 1975; Center for Research on Criminal Justice, 1977: 26–27).

The Rise and Growth of Private Policing

A discussion of nineteenth-century developments would be incomplete without some reference to the phenomenon of private policing. Private policing emerged during the same period as public police forces. Thus, pri-vate policing arose with the growth of industrial capitalism and working-class protests. Like the early "fee-for-service" constables, private policing enabled the rich to purchase their own protection from crime; hence, it is a "class-based institution" (Lynch and Groves, 1989: 90–91). While the "pub-lic" police concentrated their efforts on maintaining social order, the "pri-vate" police concentrated on the protection of the private property of the capitalist class (Lynch and Groves, 1989; Weiss, 1978).

What is important to emphasize is the distinction between private and public order. On the one hand, the origin of the police—in this case, a "pub-lic" police—was related to the need for some form of "public peace." On the other hand, there has been the notion of a "private peace," which usually has been related to the idea that while "the state is the public authority and all other authorities operating within its territory are subordinate to it," the state can, at its discretion, "define separate private peaces so long as they are not in conflict with the public peace." Corporations have been legally defined as analogous with "persons" and hence "have a right to a sphere of private authority over which they have undisturbed jurisdiction" (Shearing and Stenning, 1987:11–15).

What is especially significant in this context is the emergence of the idea of the corporation as a "person" with all the rights accorded to people in general, as noted in the Fourteenth Amendment guaranteeing that all "persons" have the right to due process. This was a carefully calculated move on the part of corporate owners and their lawyers during the so-called "Gilded Age" (roughly the last twenty-five years of the nineteenth century when huge fortunes were amassed by the "robber barons"; see Josephson, 1962). This change formally came about in 1886 with the Santa Clara case in California during which the U.S. Supreme Court ruled that a corporation should be treated like a "person" and that ordinary people were conceived as having their own liberties intertwined with the corporation and, there-fore, "taking away corporate rights was equivalent to challenging their own constitutionally guaranteed rights." In other words, an "artificial person" (which was what the corporation was in fact), had the same rights as real people. Thus, the old idea that a corporation was under public control (which it was at first) was transformed into a completely new entity unto itself with all the rights and privileges of citizens. It gave unprecedented freedom to corporations to do basically whatever they wanted (Derber, 1998: 126–131).

What this development also revealed was the close connection between corporations and the state, since it was a branch of the state (i.e., the courts) that helped create the corporation as a "private" entity. But more than this, this relationship eventually expanded to include many other state entities, including the U.S. Secret Service and the Department of Justice. As union protests escalated during the late nineteenth century, the courts began to side with corporations, charging that their (the corporation) "due process" rights were being violated by strikers. The courts began to issue injunctions against strikers, while calling out the National Guard and the U.S. Army to quell disturbances, as the federal government looked the other way. It was a clear example of "usurpation of state power by private interests" (Weiss, 1987b: 111).

The first private security agency (and the most popular, even today) was Pinkertons, established in Chicago during the 1850s. The main purpose for the establishment of this agency was to provide additional protection to private corporations and, secondly, to provide supplemental services to the Chicago police department.

After the Civil War, the Pinkertons shifted from routine detective work to industrial spying, first for railroad companies and later for other private corporations. For the next several decades, Pinkertons worked for private corporations in their battles against working-class union activities. Their services were generally confined to four important strike services: (1) labor espionage (providing spies at the workplace); (2) strikebreakers (hired especially as "scabs" to replace striking workers); (3) strike guards (those who protected private properpty during strikes); and (4) strike missionaries or those who "mingled with striking employees or townspeople either to urge strikers to violence or to act as propagandists against the strike." During the period 1869–1892, this force participated in seventy-seven strikes. Among the most famous included the Homestead (Pennsylvania) strike against the Carnegie Steel Company, which left twelve dead (ten of them strikers) (Weiss, 1978: 39).

A Senate hearing (which followed the Homestead strike) culminated in several criticisms of Pinkertons, which in turn was followed by several pieces of legislation (known as "anti-Pinkertonism" laws). Most of this legislation was ineffective because several states began to establish their own private security forces to help break strikes, with Pennsylvania establishing a state police force specifically to deal with strikes.

Violence against strikers and other working-class activities reached a peak during the late 1910s and early 1920s, such as the violence against the International Workers of the World, the Palmer Raids, and the violence against striking workers in Ludlow, Colorado, in 1914.[3] As Weiss reports,

"These agencies and corporations stockpiled huge arsenals of weapons, including millions of dollars worth of machine and handguns, sickening gas, tear gas, and deadly chloropicrin." Finally, during the Great Depression when strike activity reached a new high, part of Roosevelt's New Deal reforms focused on private policing. As collective bargaining became institutionalized, violence on the part of private security forces became unnecessary, although they continued most of their anti-labor activities (especially industrial spying) (Weiss, 1978: 42).

Pinkerton's and other security forces have continued to serve the need of private industry, with their primary emphasis being on protecting firms from employee theft and shoplifting, in addition to other guard duties. Private security forces have expanded their role to include guarding buildings at night and serving as watchmen for apartment complexes and even enclosed housing districts.

The Growth of the Police Institution in the Twentieth Century

By the end of the nineteenth century, almost every major city had a full-time police force. While the police (including private police, such as the Pinkertons) were often used to suppress strikes, many of the daily duties of police officers were of the "service" variety. At times, police officers helped provide overnight lodging services for the homeless, supplied coal for poor families, and served soup in special kitchens for the hungry. (Radelet, 1977: 35). Such functions were an apparent contradiction because the police were often called on to oppress these same people. In time, most of these services were to be handled by charity organizations, so that the police could do "real police work."

Another function of the police, one which created a great deal of animosity among the people, was to control liquor. Public drunkenness became a popular form of human activity as saloons and taverns replaced the home as a favorite place to drink during the late nineteenth century. These places also became favorite hangouts of workers, often becoming places where political meetings were held. Then came the Temperance Movement. According to Parks, the Temperance Movement began by wanting the consumption of alcoholic beverages to be moderate, rather than excessive. In time, the major concern shifted to that of abstinence. Total abstinence became a "symbol of power and respectability," and those who did not abstain were to be punished. Thus came the passage of laws regulating the drinking habits of millions of Americans. More importantly, however, the Prohibition Movement that followed (resulting in a Constitutional Amendment) was an effort on the part of powerful groups to control the dangerous classes, specifically the immigrant working classes. The police were called on to enforce these laws. Because the public was sharply divided on the issue, the police were often caught in the middle. And, since many police officers engaged in drinking behavior of the type that was outlawed, many were reluctant to enforce the law. The police often solved the problem by doing no more than the minimum; eventually, this led to a great deal of corruption (Parks, 1977).

The fact that the police were often unable (or, in some cases, unwilling) to maintain order and suppress dissent led to many criticisms, which came from all segments of society. Working-class organizations, such as unions and radical political parties, complained of harassment and brutality, while business and political leaders complained of laxness and corruption. One study concluded that:

> By the beginning of the twentieth century, many Progressives in business, government, and the universities were becoming strongly critical of the police. They regarded most police departments as corrupt and ineffective, subservient to local politics, and totally incapable of providing the level of protection they felt a highly interdependent business society required. A main stimulus for their dissatisfaction with the performance of the police was the apparently rising rate of crimes against property. . . .The traditional police forces, according to the Progressives, were not only failing to put a stop to rampant crime and political agitation, but were actually aggravating them through the use of misguided and outmoded strategies. (Center for Research on Criminal Justice, 1977: 32)

The period known as the Progressive Era (1890–1920) saw numerous reforms throughout society, including the criminal justice system. Because this period of history is so important, and so many criminal justice system changes occurred during this era, some brief comments are in order. This review should be kept in mind because it also relates to the other chapters in this book.

The Progressive Era

The literature covering the period known as the Progressive Era is voluminous. There have been many different interpretations of this movement, specifically concerning (1) the origins of this movement, the nature of its leadership, and the general social objectives; and (2) the amount of success and social value to society. Taking the more conservative perspective, Link suggests that there was not a "progressive movement" as such; rather, there were several different progressive movements. There was "the effort of social workers and students of the labor question to bring the state and national governments to the side of women, children, and other unprotected groups." There was a movement aimed to rid the nation of widespread corruption in the cities and to "restore representative government" to the cities.

There was also a movement to make state governments more responsive to the people and as instruments of social welfare, rather that subservient to corporations. Finally, "there was a progressive movement on the national level, the main thrusts of which were attempts to subject railroads, industrial corporations, and banks to effective public control" (Link, 1967: 68).

Few scholars disagree, however, as to the total effect of this period on American history. "The foundations of the society we live in today were created between 1880 and 1920 by industrialization, urbanization, and immigration. Those forty years were America's 'take off' point into modernity. . . ."(Mann, 1963: 1).

Indeed, the last half of the nineteenth century and first two decades of the twentieth century witnessed widespread social problems such as poverty, unemployment, economic crises, labor unrest, crime, and delinquency. Many people were aroused to action by the works of the "muckrakers," a group of writers (e.g., Upton Sinclair, Ida Tarbell, Lincoln Steffins) who published books and articles that exposed many urban problems. Large numbers of professionals, educators, and businessmen, who came to be known as Progressives, responded by agitating for a wide variety of reforms.

Many of the problems, as perceived by the Progressives, stemmed from overcrowded slums and the high concentration of immigrants within these areas. The Progressives' solution was to educate and "assimilate" the "foreigners" (immigrants were often called worse), while improving the more pressing problems of the cities through local (mostly volunteer) action.

There has been some debate concerning the social backgrounds of the Progressives. Some historians, such as Nye, have argued that they were Midwestern, small-town people (Nye, 1951). Others, such as Hofstadter, focused on their urban origins, arguing that the leaders were among the educated middle class. Hofstadter maintains that these reformers were most concerned about their own future positions, specifically referring to their "status anxiety" as driving forces of reform activities, rather than the plight of the poor, for instance (Hofstadter, 1955).

One of the most convincing arguments is that reformers were strongly influenced (and dominated by) the business sector. Both Hays and particularly Wiebe show how business leaders strongly supported such reforms as the regulation of the railroad and communications industry, the conservation movement, anti-trust reforms, and the Federal Reserve Act (Hays, 1959; Wiebe, 1967). Wiebe showed that business, professional, and educational groups organized on a national basis to spread their desire for nationalization, integration, and regulation—in short, the efficiency of economic and political institutions.

In recent years, a group known as the "New Left Historians" has provided a radical/Marxist interpretation to this period. Kolko, for instance, described the period as a "triumph of conservatism" because "there was an effort to preserve the basic social and economic relations essential to a capitalist society. . . ." (Kolko, 1963: 2). "Progressivism," said Kolko, was "the political rationalization of business and industrial conditions, a movement that operated on the assumption that the general welfare of the community could be best served by satisfying the concrete needs of business" (Kolko, 1963: 2–3). Williams suggests that this period brought about the triumph of a new corporate order (in his words, the "Age of Corporate Capitalism"). One result was the adaptation of the major institutions of society—indeed, the life of most citizens—to this new order. This new economic order was "designed to accumulate large amounts of capital, resources, and labor and apply them to the rational, planned conduct of economic activity through a division of labor and bureaucratic routine" (Williams, 1988: 2).

It has also been argued that many reforms (especially those concerned with education, juvenile justice, and criminal justice) resulted in extending bureaucratic controls to many areas of social life in order to regulate and control those on the bottom of the social order. Piven and Cloward, for instance, argued that public relief (and other ameliorative) programs emerge during "occasional outbreaks of civil disorder. . .and are then abolished or contracted when political stability is restored" (Piven and Cloward, 1971: xiii). One of the most popular aims of reformers was that of increasing and extending the functions of the government to solve social problems. Many reforms concerned with improving the efficiency of the legal system ended up by adding several new bureaucracies, especially on the national level (with the emergence of such organizations as the FBI) (Walker, 1998).

Most of the New Left historians argued that business leaders supported most reforms (many of which were passed as compromises, following lengthy debates in the House and Senate) because they feared social revolution. This interpretation is understandable because labor unrest and the growth of the Socialist party during this period obviously threatened the interests of capitalists. Kolko argues that most of the legislation of the period in effect, if not intentionally, sought to regulate the economy in the interests of private profit and property (Kolko, 1963; see also Wienstein, 1968; and Tipple, 1970).

Link's conclusion, however, is just the opposite. He calls the Progressive Movement "one of the most significant and fruitful reform movements in American history." He particularly praises what he calls the "social justice movement," which involved the attempt to improve the lot of the underprivileged. He wrote that the accomplishments of social justice reformers "constituted perhaps the greatest single triumph of the social justice movement before the First World War." However, even judging by Link's own account, the results of these reforms were quite mixed (Link, 1967: 70–72).[4]

Zinn observed that while "ordinary people benefited to some extent from these changes," the most fundamental conditions changed very little "for the vast majority of tenant farmers, factory workers, slumdwellers, miners, farm laborers, working men and women, black and white" (Zinn, 1995: 341–342). It was clear, said Zinn, that a lot of the reforms were insti-gated to "head off socialism." Zinn quotes a privately circulated memo from the National Civic Federation, which stated that "in view of the rapid spread in the United States of socialistic doctrines," there was a need for "a carefully planned and wisely directed effort to instruct public opinion as to the real meaning of socialism" (Zinn, 1995: 346).

Indeed, there was a concerted effort by big business to preserve the capitalist system because it was being criticized so harshly. One method was the emergence of a "public relations" industry to "sell the capitalist story to the masses." Thus began, around the time of World War I, an intense pro-paganda effort, let by such experts as Walter Lippman, the "dean of U.S. journalists," who urged the "manufacture of consent" since "the common interests very largely elude public opinion entirely, and can be managed only by a specialized class. . . ." Lasswell would later note that we should not succumb to "democratic dogmatisms about men being the best judges of their own interests" (Lasswell, 1930, quoted in Chomsky 1989:16–17). Instead, the elites are the best judges and what was needed was "a whole new technique of control, largely through propaganda," mostly because of the "ignorance and superstition" of the masses of people. After all, "ratio-nality belongs to the cool observers," noted Reinhold Niebuhr, who eventu-ally became "the official establishment theologian" of the government and who suggested that what was needed was for elites, via the media and the advertising industry, to provide the "necessary illusions" so that the "right course of action" can be followed, all for the "common good" (Chomsky, 1989: 16–17). Such "necessary illusions" included intense propaganda about the emerging juvenile justice system and that such a system would act "in the best interest of the child," especially the children of the poor. [5] Those in authority would "know what's best," better in fact than the parents of these children. (See Chapter 5.)

Whether these reforms were "successful" probably depends on one's own ideological views and the period within which one is writing. From a conservative standpoint (represented by Link) they were, in fact, "progres-sive," while from a radical standpoint (represented by Kolko, Zinn, and oth-ers), they were failures or—at best—uplifted only a handful of the under-privileged. The latter interpretation better fits the available evidence because so many people (as Zinn notes), especially blacks and immigrants, benefited little and experienced a wave of repression throughout the period (e.g., the rise of the Ku Klux Klan, the Red Scare, the Palmer Raids on immi-grants, and the passage of anti-immigration laws). The benefits of reforms aimed at children and youth also can be questioned, as discussed in Chapter 5 (Walker, 1998: 151–152).

There is no questioning the fact that American society underwent some radical transformations during this period. What occurred was the "bureaucratization" of many areas of social life, resulting in the control, regulation, and efficient functioning of the major institutions of society and the establishment of many regulatory agencies of social control (Weber, 1946; Haber, 1964).

Police Reforms During the Progressive Era.   Concerning the police, some of the major goals of reformers included the following:

1. *Centralization.* This was necessary because, said reformers, the existing police were "too close" to local communities and under the control of local politics. Apparently, the police institution had not as yet become completely separated from influences of local communities, although, to be sure, such a process was by this time well underway. Reformers aimed to tighten the control of the police, leaving it in the hands of high-level administrators, such as police commissioners.

2. *Professionalism.* Reformers sought to "professionalize" the police by filtering out incompetent or unskilled police and replacing them with educated and highly skilled officers. This tactic also included the abolition of community residence requirements, which no doubt contributed to many officers' inability to control working-class strikers. This reform should sound familiar since "professionalism" has been strongly recommended by many special crime commissions, including the Wickersham Commission in the 1930s and the President's Commission in 1967, as well as the National Advisory Commission in 1973.

3. *Technology.* A third method of improving the police was to increase the reliance on the use of technology. This strategy was supposed "to replace the traditional police reliance on fear and brute force," especially in dealing with riots and other forms of protests. One of the most notable changes was the introduction of the call-box system in the 1880s and the two-way radio in 1929 (Kalmanoff, 1976: 42).

4. *Crime Prevention.* A fourth tactic was to beef up efforts toward *preventing* crime. Two specific methods were to be developed: (1) cooperation with schools, welfare agencies, and the like in order to identify "potential delinquents" and other "troublemakers" (e.g., in the schools); and (2) increasing contacts with "troublesome" groups directly, especially youth. One example of these efforts was the "crime prevention division" of the Berkeley police, which worked closely with the "child guidance clinic." (Center for Research on Criminal Justice, 1977: 35–39)

Police departments all over the country were plagued with problems of graft and inefficiency during the late nineteenth century. One of the most common solutions to this and other internal problems was the introduction of the civil service system. At times, civil service (and other re-

forms) was aimed at "throwing the rascals out." Indeed, police and political corruption (e.g., Tammany Hall in New York City) were believed to
go hand in hand. But civil service reform involved more than this. As
Richardson states: "The civil service program became intertwined with a
larger program to eliminate 'politics' from the government of cities, to
make urban government a matter of administrative efficiency rather than
political conflict." In effect, such a form of government was to take away
influence from poor and working-class (especially immigrant) neighborhoods. As far as the police system was concerned, promotions began to
be made through competitive examinations (before promotions were largely
made based on who you knew). Yet the reality was much different from
what the new laws stipulated, for "political influence remained strong in
promotions. . . . Police commanders exercised too much power in too many
sensitive areas. . .and politicians and others constantly sought to get
'their' policemen promotions and the right assignments" (Richardson,
1974: 64).

New Developments in Private Policing

Labor struggles continued well into the twentieth century and the police—
both public and private (including state police, the National Guard, and the
U.S. Army)—continued to be used to control labor unrest. However, during
the Depression Era of the 1930s, the rights of labor were finally recognized
with the passage of the Wagner Act (i.e., the National Labor Relations Act)
in 1935, which backed up workers' right to organize. But corporate America
immediately began to resist and fight back with the beginnings of intensive
"corporate propaganda" (Fones-Wolf, 1994: 5–25; Carey, 1995). This
involved a large public relations industry to sell the capitalist story, including "convincing workers to identify their social, economic, and political
well-being with that of their specific employer and more broadly with the
free enterprise system" (Fones-Wolf, 1994: 6). This was perhaps best summarized with the famous phrase, "what's good for General Motors is good
for the country." Certainly corporations had a lot to worry about: between
1936 and 1944, membership in unions went from about four million to
around fourteen million, as strikes continued throughout the 1930s—four
thousand in 1937 alone (Weiss, 1987b: 112).

Henry Ford, while considered by some a "great innovator," among
workers he was known as a tyrant "who demanded from his workers
absolute obedience and machinelike behavior to complement his technocratic vision of the ideal factory" (Weiss, 1987b: 113). An illustration of this
can be seen at his River Rouge plant, where eighty thousand workers were
employed in what can be called, for all practical purposes, a prison-like
environment. Weiss quotes the following description, which summarizes
what this factor was like:

They do not whistle while they work; they do not even whisper. Only the tools they use make any sound as they demonstrate the efficiency of mass production. Their silence is a tribute to the Machine-Age Pavlovs who determine from week to week just how much men can stand before running amok. (Weiss, 1987b: 114)

To enforce this prison-like atmosphere, corporations like Ford and Bethlehem Steel hired thousands of spies and "sluggers" (i.e., private detectives) who were working with hundreds of private detective agencies. At one point, Henry Ford had his own in-house police department, with as many as 3,500 men employed (Ford called this the "Ford Service Department"). At times, this was augmented by various community groups, including the Knights of Dearborn and the Legionnaires. In response to this, the American Civil Liberties Union (ACLU) pressed for a Congressional investigation. Finally, in the face of incredible opposition from a strengthened union movement and the Roosevelt Administration, there began a turnaround in both the philosophy and strategy of corporate management. What occurred was a shift toward what became known as *public relations* (actually a nicer sounding word than *propaganda*) from the usual "robber barons" approach known as *slugging* (Weiss, 1987b).

As World War II ended, there were expectations of the lowering of wages and the inevitable strikes by workers as a response. Management was understandably concerned with the new power of labor. Instead of relying on old methods of social control (discussed previously), the new head of Ford (i.e., Henry Ford II, who took over in September 1945) created a new "industrial relations" position within Ford. This method entailed recognizing unions, but putting union leadership "on the defensive" where they would be "held accountable to the *company's* demands" (Weiss, 1987b: 122).

Despite this effort, more strikes occurred in 1946. One result was Congressional action culminating in the passage of the Taft-Hartley Act in 1947, which included sanctions against unions for activities such as mass picketing, wildcat strikes, and walkouts. The act increased union power over their own members, which transformed them into not only "agents of labor peace, *but also agents of the state as well*" (Weiss, 1987b: 124, quoting Lipsitz, 1982). In short, labor officials became policemen in effect, so that reliance on private police, state police, and the like would no longer be required. As Weiss notes, "the slugging-detective style of labor discipline became inappropriate and dangerous. Under the new system, as long as union bosses limited contract demands to wage and hour considerations, negotiations could be 'reasonable' " (Weiss, 1987b: 125). Various strike-breaking efforts of union leaders (i.e., their *policing* activities) were supported by federal law under the Taft-Hartley Act. This style of policing represents a *continuum* of policing from public forms of policing with public accountability at one end, to those forms with "special powers and accountable only to private interests" at the other end (Weiss, 1987b: 127).

One of the most important changes in the police institution during this century has been its increasing bureaucratization. There are more specialized areas and more tasks to be performed. The emergence of special detective bureaus is an example of this. We have, in most police departments, such detective divisions as burglary, robbery, homicide, vice, and juvenile, to mention just a few. The average police officer now spends most of his or her time performing rather routine clerical tasks, such as interviewing victims of crimes (in which long and detailed crime reports often have to be filled out) and writing traffic tickets.

One result of these changes is the growing alienation of the beat police officer. The automobile, along with the geographical mobility of citizens and the emergence of suburbs, has contributed to this alienation. In particular, the uniformed police officer is alienated from "real police work" (e.g., conducting investigations and making important arrests) and from the people he or she is supposed to serve. Gone are the days of the walking beat cop who knew everybody (e.g., Bumper Morgan in Joseph Wambaugh's *The Blue Knight*, 1974). Now the beat is an impersonal one and the city is seen through the glass windows of a squad car. Yet the functions remain basically the same.

This does not mean, however, that uses of certain police forces to control those defined as dangerous ceased to exist, because in the era following World War II, various efforts were made to control a new "dangerous class" that had emerged in the 1960s; namely, urban, lower-class African Americans.

Policing the Ghetto in the 1960s

In the 1960s, many began to conceive of the ghettos within the inner cities of America as analogous to imperialized "colonies" (Blauner, 1972; Tabb, 1970). Not unlike today, such ghettoes are almost totally separated from the rest of society (both literally and figuratively). Part of this separation can be seen in some of the most common problems that plague these areas, including poverty, unemployment and underemployment, substandard housing, inadequate social services, high crime rates, and high rates of alcohol and drug abuse.

Blauner described the "colonization" of African Americans in terms of five major components. First, there is a "forced, involuntary entry." Second, the colonizers carry out policies that constrain, transform, or destroy the culture of the colonized. Third, government bureaucracies and the legal system itself administer control over the lives of the colonized. "The colonized have the experience of being managed and manipulated by outsiders who look down upon them." Fourth is the element of *racism*. "Racism is a principle of social domination by which a group seen as inferior or different in alleged biological characteristics is exploited, controlled, and oppressed socially and psychically by a superordinate group." Finally, there is a separation according to labor status, with the colonized assigned the menial and unskilled tasks and often relegated to the "surplus labor force" (Blauner; 1972: 84).

The colonial model was extended to explain the role of the police in the ghetto as an "army of occupation," in that they began to be viewed as an "alien force of soldiers in enemy territory." Several studies during the late 1960s demonstrated that the police were not only *perceived* by ghetto residents as "outsiders," but they actually were outsiders in many respects (i.e, not from the same neighborhood). This was true even when applied to African American officers (Kelly, 1976).

Another element of a "colonial" police force noted by Blauner was expressed as the goals of containment, regulation, and control. Blauner noted that "they constrict Afro-Americans to black neighborhoods by harassing and questioning them when they are found outside the ghetto. . . ." (Blauner, 1972: 97–98). In the survey by Kelly discussed previously, it was found that ghetto residents believe that the police virtually ignored serious crime (especially crimes against residents by absentee merchants, landlords, and other representatives of the business community, as well as government) and spent too much time on relatively minor offenses. Many also believed that most police ignored serious personal crimes, as long as it was black against black.

The goal of containment was most apparent with regard to collective disorders, such as the riots of the 1960s in locations such as Watts, Detroit, and Newark. Blauner noted at the time that "in the final analysis, they [the police] do the dirty work of the larger system by restricting the striking back of black rebels to skirmishes inside the ghetto, thus deflecting energies and attacks from the communities and institutions of the larger power structure" (Blauner, 1972: 99; see also Balbus, 1973).

Police Corruption: A Continuing Problem

Corruption has been a constant within the police institution. During the early years of the American police, there were constant problems associated with various kinds of corruption among not only individual police officers but also entire departments. As Walker notes, one could easily conclude that corruption was the main business of the police in the nineteenth century. Police routinely received payoffs to "look the other way" at various illegal activities. This was, of course, during the era when almost entire local governments were in one way or another corrupt. It was the era of Tammany Hall and other political machines that made corruption seem almost normal (Walker, 1998).

Various "reforms" during the Progressive Era and after did little to stem the tide of police corruption. Evidence of this comes from the first of many "blue ribbon" government commissions investigating corruption and other aspects of the criminal justice system throughout the twentieth century. The first was the Wickersham Commission in 1931 (National Commission on Law Observance and Enforcement, 1931), which found corruption within police departments to be common. President's Johnson's Crime Commission in the 1960s (e.g., the Task Force Report on the Police) came up with findings almost identical to the Wickersham Commission (President's Commission, 1967b).

Greater detail of corruption has often come with investigations that focused on one city. One of the most popular was the Knapp Commission on Police Corruption in New York City in the early 1970s. This investigation stemmed from allegations brought forth by plainclothes patrolman Frank Serpico who became quite a celebrity (his story became a bestselling book, a movie starting Al Pacino, and even a television series). In the words of the Commission's final report: "We found corruption to be widespread" (Knapp Commission, 1975: 235).

Specifically, they found that plainclothesmen were involved in a "pad" or collections of payments (up to $3,000 per month) from several gambling establishments. The share per month per officer ranged from $300 to $400 in midtown Manhattan to $1,500 in Harlem. Serpico charged that nineteen Bronx plainclothesmen received an average share (called a *nut* by the police) of $800. The Commission also found that Brooklyn plainclothesmen brought in an average nut of $1,200 (see also Maas, 1975).

Payoffs in narcotics enforcement (known as *scores*) were common. The Commission found a pattern "whereby corrupt officers customarily collected scores in substantial amounts from narcotics violators. These scores were either kept by individual officers or shared with a partner and, perhaps, a superior officer. They ranged from minor shakedowns to payments of many thousands of dollars. . . . " (Knapp Commission, 1975: 235). The largest payoff discovered was $80,000.

In Reading, Pennsylvania, back in the 1950s, the entire city was controlled by organized crime. In the 1960s, in New City, a close advisor of Mayor Lindsay, James Marcus, was deeply meshed in corrupt political activities with organized crime figures. In Newark, New Jersey, in 1969, a scandal broke out involving the mayor, other city officials, and the police department (Quinney, 1979: 211–212).

In a study conducted for the President's Commission, Gardiner reported on one medium-sized city (he used the pseudonym of "Wincanton") where it was found that corruption had been common for many decades. Specifically, it was found that "mayors, police chiefs, and many lesser officials were on the payroll of the gambling syndicate. . . ." (Gardiner, 1969: 104). According to this report, the head of these illegal operations "controlled the police department." A police chief was quoted as saying, "Hollywood should have given us an Oscar for some of our performances when we had to pull a phony raid to keep the papers happy" (Gardiner, 1969: 111). The leader, Irv Stern, was able to "secure freedom from state and local action." One investigation found "that Stern had given mortgage loans to a police lieutenant and the police chief's son" (Gardiner, 1969: 112). Finally it was found that "most policemen. . .began to ignore prostitution and gambling completely after their reports of offenses were ignored or superior officers told them to mind their own business. State policemen, well informed about city vice and gambling conditions, did nothing unless called upon to act by local officials" (Gardiner, 1969: 114).

As the Knapp Commission suggested, officers tend to be socialized into a police subculture that supports various forms of deviant activities. The Commission distinguished between the *bad-apple theory* and the *group-support theory* of police corruption. In another study (of a police department in the Southwest), Stoddard found widespread support for certain forms of deviance among officers. Specifically, Stoddard found the existence of an informal code that supported deviancy. Rookies were pressured to go along with this code; failure to do so resulted in group ostracism. "Lack of acceptance not only bars the neophyte from the inner secrets of the profession but also may isolate him socially and professionally from his colleagues and even his superiors" (Stoddard, 1975: 262). Thus, while the bad-apple theory suggests that police corruption stems only from a few bad apples in an otherwise clean barrel, the group-support theory suggests that the barrel is not so clean after all and that deviancy, while not indulged in by all police officers within a department, is nevertheless condoned by most officers.

The study by Stoddard, as well as the Knapp Commission's findings, suggests that it is the honest policeman who is the exception. Stoddard quotes one policeman who, in reference to a fellow officer, said: "You've got to watch him, because *he's honest!*" (Stoddard, 1975: 268) The Knapp Commission found an intense amount of group support within the police department in New York City and "a stubborn refusal at all levels of the department to acknowledge that a serious problem exists" (Stoddard, 1975: 238).

However, both the bad-apple and group-support theories fail to adequately explain police corruption as a persistent phenomenon throughout our history. Both perspectives imply that a new kind of police officer is all that we need (perhaps of the Serpico variety). But the historical consistency of corruption and the social, political, economic, and legal contexts suggest that this type of reform will not solve the problem. One reason is the fact that so much money is involved and that there are very powerful interests (usually on the part of "respectable" people) enmeshed in police corruption. In other words, there is evidence to suggest that police corruption is not the problem; the problem appears to be that the economic and political structure of our society breeds corruption. A study by Chambliss lends support to this view (Chambliss, 1975b).

Chambliss found corruption to be widespread in Seattle, Washington, as he studied the problem through personal observation over a period of several years. This corruption did not involve only police officers, it also involved members of organized crime, key political and business figures, and high-ranking police officials. In particular, Chambliss discovered that all of these individuals participated in illegal activities such as gambling, prostitution, loan-sharking, and many more, while individual police officers took bribes of substantial amounts. Most of these activities were restricted to the fringes of slum communities, where "respectable" citizens could participate but not be seen by their fellow citizens. The police made a few token arrests and even some "well-publicized raids," but of course, they avoided involving influential citizens.

Chambliss suggests that there existed a symbiotic relationship between the law enforcement bureaucracy and the major suppliers of vice in Seattle. He concluded:

> The gambling, prostitution, drug distribution, pornography, and usury that flourish in the lower-class center of the city do so with the compliance, encouragement, and cooperation of the major political and law-enforcement officials in the city. There is in fact a symbiotic relationship between the law enforcement-political organizations of the city and group of *local*, as distinct from national, men who control the distribution of vices. (Chambliss, 1975b: 150)

The implications of Chambliss' findings are far-reaching. He further concludes that in the study of organized crime, there has been an overemphasis on the *criminal* and

> . . . a corresponding de-emphasis on corruption as an institutional component of America's legal-political system. Concomitantly, it has obscured perception of the degree to which the structure of America's law and politics creates and perpetuates syndicates that supply the vices in our major cities. (Chambliss, 1975b: 144)

Continuing, Chambliss concluded:

> Organized crime becomes not something that exists outside law and government but is instead a creation of them, or perhaps more accurately, a hidden but nonetheless integral part of the governmental structure. The people most likely to be exposed by public inquiries (whether conducted by the FBI, a grand jury, or the Internal Revenue Service) may officially be outside of government, but the cabal of which they are a part is organized around, run by, and created in the interests of economic, legal, and political elites. (Chambliss, 1975b: 144)

Another implication of this study is that it becomes evident that law enforcement is a form of class domination, especially in the case of vice laws. As Chambliss found out (and as most observers have noted), those who were arrested were mainly small-time, lower-class people. The well-to-do who actively participated in these vices were rarely if ever arrested. From this perspective, the police serve to perpetuate profit-seeking ventures of the "private enterprise system" (i.e., privately run by a small minority).

The average police officer is, of course, caught in a bind between demands by the powerless for a more equal share of the wealth and power and the powerful and propertyholders who want to keep what they have. The most common solution is to practice "crime control" when dealing with the poor but to observe "due process" when dealing with the privileged (Chambliss and Seidman, 1971: 365). In his study, Chambliss found:

> . . . the law enforcers do what any well-managed bureaucracy would under similar circumstances—they follow the line of least resistance. Using the discretion inherent in their positions, they resolve the problem by establishing procedures which minimize organizational strains and which provide the greatest promise of rewards for the organizations and the individuals involved. Typically, this means that law enforcers adopt a tolerance policy toward the vices, selectively enforcing these laws only when it is to their advantage to do so. Since the persons demanding enforcement are generally middle-class persons who rarely venture into the less prosperous sections of the city, the enforcers can control the visibility and minimize complaints by merely regulating the ecological location of the vices. (Chambliss, 1975b: 146–147)

In case you think that this problem has disappeared, still another police corruption scandal in New York City (actually the Bronx) prompted yet another commission in 1994, known as the Mollen Commission. Once again, widespread corruption was discovered. Not only this, police brutality was apparently normal. One officer was known as "the Mechanic" because "I used to tune people up" (police jargon for a beating). As usual, most of the recipients of this "tune up" were African Americans or Hispanics (Cole, 1999: 23). In the same city of New York still another scandal has occurred; in fact, two big scandals that began to make the headlines in 1999. One involved the arrest and "gang rape" of a Haitian man, while another involved the killing of another man, who was riddled with no less than 41 bullets! As of this writing (February, 2000), both cases are still pending.

Finally, a scandal of huge proportions emerged in Los Angeles in late 1999, involving potentially up to 70 police officers. As of this writing (March, 2000) at least 20 police officers have either quit, been fired, or been suspended. It has been alleged that police officers affiliated with an anti-gang unit known as Community Resources Against Street Hoodlums (CRASH) might have been involved (either engaging in the illegal conduct or knowing about it and doing nothing). The scandal involved a group of officers (called by one source "rogue officers") who made false arrests, put many innocent people in jail, extorted drug money from drug dealers, and engaged in unjustified shootings and beatings. Investigators found evidence that at least 99 people had been framed, with a total of 32 convictions having been overturned. A Los Angeles city councilman has called for an independent investigation (Los Angeles Times, 2000; Washington Post, 2000). It also has been suggested by the mayor of Los Angeles that, in order to settle the law suits that have already begun (with more predicted to follow), money from the tobacco industry settlement (up to $300 million) be used to help cover these lawsuits. What is important to note here is that this money was supposed to be used for health, education, and other social programs (Jablon, 2000). It should also be noted that the victims of this corruption have been overwhelmingly the poor and racial minorities, especially Hispanics.

That corruption has become almost synonymous with government and big business has been documented by the Watergate and other scandals during the past several decades. For instance, several reports concluded that the men involved in Watergate had several things in common. First, many of the Watergate defendants were or had been employed by either the CIA or the FBI or both. Second, many of these men had been involved (at least indirectly) with such incidents as the Bay of Pigs, a plot to assassinate Fidel Castro, and the assassinations of John and Robert Kennedy. Third, many of these men had close ties to organized crime figures. In fact, several reports have indicated that there is strong evidence linking the Office of Strategic Service (OSS), which eventually became the CIA, with Lucky Luciano, Meyer Lansky (two famous Mafia members), Thomas Dewey (former governor of New York and presidential candidate against Truman in 1948), John and Allen Dulles, and Richard Nixon. According to one report, Lucky Luciano, with help from the CIA, "began an international smuggling ring for the syndicate's narcotics industry" (Leslie, 1977; see also Nohn, 1976). Further, "the CIA called on Luciano in 1947 when Communist strikers shut down the port of Marseilles to American shipping. He supplied hitmen while the CIA supplied money and weapons" (Leslie, 1977: 9). Frank Sturgis, one of the Watergate burglars, had been a gun smuggler for Castro and later became a CIA undercover agent. He and Robert Maheu (FBI agent, Howard Hughes' assistant, involved in Watergate), John Roselli, Sam Giancanna, and Santo Trafficante (all connected with organized crime), Richard Helms (former CIA director), and E. Howard Hunt (CIA agent, consultant to White House counsel Charles Colson, Watergate burglar) were involved in the Bay of Pigs incident (an attempt to overthrow the Castro regime).[6]

More recent examples of the CIA and FBI involvement in corruption include the overthrow of the Allende government in Chile (with the help of IT&T) and the FBI's counter-intelligence efforts to subvert the Black Panthers and other radical groups in the 1960s, an effort known by the code word COINTELPRO (counterintelligence program) (Blackstock, 1975).

Quinney summarizes the connection among big business, organized crime, politics, and law enforcement as follows: "The connection among crime, business, and the state continues to be covered up by the federal government's law-enforcement agencies. . . . To disclose a nationwide criminal conspiracy would require the FBI to investigate and expose gangster friends and supporters deeply involved in business and politics" (Quinney, 1979: 215).

COINTELPRO reveals something far more sinister than street cops taking bribes or receiving "kick-backs." Revealed in numerous studies (Chomsky, 1999b; Blackstock, 1975: Davis, 1992; Churchill and Vander Wall, 1988, 1990) was the systematic repression of the Black Panther Party and other radical groups throughout the 1960s and early 1970s. To give but one example, in 1971 there were several burglaries of members of the Michigan Socialist Workers Party (in Detroit), which involved the theft of membership lists rather than valuables ordinarily taken in burglaries. Several years later, a U.S. District Court Judge ruled in favor of the Socialist Workers Party in its suit against the Attorney General of the United States. The judge stated that the FBI's activities constituted a violation of the constitutional rights of the party. The judge identified many crimes committed by the FBI, including at least 208 "surreptitious entries" (this did not include the Michigan case). The Detroit case (and many others like it) barely made a ripple in the national press. At about the same time that these cases (including the breakup of the Black Panther Party) were occurring all over the country, Watergate made the headlines and dominated the news for several years (Chomsky, 1999b).

It should be obvious why Watergate received so much attention: those subjected to the FBI's terroristic tactics were among the dangerous classes (i.e., radicals trying to form an alternative political party and African Americans seeking justice), whereas the victims of Watergate (and most of the perpetrators) were men of power (see Chomsky, 1999b; Blackstock, 1975 for details). This crime was rather petty in comparison to those committed by the state during the same period.

Space does not permit a complete discussion of COINTELPRO, but it should be mentioned that the FBI has had a history of involvement in these kinds of activities. The Bureau of Investigation was founded in 1908, ostensibly to enforce the Sherman Anti-Trust Act, and the Alien and Sedition Acts, and was immediately involved in controversy and various illegal and quasi-legal behavior. It served primarily as an instrument for the *protection* of big business. The Bureau was also involved in many anti-union activities. For example, the first time that the Sherman Act was enforced was against a labor union, charging it with "restraint of trade" (Michalowski, 1985: 178). This agency was involved in gross violations of civil liberties during the infamous Red Scare of 1919–1920, largely under the leadership of one of its staff members, a man named John Edgar Hoover. Hoover took over as head of a new organization called the Federal Bureau of Investigation in 1924; the bureau has been involved in numerous scandals ever since (Donner, 1980; Garrow, 1981). COINTELPRO was the FBI's largest undertaking. It was modeled after successful programs to disrupt the American Communist Party during the 1950s and other radical organizations during the 1960s (Churchill and Vander Wall, 1988, 1990).

Mention should also be made of what is commonly known as *state crime,* a topic rarely discussed. Yet the death toll and economic devastation of crimes committed by the U.S. government is beyond description. Crimes of the state include several different kinds of harmful behaviors and they all have at least this in common: they are generally committed against power-less people and they are rarely, if ever, called "crimes." Although there are several definitions, I generally accept one offered by Kramer and Michalowski, who call this *state-corporate crime* because there is some rela-tionship between corporations and the government, as when "one or more institutions of political governance pursue a goal in direct cooperation with one or more institutions of economic production and distribution" (Kramer and Michalowski, 1990: 3). Admittedly, this definition is a little vague, so let's just say that *state* crimes involve harmful behaviors committed by the government itself (sometimes in collusion with private corporations, some-times not), whether it be on a national level (e.g., the CIA, the State Department) or on a local level (i.e., state and local governments).

Examples of these harms include the following: the violation of en-vironmental, safety, and health standards at federal nuclear-weapons pro-duction facilities by private contractors; the famous Iran-Contra Affair (cooperation between the CIA and private arms dealers); and the interven-tion by our government into the affairs of Third World countries in support of dictatorships and the overthrow of democratically elected governments, all in support of private corporate interests. The last category is particularly interesting because our government is supposed to be "making the world safe for democracy." Specific examples of these interventions include Guatemala (1950s), Zaire (1960s), Dominican Republic (1961–62), Indonesia (including East Timor, 1960s-1970s), Greece (1967), Chile (1973), Angola (1975), Libya (1980), Grenada (1980s), El Salvador (1980s), Nicaragua (1980s), Haiti (late 1980s, early 1990s)—to name just a few in a long list of mostly CIA-backed atrocities, all in the name of private profit and political domination.[7]

One particularly gruesome example—and one almost completely ignored by the mainstream press (however, it has finally received world-wide attention in light of elections for independence in August 1999)—was what amounted to genocide in a little country known as East Timor. East Timor, a part of Indonesia, just north of Australia, was a country of around 600,000. This country, rich in oil and other resources, became a pawn of the Indonesian dictator Suharto (who had overthrown the democratically elected President Sukarto, with CIA backing). Suharto, along with abundant arms from the United States, killed approximately 200,000 innocent citizens in what has been described as the worst example of genocide (on a per-capita basis) since the Holocaust. [8]

Still Controlling the "Dangerous Classes": the War on Gangs and the War on Drugs

The War on Gangs

Since the police are often viewed as society's "first line of defense" against crime, it obviously follows that they are the first segment of the criminal justice system that responds to the youth-gang dilemma. The police have responded to gangs with a multitude of maneuvers. California's "State Task Force" offered a number of policy (and legislative) suggestions to combat youth gangs: (1) design and develop statewide gang information systems; (2) launch school-based gang and narcotics prevention programs; (3) provide technical assistance to local law-enforcement agencies in gang analysis; (4) identify gang members under the supervision of the Department of Youth Authority and intensify parole supervision; (5) establish and expand special units in probation to supervise gang members; (6) create a Southeast Asian youth-gang prevention and intervention program; (7) establish standards throughout the correctional system that discourage gang membership; and (8) using ex-gang members and community street workers, establish a model gang intervention program (State Task Force, 1986: 37). Although many of these suggestions do not affect law enforcement *directly*, they all have an impact on law enforcement's role in "policing" youth gangs.

In a desperate attempt to find solutions to the problem of youth gangs, violence, and drugs, law enforcement has embarked on a voyage that starts from the proactive-policing approach of creating and sponsoring new programs with "catchy" acronyms like D.A.R.E. (Drug Awareness Resistance Education) and S.A.N.E. (Substance Abuse Narcotics Education) to paying gang members to "fight crime." Some promote the notion that "foot patrols" should be a major tactic used against gangs (Wilson and Kelling, 1989); others (Boyle and Gonzales, 1989) embrace police programs that target schools and neighborhoods and provide instruction on developing self-esteem, dealing with peer-group pressure, decision-making, and the like.

Many police officers in a major Midwest police department agree that a dual-strategy approach is crucial, but both dimensions must be implemented simultaneously: (1) an immediate response that requires interdiction (i.e., monitor and/or arrest) to preserve the peace and save lives; and (2) implementation of long-range plans that include "realistic" options from which these youth may choose (e.g., preventive measures such as job training and creation, and recreation facilities that provide supervised activities for youth). One officer, who has worked with gang members for nearly eight years in the course of his regular patrol duties, stated, "Many of these kids have zero options. They live in a shit hole. I can arrest them. They may, in rare instances, actually do some time. When they get out, they are dumped back into the same shit hole" (Shelden et al., 1997: 209). Another officer pointed out that "these kids have no place to play. They find some structure (e.g., a street-light pole) to nail a backboard and hoop, and play basketball in the middle of the street. They disrupt traffic and make drivers mad. Pretty soon, the kids just say fuck it and go find something else to do—they go banging" (Shelden et al., 1997: 209). Most interesting is the reference to "kids," suggesting an acknowledgment by these officers that these youth are not necessarily gangsters or criminals; rather, many are children. This language is qualitatively different from the rhetoric used by those who have transposed the term *kids* (a term frequently associated to a stage within the human development process) to other less flattering abstractions like *scavengers*, which is used by Taylor (Taylor, 1990: 105). Of course, in a broader sense, these officers are drawing attention to structural issues germane to many neighborhoods in the inner city.

The interdiction dimension of law enforcement's response to youth gangs is a reflex of the tremendous pressure placed on police to produce results. Many law-enforcement agencies have come to rely on special units. Several scholars have pointed out advantages in the creation of these units (Skolnick 1994; Skolnick, and Bayley, 1986), others are less than enthusiastic about the special-unit approach (Walker, 1994; Goldstein, 1990). With a nearly impossible mandate (to eradicate or at least control youth gangs), many law-enforcement administrators and local governments often find themselves financially driven to replenish insufficient resources. Many have had to tap into funding sources that are provisional to the "exploitation" of America's youth gangs.

During the past few years, the federal government has provided assistance in funding through block grants designated for youth-gang interdiction. Most often, these grants are used to create and support social-control strategies rather than solution-oriented approaches. One law-enforcement agency formed a special "gang unit" to compete for a piece of the block-grant "pie." Surprisingly, this particular jurisdiction did not have a youth-gang problem at the time of application nor does it have a gang problem now. During an interview with the detective in charge of the newly formed "gang unit" it was revealed that "the mayor wanted a gang unit because he had heard that federal grant money was available for police departments that had adopted this sort of special unit." When asked what his gang unit did, he responded, "Nothing. We don't have any gangs in this community. We have some kids who play with spray paint. At best, we have a few gang 'wanna-bees'" (Shelden et al., 1997: 209).

In another example, one major Midwestern urban police department has a gang unit consisting of more than sixty officers. This unit consists of five components: administrative, enforcement, investigation, intelligence, and surveillance (Shelden et al., 1997: Chapter 8). The general responsibilities of this unit include the following:

1. Identification and patrol of high youth-group activity, and "shooting scenes" that do not result in death and are not dealt with by other special units.
2. Identification of active criminal youth and their leaders.
3. Collection, analysis, and dissemination of all information related to youth-group problems.
4. Investigation, enforcement, and intelligence-gathering related to all youth-group criminal activities.
5. Deploying both uniformed and plainclothes officers as required to respond to scenes of youth-group criminal problems. This includes planned youth events that have the potential for youth criminal problems and violence (e.g., rock concerts, rap concerts, high school sporting events, ethnic festival events).
6. Surveillance responsibilities are restricted to youth-oriented activities.
7. The gang unit shall have sole responsibility for handling, investigating, and securing warrants in probate and recorder's court for all arrests and detentions stemming from firearms offenses occurring in and around public and private schools in the city.

Specific enforcement-unit duties include aggressive enforcement that targets areas that have a *potential* for youth crime activity (e.g., schools, gatherings of youth for social functions, and neighborhoods experiencing high incidents of street shootings and gang activity); and aggressive techniques such as traffic stops, and stop and frisk.

Duties of the investigative unit include conducting live "show-ups" and preparing warrant requests for the prosecution of gang members and their associates. Among the surveillance-unit duties are those that target individuals, vehicles, groups or locations, based on information provided by the investigation and intelligence units.

The intelligence unit is responsible for preparing "profiles" on perpetrators of criminal acts who are involved with various gangs and maintaining files with information relevant to gangs (e.g., nickname file, vehicle file, gang membership, affiliation with other gangs).

Gang members are identified by this special unit using the following criteria (which are similar to many other jurisdictions): (1) an individual admits membership in a gang; (2) when a reliable informant identifies an individual as a gang member; (3) when a reliable informant identifies an individual as a gang member and this information is corroborated by independent information; (4) when an individual resides in or frequents a particular gang area and adopts their styles of dress, use of hand signs, symbols, and tattoos, and associates with known gang members; (5) when an individual has been arrested several times in the company of identified gang members for offenses that are consistent with usual gang activity; and (6) when there are strong indications that an individual has a "close relationship" (how this is to be determined is not specified) with a gang but does not fit the previous criteria, he or she shall be identified as a "gang associate."

An obvious paradox exists for this gang squad when one considers the specific duties of each element within the context of what the unit calls its underlying philosophy. The gang unit is essentially a *proactive* unit that curtails the activity of youthful offenders through *proactive enforcement in areas that are heavily concentrated with gang members* (Shelden et al., 1997: 211). What should also be obvious is that such a philosophy results in concerted efforts to maintain control and surveillance in mostly minority and lower-class communities, because these individuals have the greatest probability of being identified as "gang members."

On any given day, rarely are there more than four or five officers actually working on gang-specific cases within their jurisdiction. Typically, "working gangs" for this unit is limited to conducting investigations when alleged gang members are possible suspects in a crime. Moreover, it is common knowledge among police officers throughout this department that assignment to the gang unit provides strong credentials for promotion—thus, the gang unit in this jurisdiction is little more than a political position. Several officers agreed with one officer's perception: "Members of the gang unit profile around and play cowboy. When they do make contact with gang members, they do little more than harass them." Another officer stated, "We [patrol officers] are the ones who work the gangs. We deal with them on a daily basis. The gang squad is too busy dealing with the media and kissing the Chief's ass." Suggesting that this perception may extend beyond this Midwestern jurisdiction, a San Jose police veteran of twenty-two years said, "Gang units are like every other special unit in policing—full of bullshit and totally political" (Shelden et al., 1997: 212).

Conducting "sweeps" or "rousts" of targeted areas is another strategy employed by police. Sweeps or rousts are tactics whereby many police officers converge on a target area for the purpose of eradicating (or relocating) specific forms of criminal or undesirable behavior. Similar methods were employed by the SS to "relocate" the Jewish population in Nazi Germany; however, I suspect that the American public, including political officials, are not willing to go quite that far to provide a solution to the youth-gang problem. Following public outcries to local officials about prostitution, police have had some success in relocating prostitutes using these maneuvers. In the case of youth-gang interdiction, this tactic is analogous to an attempt to

put out a forest fire with a water bucket. While it is possible to remove prostitutes from a particular neighborhood (at least for a period of time), it is
more difficult—and legally and morally questionable—to remove youth
gang members from their neighborhoods, homes, and/or families. Often
this tactic can do more harm than good; this is particularly true when local
citizens view this approach as an example of racism (e.g., Watts, Newark,
and Detroit during the 1960s, and events leading to South Central Los
Angeles in 1992).

An example of suppression tactics can be seen in the case of
"Operation Hammer" and similar police suppression tactics in Los Angeles
during the late 1980s.This was a major police response to gangs in South
Central Los Angeles under the administration of Police Chief Daryl Gates.
The crackdown began in April 1988 and focused on 10 square miles in the
South Central area. It was like a "search-and-destroy" mission in Vietnam
(Miller, 1996). A total of 1,453 arrests were made, mostly for minor offenses
like curfew, disturbing the peace, and the like. Hundreds more had their
names and addresses inserted into an electronic gang roster for future intelligence (Davis, 1992: 268). To aid in this repressive activity, the police used a
special mobile booking operation next to the Los Angeles Coliseum. The
overall purpose was merely social control (of African American youth)
rather than a serious attempt at reducing crime. Proof of this is the fact that
of the 1,453 arrests, 1,350 (93 percent) were released without any charges
filed. More interesting is that half of them turned out *not* to be gang members. Only sixty felony arrests were made and charges were filed on only
thirty-two of these. Around two hundred police officers were used, while
during the same period there were two gang-related homicides (Klein, 1995:
162).

Similar suppression efforts in the "war on gangs" and the "war on
drugs" in Los Angeles have met with similar results. For instance, Chief
Gates launched the so-called Gang-Related Active Trafficker Suppression
(GRATS) program in February and March of 1988, just before Operation
Hammer took place. This program targeted so-called "drug neighborhoods"
for raids by two hundred to three hundred police officers. They stopped and
interrogated anyone suspected of being a gang member, based on how they
dressed or used gang hand signals. Nine sweeps took place, resulting in five
hundred cars being impounded and approximately 1,500 arrests. Gates
wanted to "get the message out to the cowards out there. . .that we're going
to come and get them." Apparently the message didn't get through, for after
the Chief gave a speech praising his sweeps, a few Crips fired on a crowd
on a street corner in South Central, killing a nineteen-year-old woman
(Davis, 1992: 268–274).

Such a crackdown was supported by many conservative leaders,
including County Supervisor Kenneth Hahn, who asked for the use of the
National Guard, suggesting that Los Angeles was "fighting the war on gang

violence. . . that's worse than Beirut," while a state senator's press secretary argued that "when you have a state of war, civil rights are suspended for the duration of the conflict." Meanwhile, the NAACP reported that during these events there were hundreds of complaints about unlawful police conduct and that the police were, in effect, contributing to gang violence by leaving suspects stranded on enemy turf—even going so far as to write over Crip graffiti with Blood graffiti and vice versa (Davis, 1992: 274).

Moore notes a similar crackdown on gangs in Los Angeles that took place on four consecutive weekends in the late 1980s, which netted a grand total of 563 arrests (mostly on outstanding warrants), 3 ounces of cocaine, and a total of $9,000 in cash related to the drug trade (Moore, 1991: 3–4). In San Diego, a similar sweep resulted in 146 arrests during a one-week period (mostly minor offenses), and only seventeen were still in custody at the end of the week. Similar suppression efforts have been tried with the same results in cities such as Chicago, Milwaukee, Baltimore, and Boston (Klein, 1995: 162, 166).

In still another crackdown, Chief Gates ordered a raid that turned into what some called an "orgy of violence" as police punched and kicked residents, threw washing machines into bathtubs, smashed walls and furniture with sledgehammers and axes, and even spray-painted slogans on walls, including "LAPD Rules." The result: two minor drug arrests. The police took disciplinary action against thirty-eight officers, including a captain who ordered his officers to "level" and "make uninhabitable" the apartments that were targeted (Davis, 1992: 276)—another example of a search-and-destroy type of activity, similar to those used in Vietnam.

Another Gates program was called CRASH (Community Resources Against Street Hoodlums), which was originally called TRASH, with the "T" standing for Total, but the name was changed for obvious reasons. Under this program, the police engaged in "surveillance and harassment" with the explicit purpose being, to use one officer's words, to "jam" suspected gang members (i.e., harass and then move on, with no arrest being made in most cases). The officers were rotated out after two or three years and, thus, never had a real opportunity to develop detailed knowledge about the communities (Klein, 1995: 164–165).

Operation Hammer and other suppression efforts resulted in the arrests of an estimated fifty thousand African American youth, with as many as 90 percent never being formally charged. Yet Chief Gates nevertheless continued such sweeps as a sort of "semi-permanent community occupation" or "narcotic enforcement zones," one known as "Operation Cul-de-Sac." These "zones"—similar to the Berlin Wall—were extended all the way from South Central to the San Fernando Valley just to the north (Davis, 1992: 277).

Behind such crackdowns—and the war on gangs in general—is a widespread racist belief system. Typical of such racist beliefs was one expressed by Chief Gates, chief architect of gang suppression efforts in Los Angeles. Concerning the scandal involving the deaths of African American men because of the police use of the "chokehold," he remarked, "We may be finding that in some blacks when [the carotid chokehold] is applied, the veins or arteries do not open up as fast as they do on normal [sic] people" (Davis, 1992: 272).

What about the deterrent effect of such efforts? Concerning the effects of sweeps such as Operation Hammer, Klein offers the following humorous scenario that may take place. It begins with a gang member, upon release from the mobile booking area near the Coliseum, returning to his neighborhood and meeting up with some of his homies. Klein continues:

> Does he say to them, "Oh, gracious, I've been arrested and subjected to deterrence; I'm going to give up my gang affiliation." Or does he say, "Shit man, they're just jivin' us—can't hold us on any charges, and gotta let us go." Without hesitation, the gangbanger will turn the experience to his and the gang's advantage. Far from being deterred from membership or crime, his ties to the group will be strengthened when the members group together to make light of the whole affair and heap ridicule on the police. (Klein, 1995:163)

Ironically, one of America's gross social injustices (also believed to be a contributing factor in the proliferation of youth gangs) may actually assist law enforcement in its quest for "victory" over youth gangs—racial segregation. There are social-control advantages reached through segregation. Jackson writes, "Segregation may reduce the pressure on authorities to police minority populations, since segregation reduces interracial crime, the phenomenon most likely to result in pressure on crime control-authorities." Moreover, she adds, "Fear of crime, coupled with fear of loss of dominance, provides fertile ground for a mobilization of policing resources" (Jackson, 1992: 90).

The War On Drugs

The "war on drugs" has similarly targeted minority groups, but especially African Americans. Indeed, there is abundant evidence that the war on drugs has been in reality a war on African Americans, on a scale that is unprecedented in American history. As the research by Miller shows, young African American males have received the brunt of law-enforcement efforts to "crack down on drugs." He notes that in Baltimore, for example, African Americans were being arrested at a rate six times that of whites, and more than 90 percent were for possession (Miller, 1996: 8; see also Currie, 1993; Tonry, 1995; Mann, 1995; Chambliss, 1995; Lockwood, Pottieger, and Inciardi, 1995). While the arrest rate for both races among juveniles for heroin and cocaine possession was virtually the same in 1965, by the 1970s the gap began to widen, and by 1990 the arrest rate for African Americans stood at 766, compared to only sixty-eight for whites. Overall, in 1980, the national rate of all drug arrests was about the same for black and white juveniles; during the early 1980s, the arrest rate for whites dropped by one third, while the rate for blacks remained about the same. But as the war on drugs expanded, the arrest rate for black youths went from 683 in 1985 to 1,200 in 1989, which was five times the rate for whites; by 1991 it went to 1,415.[9]

Another study found that "black youths are more often charged with the felony when [the] offense could be considered a misdemeanor. . . ." Also, those cases referred to court "are judged as in need of formal processing more often when minority youths are involved." When white youths received placements, they are more often than not "group-home settings or drug treatment, while placements for minorities more typically are public residential facilities, including those in the state that provide the most restrictive confinement." A study by McGarrell found evidence of substantial increases in minority youths being referred to juvenile court, thus increasing the likelihood of being detained. However, cases of the detention, petition, and placement of minorities nevertheless exceeded what would have been expected, given the increases in referrals. There has been an increase in the formal handling of drug cases, which has become a disadvantage to minorities. "Given the proactive nature of drug enforcement, these findings raise fundamental questions about the targets of investigation and apprehension under the recent war on drugs" (McGarrell, 1993, quoted in Miller, 1996: 258). As noted in a study of Georgia's crackdown on drugs, the higher arrest rate for African Americans was attributed to one single factor: "It is easier to make drug arrests in low-income neighborhoods. . . . Most drug arrests in Georgia are of lower-level dealers and buyers, and occur in low-income minority areas. Retail drug sales in the neighborhoods frequently occur on the streets and between sellers and buyers who do not know each other. Most of the sellers are black. In contrast, white drug sellers tend to sell indoors, in bars and clubs and within private homes, and to more affluent purchasers, also primarily white" (Fellner, 1996: 11).

Not surprisingly, this has had the same impact when considering adult minorities, as they have been systematically singled out in this "war." Drug offenses have accounted for most of the increase in prison populations in recent years, and it not surprising to find that the prison and jail populations have become increasingly dominated by minorities, especially African Americans. (Imprisonment rates are discussed in more detail in Chapter 4.) Looking at a long-term trend, between 1960 and 1992, the percentage of non-white inmates went from around one third to more than half, while the proportion of inmates convicted of drug offenses went from a mere 5 percent to almost 30 percent. More alarmingly, from 1986 to 1991, right in the middle of the crackdown on drugs, the proportion of African Americans incarcerated for drug offenses went up an incredible 465.5 percent.

Not surprisingly, the overall arrest rate on drug charges has zoomed upward since the early 1980s, especially for African Americans. Among juveniles, whereas the arrest rate for whites on drug charges was greater than the rate for African Americans in the early 1970s, the most recent data (1995) show that the arrest rate for African American juveniles is about four times greater than the rate for whites.

Clearly, the police are continuing to carry out their historical mandate to control the dangerous classes, which today means African Americans and other minorities, in addition to the poor in general.

Notes

1. There was an apparent rise in crime immediately preceding the formation of the new police force. However, most of the crime (as reflected in arrest and court data) was of a rather petty nature and grew out of the class conflicts of the period. For instance, the rate of males going to trial went from 170 per 100,000 population in 1824 to 240 in 1828 and 250 in 1830. The proportion committed for vagrancy increased by 34 percent between 1826 and 1829, and it rose by 65 percent between 1829 and 1832. Over half of the prison population during this period were those convicted of vagrancy, poaching, petty theft, disorderly conduct, and public drunkenness. Only 25 percent of those awaiting trial in local jails or serving actual sentences were there for indictable crimes; deserters and debtors constituted the rest. The new police *increased* the already growing crackdown on minor offenses. Thus, during the 1830s, about 85 percent of all arrests were for drunkenness, disorderly conduct, and similar minor crimes (Ignatieff, 1978: 179–185). The heavy emphasis on minor offenses, which were committed mainly by the poor and working class, reflected the trend toward the regulation and control of the laboring population, so often referred to as the "dangerous classes."

2. For a good description and summary of this period of labor unrest, see Zinn (1995), especially Chapter 11.

3. For a more complete discussion of the "Ludlow Massacre," see Zinn (1990: 79–101).

4. For opposing views on the outcome of progressivism, see Mann (1963). For a radical critique of "progressivism," see Zinn (1990, 1995).

5. Corporate propaganda is rarely discussed and in fact the first serious academic studies of this phenomenon did not appear until recently (Carey, 1995; Fones-Wolf, 1994), although it had been used at least since around the time of World War I. As Carey noted, corporations and political leaders have actually feared true democracy and thus corporate propaganda has been used, as the title of Carey's book suggests, to "take the risk out of democracy." (See also Herman and Chomsky, 1988.)

6. The connection between the participants in Watergate and other scandals has been amply documented. See the following for examples: Borosage and Marks, 1976; Agee, 1974; Marchetti and Marks, 1974; Smith, 1972; and Nohn,1976.

7. A complete listing and detailed discussion of these and other state crimes can fill an entire book—in fact they fill several books. See, for example, the following works: Parenti, 1995; Chomsky, 1993; Zepezauer, 1994; Barak, 1991).

8. Extensively documented in Chomsky, 1996a: Ch. 7; Parenti, 1995: 26–27; and Zepezauer, 1994: 30–31.

9. An alarming study in Baltimore found that total arrests for black youths was around eighty-six in 1981 (versus fifteen for whites); by 1991, that number had increased to 1,304 for blacks compared to a mere thirteen for white youths. Nationally, between 1987 and 1988, the number of whites brought into the juvenile court remained virtually the same (up 1 percent), but the number of minorities referred to the court increased by 42 percent (Miller, 1996: 84–86). In Miller's own study of Baltimore, he found that during 1981, only fifteen white juveniles were arrested on drug charges, compared to eighty-six African Americans; in 1991, however, the number of whites arrested dropped to a mere thirteen, while the number of African Americans skyrocketed to a phenomenal 1,304, or an increase of 1,416 percent. The ratio of African American youths to white youths went from about 6:1 to 100:1 (Miller, 1996: 86).

Processing the
Dangerous Classes

The American Court System

Introduction

In the late spring of 1999, in a Michigan court, a young African American male was sentenced to prison. An observer of this sentencing wrote the following words:

> In the spring of 1999, a young African American male was sentenced to prison for the crime of burglary in a Michigan court. Sitting behind the young man was an older woman who wept and an older man who simply placed his head in his hands and just sat there. The couple appeared to be the young man's parents. After informing the young man of his sentence, the judge made a profound, concluding statement that "justice had been served." After the judge left the courtroom, two officers of the court walked over to the young man—one on each side—and instructed him to "come with us." The defense attorney patted the young man's shoulder, turned, and walked away. There was no exchange of words between this young man and his white attorney. The older couple stood up. The woman reached out to her son, but the officers would not allow the young man to take her hand. He was quickly ushered out of the courtroom. The older man put his arm around the woman and they walked out of the courtroom. The woman was crying profusely. He tried to comfort her. Outside the courtroom, they got into a very old vehicle and drove off. Exhaust fumes could be seen for nearly a block before they turned at an intersection and disappeared. This observation is not an isolated event in the annals of American jurisprudence. It is jurisprudence history, and it is repeatedly enacted in criminal courtrooms across America. Some form of "justice" may have been served in this courtroom episode, but it was not *social* justice.[1]

The American criminal courts are a major link within the criminal justice system; they stand between the police and the correctional system. This system is a major institution in American society.

One does not have to travel very far in America without a reminder of the central role of the courts. Pass through any town of any size in this country and the local courthouse will often stand out among all of the buildings. In many towns, the courthouse lies literally in the center of town, often with many other important government offices found within (or in proximity to) this building (e.g., local police or sheriff's department, jail, city hall, post office). In many small towns, the courthouse is surrounded in a circular fashion by several small businesses. The courthouse grounds is often neatly landscaped, with park benches and picnic tables. Invariably displayed in huge letters is the phrase, "Justice For All" or similar words, along with the symbol of the "blind lady of justice" and the American and state flags.

The courts are certainly one of the busiest of all government institutions, and they differ from most other institutions in at least two important ways. First, the courts are places where citizens most directly interact on an individual basis rather than in groups (with some exceptions, to be sure). Second, it is where people go to "get what is their due" or "have their day in court," whether a small claims case or a traffic case or even as victims in a criminal case. Yet, at the same time, the courts are perhaps one of the least understood institutions—at least as far as the general public is concerned. Public-opinion polls consistently find that the public is more ignorant of the court system than any other institution. Also, surveys consistently show that the public often feels mistreated by the courts and dealt with in a disrespectful way. The public comes to the court system wanting some resolution, either protection or punishment; too often they get neither and their claims are often treated as "trivial" or "frivolous." This is especially the case among ordinary, working-class citizens (Merry, 1990).

In the United States today, there are federal and state courts, each with its own hierarchy and jurisdictional distinctions. The Supreme Court is at the top of the federal court hierarchy, followed in succession by the U.S. Courts of Appeal (with thirteen circuits), an assortment of district courts (some have both federal and local jurisdictions, others have only federal jurisdiction), and administrative quasi-jurisdictional agencies (e.g., Federal Trade Commission, National Labor Relations Board). The U.S. Supreme Court is composed of eight associate justices and one chief justice. Cases are advanced to the U.S. Supreme Court through a *writ of certiorari* from the U.S. Courts of Appeal, and from state supreme courts (Vago, 1997; Neubauer, 1996). At the very bottom of the federal court hierarchy are U.S. magistrates, who adjudicate minor criminal cases, conduct preliminary stages of felony cases, and oversee numerous civil cases. State supreme courts head the state court hierarchy. Some states also have intermediate appellate courts. State supreme courts are courts of last resort for appeals requiring interpretation of state law.

Below these higher courts are, in order of succession, trial courts of original and general jurisdictions, and at the bottom are courts of limited jurisdiction. The trial courts typically deal with serious felony and major civil cases, but they also adjudicate misdemeanor cases. A simpler way to view the institution of courts is to recognize that in both the federal and state court systems, there are trial courts (with varying degrees of jurisdiction) and appellate courts. Trial courts serve as a trier-of-fact body of this institution (e.g., take witness testimony, examine evidence, apply procedural rules), whereas appellate courts base decisions on the trial court's record and the constitutionality of lower-court decisions made within that record (Vago, 1997; Neubauer, 1996).

The court has been defined as "an agency or unit of the judicial branch of government. . . which has the authority to decide upon cases, controversies in law, and disputed matters of fact brought before it" (Rush, 1994: 78). Such a definition is frequently associated with concepts like justice, fairness, impartiality, objectivity, and other superlatives. Actually, the court is not an agency, nor a component of any agency, but more like an independent branch of government "stipulated in both the Constitution of the United

States and in state constitutions" (Turkel, 1996: 139). On the surface, this statement suggests that the court is autonomous to other branches of government and other institutions but, as will be shown, the court is simply another political government institution—often with an agenda far removed from any notions of justice and impartiality.

Criminal courts have been described as "marketplaces in which the only commodity traded seriously is time" (Jackson, 1984: 77). Civil courts can be viewed in a similar vein, with the exception that the commodities traded are power and privilege, which allow corporations to do pretty much as they will. It removes people from their homes (e.g., relocation of Native Americans). It decides which parent receives custody of children in divorce cases. It controls women's bodies (e.g., abortion issues). It decides who can work and who cannot (e.g., labor issues). It keeps people living in poverty (e.g., welfare issues). This commodity controls and impacts many other social issues that face contemporary society. Obviously, this view implies, at the very least, that the court is not justice-oriented, objective, or impartial; rather, it suggests that the court operates in a stock-market atmosphere with justice reduced to the "eyes of the beholder," where fairness is replaced by whims of power. Such a definition also considers the ideology of the court to be interest-serving. The function of the court is limited to efficiency. This is not any different than many other institutions within capitalist society.

Most people do not think of the court as a self-serving institution that conceals its true identity behind a cloak of justice, fairness, and impartiality. Rather, most people choose to view the court as simply a guardian of justice. Of course, justice is whatever we want it to be at a given point in time. It is typically said that "justice is served" if the court's decision favors us or our ideas about the disposition of a case in which we are familiar. We tend to turn on that definition when the court's decision is against us or against what we think the court ought to have done, resulting in the charge of "injustice." Thus, when a defendant stands before the sentencing judge after being found guilty of a crime and is informed that he or she is sentenced to a term in prison, many applaud the decision and say that justice has been served. Few consider another form of justice relevant to most criminal cases, that of *social justice*, which necessitates the consideration of concepts such as race/ethnicity, sex/gender, and social class. When the topic of social justice is brought up, it is generally rejected with contempt or dismissed as simply another example of liberal thought that fails to recognize that all poor or disadvantaged people do not commit crimes.

A review of the history of the courts demonstrates that while justice has often been served, social justice has not generally been served. This problem can be traced back to the very beginning of the American court system during colonial times.

The Development of the Modern Court System: The Colonial System

Although there were significant changes within the entire governmental structure following the American Revolution, including the criminal justice system, our modern courts have their roots within colonial society. Early American courts and their administration of justice process were microcosms of the British judicial system. As in England, which regarded the Parliament as the highest court, colonial legislatures were the highest courts and one of their legal functions was to serve as courts of appeal. Throughout the seventeenth century, colonial courts emerged into a three-tiered court system (much like state courts are arranged today). Below the legislature high courts were Superior courts, where governors or their designates presided over criminal trials and civil trials that were previously heard in lower courts. The lower courts handled most of the trials, and levied and collected taxes. These lower courts also provided residents with socializing opportunities and a place to conduct business and engage in lively political discussions (Knappman, 1994). "Ordinary people *used* the courts to get justice for themselves, vindication, restitution; and in criminal as well as civil matters" (Friedman, 1993: 31). The courts were also used as places to vent frustrations and anger, thus assisting in the stability of colonial society (Chapin, 1983, 1996). These in turn were copied, with a few modifications, from England's court system.

The original charter of the Massachusetts Bay Colony created two types of courts: a "general court" and a "court of assistants." The former acted as both a legislative body and the highest court, while the latter (which consisted of the governor, deputy governor, and magistrates) was in charge of appeals from the lower courts, which came to be known as "county courts." These county courts were the heart of the local system of criminal justice—the same kinds of courts found in most cities and towns today. What is perhaps most interesting about these courts was the fact that they performed so many different functions: probate, spending money on road and bridge repairs, various forms of licensing, maintenance of the local ministry, regulation of wages, and, of course, all matter of criminal cases (Friedman, 1973: 35).

Within these county courts, the person who performed most of the day-to-day duties was the *justice of the peace*. These individuals were appointed by the governor (who was himself an appointee of the English king) and were controlled, for all practical purposes, by the local elites. Actually, this office took the place of the local magistrate in the 1860s (Friedman, 1973: 35).

For all practical purposes, judicial authority within the colonies was in the hands of the governor, who in turn was under the control of England.

Not surprisingly, as British rule became increasingly unpopular, the courts (and the entire legal system itself, but especially judges and most lawyers) were viewed as mere extensions of the King of England. In fact, lawyers were not exactly welcomed within the colonies, although as time passed, their knowledge and skills became more appreciated and in demand (Glick, 1983: 36; Friedman, 1973: 84).

Elite Dominance of the Legal Profession in Colonial America

As the legal profession grew during colonial times, it became more specialized as increasing numbers of lawyers participated in formal training. At first, of course, few attended college, because there were no law schools in the early years of the colonies. Lawyers either had no training at all, except for informal reading, or they went to England for their training, attending what was known as the Inns of Court in London. These were not law schools as we know them today; in fact, they were "little more than living and eating clubs" where in theory "a man could become a counselor-at-law in England without reading a single page of any law book." However, they did "read law and observed English practice" (Friedman, 1973: 84).

Most other lawyers learned the trade through apprenticeships with older lawyers. In fact, some of the most famous lawyers of the eighteenth century, many of whom directly participated in the writing of the Constitution, received their training this way. Among the notables were Thomas Jefferson and James Wilson (both signed the Declaration of Independence). Some lawyers were actually imported directly from England to assist in the governance of the colony, such as Nicholas Trott, who came to South Carolina in 1699 as its attorney general. Most lawyers worked on a part-time basis, as they usually were men of considerable means and had to spend a lot of their time managing their property. In Maryland, for instance, most of these part-time lawyers listed their regular occupations as "planters." This is not to say that lawyers were not poor and struggled with their finances, as so many did. Yet the legal profession, then as now, soon began to be dominated by an upper crust of wealthy and powerful lawyers, such as those classified as "founding fathers." Of the thirty-five men listed as "founding fathers," twenty were lawyers (Friedman, 1973: 85; Wilson, 1974).

An excellent illustration of the domination of the legal profession by the upper class comes from two studies of Massachusetts lawyers during the latter part of the eighteenth century (McKirdy, 1984; Flaherty, 1984). The author of one study focuses on some of the first lawyers to practice *criminal* law in the state. He notes that there were only fifteen practicing lawyers in 1740, which increased to twenty-five by 1762 (this group achieving the newly created rank of "barrister") and seventy-one by 1775. During the first years of the Superior Court (1692–1710), there were few lawyers that did any criminal cases. There were only a few lawyers considered the "leading practitioners" during the first half of the eighteenth century, including Thomas Newton, John Valentine, John Read, Robert Auchmuty, and John Overing. Each man either came from prosperous families or became prosperous on his own, many achieving prestigious positions in Massachusetts politics and the legal profession (e.g., Attorney General, Advocate General, Judge of the Admiralty Court) (Flaherty, 1984).

The other study provides a detailed profile of every lawyer (including judges) during the ten years immediately prior to the American Revolution. The results are revealing—yet not too surprising. There were thirty-three judges in the sample and eighty-one lawyers. As for the judges, twenty-two went to Harvard College (in itself indicative of a wealthy background). As for their occupational background, of those with a listed occupation other than lawyer, all but one was either a physician, merchant, or other businessman, or a "gentleman." One was a minister, one was a soldier, and one was a tutor at Harvard (Mc Kirdy, 1984).

As for the lawyers, most read like a "who's who" in Massachusetts society. Almost all (89 percent) attended college, either Harvard (72 percent) or Yale (17 percent). Practically all of them either came from wealthy families (e.g., owners of much land, proprietors, well-known ministers) or rose to positions of power and influence (e.g., judges, attorneys general, senators). Included are some rather famous names, such as John Adams (one of the founding fathers), David Noble (famous as a judge and merchant), James Otis (Speaker of the House, Attorney General, member of the First Revolutionary Council), James Otis, Jr. (famous patriot, Representative to the General Court, elected Speaker of the House), Robert Paine (son of Thomas Paine), Timothy Pickering (Adjunct General of the Continental Army, U.S. Senator, U.S. Congressman, U.S. Postmaster General, Secretary of War), Josiah Quincy, Jr., and Samuel Quincy (of the famous Quincy family), William Read (son of John Read, one of the leading lawyers in the state, Deputy Judge of the Vice Admiralty Court, Judge of the Suffolk Inferior Court of Common Pleas), Timothy Ruggles (Brigadier General of the state militia, Speaker of the House), and Theodore Sedgwick (Representative to the General Court, state senator, member of the Continental Congress, U.S. Congress, U.S. Senate, Massachusetts Supreme Judicial Court) (McKirdy, 1984: 339–358).

Processing Criminal Cases: The Justice of the Peace in Colonial America

A particularly fascinating case study was done on a specific justice of the peace by the name of John Clark (Osgood, 1984). This study is based on some rare records left by Mr. Clark himself in a 269–page book, which contain 1,379 entries. The entries cover the period between 1700 and 1726. What is most revealing from the data contained in these entries is the kinds of cases handled in Clark's court. Although it does not provide much detail about the backgrounds of criminal defendants, the occupations of some are presented (more detail is provided for civil cases, including the occupations of those who won the case and those who lost).

As far as criminal cases are concerned, of 264 cases, 127 (48 percent) involved the crime of "breach of peace." Typical of the religious influence of the times, three offenses taken together constituted almost one third of the cases (31.8 percent)—"profane swearing," "profane cursing" (it is not clear what the difference was), and "profaning the Sabbath." Theft cases were 11 percent of the total.

Other cases that were handled included various civil (mostly violation of contracts) and administrative matters, the most common of which was a category called "violating a municipal ordinance". Grand Jury presentments amounted to a total of thirty-five cases, with the most common being "selling liquor without a license." However, it is interesting that two cases were presented by the Grand Jury that involved the charge of "uncleanness," and one each of the following charges: "bawdy house," "neglect of worship," and a "man and wife fornicating" (*where* they fornicated was not specified!) (Osgood, 1984: 148–149).

The occupations of those involved in criminal matters are given for only thirteen cases, the most common of which was the category "unknown" (five cases). The occupations of those involved in civil cases were more often listed, and included such varied occupations as "innholders," "cordwainer," "mariner," "victualler" (tavern keeper), "joiner" (a carpenter who specializes in doors and windows), and "shipwright" (Osgood, 1984: 150–151).

Upholding Morality

It is obvious that during the colonial era, cases involving various "morals" charges tended to dominate the courts. Religion and sex influenced early American courts and processes. Religion was woven into codes throughout the colonies, but was most evident in the northern colonies, as reflected in the Massachusetts Bay Colony. "In one part of the *Laws and Liberties of Massachusetts* . . . the code contained a list of 'capital laws.' Each one came equipped with citations from the Bible" (Friedman, 1973: 34). This is not surprising given the fact that the Bible had such a profound impact on the earliest settlers, especially among New England Puritans. The Massachusetts Code of 1648 made the following offenses punishable by death: "Idolatry, witchcraft, blasphemy, bestiality, sodomy, adultery, rape, man stealing, treason, false witness with intent to take a life, cursing or smiting of a parent, stubbornness or rebelliousness on the part of a son against his parents. . . " (Haskins, 1969: 37). Most of the codes were more or less reproductions straight out of the Bible.

However, when it came to enforcing these laws during actual court cases, the bark of the rulers was louder than their bite, as juries usually refused to convict on these charges or simply refused to convict at all. Apparently, these laws were established to instill *fear* more than anything else (Haskins, 1969: 44). Those that were convicted were usually sentenced to pay restitution (in cases of theft) and/or to receive punishment such as whipping, the stocks, the pillory, and other forms of *public* punishment. It was probably also the case where many citizens refused to go along with the repressive laws laid down by the rulers. Many jurors showed disrespect toward authorities, such as judges, while many a citizen simply chose to ignore the "immorality" of their fellow citizens, perhaps because they engaged in similar behavior. Indeed, as several studies have noted, the sexual behavior of colonial citizens was often quite loose. Also, there was much drinking and carrying on among citizens. In Essex County, Massachusetts, many brides were pregnant on their wedding day and about 60 percent of them were prosecuted, apparently without much success (Walker, 1998:30; see also Chapin, 1983; Flaherty, 1972).

In most other cases, justice was quite individualized, with several dismissed outright. One study found that about one third of the cases examined virtually "disappeared" from the records, presumably having been dismissed (Walker, 1998: 30; see also Greenberg, 1974). This was perhaps most clearly in evidence in capital cases, as most were reduced to a lesser offense (e.g., reducing murder to manslaughter), and most of those who were actually sentenced to death were eventually pardoned. Evidence of such leniency can be seen in the fact that between 1624 and 1664 in New York, there was only one execution (Walker, 1998: 35; see also Greenberg, 1974; Hindus, 1980; Mackey, 1982).

If there was one area where there was evidence of the occasional repressive features of colonial (especially Puritan) law, it was in the case of the famous witch trials in Salem, Massachusetts.

Hunting for Witches and Religious Dissidents: Colonial Court Processes

In early Massachusetts society, several typical religious-based offenses were heresy (which was often the foundation for the offense of witchcraft), blasphemy, Quakerism, and violation of the Sabbath (Friedman, 1973; Knappman, 1994; Dailey, 1991; Evans, 1989; Chapin, 1989; Morgan, 1958; Semmes, 1970). Women were often singled out for the prosecution of these offenses. This is not too surprising, because women were considered property and lived an existence of servitude and compliance. When they failed to comply with these rigors, they were brought before the court.

In 1637 and 1638, Ann Hutchison was charged with traducing the ministers and their ministry and heresy. Tried twice, the civil trial took place in November 1637 and the religious trial was held on March 22, 1638. She was placed on trial for her religious views and because she crossed the boundary established for women—she had held religious meetings. Mrs. Hutchison was found guilty and the sentence was banishment (Evans, 1989; Dailey, 1991). Because it was winter, her sentence was modified; she remain confined in the colony until spring. Throughout her confinement, Mrs. Hutchison continued to express her views. This demonstration of defiance resulted in the second trial where, after being found guilty on the basis of her spiritual views, she was excommunicated and ordered banished. In 1643, Mrs. Hutchison was killed by Indians in what eventually became New York. The historical significance of these trials exhibit the interest in curtailing religious dissent and the control of women in the Massachusetts Bay Colony (Knappman, 1991; Dailey, 1989).

Judith Catchpole was an indentured servant. She arrived in Maryland in January 1656. Eight months after her arrival, she stood trial for infanticide and witchcraft. Her accuser, William Bramhall, himself an indentured servant, had arrived in Maryland with Ms. Catchpole. He had made allegations that she had given birth and subsequently murdered the child. He also accused her of several acts of witchcraft. Before the trial began, Mr. Bramhall died. Interestingly, an all-woman jury was selected. After hearing the testimony of this case, the female jurors took it upon themselves to examine Ms. Catchpole, after which they testified under oath that Ms. Catchpole had never been pregnant. The jurors discarded the witchcraft charges outright and found her not guilty of infanticide. This case presents an interesting paradox. On one hand, we see women subjected to the judicial process without any substantiated evidence. One the other hand was the pragmatic response of the court to use women jurors for expert evaluation (Knappman, 1991; Semmes, 1970).

During the summer of 1659, upon visiting two imprisoned Quakers in Boston, Mary Dyer found herself imprisoned and charged with the offense of Quakerism. She was found guilty and sentenced to banishment. Several months later, Mary Dyer returned to Boston. Perhaps her fate had been sealed nearly twenty-two years earlier when she stepped forward and clutched Ann Hutchison's hand after the latter had been excommunicated and banished. Nevertheless, for her act of defiance against judicial authority, Mary Dyer was sentenced to death and was hanged on June 1, 1659. In 1959, the Massachusetts General Court authorized the construction of a 7-foot statue of Mary Dyer; the inscription reads, "Witness for Religious Freedom." Today this monument rests on the lawn of the Boston State House (McHenry, 1983; Tolles, 1971). The Puritans, who left England to avoid religious persecution, became religious persecutors, and the judicial process gave that persecution legitimacy.

In 1692, two hundred people were brought to trial in Salem, Massachusetts; their charge was witchcraft. Charges of witchcraft were not alien to the colonies; it was a crime in England and was an offense in the colonies. This case is significant in the history of American jurisprudence for several reasons. First, it demonstrates the court's willingness to support religious persecution and to wage war against women. Second, it demonstrated that the Massachusetts Bay Colony was willing to engage in witch-hunts very much like Europeans had done for centuries, but with less frequency. But most of all, it reflected the court's willingness to respond to times of anxiety and social unrest—the same causes of "witch" persecutions in Europe—through violence. In 1684, the Massachusetts Bay Colony had lost its charter and become a component of the New England Dominion. Political autonomy and the titles to land were threatened.

During the winter of 1691–92, Betty, the daughter of Reverend Samuel Parris, and her eleven-year-old cousin were being entertained by a Caribbean slave girl named Tituba. Other girls were invited, and their ages ranged from twelve to twenty. The girls began exhibiting strange behavior. Tituba, falling to the floor and experiencing convulsions, began barking like a dog. Thereafter, the other girls began acting "strangely." The entire community was horror-stricken. After a thorough investigation, the girls named the slave girl, Sarah Good who was a near derelict, and Sarah Osburn. On February 29, 1692, the three were arrested. Several months later, the jails of Salem were packed with people accused of witchcraft. The trials were conducted from June through September 1692. Some of the evidence allowed in the trials included visions seen by the townspeople. Twenty-nine people were convicted. Nineteen people were hanged, and the remaining convicted persons were released over a period of years. The significance of these trials champions the notion that women were obviously persecuted, and that in times of social peril, looking for scapegoats proved an adequate distraction. It was the court, in all of its legal splendor, that legitimated the persecution and scapegoating (Knappman, 1991; Friedman, 1993; Starkey, 1949). The persecutions and scapegoating did not cease as the colonies entered the eighteenth century.

After the Revolution: The Establishment of the Federal System and the Supreme Court

After the American Revolution, a federal court system emerged, complete with various appellate courts and, of course, the U.S. Supreme Court. This was an important development in the history of criminal justice. Following the American Revolution, there was quite a debate between those who believed that there should be a federal court system and those who did not. This debate was actually part of the much larger debate concerning whether there should be a strong central government;. thus, it was the "anti-federalists" versus the "federalists." In time, the federalists won out, although with some compromises, such as establishing district courts (via the Judiciary Act of 1789 and the Reorganization Act of 1801), which were empowered to enforce federal laws but structured along state lines, and judges had to be residents of that state. Various state courts were soon established by state legislative bodies (Neubauer, 1996: 41–42).

Of major importance was the creation of the highest court of the country, the Supreme Court, established in 1789 with the passage of the Judiciary Act. If there was ever an instance where evidence of the upper-class bias of the legal system was the clearest, the composition of the U.S. Supreme Court is just such an instance. It was created by a special Senate committee, headed by Oliver Ellsworth (who wrote the bill), who later became the third Chief Justice (Schwartz, 1993: 14). Throughout the history of the Supreme Court, its members have been drawn overwhelmingly from the upper crust of society. This was especially the case in the nineteenth century, as almost all came from the "landed gentry" and were schooled in the most prestigious, mostly Ivy League universities (Schmidhauser, 1960). The very first court, 1790–1801, reflects this class bias, as did the second court (one of the most influential in the early years), the Marshall Court (1801–1836). Those selected for the first Supreme Court were William Cushing (a Harvard graduate, ranked third in his class, Chief Justice of the Massachusetts highest court), John Jay (one of the founding fathers, member of the Continental Congress, the first Secretary of State, appointed by George Washington as the first Chief Justice), John Rutledge of South Carolina (a large slaveholder, a founding father and signer of the U.S. Constitution), James Wilson of Pennsylvania (another founding father, born in Scotland and attended the University of Edinburg, taught the classics at the College of Philadelphia, member of the Continental Congress), James Iredell of North Carolina (served as state judge and attorney general), and John Blair of Virginia (a judge on the Virginia Supreme Court of Appeals). Subsequent appointments to this first court (because of resignations of Jay and Rutledge) included Samuel Chase (a founding father who served in the Continental Congress, Chief Judge of the Maryland General Court, and one of the signers of the Declaration of Independence) (Schwartz, 1993: 17; Wilson, 1974).

The 1801–1836 court was headed by none other than John Marshall. Marshall, of Virginia, was one of the founding fathers and was a member of the Virginia Ratification Committee, who eventually served as the U.S. Commissioner to France, in the U.S. Congress, and as Secretary of State. Marshall's biggest case was, of course, the famous *Marbury v. Madison* in 1803, established the Supreme Court's power to review the constitutionality of cases (Schwartz, 1993: 39–41).

The Supreme Court has been a consistent supporter of the concept of private property; it is not unusual that the very first case it heard involved property. In the case of *Chisholm v. Georgia,* argued in 1793, the Court considered a suit concerning the claim for the delivery of goods. The issue was whether a state could be sued in federal court by a citizen of another state (the court ruled that a state could in fact be sued) (Schwartz, 1993: 20–21). While a complete review of Supreme Court decisions is beyond the scope of this chapter, suffice it to say that, in time, the Court "was doing its bit for the ruling elite." Zinn argues,

> How could it be independent, with its members chosen by the President and ratified by the Senate? How could it be neutral between rich and poor when its members were often former wealthy lawyers, and almost always came from the upper class? Early in the nineteenth century, the Court laid the legal basis for a nationally regulated economy by establishing federal control over interstate commerce, and the legal basis for corporate capitalism by making the contract sacred. (Zinn, 1995: 254)

A review of some key Supreme Court decisions in the nineteenth century demonstrates Zinn's point. Two cases typify the court's bias. One is the now infamous "separate but equal" case of *Plessy v. Ferguson,* discussed in Chapter 1. The obvious racist nature of this decision needs no elaboration. The other is the court's handling of cases falling under the Sherman Anti-Trust Act passed by the Senate in 1890, following years of agitation and protests. It came about during the infamous "Gilded Age," described by Friedman as "the factory age, the age of money, the age of the robber barons, of capital and labor at war" (Friedman, 1973: 296). It began soon after the close of the Civil War, and it marked, in a sense, the *triumph of capitalism.* What followed was an era that witnessed the amassing of great wealth, mostly off the backs of immigrant workers, many very young. The result was the concentration of wealth in the hands of a small, very ruthless minority of capitalists, appropriately called the *robber barons.*[2] There was such a public outcry at the ruthlessness of these capitalists that the U.S. Senate had to do *something.* That "something" was the Sherman Act, which theoretically was supposed to make illegal the crux of the problem: monopolistic practices (often referred to as "the trusts") and restraint of trade.

Unfortunately—and typically—this act did little to alleviate the problem. The wording was so vague as to be almost meaningless—it never defined *monopoly* or *restraint of trade,* which was what it was supposed to regulate. Further, the act failed to set up an enforcement mechanism—no separate administrative agency was established. Mostly it was "smoke and mirrors," mere public relations. What is really important to realize is that this law was ultimately most often used *against labor unions and especially as a strike-breaking tool* (Friedman, 1993: 118). The result is summarized by Zinn as follows:

In 1895 the [Supreme] Court interpreted the Sherman Act so as to make it harmless. It said a monopoly of sugar refining was a monopoly in manufacturing, not commerce, and so could not be regulated by Congress through the Sherman Act (*U.S. v. E. C. Knight Co.*). The Court also said the Sherman Act could be used against interstate strikes (the railway strike of 1894) because they were in restraint of trade. It also declared unconstitutional a small attempt by Congress to tax high incomes at a higher rate (*Pollock v. Farmers' Loan & Trust Company*). In later years it would refuse to break up the Standard Oil and American Tobacco monopolies, saying that the Sherman Act barred only "unreasonable" combinations in restraint of trade. (Zinn, 1995: 254)

Zinn goes on to quote a New York banker who gave a toast to the Supreme Court for ruling in the interests of those in power and who were the "important people," saying that the Court was the "guardian of the dollar, defender of private property, enemy of spoliation, sheet anchor of the Republic." Yes, indeed, private property was indeed defended against the unreasonable restraints placed against the rulers by those merely trying to earn a decent wage (Zinn, 1995: 254). But, after all, it was what judges wanted, what big business wanted, and it was (and still is) their views and interests that are important.

The Supreme Court continued to make these kinds of interpretations of the law so as to favor, more often than not, those with power. Consider the Fourteenth Amendment, which declared that no person shall be deprived of property, "nor shall any State deprive any person of life, liberty, or property without due process of law." Eventually, the Court began to interpret this amendment not as a protection for blacks but as a protection for corporations, ruling on many occasions that a corporation was a "person." This they did in convincing fashion in the case of *Wabash Railway v. Illinois* (1886), in which the court ruled that states could not regulate commerce, only the federal government could (Friedman, 1993: 394; Zinn, 1995: 255). Between 1890 and 1910, of all the Fourteenth Amendment cases brought before the Supreme Court, 288 dealt with corporations and a mere nineteen dealt with black citizens (Zinn, 1995: 255). One Supreme Court Justice, Samuel Miller, said in 1875 that it was useless to "contend with judges who have been at the bar, the advocates for forty years of railroad companies. . . " A statement by Supreme Court Justice David J. Brewer in 1893 summarizes the dominant view of how the law reflects the will of the rich and powerful. He stated quite matter-of-factly that:

It is the unvarying law that the wealth of the community will be in the hands of the few. . . . The great majority of men are unwilling to endure that long self-denial and saving which makes accumulation possible. . . and hence it always has been, and until human nature is remodeled always will be true, that the wealth of a nation is in the hands of a few, while the many subsist upon the proceeds of their daily toil. (Zinn, 1995: 255)

How can one in any way conclude that the courts could ever be dispensers of "equal justice," given these attitudes and the distribution of wealth and power?

Post-Civil War Changes in the Court System

The biggest changes in the American court system came after the Civil War, largely because of the huge growth in population, especially the emergence of large cities. The old agrarian court system of small-town America could no longer handle the changes. New courts emerged, including small claims courts, so-called "lower courts" (often called municipal courts or justice-of-the-peace courts, which handle misdemeanors, including traffic citations), felony courts (often called Superior Courts, District Courts, and the like), and juvenile courts (begun in 1899). Just to give an idea of this growth, in Chicago alone by the early 1930s there were more then five hundred separate courts (Neubauer, 1996).

Along with the general growth in the court system came the emergence of the grand jury. The grand jury originated in the twelfth century as a result of a struggle between Henry II and the church. Henry wanted to remove the jurisdiction of the church in cases in which members were charged with a crime (and received the "benefit of clergy"). The church was generally more lenient and gained money through the collection of fines. The grand jury consisted of a panel of sixteen men created by the king to investigate and bring charges against people who were suspected of law violations. The king created a "citizens police force" to gain control over the prosecution of criminal cases. In time, an accusation by a grand jury became equivalent to a guilty verdict, since the king had so much control over it (Clark, 1975: 9).

By the seventeenth century, two changes in criminal justice had altered the role of the grand jury. First, petit juries (trial juries) began to replace "trial by ordeal" (e.g., placing an accused's hand in boiling water). Second, Parliament emerged and its taxing power replaced the grand jury's function of levying fines. However, during the seventeenth century, the grand jury continued to be used as a means of political control and repression, such as when Charles II used it to attempt Catholic control of the Protestants by seeking indictments against the Duke of York (Clark, 1975: 9–10).

The first grand jury in America was instituted in Massachusetts in 1635; by 1683, all the colonies had them. During the colonial period, grand juries initiated investigations frequently because there were no police forces and no office of public prosecutor as we know it today. Grand juries, moreover, were quite independent at this time.

After the American Revolution, the grand jury was included in many state constitutions and in the Fifth Amendment ("No person shall be held to answer for a capital or otherwise infamous crime, unless on a presentment or indictment of a Grand Jury. . . "). The purpose of a grand jury was to have a body that would shield the citizen against abuse by the state. In reality, however, it tended to be more protective of the privileged and powerful than the average citizen. For instance, when the Federalists were in power (e.g., John Adams), the grand jury was used to indict the Republicans (or anti-Federalists), especially for charges of treason under the Sedition Laws. However, even the Republicans, when they came to power, used the grand jury against their political enemies (e.g., Thomas Jefferson indicting Aaron Burr) (Clark, 1975: 20–21).

The prosecutor has had a unique role within the court system, often viewed as the "gatekeeper" of the system in that he or she is in charge of screening cases and deciding whether to prosecute. Historically, the domain of the prosecutor (i.e., the functions, roles, duties, jurisdiction of the prosecutor) has changed drastically. In colonial times, the victim had a much larger role. Usually, the victim hired a private prosecutor (usually a privately retained lawyer) for the case. Judges and juries played a more influential role. Trials were the order of the day, and these were of a very swift duration, after which the convicted offender was "hanged, banished, lashed, or given in servitude to the victim until he made good his debt." At this time, of course, there were no prisons as such, no fully authorized police force (as discussed previously), and no public prosecutor. In other words, the *state* had not as yet stepped in to dominate the criminal justice process. In a small, relatively homogeneous and agriculturally based society, there was little need for a centralized state apparatus. All of this was to change during the nineteenth century, with the coming of the Industrial Revolution (McDonald, 1979: 22).

In the nineteenth century, the entire criminal justice system underwent some noteworthy changes. By the end of the eighteenth century, shortly after the American Revolution, the states began to enact legislation creating public prosecutors and state prisons. The result was that the "domain of the victim of crime in the criminal justice system was greatly reduced. He no longer played a correctional role; and his role in the investigation and apprehension of criminals was minimized" (McDonald, 1979: 24).

We have already seen how the police emerged as a distinct occupation in the nineteenth century. The use of the grand jury began to diminish as the states, in their constitutions, "either did not provide for a grand jury system or provided for one but also allowed for the option of proceeding by way of information filed by the prosecutor." The prosecutor's domain expanded considerably. The victim of a crime was beginning to be largely ignored, while the criminal justice process was placed into the hands of experts, a group of trained professionals who ostensibly would have the knowledge and motivation to serve the public (McDonald, 1979: 24). Also in the nineteenth century there was an increase in the police's authority in the charging decision. In fact, until the present century, the police had almost total control of this crucial decision. Today, however, the functions of the police, the prosecutor, judges, and juries, as well as the penal system, are fairly distinct.

An overview of the history of the courts would not be complete without some reference to an important component of the criminal justice system that is critically related to the courts: the jail. The jail is important—and should be discussed in connection to the courts—for at least two reasons. First, it is usually the second stage of the criminal justice process following an arrest. Throughout history, the jail has been used primarily as a place of temporary detention prior to a defendant's first appearance in court. Second, the length of time a defendant spends in jail is strongly related to the final disposition by the court. Indeed, in the majority of cases, the real reason people are held in jail awaiting trial is that they simply cannot afford to post the bond, not because they are dangerous or likely to commit further crimes. Numerous studies, covering more than forty years, have consistently demonstrated two major points: (1) whether one is released from jail pending the final disposition of the case depends strongly on both the class and race of the defendant—minorities and the poor are far more likely to remain in jail; and (2) comparisons of those who remain in jail and those released show that those released fare much better in terms of the likelihood of being convicted and, if convicted, the likelihood of being sentenced to a term of imprisonment. These studies are too numerous to summarize in their entirety here.[3]

The Jail: A Clear Case of "Rabble Management"

In his study of the modern jail, Irwin argues that one of the main functions of this institution has been to manage the *rabble* or the *underclass*—two terms that can be used synonymously with *dangerous classes* (Irwin, 1985). A common procedure for releasing a defendant pending his or her court appearance is that of *bail*, which is a form of "security" that a defendant puts forth guaranteeing that he or she will appear in court whenever requested. In most jurisdictions, a defendant can, in effect, *buy* his or her freedom. In most jurisdictions, bail is set on misdemeanor charges by a police official, usually a desk sergeant at the stationhouse where the defendant was booked. For felonies, bail is typically set by a judge in a courthouse during the initial appearance (Neubauer, 1996: 177).

According to the Fifth Amendment to the U.S. Constitution, no person can be held, "nor deprived of life, liberty or property, without due process of law." Also, according to legal principles, one is presumed innocent until proven guilty "beyond a reasonable doubt," and there can be no punishment without conviction, nor can one be detained for the purposes of punishment. The reality of criminal justice is often just the opposite. On any given day, thousands of people are held in jail awaiting court appearances (sometimes for several months). They have not been proven guilty; they are there simply because they cannot afford bail.

This is nothing new, as any cursory review of the history of jails, both in America and elsewhere, will show. The modern jail actually originated in England with the Norman Conquest in the eleventh century. Under Henry II, the jail (or to be more precise, the English term *goal*) began to take on characteristics and functions known today. Henry II sought to establish at least one jail in each county, under the control of a local sheriff. By the thirteenth century, all but five counties had a jail. The county sheriff was a royal appointment, "a functionary who upheld his master's interests against local powers" (McConville, 1998: 268).

It is obvious that from the very beginning, jails were almost exclusively used to house the poor. In fact, a term often used interchangeably with jail was that of *debtor's prison*. McConville notes that it was ironic that, on the one hand the financing of local jails depended on user fees paid to jailers, yet on the other hand, the majority of jail inmates "were drawn chiefly from the poor and powerless classes." One eighteenth-century reformer noted that such fees were extracted "from misery" (McConville, 1998: 269). Not surprisingly, corruption was rampant during this entire period, yet little was done to correct the problem. This was probably because, then as now, much profit was to be made from the existence of crime. The jails of London functioned as "brothels, taps, criminal clubs, and asylums for thieves, robbers, and fraudsmen, and when their raw material—prisoners—threatened to run out, minions would bring false charges to replenish the supply." Also not surprisingly, the well-being of the prisoners was virtually ignored. As a result of their poverty, many either starved to death or died from disease (McConville, 1998: 270).

By the middle of the fourteenth century, London jails became used as a method to extract payment from those in debt—hence, the term *debtor's prison*. Even though most who ended up in jail because of this could not pay their debts—since the means to do so were taken away by the mere fact of being in jail—the actual function of the jail in this case was more as a threat than anything else. Some debtors selected to remain in jail until their death, because this would thereby cancel their debts and save their families from being charged (McConville, 1998: 271–272).

Even though technically the jailing of people because of their debts ceased to exist by the nineteenth century, nevertheless many still went to jail on the charge of "contempt of court," which essentially served the same purpose as before and still does today—usually for failure to pay a fine.

Jails in the American colonies served similar functions, but in time became temporary holding facilities for those awaiting court appearances or those serving short sentences. The use of bail dates back to early English society (at least as early as 1000 A.D.) and was originally established to ensure that an accused appeared for trial (Goldfarb, 1965, 1975). This practice goes back to the practice of mutual responsibilities of the collective; more specifically, groups of ten families under the control of the *tithingman* (see Chapter 2) to ensure obedience to the law. The families in effect "pledged" to ensure that the defendant appeared in court. Crime prevention in those early years was a collective responsibility, which was very practical in small, agrarian communities. Such a concept no longer applies in modern societies, characterized by much mobility and anonymity. Bail has thus come to stand for a different sort of pledge—a monetary or property form of pledge, often through the defendant's family, relatives, or friends. The problem today is, of course, the fact that most accused people come from the poorest sectors of society (McConville, 1998: 279).[4]

Jails historically served still another function. For years, starting at least as far back as the mid-fourteenth century, jails were almost synonymous with what were then called *workhouses* or *poorhouses* (see Chapter 4 for a more detailed discussion of these institutions). More specifically, this function of the jail can be traced directly to the Ordinance of Labourers (or Statutes of Labourers) passed in England in 1349, brought about in part because of the Black Death (see Chapter 2 and the discussion of the "Law of Vagrancy), which forced "vagabonds" and other undesireables to accept work at the prevailing wage or go to the workhouse. The Elizabethan Poor Law of 1572 further contributed to this development. This law distinguished between the common criminal and the "unworthy poor." "Hard labor" (which evolved into the infamous "rock pile," the "chain gang," and similar punishments of our modern era) became a standard form of punishment for those not even convicted of a crime, but only because of their poverty. In time, it became difficult to distinguish between the *pauper* (the common term for a person living in poverty) and the *vagabond* (those who wandered about the country without working). Eventually, in the United States, these two terms were replaced by *welfare dependent* and *petty persistent offender,* and in time even the *mentally ill* (McConville, 1998: 282–284).

A recent case reported in the *New York Times* illustrates the charge that the modern jail functions like a poorhouse and that bail is a form of ransom. The case involves an Hispanic man charged with "sexually assaulting a quadriplegic man for whom he worked as a home-health aid." He was unable to raise the $5,000 for his bail. Consequently, he spent nineteen months in jail awaiting his trial because he refused to plead guilty. He was finally found not guilty. Ironically, he spent more time in jail awaiting this decision than he would have spent had he pled guilty to a lesser charge. After some careful investigation (by a member of the public defender's office, who was finally able to find time to conduct an investigation because his caseload was so high), it was discovered that the alleged victim had made similar complaints to the home-care agency that hires helpers to take care of people, like the victim, who need constant care (Finder, 1999).

This brief history of the jail clearly illustrates the theme of this book. Jails have been used mostly, in Irwin's term, to manage the *rabble*—another term for the *dangerous classes*. And, by logical extension, the criminal courts (especially the so-called lower courts) have served the same purpose.

The 1960s: The Warren Court and the Reaffirmation of the Right to Counsel

A history of the American court system would not be complete without a review of the significant events of the 1960s, during what became known as the "Warren Court," named after the Chief Supreme Court Justice, Earl Warren. This was a period marked by tremendous upheavals and social movements: civil rights, women's liberation, anti-war, and others. Many began to take a close look at issues that had long been smoldering under the surface, issues related to the core of American democracy. The criminal justice system, not surprisingly, stood squarely in the center of the debate. Several significant Supreme Court decisions were made during this time. The first had to do with the Sixth Amendment guarantee of the "right to counsel," among other rights.

In a 1932 decision, the U.S. Supreme Court ruled that defendants had a right to counsel in cases in which the death penalty might he imposed (*Powell v. Alabama*, 1932). This case left unanswered the problem of providing counsel in cases in which the defendant was too poor to afford a lawyer in noncapital cases. This was partially answered in *Betts v. Brady* (1942), in which the Court ruled that there was no such guarantee in state courts unless the defendant could show that if he were deprived of counsel, it would result in a denial of due process. This decision was overturned in a landmark decision in *Gideon v. Wainwright* (1963), in which the court ruled that a defendant accused of a felony even in a noncapital ease should be provided counsel.

In *Gideon*, the court was faced with an ideological challenge to the myth of "equal justice for all." It was shown that Clarence Earl Gideon, who had asked for counsel but was denied, had to act as his own lawyer and that he was no match against an experienced prosecutor. It was found that any lawyer would have been able to prove that Gideon was innocent (as a subsequent trial was to show). It was a clear case of the fact that being poor (which Gideon was) led to a denial of due process (for a fuller treatment of this case, see Lewis, 1964). The Supreme Court stated the obvious:

> Reason and reflection require us to recognize that in our adversary system of criminal justice, any person hauled into court who is too poor to hire a lawyer

cannot he assured a fair trial unless counsel is provided for him. This seems to us an obvious truth. Governments, both state and federal, quite properly spend vast sums of money to try defendants accused of crime. Lawyers to prosecute are everywhere deemed essential to protect the public's interest in an orderly society. Similarly, there are a few defendants charged with a crime, few indeed, who fail to hire the best lawyer they can get to prepare and present their defense. That government hires lawyers to prosecute and defendants who have the money hire lawyers to defend are the strongest indications of a widespread belief that lawyers in criminal courts are necessities, not luxuries. . . . From the very beginning, our state and national constitutions and laws have laid great emphasis on procedural and substantive safeguards designed to assure fair trials before impartial tribunals in which every defendant stands equal before the law. This noble ideal cannot be realized if the poor man charged with crime has to face his accusers without a lawyer to assist him. (*Gideon v Wainwright*, 372, U.S., 1963, at 344)

Several years later (1972), the Supreme Court ruled that indigents accused of misdemeanors must also be provided with counsel in cases that can lead to imprisonment (*Argersinger v. Hamlin*, 1972). The right to counsel was eventually extended to various "critical stages" of the criminal justice process, starting with custodial interrogation (*Miranda v. Arizona*, 1963), continuing through subsequent hearings, such as the preliminary hearing (*Coleman v. Alabama*, 1970) and police lineups (*United States v. Wade*, 1972).

In theory, all defendants, rich and poor alike, have a guarantee of counsel. But the real issue is the *quality* of counsel and the question of whether justice is being served. Can the average defendant receive the best counsel, given the bureaucratic nature of the court system? Can every defendant get the kind of counsel that O.J. Simpson had? Obviously not, given the degree of inequality existing in our society. Do public defenders and other lawyers for the poor provide the same kind of defense that a rich man would receive from a retained lawyer, as was the case for Simpson? Given the fact that the majority of those in prison come from poor backgrounds, had public defenders, and had to await their trial in jail, the answer to these questions has to be no.

Soon after the *Gideon* decision, both state and federal courts began making policy changes concerning the effectiveness of counsel issue, one of which included the adoption of what became known as the *mockery of justice standard*. This standard means that "only circumstances so shocking that they reduce the trial to a farce satisfied defendants' claim of ineffective counsel." However, critics immediately charged that this was too vague, subjective and narrow to be of any practical use. Under this guideline, even defense lawyers "who appeared in court drunk did not violate this standard" (Samaha, 1999: 541–542). The courts have even failed to fine ineffectiveness when the defense counsel used heroin and cocaine during the trial, even when the counsel stated that he was not prepared, when an attorney on a capital punishment case could not name a single Supreme Court decision concerning the death penalty, and even when the attorney was suffering from Alzheimer's disease! (Cole, 1999: 78–79).

Most jurisdictions eventually abandoned this guideline and adopted the *reasonably competent attorney standard*. This was not much of an improvement, as it states that a lawyer's performance would be measured against the "customary skills and diligence that a reasonably competent attorney would perform under similar circumstances." The Supreme Court attempted further clarification in *Strictland v. Washington* (1984), but without much success at operationalizing "effective counsel" (Samaha, 1999: 542).

There are still serious gaps in the right to counsel. The Supreme Court has ruled that this right applies to all critical stages in the criminal justice process. But *critical stages* only include those that occur *after* formal charges have been filed; they do *not* include the investigative stop, the actual arrest, a search following an arrest, and even custodial interrogation. This is because the Sixth Amendment guarantees the right to counsel in all criminal prosecutions—in other words, *after* the defendant has been formally charged by the prosecutor (Samaha, 1999: 354–355). The "trumpet" of Gideon (to use the title of Anthony Lewis' book) has been muted considerably over the years (Cole, 1999: Chapter 2).

Even though defense counsel is a right at each of these critical stages of the criminal justice process, most defendants do not have attorneys to call upon immediately following arrest (probably the case for the majority of defendants). What happens in the majority of cases is that counsel is assigned by the court (or the case assigned to the public defender's office) during the initial court appearance (Benner, Neary, and Gutman, 1973: 24; Neubauer, 1996). The average defendant is allowed just *one* lawyer rather than an entire *team*, as is the case during celebrity cases like Simpson's (not to mention the dozens of investigators and expert witnesses).

Under the *assigned counsel* system, a court appoints a specific attorney to handle a case. This is common throughout America, especially in large urban courts where about three out of every four defendants are "indigent"—too poor to hire their own attorney (Wice, 1985). In some areas, the percentage is even higher, such as in Seattle, where the proportion of felony defendants who were indigent in a recent year was eighty-eight percent; in Monterey, California, 92 percent of felony defendants were indigent (Hanson and Chapper, 1991).

The judge usually has a list of lawyers in private practice in a particular county or a list of those who have volunteered to serve as counsel for indigents. Unfortunately, these lawyers are typically young and inexperienced and take the cases because they need the money or the experience or both. And the money won't make them rich, as their hourly fees generally range from $25 to $40. This system is similar to "managed care" in the health system, where in cases of psychotherapy, therapists are hired by insurance companies to see eight to ten clients each day for a much lower rate. Not surprisingly, the care received by clients in each case suffers. This is another instance of "money talks." Thus, justice is itself a commodity and fits within the overall capitalist framework of commodity production (Lynch and Groves, 1989: 103).

A more recent system that has emerged is the *contract system,* used in a few but growing number of counties. As implied by the term, local governments sign contracts with local attorneys to handle indigent cases. This represents a sort of privatization of due process, as one study concluded (Worden, 1991, 1993). It is a process where a system of *competitive bidding* is often done, with the result being that the lowest bidder, and not necessarily the best bidder, wins the contract. It should come as no surprise that several states have filed suits and, in one case, the practice was ruled unconstitutional (*Smith v. State,* 1984).

It is apparent that providing attorneys for indigent defendants is not a high priority. To begin with, among the three major components of the criminal justice system, the *least* amount of annual expenditures goes to the general category of "judicial and legal." In 1993, this segment received approximately $21 billion, compared to $44 billion for police and just under $32 billion for corrections (Maguire and Pastore, 1997: 3). Expenditures on counsel for the indigent represent a small percentage of this total. According to most recent data (1986), only about $1 billion went toward public defenders' offices, which represented an increase from only $200 million in 1976, ironically prompting some critics to complain about the rising costs (Neubauer, 1996: 113). A study in Virginia found that, after accounting for overhead costs, the hourly rate for court-appointed attorneys came to $13; in Kentucky, the rate is around $8.50 per hour; in Alabama, there is a statutory limit of $1,000 for all felonies and only $2,000 for capital crimes; and in Kentucky and Tennessee, there is a $1,000 minimum for all noncapital felony cases; in Mississippi it is $1,000 per case, which amounts to just over $2 per hour (Cole, 1999: 83–84). In short, poor people get attorneys working for poverty wages.

The retained-counsel system is generally far superior, especially if a defendant can afford the fees. The main reason for this is that with enough money, private attorneys can hire investigators and spend more time collecting evidence, finding witnesses, and taking other measures to ensure an adequate defense. This is particularly true if the attorney works for a law firm and the defendant is out on bail to assist in his or her own defense.

The American court system was put to some rather severe tests during the late 1960s and early 1970s during what have been called *radical-criminal trials.* This marked an important segment of the history of criminal justice.

Traditional versus Radical-Criminal Trials

The Traditional Criminal Trial

In the more traditional trial of a criminal case, there are a number of roles, each with its own behavior expectations. We can conceive of the trial as analogous to a theater production. The major roles are those of judge, prosecutor, defense attorney, bailiff, marshal, defendant, member of the jury, spectator, and member of the press.

The judge's role is that of a "neutral" arbitrator, the defense attorney's role is that of one speaking out "on behalf" of the client, the prosecutor represents "the people" or the "state" (which is supposed to be synonymous), and the defendant is supposed to be passive and is not expected to want (or have the ability) to defend himself or herself. The spectator is supposed to be passive, sit quietly, and observe (as do all others) "proper" courtroom demeanor.

The judge is perhaps the most interesting actor and the most symbolic. He or she sits high above all the action, with the American flag on one side and the state flag on the other. The judge dresses in a black robe and is addressed as "Your Honor." All are supposed to rise when the judge walks in. The traditional symbol of justice, a woman with blindfolds, is prominently displayed either inside the courtroom or near the main entrance outside the building.

Adherence to these symbols and the formalities and power relations within the courtroom processes themselves serve to legitimize (if not to mystify) the existing judicial system and the law. The judge, the court, and the law often become synonymous with or symbolic of God and country. Failure to adhere to these symbols can result in a "contempt of court" citation and/or removal from the courtroom.

Until the late 1960s and early 1970s, the social, political, and/or economic context within which justice was meted out rarely entered into the courts (notable exceptions include the trials of the International Workers of the World and Sacco and Vanzetti during the early part of this century) (Zinn, 1995: 367). Usually the issues focused on the narrow concerns of individual criminal acts and the guilt or innocence of individuals. This, of course, corresponded with the traditional legal notions of *mens rea* (individual guilt), begun around the eleventh century in England (see Chapter 1). During the late 1960s and early 1970s, several radical-criminal trials questioned the legitimacy of the judicial system.

Challenging the System: Radical-Criminal Trials

During the late 1960s and early 1970s, several major trials sent shockwaves through the legal establishment. The defendants in these radical-criminal trials or political trials were already in contempt of society's traditional economic and political institutions, and desired to create very fundamental changes. Eventually, as Sternberg noted, "It dawned upon these defendants that far from being 'agents' of the other institutions of power, the courts themselves were another creator and center of the very status quo they were determined to change" (Sternberg, 1974: 279). These defendants viewed the criminal courts as agents of powerful interests or, more specifically, representatives of a ruling class and an oppressive institution itself.

Many defendants sought to raise what they believed to be important moral and political issues "in an effort to generate jury sympathy for the defendants and the cause they represented" (Barkan, 1977: 324). Indeed, many did not attempt to deny that they had committed the alleged criminal act. What they often did was deny that the act was, or should be, in itself "criminal." Thus, to them "legal" guilt or innocence was not the issue. A defendant in the 1969 Milwaukee Twelve draft-card–burning case said:

> I'm not saying the jury should find us innocent. I'm simply hoping that the court will allow us to demonstrate the reasonableness of our belief and to (let the jurors) decide for themselves whether, in fact, it was reasonable. (Barkan, 1977: 325)

Phillip Berrigan, one of the Baltimore Four accused of draft-card burning and sentenced in April 1968, tried, in his remarks to the court, to place this conviction in a larger perspective. He wrote:

> But whatever work is useful to describe our nation's plight, we ask today in this court: What is lawful about a foreign policy which allows economic control of whole continents, which tells the Third World, as it tells our black people, "You'll make it sometime, but only under our system, at the pace we decide, by dole, by handout, by seamy charity, by delayed justice. Don't try it any other way!" What is lawful about peace under a nuclear blanket, the possible penetration of which impels our leaders to warn us of one hundred million American casualties? . . . What is lawful about the rich becoming richer, and the poor poorer, in this country or abroad? . . . These are not times for building justice; these are times for confronting injustice. This, we feel, is the number-one item of national business—to confront the entrenched, massive, and complex injustice of our country. And to confront it justly, nonviolently, and with maximum exposure of oneself and one's future. (Berrigan, 1970: 11–12)

For Berrigan, then, the burning of draft cards was an act of civil disobedience and the fact that it was unlawful was irrelevant. What was relevant was the war in Vietnam, racism abroad and at home, the discrepancy between the rich and the poor. However, the court, ostensibly being "above politics," could only decide on the issue of guilt or innocence and, as a result, sentenced the Baltimore Four to prison.

In some cases, the defendants sought to show the jury that the federal government itself was involved, in the sense that FBI agents (with its agent provocateurs) were responsible for the alleged crimes or, in some cases, even set up the defendants. This was especially true with the Gainesville Eight trial against the Vietnam Veterans Against the War. The government charged them with conspiring to disrupt the Republican Convention in 1972. However, the government itself ended up on trial. In this case, as Cook states, "The government, in effect, was found guilty" (Cook, 1974: 75).

In some radical-criminal trials, the tactics used by the defendants confronted the authority of the court and court officials, to the utter disbelief of the latter. The large number of contempt citations, the "gagging and shackling" of Black Panther Bobby Seale during the Chicago Seven trial, and other forms of punishment demonstrate "the depth and breadth of a culture shock experienced by officers of the criminal court" (Sternberg, 1974: 280). The Chicago Seven trial perhaps best illustrates these points and exposes the often farcical nature of court proceedings.

The defendants, for instance, used several methods of challenging the legitimacy of the court, including (1) direct and verbal attacks on judges and other officials, or the judicial process itself, often insisting that they (the defendants) be allowed to speak for themselves (on 665 separate occasions during the first twelve days of the Panther Twenty-One hearing, the defendant interrupted the proceedings); (2) ignoring proceedings (e.g., refusing to stand when Judge Hoffman entered the courtroom, reading books or magazines during the proceedings); (3) mocking legal procedures, such as when Jerry Rubin (Chicago Seven case) appeared in a black robe, or when unresponsive answers were given to what court officials thought were "straightforward" questions, such as when Abbie Hoffman (Chicago Seven) gave "Woodstock Nation" as his address; (4) refusing to confine interactions with traditional role members inside the courtroom (in the Chicago Seven trial, the defendants often argued with prosecution staff in the hallways, and many gave speeches attacking the proceedings, to large audiences often in front of the courthouse); (5) attempts to restructure and even reverse traditional roles (as when Bobby Seale charged Judge Hoffman with "contempt of the American people"); and (6) defendants planning and standing together in solidarity in their challenges to the court (with shouts of "Right on!").

Defendants in radical-criminal trials often helped their lawyers with defense strategy and discussed moral and political issues while on the witness stand (often bringing charges of "immaterial" and "irrelevant" from prosecutors and judges who would warn them to "stick to the issues"). Many defendants chose to represent themselves because of certain restrictions placed on lawyers. A lawyer, having been socialized into courtroom procedures, typically seeks a purely *legal* remedy (e.g., acquittal, shortened sentences), which often involves compromises and accommodations. A lawyer who behaves otherwise is likely to be disbarred. The defendants in the White House Seven trial (1973), charged with praying for peace on the White House lawn, stated:

> We could not bring ourselves to be represented by counsel, feeling that to do so would be participating in a kind of cat-and-mouse game with the government. We felt that rather than seeking to support our legal innocence in court, it was our simple duty to speak the truth of how we were led to that place. . . . (Barkan, 1977: 328)

When defendants act as their own lawyer, they are often given some latitude by judges because such defendants are considered ignorant of "traditional rules of evidence and proper courtroom procedure." However, the defendants' ignorance of proper courtroom procedures can be turned to their own advantage, enabling them "to inject political or moral issues into the proceedings" (Barkan, 1977: 329–330).

The role of spectator underwent rather drastic changes and, in fact, changed from one of mere spectator to one of active participant in delegitimizing the court. Audience participation was almost a daily event at most trials. Attempts to control spectators are largely unsuccessful. Most of them had ideologies similar if not identical to those of the defendants. Defendants, then, viewed audiences as "their people" and their interventions as "the will of the people." Sternberg comments as follows:

> It follows that the intervening audience in the radical trial was invariably on the side of the defendants and hostile to the institutionalized judiciary. In the progressive and interactive dialogue among and between defendants and members of the audience. . . an increasingly strengthened structure of "resonating sentiments" emerged. At the same time, the dissonance of sentiments between the court on the one hand and the defendants and the audience on the other became magnified. Examples were the massive support the audience gave to Bobby Seale in the courtroom, time after time answering his defiant raised and clenched fist with cries of "Right on"; the solidarity the New York Panther defendants displayed with a spectator whom Judge Murtaugh ordered removed for interrupting the proceedings, one defendant saying, "If she goes out, we go out!"; the concerted outrage of the entire audience when Judge Hoffman bound and gagged Seale; the continuous open as well as sub rosa exchange between defendants and audiences in New York and Chicago, as if the official court personnel were either absent or simply did not count. In all these instances, audience and defendants constructed a mutually supportive and subversive social reality under the very gavel and noses of the judge, prosecutors, and marshals. (Sternberg, 1974: 285–286)

From the perspective of judges and other court officials, nothing like this had ever happened. So entrenched were they in the formal rules and regulations that they utterly failed to comprehend the radical position. Moreover, the trials themselves raised some important constitutional issues, such as the Sixth Amendment guarantee of the right to confront witnesses *directly,* and both the Sixth and Fourteenth amendments, which guarantee a public trial. In 1970, the Supreme Court ruled (*Illinois v. Allen,* 397 U.S. 337) that defendants waived the right to confront their accusers by "disorderly behavior," and that they could be bound and gagged or even expelled. The Court did not rule on the other issue. From the defendants' perspective in these cases, a public trial meant just that—a truly *public* hearing with active participation by members of the audience.

These trials did, however, reveal the court system for what it is: a system in which dissent is stifled; in which the "rule of law" and corresponding ideologies are legitimized; and in which larger issues of social, economic, and political justice are ignored. In short, the court system merely processes defendants and does nothing about the causes of crime. It is a court system resembling a microcosm of a capitalist society in which exchange and bargaining between unequals goes on, all in the name of justice.

This is quite typical in a capitalist society, where commodities are *produced socially but owned privately.* In other words, commodities are produced mainly for *private profit* rather than for *social good.* Within the justice system, "justice will be pursued socially, but the benefits of justice will accrue to particular individuals," especially those with power (Lynch and Groves 1989: 99). The courts are agencies that attempt to rectify problems caused by the capitalist system itself, such as gross social inequalities. As such, the courts are attempting to solve a *social problem* by merely *punishing individuals.* By focusing almost exclusive attention on individual offenders, the courts merely reinforce the myth that individuals need correcting rather than the surrounding social system. This ideology is further reinforced by the mystique of the "law" displayed every day in every court—the extreme formalism of the court process, with the swearing on the Bible, the robes of the judges, the ubiquitous scales of justice signified by the "blind lady"—which masks what is really occurring in the outside world (Lynch and Groves, 1989: 98–99). The various radical-criminal trials of the 1960s and 1970s, along with the system's response to mass civil disobedience during the riots of the 1960s and, more recently, the riots following the Rodney King decision, demonstrated clearly how the courts are unable to deal with these outside issues (Feagin and Vera, 1995: 83–108; Balbus, 1973).

Moving into the last years of the twentieth century, we find that little has changed. However, one significant change has been that the people who are increasingly appearing in the nation's courts—and hence, jails—are racial minorities (especially African Americans) charged with drug-law violations. This is the result of a war on drugs that has been rather successful, since it appears that the intent was to control the minority population, especially those included among the growing "underclass"—the modern equivalent of the dangerous classes of a century or more ago.

The Modern Era: The War on Drugs and African Americans

As the two previous chapters point out, the war on drugs has had a huge impact on the criminal justice system. With the emphasis placed almost totally on a legalistic response to the "drug problem," the police have responded with literally millions of arrests for drug possession and sales during the past two decades. Not surprisingly, there has been a predictable impact on the criminal courts and the rest of the criminal justice system.

Data on court commitments to state prisons during the 1980s and early 1990s clearly show the dramatic changes for drug offenses. Between 1980 and 1992, sentences on drug charges increased by more than 1000 percent. In contrast, there was a more modest increase of 51 percent for violent offenses. Race played a key role in these increases, especially during the late 1980s and early 1990s, as the number of African Americans sentenced to prison for drug charges increased by more than 90 percent, almost three times greater than white offenders (Maguire and Pastore, 1996: 550). Currie noted that between 1985 and 1995, the number of African American inmates who had been sentenced for drug crimes increased by 700 percent (Currie, 1998: 12–13). Tables 3.1, 3.2, and 3.3 illustrates these figures.

Not only were more African Americans sentenced for drug crimes, but also the *severity* of their sentences increased compared to whites. In 1992, in the federal system, the average sentence length for African American drug offenders was about 107 months, compared to 74 months for white drug offenders. There has been a huge discrepancy when comparing powder and crack cocaine sentences in the federal system. In 1995, for instance, African Americans constituted a phenomenal 88 percent of those sentenced for crack cocaine, compared to less than 30 percent of those sentenced for powder cocaine. (See Tables 3.4 and 3.5.)

Sentencing in the federal system for drug offenses shows some startling changes during the past half century. As shown in Table 3.6, between 1945 and 1995, the proportion of those going to prison for all offenses rose from 47 to 69 percent, compared to a decrease of those granted probation (from 40 percent to 24 percent), while the average sentence has risen by more than 300 percent. The changes in the sentences for drug-law violations are most dramatic. As noted in Table 3.7, whereas in 1945 the percentage of drug offenders going to prison was high enough at 73 percent, by 1995 fully 90 percent were going to prison. The average sentence for drug cases went from only twenty-two months in 1945 to almost ninety months in 1995, an increase of 300 percent. Finally, while in 1980 the most serious offense for

TABLE 3.1   *Court Commitments to State Prison, 1988–1992.*

Offense *Violent:*	1988	1992	% Increase
White	26,299	33,376	26.9
Black	30,677	40,803	33.0
Property:			
White	37,978	44,344	16.8
Black	33,901	39,085	15.3
Drugs:			
White	18,851	25,474	35.1
Black	26,769	51,970	94.1

Source: Maguire and Pastore, 1996: 550

TABLE 3.2   *Court Commitments to State Prison, by Crime Type, 1980–1992.*

Offense	1980	1992	% Increase
Total	131,215	334,301	155
Violent	63,200	95,300	51
Property	53,900	104,300	94
Drugs	8,900	192,000	1046
Public Order	5,200	29,400	465

Sources: Gilliard and Beck, 1994

TABLE 3.3   *Average Sentence Length for Offenders Convicted of Various Crimes in U.S. District Courts, by Race, 1992 (sentences in months).*

	White	Black	Other
All Offenses	56.8	84.1	60.8
Violent Offenses	92.4	103.9	76.1
Drug Offenses	73.6	106.9	77.2

Source: Maguire and Pastore, 1996: 474

TABLE 3.4   *Drug Offenders Sentenced Under the U.S. Sentencing Commission Guidelines,*
by Race, Powder Cocaine and Crack, 1995.

	Powder Cocaine		Crack Cocaine	
	N	%	N	%
White	977	22.0	168	4.5
Black	1,274	28.6	3,330	88.4
Hispanic	2,166	48.7	245	6.5
Other	33	0.7	23	0.6

Source: Maguire and Pastore, 1996: 492

those admitted to federal prison was a violent crime in about 13 percent of
the cases and a drug offense in just over one fourth of the cases, by 1992 in
almost half of the cases (48.8 percent), the most serious offense was drugs,
compared to a violent crime in less than 8 percent of the cases. In the meantime, the average maximum sentence *declined for violent crimes (from 125 to 88
months) and almost doubled for drug offenses (from 47 to 82 months)* (Beck and
Brien, 1995:59).

More detailed data from U. S. District Courts (i.e. federal system) show
that whereas in 1982 about 20 percent of all convictions were for drugs, by
1994 this had increased to about 36 percent. During this same period, the
proportion of those convicted on drug charges who were sentenced to
prison increased from 74 percent in 1982 to 84 percent in 1994, and their actual sentences increased from an average of 55 months in 1982 to 80 months
in 1994. The average sentences for murder during this period actually *decreased* from 162 to 117 months, while for all violent offenses, the average

TABLE 3.5   *Sentences to Federal Prison, by Offense and Race, 1995.*

Offense	*White*	*Black*	*Hispanic*	*Total*
Total	*100.0%*	*100.0%*	*100.0%*	*100.0%*
Drug Offenses	27.9	47.6	52.8	40.0
Fraud	23.7	13.2	4.9	15.4
Immigration	1.0	2.0	25.4	8.2
Firearms	7.7	9.3	3.0	6.7
Larceny	8.1	8.0	1.9	6.5
Robbery	4.6	6.8	1.2	4.2
Total Violent	6.2	8.3	1.9	6.2

Source: Maguire and Pastore, 1996: 484

TABLE 3.6   *Getting Tough on Crime in the Federal System, 1945–1995.*

Year	% Probation	% To Prison	Avg. Sentence (months)
1945	39.8	47.3	16.5
1955	41.6	50.0	21.9
1965	37.5	47.5	33.5
1975	47.9	46.2	45.5
1985	37.4	48.5	60.2
1995	24.4	69.1	66.4
% change (1945–95)	−15.4	+21.8	+302

Source: Maguire and Pastore, 1996: 477

sentence declined from 133 to 88 months. Incidentally, on any given day, almost 60 percent (58.6 percent) of all federal prisoners are serving time for drug offenses; of these, 40 percent are African American (Maguire and Pastore, 1995: 468, 472, 576).

The trend in getting tougher on drugs is further illustrated by the proportion of sentences relative to arrests. For instance, between 1980 and 1992, the number sentenced to state prisons for murder per 1,000 arrests *decreased* from 621 to 521 (i.e., in 1980, 62.1 percent of those arrested for murder went to prison compared to 52.1 percent in 1992). For drug offenses, the number going to prison per one thousand arrests was only nineteen in 1980, but 104 in 1992 (from 1.9 to 10 percent). In other words, *it has become progressively more serious to have been caught with drugs than to kill someone* (Beck and Brien, 1995: 55).

TABLE 3.7   *Sentences in Federal Courts for Drug Law Violations, 1945–1995.*

Year	% Probation	Prison	Avg. Sentence (months)
1945	24.2	72.7	22.2
1955	18.2	80.8	43.5
1965	27.4	71.6	60.3
1975	39.4	60.0	45.3
1985	23.7	75.1	64.8
1995	9.3	90.1	88.7
% change (1945–95)	−14.9	+17.4	+300

Source: Maguire and Pastore, 1996: 491

One of the most recent sources of data on court cases comes from a U.S. Department of Justice report that examined felony defendants in the largest seventy-five counties in 1994 (Reaves, 1998). We can see the effects of the war on drugs and its impact on the nation's court system; we also can clearly see the effects of race. The most serious charge in just over one third (34.6 percent) of the cases was a drug offense, with nontrafficking drug offenses being the most common (58 percent of all drug charges), followed closely by a property crime (31.1 percent), and with about one fourth (25.7 percent) being violent offenses, mostly assaults (constituting 45 percent of all violent crimes).

Not surprisingly, race figured prominently in these cases. African Americans constituted more than half (56 percent) of all defendants and 62 percent of those charged with drug offenses. Another study noted that almost *all* (99 percent) drug-trafficking defendants between 1985 and 1987 were African Americans (Baum, 1997: 249). In some cities, the proportion of felony defendants who were African American was quite high. For example, African Americans constituted 93 percent of all felony defendants in Wayne County (Detroit), 90 percent in Baltimore, and 85 percent in Cook County (Chicago) and Kings County (Seattle), but only 14 percent in Maricopa County (Phoenix) and 9 percent in Honolulu (Reaves, 1998: 43).

Many of these defendants had prior experiences with the justice system. For example, about one fourth (24 percent) were either on probation or parole, while another 12 percent were on pretrial release status at the time of their most recent arrest. These figures varied by offense, with 39 percent of the drug defendants having an active status within the criminal justice system at the time of their arrest, while 45 percent of those were charged with "public order" offenses. Also, about two thirds (68 percent) had at least one prior arrest, with 23 percent having had ten or more. The most likely persons to have had prior arrests were drug offenders and public order offenders (72 percent). Just over half (56 percent) had at least one prior felony arrest, with about one fifth (22 percent) having had five or more. Moreover, more than half (55 percent) had at least one prior conviction, with 38 percent having prior felony convictions (mostly of a nonviolent nature). Clearly, these defendants were no strangers to the criminal justice system (Reaves, 1998: 8–14).

The majority of these defendants (62 percent) were released pending the final disposition of their case. Of these, the most common form of release was on their own recognizance and through some form of financial release (e.g., surety bond). The median bail amount for those released was $5,000, while the median for those detained was $15,000. Most of the defendants who were released were set free within twenty-four hours (51 percent), with more than three fourths (79 percent) being released within one week (Reaves, 1998: 19). Most (76 percent) of those released made all of their court appearances, with those charged with violent crimes being the *most likely* to make all of their court appearances (85 percent), with drug defendants the *least likely* (71 percent). Of those who were rearrested while on release status, only 15 percent were rearrested for a new offense.

A total of 72 percent of these defendants were ultimately convicted—61 percent on a felony charge and 11 percent on a misdemeanor charge. Not surprisingly, few of those convicted ever went to trial (4 percent of those convicted of a felony and none of those convicted of a misdemeanor). Of those not convicted, most had their cases dismissed. Those *charged with violent offenses were the most likely to have their cases dismissed* (36 percent). Also not surprisingly, more than three fourths (79 percent) of those who were detained were convicted, compared to only 67 percent of those released; 84 percent of the drug defendants who were detained were convicted, compared to 69 percent of the violent offenders (Reaves, 1998: 24).

Looking at those convicted, the largest percentage of convictions were for drug offenses (31 percent), with property crimes ranking second (accounting for 29 percent of the total), and violent crimes ranking third at 16 percent. In terms of sentencing, those convicted of violent crime were the most likely to be sent to prison (76 percent), with public order offenders a close second (71 percent) and drug offenders third (68 percent, with 75 percent of those convicted of trafficking sent to prison). All together, two thirds (67 percent) of those convicted were sentenced to prison. Not surprisingly, violent offenders received the harshest sentences (i.e., a median of 72 months), while the median sentence for drug offenders was 36 months (48 months for traffickers). Unfortunately, no cross-tabulations are provided for race and sentencing in this study, but given data presented in other tables in this chapter, race is obviously an important variable.

One of the explanations for these trends can be found in recently enacted "get tough" sentencing legislation. One example is called *mandatory sentencing*. These types of sentences result from mandates by state legislatures (almost always resulting from local or even national political moods, frequently during election years) that certain kinds of offenders who commit certain types of crimes be sentenced to a term in prison for a set minimum amount of time. In some states there are laws such as "use a gun, go to prison," which gives neither judges nor prosecutors any discretion.

A popular variation of this is known as *habitual offender laws*. These sentencing laws stipulate that after an offender is convicted of so many serious crimes (usually two or three major felony convictions), the individual is sentenced to a very lengthy term in prison, often for life (sometimes without the possibility of parole). Perhaps the most infamous of these laws is *Three Strikes and You're Out*, which began in California in the early 1990s. A product of political posturing and the cynical desire among politicians to get votes by playing on public fears of crime, legislation in

California and elsewhere used the popular baseball phrase to obtain the needed support. Almost instantly, the catchy phrase became part of American popular culture. This would be the ultimate "get tough" stance on crime, showing little regard for the consequences. Originally passed in 1993 in California, the legislation was supposed to impose extremely harsh sentences after a conviction for a third felony (specifically, in California the "third strike" would result in a sentence of 25 years to life). Theoretically, it was supposed to "get tough" on the toughest criminals—mostly repeat, serious, especially violent offenders. It was, unfortunately, based on the erroneous assumption that the criminal justice system was too lenient on criminals (when in fact just the opposite was occurring); it was also based on a few celebrated cases, especially the kidnapping and murder of Polly Klass (Walker, 1994).[5] It has also been described as "politicized crime-control policy" (Benekos and Merlo, 1995).

The consequences of *Three Strikes and You're Out* have been as follows: (1) it has had virtually no impact on crime; (2) instead of locking up serious offenders, the bulk of those sentenced have not fit the stereotype of the superpredator and many have been relatively minor offenders (in California, by March 1999, more had been sentenced for marijuana possession than the combined total for those sentenced for murder, rape, and kidnapping); (3) a very uneven application of the legislation across different jurisdictions; (4) it has resulted in both jail and prison overcrowding, especially in California (not to mention the increase in court costs because of a decline in plea bargaining caused by an increase in cases going to trial); and (5) not surprisingly, a huge discrepancy when it came to race and class, with the impact being felt on those who are poor and/or racial minorities (in California, while African Americans accounted for only 7 percent of the total population, they accounted for 20 percent of all felony arrests, 31 percent of the state's prisoners, and 43 percent of those sentenced for the third strike) (Campaign for an Effective Crime Policy, 1998).[6]

Whether we are talking about early English society or the modern criminal courts, the court system in the United States tends to focus its attention primarily on those from the less-privileged sectors of society. The courts have been dominated by persons drawn primarily from the more privileged sectors of society, especially the highest court, the U.S. Supreme Court. The recent war on drugs has been, in effect, a war on minorities, especially African Americans. This will become especially apparent when the history of the next component of the criminal justice system is examined: the prison system.

Before turning to the prison system, some attention should be paid to the ultimate penalty: capital punishment. Not surprisingly, the most likely recipients of this penalty have been the dangerous classes, especially African Americans.

The Ultimate Sanction for the Dangerous Classes: The Death Penalty

Capital punishment is one of the oldest forms of punishment, dating back several thousands of years. It has had a long and turbulent history in America. It has gone through periods in which most states either abolished it altogether or never used it and periods in which it was commonly used (Sellin, 1967; Bedau, 1964). Two landmark Supreme Court decisions in the 1970s rekindled the controversy surrounding the death penalty: *Furman v. Georgia* (1972) and *Gregg v. Georgia* (1976). After these two decisions were handed down, the use of death-penalty sentences increased dramatically. Between 1977 and 1995, there were 4,857 sentenced to death, with 313 of these were actually executed. (Between 1930 and 1967, there were 3,860 prisoners executed in the United States, more than in any other democratic nation.)

In *Furman v. Georgia*, there were nine separate opinions, one from each justice. Overall, the court ruled that the death penalty *as it was administered* constituted cruel and unusual punishment, in violation of the Eighth and Fourteenth amendments of the Constitution. The court did not rule that the death penalty *in and of itself* constituted cruel and unusual punishment. The response by the states was almost immediate. Appeals began flowing into the court system and within four years of *Furman,* the Supreme Court made perhaps its most significant ruling on the matter.

In the case of *Gregg v. Georgia,* the court upheld the Georgia statute calling for the death penalty for murder. The court ruled: "A punishment must not be excessive, but this does not mean that the states must seek the minimal standards available. The imposition of the death penalty for the crime of murder does not violate the Constitution." In two other decisions, the court ruled similarly (*Proffit v. Florida*, 1976, and *Jurek v. Texas*, 1976). However, in *Coker v. Georgia* (1977), the court ruled that the death penalty for rape constituted cruel and unusual punishment.

After a *de facto* abolition of the death penalty, it was reactivated in 1977 with the execution of Gary Gilmore by a firing squad in Utah (this state is the only one that allows the prisoner a choice between the firing squad and hanging). As of the end of 1995, thirty-eight states and the federal government had the death penalty. As of October 1999, there were about 3,600 under the penalty of death, awaiting their appeals; eighty-three had been executed during the year as of this date.[7] During 1995, fifty-six were executed, with Texas leading the way with nineteen. Three states—California, Texas, and Florida—together accounted for almost 40 percent of those on death row (38.8 percent). Since it resumed executions 1982, Texas leads the nation with more than one hundred executions, far ahead of the state ranked second (i.e., Florida, with thirty-six executions). Virtually all of those on death row today have been convicted of murder (Mays and Winfree, 1998: 80–81). A total of three hundred fifty-eight were executed between 1977 and 1995 (Walker et al., 2000: 232).

Race figures prominently in the imposition of the death penalty. For instance, of the 4,172 prisoners executed between 1930 and 1995, more than half (52 percent) were African Americans. Between 1930 and 1972, a total of four hundred fifty-five were executed for rape, and 89 percent were African Americans. When considering the race of the victims, race once again enters the picture. For instance, 82 percent of the victims of those executed were white, whereas about 50 percent of the victims of *all* homicides were African American. Several studies have noted that there are vast discrepancies in the application of the death penalty according to the race of the victim and the race of the offender. When the victim is white and the offender is African American, the death penalty will be given about 35 percent of the time, compared to only 14 percent when the relationship is reversed (i.e., African American victim and white offender). The death penalty will be given in 22 percent of the cases when whites kill whites and in only 6 percent of the cases when African Americans kill African Americans (Baldus et al., 1990; cited in Walker et al., 2000: 242). The study by Baldus also found that the race of the victim played a key role in the prosecutor's decision to seek the death penalty and a jury's decision to impose it. Even after controlling for an astounding two hundred variables, Baldus still found race to be the most significant variable. Other recent studies have arrived at identical results. These studies, by the way, examined data from several different states (Gross and Mauro, 1989; Radelet, 1981; Amsterdam, 1988).

It is not as if these findings are new. Almost forty years ago, Wolfgang, Kelly, and Nolde (1962) studied four hundred thirty-nine cases of men sentenced to death in Pennsylvania for murder between 1914 and 1958. They found that 20 percent of the whites had their sentences commuted to life imprisonment, whereas only 11 percent of the blacks did, a statistically significant relationship. In an even earlier study, Johnson (1941) examined homicide cases in Richmond, Virginia, and in five counties in North Carolina during the 1930s. He found that the death penalty was most often applied when the victim was white and the offender was black, and least likely when both the offender and the victim were black (see also Garfinkel, 1949).

Studies of rape have also found a strong relationship between the race of the victim and the imposition of the death penalty. Johnson, in a study of rape cases resulting in the imposition of the death penalty in North Carolina between 1909 and 1954, found that blacks were more likely than whites to be executed (Johnson, 1941). A study of Florida cases found that blacks who raped whites were much more likely to receive death than if the situation were reversed (cited in Wolfgang and Reidel, 1975: 369). Wolfgang and Reidel also studied three thousand rape convictions in eleven southern states between 1945 and 1965. The found: "Among 1,265 cases in which the race of the defendant and the sentence are known, nearly seven times as many blacks were sentenced to death as whites" (Wolfgang and Reidel, 1975: 371–372). They also found that 36 percent of the blacks who raped whites were sentenced to death, while all other racial combinations resulted in only 2 percent being sentenced to death. These relationships held true even when they held constant such other factors as prior record and contemporaneous offenses (e.g., murder while committing robbery) (see also Bowers, 1974).

Many of these studies gained some prominence in one of the most significant Supreme Court cases concerning the death penalty, that of *McCleskey v. Kemp* in 1987. It was here that research concerning the race of the victim was cited. Not surprisingly, the case originated in Georgia, just as did *Furman* and *Gregg*. The defendant was Warren McCleskey, an African American who was convicted of killing a white police officer. Part of the defense strategy was to use the study by Balbus. Despite the overwhelming evidence in support of the importance of the race of the victim, the Supreme court rejected the appeal. While accepting the validity of the Balbus study, the Court nevertheless ruled that—regardless of statistical correlations—in the case of McCleskey, there was no evidence that *"any of the decision-makers in McCleskey's case acted with discriminatory purpose"* (quoted in Walker et al., 2000: 248, emphasis added). The court also suggested that, *at best,* all that could be shown was a "discrepancy that appears to correlate with race."

What is perhaps most interesting about this ruling is that the court appeared to be afraid of what the logical conclusions of such evidence might be. Justice Powell, writing for the majority, noted that such evidence "throws into serious question the principles that underlie our entire criminal justice system. . . . If we accepted McCleskey's claim that racial bias impermissibly tainted the capital sentencing decision, we would soon be faced with similar claims as to other types of penalty." Not surprisingly, the ruling came in for immediate attacks, including four dissenting justices (i.e., Blackmun, Marshall, Brenan, and Stevens). Heaven forbid, they suggested, that others may challenge such obvious biases, "even women" (wrote one justice). One scholar noted sarcastically that concluding that "at most" there appears to be a "discrepancy" is like saying that "at most" the many studies on lung cancer "indicate a discrepancy that appears to correlate with smoking" (Kennedy, 1997: 336). Most of the critics voiced the opinion that this ruling sent a message that racial bias is perfectly constitutional. McCleskey was eventually executed in the electric chair on September 26, 1991. The famous Justice Thurgood Marshall, who joined two other justices in a dissent for a stay of execution, stated that it appears that "the court values expediency over human life. . . ." (Walker et al., 2000: 252).

Cole has argued that it would be nearly impossible to prove that a prosecutor and a jury have imposed the death penalty in a particular case because of the defendant's race. He notes that there are long-standing rules that prohibit defendants from obtaining discovery from the prosecution and, therefore, "unless the prosecutor admits to acting for racially biased reasons, it will be difficult to pin discrimination on the prosecutor"; similarly in the case of jurors. In short, says Cole, "defendants are precluded from discovering evidence of intent from the two actors whose discriminatory intent the *McCleskey* court required them to establish" (Cole, 1999: 135).

Subsequent cases on this issue had almost identical results. In one such case, that of *Dobbs v. Zant* (a 1989 case in Georgia), the court rejected the appeal even though several jurors referred to African Americans as "coloreds" and two admitted using "nigger" in their conversations. Even the defense attorney (a court-appointed attorney) admitted using "nigger" and believed that African Americans make good basketball players but not teachers (Cole, 1999: 135).

In other words, the Supreme Court concluded that "discrimination is inevitable," a "natural byproduct of discretion" and, hence, "constitutionally acceptable" (Cole, 1999: 137). The highest court in the country, which espouses "equal justice for all," tells us in effect that racial bias is supported by the U.S. Constitution. Some members of Congress responded to the *McCleskey* decision by adding a "Racial Justice Act" to the Omnibus Crime Bill of 1994. By a slim majority, the House voted for this provision, which would have allowed those on death row to challenge their sentence based on statistical evidence of race discrimination in capital cases, as had McCleskey. But it was defeated in the Senate and dropped from the 1994 bill. Senator Orin Hatch (R-Utah) remarked, quite candidly, that this "so-called Racial Justice Act has nothing to do with racial justice and everything to do with abolishing the death penalty. . . . It would convert every death-penalty case into a massive sideshow of statistical squabbles and quota quarrels" (quoted in Kennedy, 1997: 346). What more can be said, given this kind of worst-case–scenario logic!

One issue that is often overlooked (but fortunately not forgotten by critics of the death penalty) is that of those wrongly convicted. One detailed study found evidence of some four hundred defendants sentenced to death who turned out to be innocent, with an estimated two dozen who were actually executed—and many more spent years in prison. Not surprisingly, a disproportionate number have been African Americans (Radelet, Bedau, and Putnam, 1992).

Meanwhile, the use of the death penalty has increased, as appeals have declined and the process from conviction to execution has been stepped up. More are being executed every day. A few states, such as Texas, have turned this into a "sideshow" (to use Hatch's terminology), with crowds of people outside applauding as soon as the defendant is executed. African Americans and other minorities continue to receive the death penalty in numbers far greater than their proportion in the general population. Almost without exception, the executed are drawn from the ranks of the dangerous classes. Indeed, the death penalty is the ultimate penalty for this class.

Notes

1. The observations of a Detroit courtroom were made in February 1999 by my good friend and colleague, William B. Brown, Professor of Sociology at the University of Michigan-Flint. He provided most of the material used in the introduction to this chapter. The author gratefully acknowledges his assistance.

2. See the classic study by Josephson called *The Robber Barons* (1962). He lays bare the greed and corruption, and often criminal behavior, of the richest men in America: Rockefeller, Vanderbilt, Carnegie, Mellon, Harriman, Gould, Frick, Morgan, and a host of others. Ironically, only one other period of American history has seen such concentration of wealth in such a small number of hands—the last two decades of the twentieth century and the beginning of the twenty-first century, the period we are in as these words are written!

3. The connection between time spent in jail (and whether a defendant is detained in the first place) and final disposition has been documented by numerous studies. Among the most important of these studies are Bynum, 1982; Clarke and Koch, 1976; Foote, 1954; Ares, Rankin, and Sturz, 1963; Farrell and Swigert, 1978; Patterson and Lynch, 1991.

4. A 1992 study found that, nationwide, about 80 percent of felony defendants in the seventy largest counties were indigent (Cole, 1999: 66).

5. Ironically, the father of Polly Klass, Marc Klass, has publicly criticized this type of legislation. He has formed the nonprofit KlassKids Foundation, which, among other goals, seeks means of prevention rather than merely harsh reaction. He wrote the foreword to Peter Elikann's critique of the current "demonization" of children as "superpredators" (Elikann, 1999).

6. Space does not permit a detailed coverage of the "three-strikes" law, but the reader is encouraged to read the report by the Campaign for an Effective Crime Policy (cited in the text) plus the text by Shichor and Sechrest (1996).

7. This is according to an Associated Press story dated October 30, 1999. This story also indicated that the Supreme Court was to hear arguments concerning four death penalty cases, including one claiming that death by the electric chair constitutes cruel and unusual punishment, in violation of the eighth Amendment. The eighty-three who had been executed as of this date marked the highest ever for one year since 1954.

4

Housing the Dangerous Classes

The Emergence and Growth of the Prison System

Despite popular beliefs, imprisonment has little to do with actual levels of crime. Rather, imprisonment is one among many forms that have developed over the years to contain and house those individuals who are part of the dangerous classes. The basic argument in this chapter is that the development of the prison as a place of punishment corresponds not to crime but to much larger structural changes in the surrounding society and the specific social and historical context. In this case, the emergence and growth of the prison system corresponded to the emergence and growth of capitalism as a dominant economic form. Given that, as Marx predicted, capitalism continually produces a "relative surplus population" or "reserve army of unemployed." Certain mechanisms have been needed to somehow contain or manage this group, especially the lowest stratum, which Marx called the *lumpenpropetariat*. In the introduction, this "relative surplus population" was defined as a more or less chronically unemployed segment of the population that has become redundant or superfluous, as far as producing profits is concerned. Prisons and other forms of total institutions have been among the major mechanisms for such containment.

PART I: EARLY DEVELOPMENTS OF IMPRISONMENT, 1600–1900

In their book *Punishment and Social Structure*, Rusche and Kirchheimer state their basic thesis on the relationship between the economic base of a society (or the mode of production) and the dominant form of punishment:

> ... the mere statement that specific forms of punishment correspond to a given stage of economic development is a truism. It is self-evident that enslavement as a form of punishment is impossible without a slave economy, that prison labor is impossible without manufacture or industry, that monetary fines for all classes of society are impossible without a money economy. On the other hand, the disappearance of a given system of production makes its corresponding punishment inapplicable. Only a specific development of the productive forces permits the introduction or rejection of corresponding penalties. But before these potential methods can be introduced, society must be in position to incorporate them as integrated parts of the whole social and economic system. (Rusche and Kirchheimer, 1968: 6)

They note that in the history of punishment, several epochs can be distinguished during which different penal systems and modes of punishment were predominant. Thus, during the early Middle Ages, penance and fines were dominant; during the later Middle Ages, a harsh system of corporal and capital punishment prevailed; during the late eighteenth and early nineteenth centuries, imprisonment became the dominant form (Rusche and Kirchheimer, 1968: 6–8).

The major concern in this chapter is to examine the reasons why imprisonment became a dominant mode of punishment during the late eighteenth and early nineteenth centuries. Specifically, this chapter explains why the prison emerged as a dominant *place* for punishment. Prior to this period, punishment was harsh and *public*, often taking the form of a *spectacle*, with public whippings, hangings, and hard labor in city streets (Foucault, 1979: 9). Along with the prison system there emerged a new form of penal *discipline*. Rather than merely physical *punishment* imposed upon the *body*, we find a form of *discipline* aimed at the *mind*. This took such forms as daily rituals and routines, the inculcation of various attitudes and values (e.g., "habits of industry" and the "Protestant ethic"), hard labor, and the use of solitary confinement. This form of discipline arose simultaneously with the emergence of almost identical forms of discipline in the newly emerging factory system; both arose along with the emergence of a capitalist mode of production. The evidence suggests that the prison system and the new forms of discipline imposed on prisoners served the major function of providing a pliant and stable workforce, in addition to controlling in some way those segments of the population that do not or cannot fit into the prevailing social order (Melossi, 1978).

Early Capitalism and the Emergence of the Workhouse

To understand the rise of the modern prison system, we need to consider some of the earlier forms of imprisonment; namely, *workhouses* or *houses of correction*. These institutions emerged in the late fifteenth century and throughout the sixteenth century, during which time were the beginnings of what Marx called the "expropriation of the agricultural population from the land." It was the beginning of the transformation of a feudal society to a capitalist society. It was also a part of history written in blood and fire, "for it was literally the case that small farmers and peasants were often killed and had their homes or huts burned" (Marx, 1977: 375). It was also the beginning of the famous "enclosure movements" (in 1489), a form of robbery against the poor by landlords, which lasted well into the nineteenth century in England and Scotland as formerly common land was transformed into private property (Chambliss and Ryther, 1975: 186–187).

This process turned a mass of propertyless and powerless peasants into a mass of wage-laborers (or *proletarians*) who were forced to emigrate to the cities and towns in search of work. However, there were more people than occupations and jobs available (a condition that has remained throughout the history of capitalism). This created a problem in "social control" in terms of how to control the newly created surplus population. Marx stated the problem as follows:

The proletariat created by the breaking up of the bands of feudal retainers and by the forcible expropriation of the people from the soil, this free and rightless proletariat could not possibly be absorbed by the nascent manufactures as fast as it was thrown upon the world. On the other hand, these men, suddenly dragged from their accustomed mode of life, could not immediately adapt themselves to the discipline of their new condition. They were turned in massive quantities into beggars, robbers, and vagabonds, partly from inclination, in most cases under the force of circumstances. Hence, at the end of the fifteenth and during the whole of the sixteenth centuries, a bloody legislation against vagabondage was enforced throughout Western Europe. The fathers of the present working class were chastised for their enforced transformation into vagabonds and paupers. Legislation treated them as "voluntary" criminals, and assumed that it was entirely within their powers to go on working under the old conditions, which in fact no longer existed. (Marx, 1977: 896)

In other words, the new class of paupers, vagabonds, beggars, and vagrants was created by and in turn "criminalized" by the state and sentenced to a term of confinement at hard labor in the houses of correction. These houses of correction were among the first in a long line of institutions (including modern forms of welfare) established for the control and regulation of this "surplus population" created by capitalism (Quinney, 1980: 131–140).

The first *house of correction* was known as the *Rasphaus,* which opened in 1596 in Amsterdam (Sellin, 1944, 1976; Shank, 1978). In this and similar institutions that sprang up throughout Europe and later in America, the shift toward punishment of the *mind* began in the form of the inculcation of "habits of industry." The intention of the Rasphaus "was to discipline the inmates into accepting a regimen analogous to an 'ideal factory,' in which the norms required for capitalist accumulation were ingrained in the code of discipline" (Shank, 1978: 40). Furthermore, the organization of these workhouses "anticipated the compulsive regimens of isolation and hard labor to be pursued far more thoroughly in the penitentiary" (Ignatieff, 1978: 13–14). These workhouses, which were often appropriately called "poorhouses," were more fully developed in the late eighteenth and early nineteenth centuries in the shape of a gigantic "workhouse for the industrial worker himself," known as the "factory" (Marx, 1977: 388–389). (As will be noted later, many have suggested that the factory was at least partly modeled after the penitentiary.) When released from these workhouses, the inmates would theoretically willingly adapt to the regimentation of the factory and other forms of labor under the new capitalist system (Rusche and Kirchheimer, 1968: 42).

Most forms of punishment during the seventeenth and eighteenth centuries were harsh and public, as suggested earlier. Corporal and capital punishments were the norm, even for minor offenses. During the eighteenth century, however, the harshness of the punishments began to produce inconsistent results. Instead of acting as a deterrent and promoting respect for the law and for the ruling class, public punishments often turned into public demonstrations. For instance, the English judicial system even went so far as to engage in processionals as condemned men were transported through the streets toward the gallows at Tyburn outside of London. The ritual of such hangings "was taken over by the crowd and converted into a thieves' holiday and poor people's carnival." These hangings were constantly "attended with disruptions, threatened rescues, disorders, brawls, and riot." Such disturbances became almost weekly occurrences and, by the end of the eighteenth century, were reminding the rich of the Gordon Riots, which was "an alarming sign of a new cleavage between elite and the poor." It wasn't too long before hangings were conducted within prison walls, out of sight of the public (Ignatieff, 1978: 88–89; Linebaugh, 1975: 67; Linebaugh, 1992).

In other words, the existing methods of justice were often irrational and inconsistent, and often producing results quite the opposite of those intended. This gave rise to a series of "reforms" (ostensibly "humanitarian") toward the end of the eighteenth century, which culminated in the birth of a new system of punishment—the modern prison.

Late Eighteenth Century Reforms and the Birth of the Prison System

Crime and punishment during the eighteenth century in England was characterized by corruption, inefficiency, discretion, and local control (especially by local justices of the peace). As capitalism grew, so did the power of the capitalists, at the same time, so did the conflicts with those groups trying to resist the new forms of production and the newly emerging ruling power— the bourgeoisie.

A constant complaint of reformers centered around the inefficiency and corruption of local jails and workhouses. The management of these institutions was solely in the hands of local jailers and justices of the peace. There was wide variation in the kind of discipline used and unequal treatment of the rich and the poor; many criminal justice workers were paid fees and thus open to constant bribery. Moreover, there was an inmate subculture that exerted a great deal of control over what took place within these institutions. Those in control, however, looked the other way and as long as they reaped profits (e.g., payments for preferential treatment), these abuses were ignored. Another problem was overcrowding, which became so bad that there was much rebuilding and enlargement of facilities between 1766 and 1776 (Ignatieff, 1978: 35–43).

One attempt to relieve the overcrowding was the introduction of convict "hulks," whereby convicted offenders were sentenced to serve a period aboard ships, a form of *galley slavery*. Many convicted offenders had their sentences commuted and were placed aboard ships and even transported to newly conquered colonies, where there was a need for abundant cheap labor (Rusche and Kirchheimer, 1968: 57; Barnes and Teeters, 1959: 295–305; Barnes, 1972: 61–92; Ives, 1914; Shaw, 1966; Ekirch, 1987).

Several notable reformers, such as Cesare Beccaria, Jeremy Bentham, and John Howard, became famous for their critique of the arbitrariness, excesses, and inefficiency of the criminal justice system. These and other reformers represented two major currents of thinking within the penal reform movement. One current advocated reform of the law along rational lines; that is, they wanted the laws to be explicit and the punishments proportionate of the offense and applicable to all, regardless of the circumstances. This was the essential argument of the "Classical School of Criminology," especially Beccaria, who argued that the "punishment should fit the crime." Similarly, Bentham argued that punishment should be consistent and physical punishment should not differ according to the emotions of the punisher. For the punishment of whipping, for instance, he recommended a "whipping machine," whereby each whip would be like all the others. In other words, punishment should become a "science" (Ignatieff, 1978: 75).

Another strand of thought advocated the implementation of new modes of *penal discipline* that would more efficiently inculcate habits of industry and help maintain social order. This corresponded to new thinking about crime and criminals. Bentham, for instance, said criminals were like children and "persons of unsound mind," who lacked self-discipline. They had "infantile desires" that "drove them to ignore the long-term cost of short-term gratifications" (Ignatieff, 1978: 66–67). It was Bentham who designed the famous *panopticon* style of prison, which also became useful to those who would later design the factory, since it involved a central administration area that allowed complete surveillance of inmates at all times. Social control was complete within such a system, like similar social-control systems in the factory. Also, the regimentation within these early prisons predated almost identical regimentation in many factories. As Rothman notes, both the early prisons and the factories "emphasized regularity and punctuality" and by "instilling order in its inmates, the prison was in effect helping to guarantee discipline and regularity in those who arrived each morning at the factory gate" (Rothman, 1998: 111) (this also applied to the routine in the reformatory, discussed later in this chapter).

Along similar lines are the views of John Howard, who was perhaps the most well-known and well-traveled prison reformer. Howard was heavily influenced by Quaker asceticism, which stressed silent prayers, suffering, and self-discipline. This led him to advocate a strong disciplinary regime within the prison system. He also believed that criminals were sinful and "lost souls estranged from God." Much of his thinking was derived from a branch of knowledge known as *materialist psychology*. According to this view, what was needed was a strict regime of routinization and repetition, which would result in the internalization of "moral duties." The best place for this kind of "reformation" was within a "total institution" (Goffman, 1961). Some have even called Howard the "father of solitary confinement," who even advocated this form of punishment for his own son (Ignatieff, 1978: 49–67; McGowen, 1999). Howard's ideal of a prison was that of a "structurally secure, spacious, and sanitary" institution that would "embody a reformatory regime of diet, work, and religious exercises" and "subject to a formal code of rules and systematic inspection" (Hogg, 1979: 10).

Reformers wanted a system of punishment that would be perceived as legitimate (for there was a crisis in legitimacy at this time); to do so, the reformers needed to reconcile the apparent opposites of deterrence and rehabilitation, punishment and reform—just as factory owners had to reconcile the apparent conflict between profit and benevolence. The answer lay in the establishment of strict rules that would remove discretion of those in authority. Thus, both guards and inmates were to be routinized by an explicit system of rules. To do away with the inmate subculture, they would institute the famous "silent system." Constant surveillance of the inmates by guards, and of guards by special inspectors, and of the entire operation by the general public was also advocated (Ignatieff, 1978: 76–78).

Some prison reformers, including Howard, were influenced by hospital reformers of the period. The hospital reformers wanted to habituate the poor to cleanliness, because the sicknesses of this class of people "were interpreted as the outward sign of their inward want of discipline, morality, and honor." Physical diseases were correlated with moral problems and the poor, it was believed, needed to be taught to be clean and to be "godly, tractable, and self-disciplined." "Once the bodies of the poor were subjected to regulation, their minds would acquire a taste for order" (Ignatieff, 1978: 60–61).

It is hardly a coincidence that similar behavior was required of factory workers. Among the men who actively supported Howard's reforms were leading scientists, academics, and manufacturers. Ignatieff says that the manufacturers were:

> . . . best known as the fathers of the factory system and scientific management. Besides introducing mechanization, extended division of labor, and systematic routing of the work process, they also devised the new disciplines of industrial labor: punch clocks, bells, rules, and fines. In order to reduce turnover and stabilize the labor force in their early factories, they provided schools, chapels, and homes for their workers in model villages. Regimentation along these lines would uplift the morals of the workers and eliminate their vices, according to the reformers. If this type of regimentation did not produce the desired results, there was always the workhouse and the prison. (Ignatieff, 1978: 62)

Howard and other reformers believed that crime was a product of unregulated, undisciplined, and immoral lives and the required corrective was a strict regime of routinization and regulation, including the "repentance" of one's sins (hence, the name "penitentiary"). Foucault describes the new form of punishment, which he called a "gentle" form of punishment, as follows:

> As for the instruments, these are no longer complexes of representation, rein-forced and circulated, but forms of coercion, schemata of constraint, applied and repeated. Exercises, not signs: sign-tables, compulsory movements, regu-lar activities, solitary meditation, work in common, silence, application, re-spect, good habits. And, ultimately, what one is trying to restore in this technique of correction is . . . the obedient subject, the individual subjected to habits, rules, orders, an authority that is exercised continually around him and upon him, and which he must allow to function automatically in him. (Fou-cault, 1979: 128–129)

The prison became one among many controlling institutions "de-signed to shape an emerging industrial proletariat." It was obvious that nei-ther the control of crime nor humanitarianism was the major factor in prison developments; rather, "discipline and surveillance were the objectives of the new institutional web" (Weiss, 1987a: 338–339).

One of the most important guiding principles of prison reform was the *principle of less eligibility.* Simply put, less eligibility means that the condi-tions (or the standard of living) within the prison (or those dependent on welfare on the outside) should never be better than those of the lowest stra-tum of the working population. This would, theoretically, act as a deterrent to crime (or poverty) because people would choose to work under the pre-vailing conditions of "free labor" rather than commit crime and go to prison. In other words, people would freely choose to sell their labor power on the open market rather than seek alternative methods of subsistence and face a possible prison sentence. This principle still operates today, *even though the theory behind it has never been proved correct* (Rusche and Kirchheimer, 1968: 94; Melossi, 1978: 75; Hogg, 1979: 11).

The result of reform efforts during the last half of the eighteenth cen-tury was the passage of the Penitentiary Act of 1779 in England. This act cre-ated "hard labor houses" that would avoid the inefficiency and corruption of the old houses of correction. But the ideal workforce free from corruption and willing to accept a regime as regulated as those of the inmates could not be found. Prisoners usually refused to work as diligently as superintendents wanted them to, and guards would slack off and even accept bribes. Over-crowding, a problem common today, was also a problem then (Ignatieff, 1978: 106).

The Penitentiary Act failed to deter crime and eliminate corruption. English society continued to experience crises, which grew worse during the 1790s and the first two decades of the nineteenth century. It was during this time that the first *national* penitentiary opened at Millbank in 1813. But even the opening of this prison did not solve the problem. The regimes of hard labor, solitary confinement, and meager diets (all recommended by Howard and other "humanitarian" reformers) resulted in prisoner revolts, many of which were widely supported by those in the free society. One result was the return of whipping and other forms of physical oppression. One of the most interesting innovations in punishment during the 1820s was the *treadwheel*. The prisoners, holding onto bars, moved their feet in a walking motion in order to make the treadwheel go. The famous *silent system*, in which prisoners were prohibited from talking to one another, was also introduced at this time. Meanwhile, crime and prisoner rebellions increased.

As more *formal* systems of control replaced informal systems of control (especially with the formation of the London Metropolitan Police in 1829), sentences to prisons and jails increased dramatically. For instance, when a new prison opened at Pentonville in 1842, the rate of imprisonment was three hundred twenty-six per 100,000 population, an almost twofold increase from the rate of one hundred seventy in 1824. Among the new methods of control introduced in Pentonville were the removal of such privileges as communication with friends and family, an increase in the number of guards, and transportation to Australia following release, which almost amounted to a life sentence, even for minor crimes (Ignatieff, 1978: 179, 200).

The imposition of a new regime of penal discipline in England was part of a much larger movement to increase the hegemony of the new bourgeois society. Dominant middle-class values such as hard work, respect for law and property, thrift, and obedience were held up as analogous to a religion (in a sense it was a religion, influenced as it was by the Quakers and other religious groups). The image of the prison served to confirm the dominant values implicit in their hegemony and the devotion of "respectable," "law-abiding" citizens to such values. Perhaps more importantly, the newly emerging penal system should be viewed as part of a much larger network of institutions (e.g., family, education, religion) that would act to reproduce capitalist social order. Neither the control of crime nor altruism was the motivating force; rather, the motivation was discipline and surveillance (Staples, 1997). While some reformers were motivated by genuine concern over the poor and the downtrodden (as have so many over the years), the net result has always been the same: social (especially class) control.[1]

Crime was viewed as a moral problem and, like poverty, was a simple choice. Hogg sums up the goal of the prison system and penal discipline in early English society as follows:

> The sanctity of property and middle-class standards of propriety had little relevance to communities whose very economic survival and conditions of life involved their transgressions in myriad of everyday, and mostly petty, ways. The desire to moralize, discipline, and reform the habits of these classes was the prime motivation for penal and other reforms in the second half of the century, as it had been in the period before. (Hogg, 1979: 14–15)

Developments in America followed more or less along the same lines. The emphasis was on discipline of the laboring and dangerous classes, and the inculcation of those habits that were to be the very essence of "capitalist work management" (Melossi, 1978: 75).

The Development of the American Prison System

The Walnut Street Jail

The use of imprisonment as a mode of punishment did not occur until the late eighteenth century in America. A penal reform movement actually can be traced back as far as the efforts of William Penn in 1682. Penn was in the forefront of a movement to abolish the death penalty for many crimes and to introduce a new method of punishment modeled after the Dutch workhouse, which seemed to correspond closely to the Quaker thinking of the time (Melossi and Lettiere, 1998: 21).

Throughout colonial America, the most common form of punishment was a combination of banishment and various forms of public punishments, such as the stocks, the pillory, and branding (e.g., branding the letter "T" on a thief's forehead). The use of workhouses as a place of confinement was usually a last resort (Rothman, 1971, Chapter 2; Powers, 1966). The primary method of social control in such a society was rather informal, with local families, the community, and the church providing most forms of punishment. Toward the middle of the eighteenth century, imprisonment in jails and workhouses came to be reserved more for the poor. Many workhouses came to be called *poorhouses.* In Pennsylvania in 1766, the government established a house of employment reserved for those classified as "rogues, vagabonds, and other idle and dissolute persons" (Takagi, 1975: 20).

Shortly after the end of the American Revolution, a group of prominent citizens, including Benjamin Franklin, Benjamin Rush, William Bradford, and Caleb Lownes, came together to update the criminal code of 1718. The new law, passed in 1786, authorized a penalty of "hard labor, publicly and disgracefully imposed" (Takagi, 1975: 20; see also Barnes, 1972: 81). Prisoners were to be sentenced to perform hard labor in the city streets. However, as in England during the processionals of condemned men, convicts began to draw crowds of sympathetic people. Shortly thereafter, a group calling themselves the Philadelphia Society for Alleviating the Miseries of Public Prisons amended the law and in 1788 suggested that sentences be more private, and even called for *solitary confinement* within the confines of the Walnut Street Jail. The reason for this was that the new bourgeois class, having just gained power as the dominant class, wanted to promote stability and social order, in addition to respect for the law and for the new government. Placing prisoners on city streets did not result in such respect; placing them indoors would "export out of public view the sufferings and degradations heaped upon the poor" (Takagi, 1975: 23).

The Walnut Street Jail became the first state prison in America, and it was part of a much larger effort to create a powerful and centralized state apparatus. This state apparatus not only helped secure the new order, but it also helped perpetuate the existing class divisions. Takagi states that "the success of the Revolution at home was brought about by the creation of a class-divided society based on private property and the ratification of the new Constitution was to guarantee the privileges and power of the bourgeoisie" (Takagi, 1975: 22–23). In fact, James Madison made it quite clear when he wrote in *The Federalist Papers* that "The diversity in the faculties of men, from which the rights of property flow, is not less an insuperable obstacle to a uniformity of interests. The protection of these faculties is the first object of government." Continuing, Madison argues that one of the duties of a government or state is to regulate various interests, including "a landed interest, a manufacturing interest, a mercantile interest, a moneyed interest, with many lesser interests. . . ." (Madison, 1961: 78–79).

There were, indeed, class divisions at the end of the eighteenth century. And there was a great deal of disorder, stemming mainly from economic crises and general uncertainty over the future of American society. Shay's Rebellion was just one among several popular revolts of the time against the existing form of government and economy (Zinn, 1995: 90–96). It was also the early beginnings of the newly emerging ruling class of business people who would eventually become the "tools and tyrants" of the government, "overwhelming it with their force and benefiting from its gifts." It was a system characterized by the replacement of the old feudalistic monarchy of England (which the American Revolution fought against) by the rule of a small business elite. It was becoming obvious at that time that some of the original supporters of the American Revolution (e.g., Thomas Jefferson) became alarmed at what was occurring. It was, in short, becoming less like a democracy (which the ruling class feared) and more like a ruling oligarchy with the "new spirit of the age: gain wealth, forgetting all but self" (Chomsky, 1996a: 123–125, 154).

Prominent Americans, including those belonging to the Philadelphia Society for Alleviating the Miseries of Public Prisons, were concerned about maintaining social order. As Rothman writes: "What in their day was to prevent society from bursting apart? From where would the elements of cohesion come?" The major worry, as Rothman suggests, was whether the poor would "corrupt society" and criminals would "roam out of control." Thus, continues Rothman, comprehension and control of deviance "promised to be the first step in establishing a new system for stabilizing the community, for binding citizens together. . . . And here one also finds the crucial elements that led to the discovery of the asylum." In the end, the prison system became one among several methods of reforming and controlling the dangerous classes (Rothman, 1971: 58–59).[2]

While imprisonment slowly became a dominant method of punishing offenders, there also began to be some changes in the methods of "penal discipline." Specifically, there was for a time two contrasting methods, which came to be known as the Pennsylvania and Auburn systems.

The Pennsylvania and Auburn Systems of Penal Discipline

Many reformers of the period believed that criminals lacked respect for authority and proper work habits, which could only be accomplished through a system of penal discipline emphasizing hard labor. Other reformers believed that the criminal was a "sinner" and needed to "repent" for his crimes. The idea of "penance" is said to have originated in the medieval monasteries of Europe for monks who had sinned or committed crimes (Mellosi and Lettiere, 1998: 22). This could only be accomplished through the use of solitary confinement and no contact with other prisoners or the outside world. These two views (although having more similarities than differences) came to be known, respectively, as the Pennsylvania and Auburn systems of penal discipline and prison construction.

The *Pennsylvania system* was modeled after some of the beliefs of John Howard. Two prisons were constructed during the early nineteenth century in the state of Pennsylvania. The first was opened in 1826 in Pittsburgh (known as the Western Penitentiary); the other was opened in 1829 in Cherry Hill, near Philadelphia (known as the Eastern Penitentiary). The architecture of these prisons (especially the one at Cherry Hill) reflected the basic plan for solitary confinement. The cells were arranged like spokes on a wheel, all radiating from a common central area. Each cell had an outside exercise yard. Each prisoner was allowed short periods in this yard for daily exercise, but most of the time was spent inside the cell working at some menial task. Each prisoner was blindfolded as he entered the prison to begin his sentence and was prohibited from contact with other prisoners. Only approved visitors from the outside were allowed to visit the prisoner (Barnes and Teeters, 1959: 338–339).

The *Auburn system*, which emphasized work in association with other prisoners, began in New York and was supported by some of the most prominent citizens of the state, including Thomas Eddy (noted financier and philanthropist), political leader and one-time governor De Witt Clinton, and governor and jurist John Jay. The first prison modeled after this plan was called the *Newgate Prison,* which opened in New York in 1797. In 1821, the second prison was opened in Auburn (Barnes, 1972: 132).

The Pennsylvania model soon came into disfavor because so many prisoners died or became insane, and there was a significant rise in the number of suicides as well. In the Auburn system, prison administrators developed what has become known as the *congregate system* and the *silent system*. Prisoners worked together during the day but were not allowed to speak to one another and they were kept in solitary confinement at night. This system became the dominant one and was followed by hundreds of prisons throughout the nation during the nineteenth century.

While ostensibly calling themselves and their new system at Auburn "humanitarian," supporters of the system were as cruel as those who had come before them, and the system they created was almost as repressive as those that existed in previous years. Elan Lynds, the first warden at Auburn, introduced the famous "lock-step" (prisoners would march single file while shuffling their feet and keeping their eyes right) and was a strong advocate of the use of whipping, including the use of the "cat-o-nine-tails." Lewis Wright, head of the Prison Discipline Society of Boston, was a firm believer in the Auburn system and published several tracts in support of it. In one he wrote as follows about the Auburn prison:

> The whole establishment, from the gate to the sewer, is a specimen of neatness. The unremitted industry, the entire subordination and subdued feeling of the convicts, has probably no parallel among an equal number of criminals. In their solitary cells they spend the night with no other book but the Bible, and at sunrise they proceed, in military order, under the eye of the turnkeys, in solid columns, with the lock march, to their workshops: thence, in the same order, at the hour of breakfast, to the common hall, where they partake of their wholesome and frugal meal in silence. . . . When they have done eating, at the ringing of a little bell, of the softest sound, they rise from the table. . . . From one end of the shops to the other, it is the testimony of many witnesses, that they have passed more than three hundred convicts, without seeing one leave his work, or turn his head to gaze at them. There is the most perfect attention to business from morning till night, interrupted only by the time necessary to dine, and never by the fact that the whole body of prisoners have done their tasks, and the time is now their own, and they can do as they please. . . . (Barnes, 1972: 136–137)

The famous Frenchmen Gustave de Beaumont and Alexis de Tocqueville, who toured American prisons during the first half of the nineteenth century, noted that while the Pennsylvania system produces "more honest men," the New York system (i.e., Auburn) produces "more obedient citizens" (de Beaumont and de Tocqueville, 1964). They also could have added that the Auburn system attempted to produce an ideal worker for the factory system, a worker who was obedient, passive, silent, and who would not complain about the grueling work conditions.

In time, the Auburn system became the most dominant not simply because it was more profitable, but also that it fit within the larger structure of capitalism, characterized as it was by the need for cheap labor. Early prison factories resembled factories on the outside and, for a time, prisoners produced goods that were sold in the free market on the outside. While this may have been an important factor, it was certainly not the only factor. Perhaps even more important was the fact that as a mode of penal discipline, the Auburn system was ideally suited for an emerging capitalist society in that it attempted to inculcate habits of hard work, punctuality, and other routines that would fit into the regime of the factory system.

The penitentiary also fit into the overall pattern of *republicanism*, the view that society can be held together only through a "free market," promoted by an active state. Consistent with this belief system was the need for individuals to become "self-governing." Benjamin Rush had suggested the penitentiary might become a sort of gateway to the new republic by producing "Republican machines"—that is, human beings who were uncivilized or had "lost their civilization" and who would be transformed "into good workers and citizens." To accomplish this task, the very souls of these men "had to be conquered" so that they could "enter into a conversation with the other members of the American covenant." (Melossi and Lettiere, 1998: 25)

One consequence of such a plan was "the extermination of those whose souls (if they indeed had been endowed with one) could not be reached, such as the native inhabitants of North America"; in other words, those who were unable or unwilling to accept the new order. de Tocqueville, in his classic work, *Democracy in America*, had noted that while the Native American was much too *different* to become part of this new order, the "other race" (the "colored") would, once freed, be exposed to the new penitentiary regime—which is exactly what happened. As to the Native Americans, genocide was the preferred method (Melossi and Lettiere, 1998: 25–26; see also de Tocqueville, 1961).[3]

While the penitentiary was objected to by many Christian ministers, it was widely supported by state governments and the wealthy as an important mechanism to protect private property. Moreover, the apparent love for punishment was closely related to the love for democracy on the part of Americans. Furthermore,

> Democracy is the expression of the will of the people. Who counters that will, which expresses itself into the law, has to be punished. . . . Right or wrong, black or white: who is (or is perceived to be) on the wrong side of the law, shall be punished. But alas, as with everything else in society, who breaks the law and is powerful (economically, politically, ethnically, racially, culturally, and in regard to gender, and so on and so forth), can afford a full use of the safeguards that a developed legal system provides them with. For others, tough luck. (Melossi and Lettiere, 1998: 28)

Finally, a capitalist system, based as it is on competition, cannot survive without various rewards and punishments. Those at the bottom of that order are viewed as being more tempted to violate the law in order to get ahead, based on the notion that they have less to lose and more to gain. Thus, those individuals need to be more carefully watched and controlled. This was noted by many observers, including de Beaumont and de Tocqueville (Melossi and Lettiere, 1998: 28; de Beaumont and de Tocqueville, 1964).

The Rise of the Reformatory

During the first half of the nineteenth century, several reformers and students of the prison system noted with dismay the brutality that existed within these institutions. The Frenchmen de Beaumont and de Tocqueville commented that while American society provided the most extended liberty, the prisons offered the spectacle of the most complete despotism (de Beaumont and de Tocqueville, 1964). As crime and disorder continued to rise in America, reformers searched for some alternative to the existing regimes of custody that prevailed. Some began to believe that prisoners should be "rehabilitated" and "reeducated," and should be allowed to earn their freedom while learning a specific trade. These beliefs led to the introduction of such well-known practices as the indeterminant sentence, parole, and vocational and educational training. All of these programs emerged with the rise of a new type of prison, known as the *reformatory* (Barnes and Teeters, 1959: 417ff; Barnes, 1972: 144ff).

The reformatory idea received its impetus from Captain Alexander Maconochie, who headed the penal colony on Norfolk Island in Australia. Maconochie introduced the *mark system*, whereby a prisoner's sentence would be reduced if he obeyed prison rules (the modern version is known as *good time*). This worked as follows:

> Every convict, according to the seriousness of his offense, instead of being sentenced to a given term of years, had a certain number of marks set against him which he had to redeem before he was liberated. These marks were to be earned by deportment, labor, and study, and the more rapidly they are acquired the more speedy the release. (Barnes, 1972: 145)

About the same time in England, Sir Walter Crofton introduced the so-called *Irish system*, which included the indeterminant sentence and parole. In the reformatory system in America, the ideas of Crofton and Maconochie were combined with such innovations as classification of inmates according to offense, personality, and other characteristics. If the prisoner proved he was *reformed* (a term that has never been precisely defined), he was given a pardon or what was known as a *ticket-of-leave*. The prisoner was still under some sort of supervision by the state until the expiration of his sentence. This practice was copied in America and came to be known as *parole* (Simon, 1993).

The reformatories were designed ostensibly to transform the "dangerous criminal classes" into "Christian gentlemen and prepare them to assume their 'proper place' into . . . hard-working, law-abiding, lower-class citizens." These institutions would also inculcate good old-fashioned "American values" such as "habits of order, discipline, self-control, cheerful submission to authority, as well as respect for God, law, country, and the principles of capitalism and democracy" (Pisciotta, 1994: 4).

All of these programs were put into practice in a new prison at Elmira, New York, called the *Elmira Reformatory*, which was opened in 1877 (an institution that still stands today). Under the administration of Zebulon Brockway (a popular prison reformer and administrator and also an author of several books), a wide variety of programs were introduced, including industrial and academic education, religious services, library facilities, an institutional newspaper, and a gymnasium. The development of the reformatory came at a time of new hope among penologists of the period, exemplified by the first annual meeting of the National Congress of Penitentiary and Reformatory Discipline, in Cincinnati in 1870 (this organization is today known as the American Correctional Association). It was here that Brockway "electrified" the audience with his presentation on "The Ideal of a True Prison for a State," which came to be called the "new penology" (Walker, 1998: 95).

Brockway's proposal was influenced by a study done by two penologists of the period, Enoch Cobb Wines and Theodore Dwight, who published *Report on the Prisons and Reformatories of the United States and Canada* in 1867 (Wines and Dwight, 1973). Wines and Dwight urged the development of a "new" type of institution to separate veteran and younger criminals, which they called an *adult reformatory*. Such an institution, they said, would "teach and train the prisoner in such a manner that, on his discharge, he may be able to resist temptation and inclined to lead an upright, worthy life" (Pisciotta, 1994: 11).

The recommendation was taken up by New York with an 1870 act that created the Elmira Reformatory, with the aim of housing "male first-time offenders between the ages of sixteen and thirty" and providing "agricultural labor" and "mechanical industry" (Pisciotta, 1994: 12). Following the "Declaration of Principles" put forth at the 1870 Congress, this institution would specifically provide "treatment" based on the new *medical model* (discussed later in the chapter) using the *indeterminant sentence*, along with a carefully calculated system of classification, "intensive academic and vocational instruction, constructive labor, and humane disciplinary methods." An intensive period of parole would follow, thereby theoretically extending treatment into the community (Pisciotta, 1994: 13).

Brockway became its first and most popular administrator and he called his new institution a "reformatory hospital" and "college on the hill." However, the Elmira Reformatory under Brockway became a military-like fortress that emphasized "coercion and restraint" and ushered in a new era of "treatment." Brockway defined *reformation* as the "socialization of the anti-social by scientific training while under completest governmental control." However, the Elmira Reformatory "became like a garrison of a thousand prisoner soldiers. . . . By means mainly of the military organization. . . the general tone had gradually changed from that of a convict prison to the tone of a conscript fortress" (Platt, 1977: 67–68). In reality, it became "benevolent repression" under a strict military form of discipline, rather than reform (Pisciotta, 1994: 22).

The Elmira Reformatory (and other reformatories) failed to live up to its promise of reforming criminals and it ". . . failed signally to provide the right sort of psychological surroundings to expedite this process [of reformation]. The whole system of discipline was repressive, and varied from benevolent despotism, in the best instances, to tyrannical cruelty in the worst" (Barnes, 1972: 147). Elmira was originally built to house five hundred inmates, but by 1899 it housed around 1,500. This prompted one writer of the period to state: "What had begun as a bold experiment lost the inspiring impulse of its first promoters, and became routine work and mass treatment" (Platt, 1977: 68). Beatings were routine, often done in the bathroom (called the "slaughterhouse" by inmates). Brockway himself administered some of the punishment. He was described by inmates as a "different man" at these times, as if he enjoyed the beatings. Brockway rationalized this by calling it part of his "scientific criminology" and renaming corporal punishment as "positive extraneous assistance"; solitary confinement was dubbed "rest-cure cells" (Walker, 1998: 97–98). This was the "new penology" of the period.

However, Elmira (and so many other "asylums") was never specifically designed for any other purpose than custody and control. More than this, it was a system of *class* control, for the prisons (then and now) were populated by the poor, the powerless, and (especially during the nineteenth century) immigrants. Commenting on the insane asylums and houses of refuge (for juveniles), Rothman states that these institutions "were two more bricks in the wall that Americans built to confine and reform the dangerous classes" (Rothman, 1971: 210).

Convict Labor

Throughout the history of prisons, the concept of "work" in its various forms has been of utmost importance. This has been part of the more general belief that "idleness is the devil's workshop" and that criminals lack the "work ethic" (Morash and Anderson, 1978). Thus, most prison regimens have utilized some form of work as a form of punishment (Miller, 1974). It also can be said that the use of inmates as a form of cheap labor has been part of the capitalist system from the beginning, as owners seek to maximize profits however they can, including using the cheapest form of labor, whether it be slaves, immigrant labor, or inmates. Such exploitation persists to the present.

In the nineteenth century, three different forms of convict labor emerged: the *contract* system, the *state-use* system, and the *convict-lease* system. The prisons in the North tended to emphasize the *contract* system, whereby prisoners produced goods to be sold (at a profit) to private companies, which in turn sold the goods in the free market. This was part of the Auburn system because the congregate style of work was more applicable for the emerging industrial system of labor. This was especially the case during the Civil War, which created a need for various products such as cloth, hosiery, and shoes (Weiss, 1987a: 336). The exploitation of convict labor was part of a much larger process of capitalist exploitation. Barnes and Teeters noted:

> But it was the rise of the merchant-capitalist in America, in the period following 1825, that breathed life into prison industry. Here was an intermediary who was glad to furnish the raw material and take the finished product at an agreed-upon rate. The system of contract labor was only one incident in the rise of the merchant-capitalist, of which home labor and the sweatshop were other phases in his attempt to obtain cheap labor. Through this system, prisons became profit-making enterprises, which was one reason why the Auburn system came to its dominant position. (Barnes and Teeters, 1959: 528)

A variation of the contract system was the *convict lease system*. Under this system, prisoners were hired out to private businesses and worked away from the prison during the day. Through this method, thousands of prisoners in several states helped build railroads, bridges, roads, and other projects. This system soon gave rise to the notorious "chain gang," which still exists in many forms, mainly in the South.

The contract system was abandoned soon after the end of the Civil War, particularly in the Northeast and Midwest, as organized labor mounted a serious campaign against the use of prison labor. What happened next was that the state took over under the so-called *state-use system*. Under this system, prisoners produced goods that would be used within the state system (e.g., other prisons, schools, and hospitals). Today this is the most common form of prison labor, although variations of the old contract system have begun to emerge with many private companies using inmate labor. (This subject is discussed further in the final chapter.)

These systems of convict exploitation soon disappeared in the North, but another system, convict leasing, had become popular in the South shortly after the Civil War.

Convict Leasing

Following the Civil War, there emerged a method of punishment that demonstrates the fact that penal changes reflect much deeper changes in the political economy of a society. In the Southern states, prisons were not used extensively prior to the end of the Civil War. After the war, however, the South was faced with some rather serious economic, political, and social problems. Political and economic recovery were among the first priorities because the economy of the South, based as it was on a slave mode of production, was being replaced by a capitalist mode. Another crucial problem was what to do with the newly "freed" slaves. The white ruling class began the systematic oppression of blacks and maintained a system of *caste* rule that would replace a system of slavery (Shelden, 1979, 1993b). The *share-cropping* system replaced slavery as a "legal" method of controlling the labor of African Americans. A system of agricultural (and eventually industrial) "peonage" emerged and was supported by such informal methods as vigilantism, intimidation, Jim Crow laws, and the like (Weiss, 1987a: 345).

Convict leasing was introduced throughout the South for one main reason: "free" blacks represented such a threat to white supremacy, convict leasing would be just another form of chattel slavery that would function to keep the black race in a subordinate position. Some might argue that this was one way to provide an abundant source of cheap labor to help rebuild the war-torn South (Shelden, 1979, 1993b). While this is no doubt partly true and an abundant supply of cheap labor was in fact readily available, this form of labor was not much help in the enormous task of rebuilding that faced the South (Sellin, 1976: 145; Weiss, 1987a: 345–347).

The subjugation of African Americans became common throughout the South after the war. Several laws were passed (or old ones were reinstituted) that helped keep the African American population in its place, including vagrancy, loitering, disturbing the peace, and Jim Crow laws. When these methods failed, the use of force was relied upon, especially lynching (lynchings *increased* after the war). Indeed, as several writers have documented, the use of force to keep African Americans in a subordinate position increased dramatically after the war, one example being the rise of the Ku Klux Klan (Cable, 1962; Johnson, 1930; Friedman, 1970; Meier and Rudwick, 1970; Woodward, 1955, 1969).

One result of this practice was the shift in prison populations to predominantly African American following the war. Data for Tennessee prisons demonstrated this change. As indicated in Table 4.1, African Americans represented only 33 percent of the population at the main prison in Nashville as of October 1, 1865, but by November 29, 1867, it had increased to 58.3 percent. By 1869, it had increased to 64 percent, reaching an all-time high of 67 percent between 1877 and 1879. A slight decrease in the number of inmates (especially African American) between 1880 and 1898 can be explained in part by the opening of two branches of the main prison, Brushy Mountain and Inman, in the 1890s. As indicated in Table 4.2, the population of Brushy Mountain Prison was predominantly African American, much more so than at the main prison. The only data available for the Inman branch are for prisoners on hand as of December 1, 1898. At that time, there were only 58 prisoners, all of whom were African American (Shelden, 1979: 465–466).

Data from other states also illustrate the predominance of African Americans in the Southern prison system after the war. In 1888, the prison at Baton Rouge, Louisiana, held 85 whites and 212 African Americans; in 1875 in North Carolina, 569 African Americans and 78 whites were sentenced to prison (Sellin, 1976: 149–159).

The actual increase in the populations within Southern prisons is staggering, as Tables 4.1 and 4.2 indicate. In Georgia, there was a tenfold increase in prison populations during a four-decade period (1868–1908); in North Carolina, the prison population increased from 121 in 1870 to 1,302 in 1890; in Florida, the population went from 125 in 1881 to 1,071 in 1904; in Mississippi, the population quadrupled between 1871 and 1879; in Alabama, it went from 374 in 1869 to 1,878 in 1903 and to 2,453 in 1919 (Mancini, 1978: 343).

Convict leasing involved leasing out prisoners to private companies that paid the state a certain fee. The convicts worked for the companies during the day (convicts were usually not paid) outside the prison and returned

TABLE 4.1   *Racial Composition at the State Prison at Nashville, Tennessee, 1865–1914.*

Date	Total	White	Black	Percent Black
October 1, 1855	200	134	66	33.0
November 29, 1867	485	202	283	58.3
October 1, 1869	551	198	353	64.0
December 1, 1874	963	380	583	60.5
January 1, 1877	997	326	671	67.3
January 6, 1879	1,183	372	781	67.7
December 1, 1880	1,241	420	621	66.1
December 1, 1898	899	324	575	63.9
December 1, 1900	1,110	418	692	62.3
December 1. 1902	923	408	525	55.7
January 1, 1910	1,060	395	671	62.9
December 1, 1912	1,206	474	732	60.7
December 1, 1914	1,243	520	723	58.2

Source: Shelden, 1982: 315

TABLE 4.2 *Racial Composition at Brushy Mountain State Prison, Tennessee, 1898–1914.*

Date	Total	White	Black	Percent Black
December 1, 1898	525	64	441	84.0
December 1, 1900	634	127	507	79.9
December 1, 1902	762	145	617	80.9
January 1, 1910	747	131	616	82.5
December 1, 1912	704	139	565	80.3
December 1, 1914	616	131	485	78.7

Source: Shelden, 1982: 316

to their cells at night. The sole aim of convict leasing "was financial profit to the lessees who exploited the labor of the prisoners to the fullest, and to the government which sold the convicts to the lessees." One example was a lease system in Alabama. As Sellin explains it: "In 1866, the governor of Alabama leased the penitentiary to a contractor who was charged the sum of five dollars and given a sizable loan. The legislature granted him permission to work the prisoners outside the walls; they were soon found in the Ironton and New Castle mines" (Sellin, 1976: 146–150). In Tennessee by 1870, convicts were being leased from the main prison at Nashville to three separate railroad companies in Tennessee. During the 1880s, the legislature appropriated about $14 million to relieve the railroad companies that had suffered great losses during the war. It is no exaggeration that convicts rebuilt Tennessee's railroads. In 1871, coal-mining companies began to use convict labor and by 1882 more than half of the convicts at the Nashville prison were leased out. In 1884, the Tennessee Coal, Iron, and Railway Company took complete control and leased the entire prison population (Shelden, 1979: 467).

Mancini describes how one company, especially the owner Joseph E. Brown, made huge profits from convict-leasing in Georgia:

> In 1880 Brown, whose fortune could he estimated conservatively at one $1 million, netted $98,000 from the Dade Coal Company. By 1886, Dade Coal was a parent company, owning Walker Iron and Coal, Rising Fawn Iron, Chattanooga Iron, Rogers Railroad, and Ore Banks, and leasing Castle Rock Coal Company. An 1889 reorganization resulted in the formation of the Georgia Mining, Manufacturing, and Investment Company. This rested largely on a foundation of convict labor. (Mancini, 1978: 342)

The convict lease system was cruel and inhumane, to say the least. Deaths were common and the treatment caused much sickness and suffering. In a coal mine in Georgia, convicts were routinely whipped if they did not produce the daily quota of coal (Mancini, 1978: 347). In Alabama, inmates were punished by being placed in a "sweat box" during the day in the hot sun. A Louisiana newspaper reported that it would be more humane to impose the death sentence upon anyone sentenced to a term with the lessee in excess of six years, because the average convict lived no longer than that. Indeed, the death rate in 1896 was 20 percent (Sellin, 1976: 150–153). The mortality rate for inmates in the South was 41.3 per thousand convicts, compared to a rate of 14.9 in the North (McKelvey, 1968: 183).

The convict lease system as such disappeared, yet other forms of convict labor continued (and still exist today) in various forms. McKelvey notes: "But the lease system was doomed by its decreasing usefulness to the state, and it was not abandoned until profitable substitutes were perfected." These other systems included plantations, industrial prisons, and the famous chain gang, which still exists today (McKelvey, 1968: 185). The chain gang actually developed alongside the convict-lease system as one of the two major forms of convict labor. Weiss provides us with the following graphic description of this system: "Chained together in fetid bunkhouses, suffering malnutrition and exposed to rampant disease, these hapless charges suffered one of history's most degrading punishments" (Weiss, 1987a: 345). The vast majority of those on the chain gangs were African Americans, often convicted merely for being black.

PART II: TWENTIETH CENTURY DEVELOPMENTS IN THE AMERICAN PRISON SYSTEM

PRISON REFORM DURING THE PROGRESSIVE ERA

As discussed in the previous chapter, the Progressive Era brought about widespread changes in how American society responded to crime and other social problems. Reformers focused on practically all emerging problems of a growing capitalist society. As with all aspects of the criminal and juvenile justice system, the prison system became the focus of the many efforts by reformers to make changes.

Inmate Self-Government

Progressive prison reformers sought to achieve the aims of rehabilitation inside the prison walls. These reformers reversed some of the principles of earlier reformers, in that the prison should be as similar to the outside society as possible. The major principle that organized their efforts was the view of the prison as a community. Thus, they set about to humanize, individualize, and democratize the prison. For instance, they wanted to abolish the lock-step and striped uniforms, liberalize visitation rules and correspondence, abolish the silent system, and introduce a number of amusements, such as movies, sports, exercise, and bands (Rothman, 1980: 118–119).

One illustration of progressive prison reforms was the Mutual Welfare League, an attempt to introduce the idea of inmate self-government into a prison. The chief organizer of this bold attempt was Thomas Mott Osborne, head of the New York Prison Reform Commission. Osborne was probably the first to spend time inside a prison anonymously, which he did at the Auburn Prison in 1913. His experiences led him to conclude that the regime in this prison was too repressive, particularly the silent system and total isolation (i.e., solitary confinement). He came away with the conclusion that inmates must learn to be responsible for their own conduct. When he became warden of Sing Sing Prison in 1914, he established a Mutual Welfare League. Under this plan, prisoners would elect a Board of Delegates, who would in turn elect an Executive Board. The Executive Board would be the rule-making and enforcement body of the prison. The League would also present inmate grievances. The aim of such a program was to make inmates "not good *prisoners,* but good *citizens. . .* "(Rothman, 1980: 121).

At first, the experiment seemed to work. Sales of products produced by prisoners increased by almost $40,000 between 1913 and 1914. Also, discipline seemed to have improved. One indication of this was that in 1914, only 155 prisoners were treated for wounds, compared to 363 the year before. In time, however, the experiment failed, mainly because disciplinary problems seemed to have increased after the first year (a charge that might be debatable), and newspapers and the prison superintendent accused Osborne of "coddling" prisoners. Charges of mismanagement were brought against Osborne, but he was exonerated. He eventually resigned in disgust. One outcome of this experiment was the discovery of the importance of an "inmate subculture," a subject that has been extensively studied since then (Walker, 1998: 152–153; Barnes and Teeters, 1959: 499–501).[4]

Classification, Diagnosis, and Treatment: A New Prison Routine

Perhaps the most enduring of all prison reforms during this era was the emergence of *individualized treatment,* based on what has become popularly known as the "medical model," which argues that the offender is "sick" or suffering from some form of "disease" and, like a physical illness, must be diagnosed and cured. The reasons for this development are many and varied. One source has to be the development of the "positive school of criminology," a major shift in the thinking about the nature and causes of crime. Coming from a variety of both European and American writers, this school of thought stressed the importance of social, psychological, and biological facts in crime causation. However, it was mainly the psychological perspective (with the parallel development of the practice of social work) that led to the development of the medical model and individualized treatment. Individualized treatment stressed the importance of viewing each offender as a separate case to be individually diagnosed and treated (just as when visiting a doctor's office with a physical ailment).

A related source was the emergence of the academic and professional fields of social work, sociology, and psychology. In the early years of these disciplines, there was a constant effort to attain respectability and to map out areas of domain. The prison eventually became a convenient laboratory for the scientific study of human behavior and social organization. In each of these disciplines, the so-called "case-study method" prevailed, which emphasizes the study of the *individual* (although it can be applied to specific groups and institutions). In the case of the problem of crime, the emphasis shifted to the study and treatment of the individual offender, largely ignoring the law itself and the surrounding social context.

Both psychologists and psychiatrists were in the forefront of prison reform during the Progressive Era. Their first goal was the establishment of diagnostic centers, where each new prisoner would be individually diagnosed and classified. "They would interview, examine, and test the inmate, determine his aptitudes and his potential for rehabilitation, then assign him to the appropriate place" (i.e., institution). To accomplish this would require the establishment of a variety of institutions. According to Hoag and Williams, two California psychiatrists, criminals could be classified according to five categories: "those capable of learning a trade, those best suited for agriculture, the insane, the defective, and the psychopathic." On the whole, then, psychologists and psychiatrists viewed the prison as analogous to a hospital (as did John Howard more than a hundred years earlier). These reformers came to view the prison as an institution that could be transformed "into treatment centers that would diagnose the ailment and deliver the appropriate antidote" (Rothman, 1980: 122–123).

For offenders to receive this treatment, reformers insisted on a sentence that would give prison personnel enough time to perform such as task. The answer was to be the *indeterminate sentence*, which entailed no fixed amount of time on a particular sentence. Reformers believed that under such a sentence, prisoners become more responsible for their own rehabilitation (Rothman, 1980: 69). Between 1890 and 1915, a total of twenty-six states had passed some type of indeterminate-sentence law (Miller, 1974).

Classification became a permanent part of the twentieth century penal institution. Some form of classification had always been used in prisons. The first known type was a simple one of segregating offenders by sex and age, which was done at the Walnut Street Jail. In the 1840s, the insane were separated and placed in separate institutions; African Americans have always been segregated from whites—if not in totally separate institutions, at least within each institution. During the last half of the nineteenth century, classification came in the form of separations according to recidivists—first offenders, sex deviates from the rest of the population, and the like. Eventually there were *grades* of offenders based on good behavior or progress (often with different uniforms or some type of insignia to distinguish them). Also, in many prisons the *trusty* system was developed, whereby a select group of prisoners is given some responsibility, the most common (and notorious) of which has been to act as a guard (Barnes and Teeters, 1959: 466–467, 496–498). This system survived until at least the 1960s, when it came under attack as a result of a series of scandals within the Arkansas prison system (Murton and Hyams, 1969).

In reality, classification was and still is based on concerns for custody. The various classification schemes appealed to prison wardens because they would simplify custody. In particular, they would segregate the troublemakers from the general population, in addition to child molesters and other sex offenders, potential suicides, and escapees (Rothman, 1980: 124).

Psychiatrists and psychologists, in all their theories about criminal behavior, never could come up with specific cures that were workable. "For all their allegiance to a medical model," says Rothman, in reality "they had no medicines to prescribe." One result was that, instead of in-depth psychotherapy and individualized attention, inmates were subjected to a highly regimented prison routine that would include work and education, with the emphasis on work. A special prison committee in New York concluded that "work is to be the foundation around which every activity revolves in every prison." The routine within these prisons would ideally keep prisoners busy and a system of rewards would, hopefully, help prisoners learn to function according to rules and regulations, therefore, making better "prisoners" rather than better "citizens" on the outside (Rothman, 1980: 125–126).

Yet even these rather modest reforms were not adopted uniformly in every prison in the country. "Change was piecemeal, not consistent, and procedures were almost nowhere implemented to the degree that reformers wished. One should think not of a Progressive prison, but of prisons with more or less Progressive features" (Rothman, 1980: 128). Probably the most consistent change was the abandonment of striped uniforms (only four Southern states still had them by the mid-1930s), the lockstep, and the silent system. Most prisons began to allow inmates "freedom of the yard" (i.e., to mingle, talk, and exercise for an hour or two each day outside of their cells in an open area), more recreation (especially baseball), and movies. However, treatment never became a reality, since most states were reluctant to spend the necessary money and custody considerations always came first. In fact, despite all the rhetoric of individualized treatment, by 1926 there were only a small handful of full-time psychiatrists and psychologists.

The failure to implement treatment programs also can be attributed to the fact that the medical model rarely went beyond diagnosis, for there was no specific "cure" available for criminal behavior. Even educational and vocational training was limited. Austin MacCormick, noted prison reformer and eventual director of the Bureau of Prisons, concluded in 1929 that "save for a few exceptions, we are tolerating a tragic failure. There is not a single complete and well-rounded educational program in all the prisons and reformatories for adults in America" (Rothman, 1980: 136). In short, the "bottom line" was (and still is) custody, because whenever the goals of treatment and custody conflicted, custody won (and still usually wins).

The reality of American prisons became one of idleness and boredom. Vocational training was at best extremely limited. The amount of work available was quite limited, which is ironic because so many had believed that work was highly reformative. An Attorney General's report in the mid-1930s found that 60 percent of the nation's prisoners were idle. One reason was the fact that most forms of inmate labor common in the nineteenth century had largely disappeared.

The Decline in Prison Industries

By the end of the Progressive Era, the lease and contract methods of inmate labor had begun to disappear from the scene. Three other systems became the most common: state account, state use, and public works.

The *state account* and the *state use* systems are very similar, the major difference being that in the former the goods are sold on the open market and in the latter the products are used by other state agencies. The latter is the most often used today. *Public works* uses prisoners in the building and/or repair of highways, streets, bridges, and similar projects. Between 1914 and 1915, there was a so-called *good roads* system, which involved using prisoners to build and improve public highways. This movement may have been related to the arrival of the automobile on a large scale during this period. Colorado and Washington, among other states, took advantage of this brief experiment (Walker, 1980: 154).

A variation of public works was the infamous *chain gang*, which emerged in the South after the Civil War in the form of prison camps. This system emerged out of the lease system when, because the convicts often refused to work and many escaped, they were placed in chains while they worked. One notorious chain gang was called by one writer "The American Siberia" (Powell, 1891). This particular chain gang was a camp in Florida, where turpentine was extracted in a semitropical-jungle atmosphere, where the only labor that could be obtained was that of convicts. "Prisoners worked in gangs, chained together in filthy bunkhouses, exposed to dysentery and scurvy" (Barnes and Teeters, 1959: 378). After several exposés covering most of the Southern states, plus government investigations, the chain gang has all but disappeared, although some form of this system still exists in the South.

The final phase of the decline of prison industries came during the 1930s. Because of the economic decline of the Great Depression, a total of thirty-three states passed various laws that prohibited the sale of prison-made goods on the open market. Two federal laws, the Hawes-Cooper Act of 1929 and the Ashurst-Summers Act of 1935, prohibited the interstate shipment of prison-made goods. As a result, the traditional forms of prison industries, for all intents and purposes, ceased to exist (Allen and Simonsen, 1998: 44–45).

Instead of a "treatment"-oriented prison, what really became dominant during the Progressive Era was a type of prison popularly known as "The Big House." An analysis of prison developments during this period would not be complete without a discussion of this type of prison.

The "Big House"

We can trace the overall growth of the American prison system in terms of six major eras: (1) 1790–1830: early American prisons; (2) 1830–1870: the Pennsylvania and Auburn systems; (3) 1870–1900: Reformatories; (4) 1900–1946: the "Big House"; (5) 1946–1980: the "Correctional Institution"; and (6) 1980 to the present: "warehousing."[5] The last two eras have seen the greatest growth in the prison system. Thus, while in 1900 the prison population stood at around 50,000, by 1935 it was more than 120,000. In 1900, there were eighty-one state prisons and reformatories; at the end of the 1930s, there were more than one hundred. In 1990, there were a total of 1,287 prisons (80 federal and 1,207 state prisons); by 1995, there were a total of 1,500 prisons (125 federal and 1,375 state prisons), representing an increase of about 17 percent. The federal system experienced the largest increase, going up by 56 percent. In some cases, the *capacity within* the prison has increased—some "megaprisons" can hold from five thousand to ten thousand inmates (Irwin and Austin, 1997: 66). As of June 1998, there were about 1.3 million prison inmates and an additional half-million jail inmates, bringing the total to more than 1.8 million prisoners (Killinger and Cromwell, 1973: 23–53; Mays and Winfree, 1998: 171; Proband, 1998).

The Big House became the dominant type of prison until the late 1940s and early 1950s. This prison was typically a huge granite structure, capable of housing two thousand or more prisoners, with some housing more than four thousand. These institutions were supposed to eliminate the most abusive forms of punitiveness and prison labor within existing prisons (Rotman, 1998: 165). Most had large cell blocks with three or more floors or *tiers* of cells, usually housing one or two men in each cell. Many were built in the late nineteenth century, such as Michigan (Jackson), California (San Quentin), Illinois (Joliet), and New York (Sing Sing), while most were built in the twentieth century, such as Stateville (Illinois) and Attica (New York) (Irwin, 1980: 3; Killinger and Cromwell, 1973: 47). Irwin provides perhaps the most graphic description of The Big House:

> This granite, steel, cement, and asphalt monstrosity stood as the state's most extreme form of punishment, short of the death penalty. It was San Quentin in California, Sing Sing in New York, Stateville in Illinois, Jackson in Michigan, Jefferson City in Missouri, Canon City in Colorado, and so on. It was the place of banishment and punishment to which convicts were "sent up." Its major characteristics were isolation, routine, and monotony. Its mood was mean and grim, perforated here and there by ragged-edged vitality and humor. (Irwin, 1980: 5)

Although it was, in a sense, an "industrial" prison, with factories producing various goods, most prisoners spent their time in relative idleness toward the end of the 1930s. When they did work, one of the major products was license plates.

Thus ends another chapter in prison "reform." The reform agenda during the Progressive Era ran up against the hard realities of the prison. The twentieth-century prison, mostly in the form of "The Big House," was this reality. Rothman concludes his analysis of prison reforms during this period with the observation that the reality of the prison "is not one of the inmates exercising in the yard or attending classes or taking psychometric tests, but of the physical presence of the walls" (Rothman, 1980: 157–158). It was these high walls (some as high as 30 feet above the ground) that helped wardens and guards keep their jobs, for legislatures and the general public seemed to be content with one thing: maintaining a "quiet joint" (i.e., no riots, no escapes, a smooth-running institution).

The Emergence of the Federal Prison System and the System of Corrections

The Federal Prison System

Until 1895, prisoners convicted of federal crimes were housed in state prisons. The number of prisoners housed in state prisons more than doubled from 1,027 in 1885 to 2,516 in 1895. During this period, federal prisoners were used as contract labor. But in 1897, Congress outlawed this practice and eventually it was decided that these prisoners should be transferred to a separate institution (Rotman, 1998: 166). Thus, federal prisoners began to be housed at Fort Leavenworth, an old military prison in the eastern part of Kansas. In time, a new prison was built nearby, which opened in 1928. In the meantime, two additional federal prisons were being built by the federal government, one in Atlanta in 1899 and the other on McNeil Island, Washington, in 1907 (Allen and Simonsen, 1998: 538–539).

The passage of several federal laws (e.g., Mann Act in 1910, Harrison Narcotic Act in 1914, Volstead Act in 1918, Dyer Act in 1919) resulted in an increase in federal prisoners. Subsequently, in 1925, Congress authorized the construction of a federal reformatory at Chillicothe, Ohio, and the construction of the first federal prison for women, which was opened in 1927 at Alderson, West Virginia (Allen and Simonsen, 1998: 538–539; Rotman, 1998: 167).

A more significant development was the overall increase in the role of the federal government in the fight against crime. This was due in part to an alleged "crime wave" during the 1920s and 1930s, most of which was created by the news media as they sensationalized various gangsters and famous criminals such as Bonnie and Clyde, John Dillinger, Ma Barker, and Alvin Karpis, not to mention organized crime figures such as Al Capone. As discussed in Chapter 2, a major role was played by the FBI. In 1929, the Federal Bureau of Prisons was officially established, thus completing the federal law-enforcement bureaucracy (Allen and Simonsen, 1998: 539–540; Walker, 1998: 159–163; Rotman, 1998: 167–168).

With the creation of the federal prison system and the passage of new federal laws, new federal prisons were constructed. The most famous of these new prisons was Alcatraz (opened in 1934), located on an island in the San Francisco Bay area, directly across from the famous Fisherman's Wharf. Probably more than any other federal prison, Alcatraz typified the new "crackdown on crime" and on "hardened criminals," especially organized crime figures and famous criminals like John Dillinger and Al Capone. An "escape-proof" prison located on a small island in the San Francisco Bay, it became one of the most notorious failures on the "new penology" as it hardly put a dent in the increasing crime rate of the next two decades. It was finally closed in the early 1960s and is now a tourist attraction. It was replaced, however, by a "super-max" prison at Marion, Illinois (Rotman, 1998: 168).[6]

The Federal Bureau of Prisons helped develop a new system of classification, new prison industries, a federal system of probation and parole, and new educational and vocational training programs. Perhaps the most important was the new system of classification. First, there was a classification system according to types of prisons. Five different types of facilities were developed: penitentiaries, reformatories, prison camps, a hospital, and a drug treatment facility. Second, within each facility, classification was ac-

cording to age, offense, sex, and other criteria. In the 1970s, the federal system established a classification system based upon security level. Five levels were established: *minimum* (mostly federal prison "camps"—many are
next to military bases where many inmates provide additional labor); *low*
(double-fenced perimeters and mostly dormitory-style living arrangements); *medium* (cell-type living arrangements and double-fenced perimeters with electronic detection systems); *high* (most commonly known as
"U.S. Penitentiaries," with high-security perimeter double fences or walls,
along with very close supervision of inmates in cell-type housing); and *administrative* (special needs institutions—pretrial defendants, noncitizen de-
tainees and, more importantly, the housing of the "extremely dangerous,
violent, or escape-prone inmates") (Allen and Simonsen, 1998: 540–546).

The System of "Corrections"

With the federal government leading the way, a new era of penology began
to emerge, especially after World War II. This "new penology" ushered in a
new type of prison system complete with a new terminology. Thus began
the age of the *correctional system* and a host of new prison workers, whom
Irwin has called *correctionalists*. These individuals were a "growing body of
college-educated employees and administrators of prisons, parole, and probation, and a few academic penologists. . . . " These individuals "were convinced and were able to convince many state governments and interested
segments of the general population that they could reduce crime by curing
criminals of their criminality" (Irwin, 1980: 38–39; Rotman, 1998: 169–171).
Instead of a prison, there was to be a *correctional system;* in place of prisoners or convicts, we would have *inmates;* and guards were magically transformed into *correctional officers* (Barnes and Teeters, 1959: 440). The prison
system remained a system to house the dangerous classes, but the new terminology seemed to be an attempt to mask its true functions and create the
false impression that something positive was being accomplished within the
walls.

Many of the Big Houses were replaced by shiny new *correctional centers*. In line with a "new" era of "treatment," there also emerged a new classification for these new prisons, according to the degree of security that was
apparently needed; thus, we find *maximum, medium,* and *minimum* security
correctional institutions. Examples of minimum security prisons (most
without walls) included the California Institution for Men at Chino (a state
institution), a federal institution at Seagoville, Texas, and another at Wallkill,
New York.

Part of the "new penology"[7] included the emergence of what many
have called the *rehabilitative ideal* or the emphasis (originally called for in
1870) on *treatment* (a term that was changed to *rehabilitation*). It appears that

after floundering for several decades, the proposals of the 1870 prison meetings were to be finally implemented. During the decades of the 1940s and 1950s, correctionalists would implement this "new penology" according to three essential procedures: the indeterminate sentence, classification, and specific treatment programs (Irwin, 1980: 40; Rotman, 1998: 169–170). Classification was to be done by a special team of psychologists, social workers, counselors, and other professionals who would form a special classification committee to determine the proper course of treatment for the prisoner. The "new penology" even went so far as to create a name change for the American Prison Association (formerly the Congress of Penitentiary and Reformatory Discipline), calling it the American Correctional Association in 1954—a name that exists to the present day. New names were invented to replace old, punitive practices; thus, the "hole" (solitary confinement) was renamed the "adjustment center." Even Soledad Prison in California was renamed the California Treatment Facility. In place of the old granite walls, they built tall fences (today reinforced with razor wire, some wired with electricity) and guard towers (Rotman, 1998: 170). But for all practical purposes, they remained essentially *prisons,* or what Goffman called *total institutions* (Goffman, 1961).

The indeterminate sentence was implemented in most states. While some reformers (e.g., psychologist Karl Meninger) advocated a sentence of zero to life for all offenders (in other words, literally a sentence of indeterminate length), most state legislatures implemented a modified version, such as one to ten years for larceny passed in California. More power was granted to parole boards as a result of indeterminate sentencing laws. Ideally, parole boards would release an offender only when they felt he or she was rehabilitated. But this assumed that those in charge of the prisons "had procedures for identifying and changing criminal characteristics, which they did not, and that parole boards had procedures for determining when these changes had occurred, which they did not" (Irwin, 1980: 41–42).

While classification was supposed to be improved so that criminal behavior could be cured, the procedures adopted never attained this ideal. On the one hand, theories of criminal behavior never have been developed sufficiently to effect an adequate "cure" for criminality and treatment programs have never been fully implemented in most prisons. On the other hand, classification (and most other prison procedures) continued to be determined by concerns over custody and security. Thus, the classification procedures tended to ignore a prisoner's treatment needs, however ill-defined.

The most common treatment program to be implemented during these years (mainly the 1950s) was group counseling. However, even this was not too successful, because the pay was insufficient and the location of most prisons was far from ideal (many were located in rural areas, many miles away from urban areas). As a result, group counseling sessions were led by those not fully qualified to do so. Further, these sessions became a sort of game played by prisoners since they were led to believe that by attending their chances for parole would be greater, and perhaps even their sentence shortened. In other words, most who attended (and not all did) did so not to change their behavior and attitudes but to get an early release.

Academic and vocational training programs were more easily implemented, yet these too were far from effective. Most of the vocational training programs did not begin to equip prisoners with marketable skills on the outside. In fact, most of the programs were tied into the daily maintenance of the prison (e.g., cooking and baking); most prisons lacked modern equipment and techniques (Irwin, 1980: 46).

For the most part, the prisons of the post–World War II era continued much the way they had before. Rotman's assessment captures the basic problems of rehabilitation within these prisons when he writes that:

> . . . despite the rhetoric of rehabilitation, this new wave of treatment euphoria shared with previous efforts the same paucity of practical realizations. Because of the limited professional possibilities offered by the penitentiary setting, the treatment staff was still generally composed of less qualified individuals. In addition, there was a permanent conflict, ideological and professional, between the custody and the treatment staffs regarding issues of discipline and security. (Rotman, 1998: 169)

Irwin's comments echo those of Rotman, as he writes that:

> The public and most government policymakers continued to demand that prisons first accomplish their other assigned tasks: punishment, control, and restraint of prisoners. In addition, the new correctional institutions were not created in a vacuum but planned in ongoing prison systems, which had long traditions, administrative hierarchies, divisions, informal social worlds, and special subcultures among the old staff. The new correctionalists were never able to rid the prison systems of the old regime, though often they tried; and the oldtimers, many of whom were highly antagonistic to the new routine, resisted change, struggled to maintain as much control as possible, and were always successful in forcing an accommodation between old and new patterns. So correctional institutions were never totally, or even mainly, organized to rehabilitate prisoners. (Irwin, 1980: 46–47)

Irwin discusses at length the history of Soledad Prison in California as an example of the failure of post–World War II developments. (Irwin himself was an inmate at this prison during the 1950s). It was originally established as a medium-security, treatment-oriented prison for younger and more trainable prisoners. Its original name implies it goals: California Training Facility. The prison had no granite walls (like Big Houses) but instead had a high fence (although with gun towers at several locations, indicating that the "new penology" was still concerned over custody and security). There was a library, a hospital, an education building, a gym, and other accoutrements of the "new penology." It offered several vocational training programs, elementary and high school programs, and a counseling program. The overall environment was not as harsh as in most of the older prisons.

It did not take too long for this new treatment-oriented prison to succumb to the realities of prison life and became just another *prison*. Prisoners became aware of the fact that the new treatment was in reality simply new methods of control and, moreover, that rehabilitation was ineffective (as evidenced by the high rate of return of prisoners who had participated in Soledad's treatment programs). Further, an influx of African Americans and Chicanos created racial divisions, which was further acerbated by a growing militancy of African American prisoners during the late 1960s. Prison administrators took advantage of these divisions (as most still do today) to better control the prison and maintain a "quiet joint" (a common "divide-and-rule" technique). Thus, by the 1960s, Soledad was like most other prisons in America, with a heavy emphasis on custody and control. It eventually fell victim to the many disturbances within the entire prison system, highlighted by the killing of the celebrated George Jackson in January 1970 (Irwin, 1980: 47–90).

The Modern Era, 1980 to the Present: Warehousing and The New American Apartheid

Most prisoners today are still drawn from the bottom of the class structure, have few marketable skills, little formal education, and poor work records, and are disproportionately nonwhite. Prisons still house the dangerous classes. More ominously, however, the modern American prison system is looking more like a "Gulag" than ever before (Christie, 1993; Richards, 1990). Also, it is clear that the prison system is becoming a form of *apartheid* because for the first time in our history, African Americans constitute a majority of prisoners.

As of December 31, 1999, the total number incarcerated in both jails and prisons was just over 1.9 million, with a rate of 725 per 100,000 population (Schiraldi and Zeidenberg, 1999). Also, around six million people were under some form of correctional supervision (i.e., probation, parole, jail, or prison) at the end of 1998 (the latest figures available), roughly double what it was in 1985. This total represented 3.0 percent of the total adult population, compared to 1.7 percent in 1985 (Gilliard and Beck, 1996). While these increases were noteworthy during the later 1980s, they were most pronounced during the first half of the 1990s, as seen in Tables 4.3 and 4.4 (Proband, 1997). What Table 4.3 clearly shows is how the rates in recent years compare over time.

TABLE 4.3   *The Growing Prison Population: 1925–1995 (Rates per 100,000 in State and Federal Prisons).*

Year	Number	Rate
1925	91,669	79
1935	144,180	113
1945	133,649	98
1955	185,780	112
1965	210,895	108
1975	240,593	111
1985	480,568	202
1995	1,085,363	411
1998	1,277,866	452

Source: Maguire and Pastore, 1997: 518; Gilliard, 1999: 3

TABLE 4.4   *Inmates Held in State or Federal Prisons or in Local Jails, 1985–1998.*

Year	Total	Federal or State Prisons	Local Jails	Rate/100,000
1985	742,580	487,594	254,986	313
1990	1,179,239	773,919	405,320	461
1998 (6/30)	1,850,052	1,298,003	552,049	660
% Increase (1985–98)	149	166	116	111

Sources: Gilliard, 1999: Gilliard and Beck, 1996

For comparative purposes, Table 4.5 illustrates population changes in other parts of the criminal justice system. Included are data on the number on probation and parole, in addition to those in prison and jail for the period 1980–1997. While the prison and jail populations were growing rapidly, so too were the other two parts of the system.

How do we explain this phenomenal growth? In a word, *drugs*. Indeed, the war on drugs, which really took off during the mid-1980s, began to have its effects on jail and prison populations by the early 1990s (Baum, 1997; Miller, 1998; Currie, 1993). In the period between 1988 and 1994, the number of prison inmates who had been convicted of drug offenses went up by 155.5 percent. By comparison, only modest increases were seen for violent and property offenders. Data on court sentencing show that between

TABLE 4.5   *Adults on Probation, in Jail or Prison, and on Parole, 1985-1997.*

Year	Total	Probation	Jail	Prison	Parole
1980	1,832,350	1,118,097	163,994	329,821	220,438
1985	3,011,500	1,968,712	254,986	487,593	300,203
1990	4,348,000	2,670,234	403,019	743,382	531,407
1995	5,335,100	3,077,861	499,300	1,078,545	679,421
1997	5,690,700	3,261,888	557,974	1,115,800	685,033
% increase (1980-97)	211	192	299	238	211

Sources: Maguire and Pastore, 1996: 540; Maguire and Pastore, 1999: 462

1980 and 1992, court commitments to state prisons on drug charges alone increased by more than 1,000 percent. Figures from U.S. District Courts (i.e., federal system) show that whereas in 1982 about 20 percent of all convictions were for drugs, by 1994 this had increased to about 36 percent. During this same period, the proportion of those convicted on drug charges who were sentenced to prison increased from 74 percent in 1982 to 84 percent in 1994, and their actual sentences increased from an average of 55 months in 1982 to 80 months in 1994. The average sentences for murder during this period actually *decreased* from 162 to 117 months, while for all violent offenses, the average sentence declined from 133 to 88 months (Maguire and Pastore, 1997: 468, 472). Put somewhat differently, while in 1980, nineteen out of every one thousand arrested for drugs were sent to prison, in 1992 an incredible 104 for every 1,000 were sent to prison (Melossi and Lettiere, 1998: 42, quoting Holmes, 1994). Incidentally, on any given day, almost 60 percent (58.6 percent) of all federal prisoners are serving time for drug offenses; of these, 40 percent are African American (Maguire and Pastore, 1997: 576).

Numbers and rates only tell half the story. To see what is happening to our prison system, we need to take a careful look at *who* is incarcerated. In general, we can conclude that modern prisoners occupy the lowest rungs on the social-class ladder, and they always have. The modern prison system (along with local jails) is a sort of *ghetto* or *poorhouse* reserved primarily for the unskilled, the uneducated, and the powerless; in increasing numbers, it is also being reserved for racial minorities, especially African Americans—which is why this system is being called the *new American apartheid*.[8]

One of the most dramatic changes in the demographics of American penal institutions in recent years has been the phenomenal increase in the proportion of African Americans and other minority groups who are locked up. Not surprisingly, this change is attributable largely to the war on drugs.

As already noted, drug offenses have accounted for most of the increase in prison populations in recent years. However, the prison and jail populations have become increasingly dominated by minorities, especially African Americans, including women. For all correctional systems (federal and state prisons, plus jails), the incarceration rate for African Americans has been far greater than for whites. In fact, for males, the black/white ratio went from 6.7:1 to 7.5:1; for females, the black/white ratio remained about the same at around 6.7:1. Table 4.6 shows the incarceration rate for jails only, and here we see that the black/white ratio has gone from about 5:1 to almost 6:1 in just ten years.

For African Americans in particular, their presence within the nation's prison system seems to be directly linked to the war on drugs, as reflected in the figures found in Table 4.7. From 1986 to 1991, right in the middle of the crackdown on drugs, the proportion of African Americans incarcerated for drug offenses went up an incredible 465.5 percent.

The most dramatic representation of the racist nature of the criminal justice system is shown in Table 4.8. The chances of going to prison for an African American male born in 1991 stood at 28.5 percent. Put somewhat differently, an African American male child's chances of going to prison was more than six times greater than his white counterpart. Such odds will not diminish over one's lifetime (in this table, until one reaches forty years of age).

Many African Americans have been unjustly subjected to some of the more repressive types of legislation passed in recent years, such as "Three Strikes and You're Out" and various "habitual offender" laws. A study by the National Council on Crime and Delinquency found evidence of systematic racial bias in Florida's habitual criminal law. Specifically, they discovered that African American offenders were about twice as likely to receive

TABLE 4.6   *Adults in Local Jails, by Race, 1985–1994 (Rate/100,000).*

Year	Total	White	Black	Ratio
1985	145	73	368	5:1
1990	218	106	568	5.4:1
1994	251	118	695	5.9:1
% change (1985–94)	73.1	61.6	88.9	

Source: Maguire and Pastore, 1996: 550

TABLE 4.7   *State Prison Inmates by Offense and Race, 1986–1991.*

Offense	1986	1991	% Increase
Violent:			
White	88,591	121,865	37.6
Black	119,694	150,972	26.1
Property:			
White	63,785	74,612	17.0
Black	58,833	70,668	20.1
Drugs:			
White	14,174	29,845	110.6
Black	14,201	80,304	465.5

Source: Maguire and Pastore, 1996: 550

this type of sentence, even when controlling for the current offense and prior record (Irwin and Austin, 1997: 52).

Finally, in 1995, it is a well-publicized statistic that around one third of all African American males in their twenties are either in jail, in prison, on probation, or on parole, a figure that stood at one fourth around 1990 (Mauer, 1995).

The American Gulag

The present American prison system is beginning to resemble in many ways the *gulags* of Russia. One of the first and most popular exposures of gulags came with the 1970 publication of Russian author Alexander Solzhenitsyn's *The Gulag Archipelago*. This book exposed literally thousands of prison camps spread throughout the Soviet Union, mostly in isolated areas like Siberia. These concentration camps originally emerged in the 1920s under Lenin and then expanded even further under Stalin. The number of prisoners grew from around 350,000 in 1929 to more than 1.5 million by 1931. These were "forced-labor" camps set up ostensibly to help the growth of industrialization following the Revolution (Conquest, 1995; Harris, 1997).

Gulags persist to the present day, not only in Russia but also in such countries as China, North Korea, and the Sudan. A recent report noted the existence of gulags in Canada during the 1930s, known as "Project 51" in Lac Seul, Northern Ontario (Collins, et al., 1996; Lilly, 1993; Pasqualini, 1993; Wu, 1996).

One might conclude that the gulag phenomenon is typically seen as either an aberration (e.g., Canada's "Project 51") or restricted to Third World

TABLE 4.8   *Chances of Going to State or Federal Prison at Some Time During the Rest Of Life, as of 1991. Percent Expected to Go to State or Federal Prison During Rest of Life among Persons Not Previously Incarcerated, by Age.*

	Birth	*20*	*25*	*30*	*35*	*40*
Totals	5.1	4.5	3.1	2.1	1.4	0.9
Sex						
Male	9.0	7.9	5.5	3.7	2.5	1.6
Female	1.1	1.0	0.8	0.6	0.3	0.2
Race						
White:	2.5	2.3	1.7	1.2	0.9	0.6
Male	4.4	4.1	3.0	2.1	1.5	1.1
Female	0.5	0.5	0.4	0.3	0.2	0.1
Black:	16.2	14.1	9.6	6.0	3.6	2.0
Male	28.5	25.3	17.3	10.8	6.5	3.6
Female	3.6	3.5	2.8	1.9	1.1	0.6
Hispanic:	9.4	8.7	6.4	4.9	3.8	2.3
Male	16.0	14.8	11.1	8.6	6.8	4.3
Female	1.5	1.5	1.2	0.9	0.6	0.4

Source: Bonczar and Beck, 1997: 2

or totalitarian societies. However, a close look at the modern American prison system might suggest otherwise; indeed, at least two recent authors have suggested as much. In the early 1990s, Norweigian criminologist Nils Christie suggested that the "crime-control industry" was beginning to look like the equivalent of the Russian *gulag* (Christie, 1993). A paper by Richards also used the term *gulag* to describe the modern prison system (Richards, 1990). We don't have to look very far back in history to find almost the exact equivalent to gulags in this country, especially in the West, with the emergence of so-called "relocation centers" to house Japanese Americans during World War II.

Today, the American prison system has many of the same characteristics of gulags. Prisons are found in just about every part of the country, with the bulk of them (especially those built during the past twenty years) in rural areas. There is also a great deal of human-rights abuses in American prisons (and jails and juvenile correctional facilities), such as cruel and unusual punishment (e.g., long periods in solitary confinement) and extreme brutality and violence. Moreover, there is much forced (and cheap) labor, much of which produces great profits for corporations.

To give the reader an idea of the gulag look of the American prison system, compare the states of Texas, Michigan, and California—three states that have obviously found building prisons a lucrative business. One of the most interesting things about the American prison system is that since the beginning, most of these institutions have been located in rural areas.

Texas is a classic example, which now boasts more than a hundred prisons (most have been built since 1980 and eighty have been built in the 1990s). An example of the rural nature of most of these facilities is seen by sampling some of the towns where they are located (populations according to the 1990 census): Iowa Park (6,072), Teague (3,268), Dilley (2,632), Brazoria (2,717), Kennedy (3,763), Dalhart (6,246), Marlin (6,386), Rusk (4,366), Richmond (9,801), Woodville (2,636), Navasota (6,296), Fort Stockton (8,524), Childress (5,055), and Cuero (6,700). A check of the 1998 Rand McNally Road Atlas reveals that several Texas prisons and other facilities are located in towns not even found on the map. Places like Lovelady, Midway, Tennessee Colony (with three separate prisons each housing more than three thousand inmates), Rosharon (with no less than *four* prisons housing more than six thousand inmates), and a privately run prison in a town called Venus (with one thousand inmates). These institutions are found in every region of the state, from the far eastern part (e.g., Woodville, located a few miles north of Beaumont along U.S. Route 190) to Lamesa (in the Texas Panhandle area about 30 miles south of Lubbock where U.S. Route 180 meets 87), and Fort Stockton (about 100 miles southwest of Odessa along Interstate 10).

The Texas prison system has more than 42,000 employees, operates its own health-services system (with more than eight thousand personnel, including two hundred doctors), and has thirty-five lawyers working for it. Farming is big business, with control of more than 134,000 acres (about 200 square miles), operating the largest horse and cattle herds in the entire state (more than ten thousand head of cattle and around 1,500 horses). The system also operates forty-two factories within thirty-two prisons under its own Texas Correctional Industries. In 1995, this system had 575,000 people under some form of community supervision, 71,000 on parole, 127,500 in state prisons, and 963 in state jails, with a grand total of more than 700,000 (Rush, 1997: 157). The most recent figures (December 31, 1997) show that there are just over 140,000 inmates in the state prison system and an incarceration rate of 717 (ranked first in the nation, except for the District of Columbia).

As of 1996, Michigan had thirty-nine prisons and fifteen prison camps, the majority of which were built in the 1980s. The rural nature of the prisons in this state is just like in Texas. Some examples include Munising (2,783), Baraga (1,231), Carson City (1,158), Grass Lake (903), Coldwater (9,607), Ionia (5,935), New Haven (2,331), St. Louis (3,828), Newberry (1,873), Eastlake (473), Freeland (1,421), Plymouth (9,560), Standish (1,377), Lapeer (7,759), and Kinchebe (not on map, nearest town is Rudyard, population 900).[9] Typical of recent trends, there are a total of *four* facilities in

Kinchebe alone, one of which is located on an abandoned Air Force Base, purchased by the state in 1978. The facility at Newbury was opened in 1995 on the site of a former state mental institution.[10] As of December 31, 1997, there were 44,771 inmates and an incarceration rate of 457 (ranked ninth in the nation, excluding the District of Columbia) (Proband, 1998b).

Not to be outdone, California also fits well into the gulag mentality. As of Spring 1996, there were thirty-two state prisons (in 1980 it had just twelve), thirty-eight forestry camps, and a multitude of community facilities. Largely as a result of the recent Three Strikes and You're Out laws, it is anticipated that by 2001 the state will have around 250,000 inmates (it had 157,547 as of December 31, 1997, and an incarceration rate of 475, tenth in the nation, excluding the District of Columbia) and around fifty prisons. Some examples of the rural nature of California's prisons include Avenal (9,770), Susanville (7,279), Techachapi (5,791), Calipatria (2,690), Baker (650), Imperial (4,113), Chowchilla (5,930), Blythe (8,428), Soledad (7,146), Ione (6,516), Crescent City (4,380), Coalinga (8,212), Jamestown (2,178), and Adelanto (8,517).

But there is more to this system than merely prisons. According to the 1997 Directory of the American Correctional Association (itself a rather large part of this "industry"), there are many different kinds of facilities that house those sentenced by the courts (both adults and juveniles), including Diagnostic/Reception Centers, Work Release Centers, and Boot Camps. As of fiscal year 1996, there were 2,499 state and 385 federal facilities, for a total of 2,883. For juveniles, there were a total of 2,297 state facilities and ninety-eight federal facilities, for a total of 2,395; all together, there were 5,278 correctional facilities—and this number does not include local jails (American Correctional Association, 1997: xxii–xxiv).

Some Concluding Thoughts

We live in times of great uncertainty and rapid social change as millions just barely eke out a living while a very small minority become richer and richer. As Reiman noted, the "rich get richer and the poor get prison" (Reiman, 1998). However, it is more than this. As we move into the new century, we find more of our citizens relegated to the ranks of what Marx once described as the surplus population, a population rendered unneeded or superfluous as far as creating profits are concerned. With more corporate downsizing has come the disappearance of semiskilled and unskilled jobs once filled by urban minorities, especially African American males. But this group is still very much with us and, from the point of view of those in power, they need to be managed in some way. The prison system seems to be the mechanism of this form of management.

It is especially ironic that we are experiencing what politicians are call-ing the "end of welfare as we know it." The irony is that we are experienc-ing a new form of welfare and it is called the prison system. Because there has not been a significant rise in the kinds of crimes that have historically re-sulted in prison sentences (e.g., burglaries, larcenies, robberies, murder) and we cannot use the crude techniques of control common in totalitarian soci-eties (e.g., torture, genocide), we have invented new "crimes" and new "criminals" to justify prison expansion—namely drugs. But, of course, only certain kinds of drugs, used by certain classes of people, are targeted.

Following the social unrest of the 1960s, the problem of *discipline* be-came greater than ever before, exemplified by the problem of crime. For con-servatives it was also a crisis in *values*—especially the values of hard work and responsibility. (Out of this concern came the hot political agenda of "family values" during the late 1980s.) As Melossi and Lettiere perceptively note, the current era has been one marked by what the famous French soci-ologist Emile Durkheim called *anomie,* a breakdown in social norms and the disjuncture between the culture (i.e., traditional goals, such as success) and the social structure (i.e., legitimate institutions that help meet these goals). Two common outcomes include an increase in various forms of crime and deviance, and a strong effort by those in power to restore and defend the "old order" through the use of various forms of social control, typically the most coercive forms (i.e., the legal system). Continuing, Melossi and Lettiere observe that during recent years, "crime"

> . . . became a master-metaphor to designate what was wrong with American society, with the criminals certainly, but also with work absenteeism, students taking over campuses, pot-smokers, free-sex lovers, rebellious minorities, "lib-erated" women, and so on and so forth. At the same time, "punishment," and the connected concept of "individual responsibility" increasingly became a master-metaphor of what "the cure" ought to be. (Melossi and Lettiere, 1998: 37–38)

This conservative reaction reached its zenith during the Reagan years in the 1980s, when the rate of imprisonment zoomed upward, and the tar-gets were mostly minorities—especially African Americans, who may face the following possible scenario within the first two decades of the twenty-first century: a majority of *all* African American males between eighteen and forty will be in prison or jail (estimate provided by Mauer, 1994; Miller, 1996; and Tonry, 1995).

Are we not engaging in our own form of slow genocide, a sort of dis-enfranchisement of urban minorities? Have we not created a new, more modern form of apartheid? In order for us to do this, it is necessary to use certain scientific-sounding labels, like *sociopath* or *criminal personality*. Of course the traditional, gut-level terms are also used, like *dangerous classes, predators, thugs, gangs,* and the like. It is not *our kind* that are being sent to prison, it is *them, those people.* This way we can wash our hands of any responsibility.

We have come a long way from the workhouses of the sixteenth and seventeenth centuries. But the functions of the modern prison system—ironically, in the richest country in world history—remain the same: providing housing for those groups deemed dangerous, a label being used more disproportionately to define people with dark skin.

Notes

1. Weiss (1987: 339). Weiss refers to a study of the emergence of the prison system in Massachusetts and South Carolina by Hindus, who argued that "The profit, production, and discipline goals of the prison [in Massachusetts] were the same as those of the factory." What is perhaps most interesting here is the fact that factory owners were often active in prison reform. Weiss reproduces an interesting quote from this source as follows: "The largest single category of arrests in Massachusetts was liquor-related offenses. Arrests for vagrancy and the entire area of sex-related crimes also show that a particular value system was being upheld through law, rather than simply that limited list of crimes against persons and property, prosecution for which few would object to." (See Hindus, 1980: 227, 251.) Virtually every major historical study has noted that the vast majority of arrests throughout the eighteenth and nineteenth centuries were for mostly "public order" and similar crimes. (See Ignatieff, 1978.)

2. Rothman (using a consensus argument) continually suggests that "Americans" wanted social order, never mentioning the fact that it was a relatively small ruling elite that wanted a *certain kind of order,* one that would primarily benefit their own class. See Chomsky (1996a) for further elaboration on this theme.

3. For a discussion on the treatment of Native Americans and evidence of genocide, see Chomsky (1993) and Zinn (1995). While the incarceration of African Americans was almost nonexistent in the South prior to Emancipation (with a rate of only 8.34 per 100,000), in the North the "free" African Americans were incarcerated at a rate of 289.91, compared to a rate of only 26.23 for whites; ironically, a difference higher than it is today (late 1990s). After 1870, of course, the South began to "catch up" with the North as far as the incarceration rate of African Americans was concerned, jumping up to a rate of 120.35 versus only 42.56 for whites. Melossi and Lettiere (1998: 27, citing Sellin, 1976: 133–144; and Sabol, 1989). In the South, the role of the penitentiary was seen as an acceptable and more "humanitarian" method of punishing *white* offenders, since most white Southerners believed capital and corporal punishments were appropriate methods of punishing *black* offenders. (See Weiss, 1987a: 343.)

4. For a more detailed story of Osborne, see Tannenbaum (1933). It is probably no accident that this experiment did not last. While the "official" goal of prisons has been to prepare inmates to be responsible and productive citizens, in actual fact, prisons have operated as if they wanted to produce just the opposite. There is a tendency to reinforce dependency and irresponsibility, which, in effect, reproduces the class structure.

5. The first five were suggested by Irwin (1980), while the last period (covering the years since Irwin's book) was suggested by Robert Weiss (personal communication).

6. This prison is located in the southern part of Illinois, within a short distance from Southern Illinois University. While a graduate student at this university in the early 1970s, the author visited this prison on several occasions as part of a special education program organized by a group of inmates (joined by fellow graduate student and now noted authority

on prisons, Robert Weiss). I recall vividly the experience of going inside this prison. It *looked* and *felt* and *sounded* like a *prison,* much more so than any other prison I have visited. The experience was at first frightening, not because the inmates were "dangerous" (some were, of course, but those I met were not), but because of the look and feel of the prison, with the steel locks, block walls, the sound of cell doors closing behind me (an unmistakable echo that gave me the message loud and clear that this was in fact a *prison*). What was particularly eerie was on the occasions when I went about the time the sun was setting—around the spacious grounds (covered with trees and freshly mowed lawns), I could see several deer roaming around. The contrast between the freedom displayed by these deer and the deprivation of freedom displayed by this very imposing prison was incredible. I have never forgotten that sight—and I wished I had a camera at the time! In time, Marion became infamous for the behavior-modification programs within its walls and the large number of political prisoners it held.

7. The reader no doubt notices that the phrase "new penology" has already been used to describe the rhetoric of the 1870 Prison Congress meetings and the reforms during the Progressive Era. This is testimony of how history so often repeats itself. The latest "new penology" was mainly "old wine in new bottles."

8. This is similar to the argument provided by Massey and Denton (1993), who were describing the "old" American apartheid.

9. There are at least *eight* prisons in the Northern Peninsula alone (located in five towns: Munising, Baraga, Newberry, Kinchebe, and Marquette) housing more than five thousand inmates.

10. It is ironic that many state mental institutions were closed in the 1960s and 1970s as part of a "deinstitutionalization" movement, only to have many of the same buildings now housing prison inmates. It has been estimated that as many as 70 percent of prison inmates suffer severe mental problems (Schlosser, 1998; interviewed by Terri Gross, "Fresh Air," National Public Radio, December 3, 1998).

5

Controlling the Young

The Emergence and Growth of the Juvenile Justice System

This chapter traces the development of the juvenile justice system from colonial times to the present. It begins with a brief discussion of how the misbehavior of children and youth was dealt with in colonial society, then turns to the buildup of institutions dealing with "juvenile delinquents" in the early nineteenth century, and then follows with a discussion of the reforms that took place in the last half of the nineteenth century, culminating in the modern juvenile court and juvenile training schools. Finally, the chapter focuses on the most significant developments during the twentieth century.

From our current historical vantage point, this is not a story with a happy ending. Indeed, we have continued to succumb to what can be called the *edifice complex*. This refers to the fact that we have continued to view the solution to many human problems as requiring some form of "edifice"—a courthouse, an institution, a detention center. Yet at the same time, we have succumbed to the *Field of Dreams Syndrome*—"If you build them, they will come." In other words, as soon as you construct these edifices, they will be filled almost immediately. This is one of the themes advanced in this chapter.

Another major theme advanced here is that "diversion," in its various forms, has been used throughout history. Each new institution (e.g., reform schools, training schools, group homes) has been established on the heels of the failure of old institutions that have become overcrowded, inhumane, and costly. Each new institution supposedly has been more "humane" and would alleviate some of the problems created by existing institutions. In time, however, these institutions have become as harsh and overcrowded as those they have replaced. The edifices have continued to be built and they (e.g., inmates, guards, administrators) kept coming.[1]

The third and major theme of this chapter is that the juvenile justice system has been used mostly to control the behavior of children of the urban poor, especially racial and ethnic minority groups. More informal—and less repressive—mechanisms have been reserved mostly for children of the more privileged classes.

Pre-Nineteenth–Century Developments

In a long view of history, even the concept of childhood is of relatively recent vintage. According to Ariès, art in the Middle Ages (A.D. 500 to 1400) did not even attempt to portray childhood, instead depicting children as little men and women (Ariès, 1962). Adolescence as a separate social category did not appear until the nineteenth century; during earlier periods (when life expectancies often went little beyond the age of forty), young adults constituted the backbone of society. Prior to this time, "infancy" ended at around seven and "adulthood" began immediately. There was no intervening stage for the simple reason that it was totally unnecessary. In fact, it was not until around the sixteenth century when there were books on the subject of child-rearing. In the medieval world, childhood was invisible (Postman, 1994: 18).

Prior to the nineteenth century, any sort of deviance on the part of children was dealt with on a relatively informal basis. Although there were often strict laws governing the behavior of youth (especially in New England), they were rarely enforced, and the severe punishment corresponding to many laws concerning children and youth was rarely administered. For example, regarding the typical response by the Quakers, Hawes reports: "When a child misbehaved, either his family took care of his discipline or the Quaker meeting dispensed a mild and paternalistic correction" (Hawes, 1971: 18). Almshouses and other forms of incarceration were rarely used for members of one's own community.

This is not to say that children were never punished, for indeed they were, and often brutally. In England, for instance, as late as 1780, children could be convicted and hanged for more than two hundred crimes. Postman recounts the hanging of a seven-year-old girl for "stealing a petticoat." What is important to note, however, is that committing crimes against one's own children was hardly noticed, but to do so against other children would be severely punished, for the simple fact that this type of crime was considered damaging the property of others. There was also a "reign of terror" against many children of the poor throughout England during the eighteenth and well into the nineteenth centuries; they were relegated to the notorious workhouses (about which Dickens often wrote), textile mills, mines, and prisons (Postman, 1994: 53–54).

Prior to around the mid-1700s, there was not much serious crime to speak of, among neither adults nor children. For the most part, the behavior and control of children was a responsibility of parents and perhaps other adults in the community. Eventually, various laws were passed calling for the punishment of parents who failed to perform their duty to control their children. In cases in which children's misbehavior was especially troublesome, apprenticeship of some form was often the punishment meted out. Also, various forms of corporal and, in rare cases, capital punishments were carried out (Bremner, 1970; Rendleman, 1974; Rothman, 1971: Chapters 1–2; Bernard, 1992: 44–45).

One of the major reasons for this type of response was the fact that the labor of children and youth was so much in demand (although in the South, slaves were more readily available). More importantly, however, children and youth were usually viewed as small adults and treated as such. As several historians have noted, there was actually no concept of *adolescent* or *teenager* prior to the onset of industrialism and the emergence of capitalism during the late eighteenth and early nineteenth centuries. Young people had relatively close ties to their families and communities until about the age of puberty. Kett has noted that in agricultural communities, "physical size, and hence capacity for work, was more important than chronological age. . . ." Autobiographies and biographies are replete with instances of young people beginning to work at ages as young as six or seven during the colonial period and well into the nineteenth century. Typically a boy between seven and fourteen would engage in minor jobs, such as running errands, chopping wood; after that age, apprenticeship into some trade was taken up (Kett, 1977: 13–18).[2]

The importance of children and youth to the family income should be stressed. As Kett noted:

> Children provided parents in preindustrial society with a form of social security, unemployment insurance, and yearly support As soon as children were able to work in or out of the home, they were expected to contribute to the support of their parents; when parents were no longer able to work, children would look after them. (Kett, 1977: 23)

There were, of course, class distinctions during this period. Many poor children were "sentenced" (because they were poor rather than their misbehavior per se) to several years of hard labor as apprentices, to either wealthy landowners or ship captains (Bremner, 1970). Kett further noted that:

> Poor farm children were forced out of the home early, children of prosperous, landowning farmers left home at a somewhat later age and returned home more frequently; children of wealthy manufacturers and merchants left early, but because of parental preference rather than necessity. The degree of freedom also depended on social class. To the extent that poor households were more frequently disrupted than wealthy ones, poor children often had more de facto freedom (unless bound as paupers), although, it must be added, there was little that they could do with their freedom. (Kett, 1977: 29)

Before the nineteenth century, then, the deviant behavior of young people was handled largely on an informal basis. This does not imply that all was well with the treatment of youths in previous centuries. For example, children were subjected to extreme forms of physical and sexual abuse (de Mause, 1974; Empey, 1982). Strict laws governed the behavior of children; however, in the United States, these laws were used only infrequently (Sutton, 1988; Hawes, 1971; Rothman, 1971). *Almshouses* (a word used synonymously for workhouses and jails until the nineteenth century) and other forms of incarceration were rarely used to handle the misbehavior of members of one's own community, and incarceration for long periods was almost nonexistent. In cases where children's misbehavior was especially troublesome, apprenticeship (i.e., sending a youth away from home to live with someone who could teach him or her a trade) was often used as a form of punishment (Rendleman, 1974). For the most part, the control and discipline of children was left up to the family unit (Krisberg and Austin, 1993: 9).

The appearance of adolescence as a social category coincided with an increasing concern for the regulation of the moral behavior of young people

(Platt, 1977; Empey, 1982). Although entirely separate systems to monitor and control the behavior of young people began to appear during the early part of the nineteenth century, differential treatment based on age did not come about overnight. The roots of the juvenile justice system can be traced to much earlier legal and social perspectives on childhood and youth. One of the most important of these was a legal doctrine known as *parens patriae.*

Parens patriae has its origins in medieval England's chancery courts. At that point, it had more to do with property law than children; it was, essentially, a means for the crown to administer landed orphans' estates (Sutton, 1988). *Parens patriae* established that the king, in his presumed role as the "father" of his country, had the legal authority to take care of "his" people, especially those who, for various reasons (including age,) were unable to take care of themselves. For children, the king or his authorized agents could assume the role of guardian to administer their property. By the nineteenth century, this legal doctrine had evolved into the practice of the state's assuming wardship over a minor child and, in effect, playing the role of parent if the child had no parents or if the existing parents were declared unfit.

In the American colonies, for example, officials could "bind out" as apprentices "children of parents who were poor, not providing good breeding, neglecting their formal education, not teaching a trade, or were idle, dissolute, unChristian, or incapable" (Rendleman, 1974: 63). Later, during the nineteenth century, *parens patriae* supplied (as it still does to some extent), the legal basis for court intervention into the relationship between children and their families (Teitelbaum and Harris, 1977; see also Krisberg and Austin, Chapter 2).

Another legal legacy of the colonial era that relates to the state's involvement in the lives of youth is the *stubborn child law.* Passed in Massachusetts in 1646, it established a clear legal relationship between children and parents and, among other things, made it a capital offense for a child to disobey his or her parents. This statute stated in part:

> If a man have a stubborn or rebellious son, of sufficient years and understanding (viz) sixteen years of age, which will not obey the voice of his Father, or the voice of his Mother, and that when they have chastened him will not harken unto them: then shall his Father and Mother being his natural parents, lay hold on him, and bring him to the Magistrates assembled in court and testify unto them, that their son is stubborn and rebellious and will not obey their voice and chastisement, but lives in sundry notorious crimes, such a son shall be put to death. (Sutton, 1988: 11)

This law was grounded in the distinctly Puritan belief in the innate wickedness of humankind, wickedness that required, for one thing, that children be subjected to strong discipline. This law was unique in several other respects: it specified a particular legal obligation of children; it defined parents as the focus of that obligation; and it established rules for governmental intervention if parental control over children broke down (Sutton, 1988).

It is important to consider the full implications of the notion of the state as parent, and more especially, father—a concept that is implied in both the *parens patriae* doctrine and, to some extent, the *stubborn child law*. The objects of a patriarch's authority have traditionally included women in addition to children (see Chapter 6 for further discussion of patriarchy). The idea of patriarchy reinforced the sanctity and privacy of the home, and the power (in early years, almost absolute) of the patriarch to discipline wife and children (Dobash and Dobash 1979: Chapter 1). Further, the notion of *parens patriae* assumes that the father (or, in this case, the state or king) can legally act as a parent with many of the implicit parental powers possessed by fathers. Therefore, governmental leaders would eventually utilize *parens patriae*, once a rather narrowly construed legal doctrine, to justify extreme governmental intervention in the lives of young people. Arguing that such intervention was "for their own good," "for their own protection," or "in the best interests of the child," the state during the nineteenth century became increasingly involved in the regulation of adolescent behavior.

In the United States, interest in the state regulation of youth was directly tied to explosive immigration and population growth. Between 1750 and 1850, the population of the United States increased from 1.25 to 23 million. The population of some states, like Massachusetts, doubled; New York's population increased fivefold between 1790 and 1830 (Empey, 1982: 59). Many of those coming into the United States during the middle of the nineteenth century were of Irish or German background; the fourfold increase in immigrants between 1830 and 1840 was in large part a product of the economic hardships faced by the Irish during the potato famine (Brenzel, 1983: 11). The social controls in small communities were simply overwhelmed by the influx of newcomers, many of whom were either foreign-born or of foreign parentage.

This was to change, slowly at first, with the transition to capitalism (specifically, the factory system in New England) during the late eighteenth and early nineteenth centuries. With the breakup of colonial society, in addition to the beginning of immigration, came an influx of poor, homeless young people, many of whom flocked to the cities of the Northeast, particularly New York. With this increase came a growing concern among prominent citizens about the "perishing and dangerous classes," as they would be called throughout the nineteenth century (Brace, 1872). With the shift from agriculture to industrialism came the age of adolescence and with this age came the problem of "juvenile delinquency" and attempts to control it.

This is an important development that needs further comment. The term *juvenile delinquent* originated in the early 1800s and referred to two different meanings: (1) "delinquent," which means "failure to do something that is required" (as in a person being "delinquent" in paying taxes), and (2) "juvenile," meaning someone who is malleable, not yet "fixed in their ways," and subject to change and being molded (i.e., redeemable). By the 1700s, with colleges and private boarding schools developing, various informal methods of social control of more privileged youth emerged, which paralleled the emergence of capitalism and the need to reproduce the next generation of capitalist rulers. Eventually, more formal systems of control emerged to control working- and lower-class delinquents around the early 1800s, including the juvenile justice system and uniformed police.[3] In other words, the attitude that even working- and lower-class offenders could be "redeemed" developed (Bernard, 1992: 49–55).

The House of Refuge Movement

During the early nineteenth century, prominent citizens in the cities of the East began to notice the poor, especially the children of the poor. The parents were declared "unfit" because their children wandered about the streets unsupervised, committing various crimes just to survive. Many believed that here was the major source of problems in social control and forerunners of even greater problems in the future. It was the class of poor and immigrant (in this era, the Irish) children and their lifestyles and social position that would soon be associated with crime and juvenile delinquency.

Rothman suggests that there was an assumption that the causes of criminality were to be found not only in these social conditions of the cities but also in family upbringing. He noted that one belief was foremost; namely, that ". . . parents who sent their children into the society without rigorous training in discipline and obedience would find them someday in prison" (Rothman, 1971: 70). Upon examining the life histories of adult convicts, reformers found that early childhood transgressions were the prelude to worse things to come. Here we find the beginnings of the use of the concept of *pre-delinquency*, a notion that has continued in its popularity to the present day.

As attention began to focus on the children of the poor, another problem was noticed. Many observers found that young children, some as young as six or seven, were locked up with adult criminals in jails and prisons and were also appearing with increasing regularity in criminal courts. It was believed that such practices were not only inhumane, but would also inevitably lead to the corruption of the young and the perpetuation of youthful deviance or perhaps a full-time career in more serious criminality.

A number of philanthropic associations emerged in eastern cities to deal with these problems. One of the most notable was the Society for the Reformation of Juvenile Delinquents (SRJD), founded in the 1820s. (This group was formerly called the Society for the Prevention of Pauperism, indicative of the common equation of deviance with poverty in this era. For a discussion of this group and a detailed description of its class backgrounds, see Pickett, 1969: 21–49). A member of this group, lawyer James W. Gerard, expressed a view that was typical of other members of this society when he commented that most of the children appearing in the criminal courts of New York were "of poor and abandoned parents" whose "debased character and vicious habits" resulted in their being "brought up in perfect ignorance and idleness, and what is worse in street-begging and pilfering" (Hawes, 1971: 28). The solution that was offered became one of the most common solutions to the problem of delinquency in years to come: remove the children from the corrupting environments of prisons, jails, "unfit" homes, slums, and other unhealthy environments and place them in more humane and healthier environments.

The SRJD, composed primarily of wealthy businessmen and professional people, convinced the New York legislature to pass a bill in 1824 that established the New York House of Refuge, the first correctional institution for young offenders in the United States. The bill created the first statutory definition of juvenile delinquency and authorized the managers of the refuge "to receive and take into the House of Refuge . . . all children as shall be convicted of criminal offenses . . . or committed as vagrants" if the court deems that they are 'proper' objects" (Hawes, 1971: 33).

The general aims of the House of Refuge, including the conceptions of *delinquents*, are reflected in the following extract from the SRJD:

> The design of the proposed institution is to furnish, in the first place, an asylum, in which boys under a certain age, who become subject to the notice of our police, either as vagrants, or homeless, or charged with petty crimes, may be received, judiciously classed according to their degree of depravity or innocence, put to work at such employments as will tend to encourage industry and ingenuity, taught reading, writing, and arithmetic, and most carefully instructed in the nature of their moral and religious obligations, while at the same time, they are subjected to a course of treatment that will afford a prompt and energetic corrective of their vicious propensities, and hold out every possible inducement to reformation and good conduct. . .(Abbott, 1938: 348)

According to the SRJD, a *juvenile delinquent* was defined as a child who broke a law or who "wandered about the streets, neither in school nor at work and who obviously lacked a 'good' home and family" (Hawes, 1971: 33).

The statutes contained vague descriptions of behaviors and lifestyles that were synonymous with the characteristics of the urban poor (especially Irish immigrants). Being homeless, begging, vagrancy, and coming from an unfit home (as defined from a middle-class viewpoint) are examples. The legislation that was passed also established specific procedures for identifying the proper subjects for intervention and the means for the legal handling of cases. According to law, the state or a representative agency or individual could intervene in the life of a child if it was determined that he or she needed "care and treatment," the definition of which was left entirely in the hands of the agency or individual who intervened.

Immigrants received the brunt of enforcement of these laws, especially children of Irish parents. Pickett notes that a House of Refuge superintendent accounted for a boy's delinquency because "the lad's parents are Irish and intemperate and that tells the whole story . . . " (1969: 15). The results of such beliefs are reflected in the fact that between 1825 and 1855, the commitments to the refuge who were Irish were as high as 63 percent (Pickett, 1969: 6).

That the delinquency statutes more often described a way of life or social status (e.g., poverty) is attested to by the fact that of the seventy-three children received at the New York House of Refuge during the first year of operation, only one had been convicted of a serious offense (grand larceny), nine were committed for petty larceny, and sixty-three (88 percent) were committed for what Abbott describes as "stealing, vagrancy, and absconding" from the almshouse (Abbott, 1938: 362).

The majority of those committed to the New York House of Refuge were children whose parents came from working-class backgrounds, many of whom could be classified as "working poor" or just plain "poor." A check of occupations of those whose parents held jobs (and most did not) shows that the most common was listed as "common laborer"; "washerwoman" ranked second and "masons, plasterers, and bricklayers" ranked third. The fact that so many parents were "washerwomen" is indicative of the common phenomenon of the period among many urban dwellers that men were forced to leave their families in order to find work elsewhere, leaving children and their mothers to fend for themselves. Women and children were the primary workforce in many factories in the Northeast (Pickett, 1969: Appendix).

It seems that the reformers and institutional officials believed that they had the qualifications not only to judge those on the bottom of the social order but also to govern or otherwise intervene in the latter's "best interest." Another method of maintaining control, says Mennel:

> Early nineteenth century philanthropists also undertook charitable work for their own protection. They feared imminent social upheaval resulting from the explosive mixture of crime, disease, and intemperance, which they believed characterized the lives of poorer urban residents. Without relieving the poor of responsibility for their conditions, these philanthropists saw in their benevolences, ways of avoiding class warfare and the disintegration of the social order. The French Revolution reminded them, however, that the costs of class struggle were highest to advantaged citizens like themselves. (Mennel, 1973: 6)

Conceptions of Delinquency: 1820–1860

The conceptions about delinquency and theories attempting to explain the phenomenon of delinquency played an important role in child-saving activities and their accomplishments during the first half of the nineteenth century.

Mennel notes that "during the eighteenth century, juvenile delinquency slowly ceased to mean a form of misbehavior common to all children and instead became a euphemism for the crimes and conditions of poor children" (1973: xxvi). By the nineteenth century, such a view became quite dominant in popular thinking. According to Pickett, the managers of the New York House of Refuge believed that the major causes of delinquency were, in order of importance, ignorance, parental depravity and neglect, intemperance, theatrical amusements, bad associations, pawnbrokers, immigration, and "city life in general." A crude environmental view prevailed throughout this period as poverty, family-rearing practices (of the poor), and other social and psychological factors were typically associated with delinquency (Pickett, 1969: 191). A report by a Unitarian minister in 1830 stated that three fourths of the young picked up by the police were from families that looked to their children to help support them. Instead of citing the inequalities that existed at the time and the exploitation on the part of factory owners (who employed large numbers of children), the report said that this condition was due to the "idleness and intemperance of the parents." The report further noted that these children "are every day at once surrounded by temptation to dishonesty. . . "(Bremner, 1970: 613).

Rothman notes that the family was generally considered a major source of the problem. He writes that phrases such as "poor upbringing," "bad habits," "drinking," and "immorality" (indicative of an anti-Catholic bias so common at that time) were commonly heard. Other factors commonly associated with crime and delinquency included the lack of respect for authority and failure to abide by the "work ethic." All of these were characteristically associated with the behavior, lifestyles, and living conditions of the urban poor (especially Irish Catholics) (Rothman, 1971: 58).

It is generally true that reformers often blamed social conditions as the primary cause and, therefore, beyond the control of individual youths. At the same time, however, they blamed the youngsters themselves (and their parents as well), at least indirectly. Time and again reformers stressed that it was up to the individual to avoid the "temptations" that such social conditions produced. A report by the SRJD noted that the youths in the refuge were "in a situation where there is no temptation to vice. . . and where, instead of being left to prey on the public, they will be *fitted* to become valuable members of society" (Hawes, 1971: 44, emphasis added). It was as if the evil conditions of the inner cities were like bacteria that were in the air and that some were immune while others were not. Therefore, the goal of reformation was to immunize individuals who had come down with the disease of delinquency or pre-delinquency. The physical analogy has been with us ever since.[4]

The Fate of the Refuge Movement

Social reformers, such as the SRJD and the "child-savers" of the late nineteenth century, have been described as "humanitarians" with "love" in their hearts for the "unfortunate children of the poor." According to the SRJD: "The young should, if possible, be subdued with kindness. His heart should first be addressed, and the language of confidence, although undeserved, be used toward him." The SRJD also said that he should be taught that "his keepers were his best friends and that the object of his confinement was his reform and ultimate good" (Hawes, 1971: 45–46).

The results of the actions by these reformers suggest that the "best interests of the child" were usually not served. Children confined in the houses of refuge were subjected to strict discipline and control. A former army colonel working in the New York House of Refuge said: "He (the delinquent) is taught that prompt unquestioning obedience is a fundamental military principle" (Mennel, 1973: 103). It was strongly believed that this latter practice would add to a youth's training in self-control (evidently to avoid the temptations of evil surroundings) and respect for authority (which was a basic requirement of a disciplined labor force). Corporal punishments (including hanging children from their thumbs, the use of the "ducking stool" for girls, and severe beatings), solitary confinement, handcuffs, the "ball and chain," uniform dress, the "silent system," and other practices were commonly used in houses of refuge (Pisciotta, 1982).

Following the lead of New York, other cities constructed houses of refuge in rapid succession. Within a few years there were refuges in Boston, Philadelphia, and Baltimore. It soon became evident, however, that the original plans of the founders were not being fulfilled, for crime and delinquency remained a problem. Also, many of the children apparently did not go along with the "benevolence" of the managers of the refuges. Inmates often staged various protests, riots, escape attempts, and other disturbances that were almost daily occurrences (Hawes, 1971: 47–48; Bremner, 1970: 689–691; Pisciotta, 1982). While at first limiting itself to housing first offenders, youthful offenders, and pre-delinquents, the refuges in time came to be the confines of more hardened offenders (most of whom were hardened by the experiences of confinement), and soon succumbed to the problem of overcrowding. Such a fate would return time and time again to plague institutions built throughout the nineteenth and twentieth centuries, even to the present day.

While the early-nineteenth-century reforms did not have much of an impact on crime and delinquency, they did succeed in establishing methods of controlling children of the poor (and their parents as well). Rothman concludes: "The asylum and the refuge were two more bricks in the wall that Americans built to confine and reform the dangerous classes" (Rothman,

1971: 210). While the poor and the working classes were usually viewed as lazy, shiftless, and dangerous, the trait that tended to strike the most fear into the hearts and minds of the privileged was "idleness." Indeed, an idle mass of underprivileged and deprived people was an obvious threat to the security of the upper class. Little wonder, then, that the major assumptions about the causes of crime and delinquency continuously stressed idleness, lack of the work ethic, and respect for authority. It is important to emphasize lack of respect for authority because "authority" usually means the ruling class and its representatives. To achieve respect for authority is to legitimize a particular order and set of rulers. When one lacks respect for authority, one has, among other things, not granted legitimacy to the existing order and ruling class. Because of this, it becomes important to instill such values in the minds of citizens, especially those who violate the law or otherwise behave contrary to role expectations. The SRJD asked citizens to visit the House of Refuge in New York "and see that idleness has become changed to industry, filth and rags to cleanliness and comfortable appearance, boisterous impudence to quiet submission" (Hawes, 1971: 44). Ideally, the result of orderly asylums such as these would be the production of passive, happy, contented workers who would gladly, upon release, submit to authority and accept their assigned place at the bottom of the social order and cause no further trouble. In the following quote, Rothman is describing the function of the prison, but his description could very easily apply to houses of refuge: "The functioning of the penitentiary . . . was designed to carry a message to the community. The prison would train the most notable victims of social disorder to discipline, teaching them to resist corruption" (Rothman, 1971: 107–108).

The rhetoric of the founders and managers of houses of refuge obviously fell far short of the reality experienced by the youth held in these facilities. A look at one of the most significant court challenges to the refuge movement provides additional insight into the origins of the juvenile justice system.

Ex Parte Crouse

Argued in 1838, *Ex Parte Crouse* arose from a petition of *habeas corpus* filed by the father of Mary Ann Crouse. Without her father's knowledge, Crouse had been committed to the Philadelphia House of Refuge by her mother on the grounds that she was "incorrigible." Her father argued that the incarceration was illegal because she had not been given a jury trial. The court noted that Mary had been committed on a complaint that said "that the said infant by reason of vicious conduct, has rendered her control beyond the power of the said complainant [her mother], and made it manifestly requisite that from regard to the moral and future welfare of the said infant she should be placed under the guardianship of the managers of the House of Refuge."[5] The court rejected the appeal, saying that the Bill of Rights did not apply to juveniles. Based on the *parens patriae* doctrine, the court asked, "May not the natural parents, when unequal to the task of education, or unworthy of it, be superseded by the *parens patriae* or common guardian of the community?" Further, the court observed that: "The infant has been snatched from a course which must have ended in confirmed depravity. . . "(*Ex Parte Crouse*, 1938: 9–11). Note here that the logic was accepted, even though one of Crouse's parents (her father) felt able to care for her. Also note that they were making predictions of future behavior based on rather vague criteria, which was becoming quite common at the time and would continue to be a common practice for years to come.

The ruling assumed that the Philadelphia House of Refuge (and presumably all other houses of refuge) had a beneficial effect on its residents. It "is not a prison, but a school," the court said, and because of this, not subject to procedural constraints. Further, the aims of such an institution were to reform the youngsters within them "by training . . . [them] to industry; by imbuing their minds with the principles of morality and religion; by furnishing them with means to earn a living; and above all, by separating them from the corrupting influences of improper associates" (*Ex Parte Crouse*, 1938: 11).

What evidence did the justices consult to support their conclusion that the House of Refuge was not a prison but a school? Not surprisingly, only testimony by those who managed the institution had been solicited. This was probably because the justices of the Supreme Court came from the same general class background as those who supported the houses of refuge and believed the rhetoric of these supporters. In short, they believed the "promises" rather than the "reality" of the reformers. A more objective review of the treatment of youths housed in these places, however, might have led the justices to a very different conclusion. For instance, subsequent investigations found that there was an enormous amount of abuse within these institutions. They were run according to a strict military regimen, during which corporal punishment (girls in one institution were ducked under water and boys were hung by their thumbs), solitary confinement, and a silent system were part of the routine (Mennell, 1973; Hawes, 1971; Bremner, 1970; Pisciotta, 1982). Work training was practically nonexistent, and outside companies contracted for cheap inmate labor. Religious instruction was often little more than Protestant indoctrination (many of the youngsters were Catholic). Education, in the conventional meaning of the word, was almost nonexistent.

A most intriguing addendum to the history of the houses of refuge—and to the Crouse case—came in 1870 with a Chicago case concerning a boy named Daniel O'Connell in the case of *People v. Turner* (1870). This young boy was incarcerated in the Chicago House of Refuge not because of a criminal offense, but because he was "in danger of growing up to become a pauper." His parents, like Mary Crouse's father, filed a writ of *habeas corpus*, charging that his incarceration was illegal. What is most intriguing about this case is that, although the facts were almost identical to the *Crouse* case, the outcome was the exact opposite.

The case went to the Illinois Supreme Court, which concluded that, first, Daniel was being *punished*, not treated or helped, by being in this institution (recall that the court had concluded that Mary Crouse was being *helped*); second, the Illinois court based its ruling on the *realities* or *actual practices* of the institution, rather than merely on "good intentions" as in the *Crouse* case; and third, the Illinois court rejected the *parens patriae* doctrine because it concluded that Daniel was being "imprisoned" and thus they based its reasoning on traditional legal doctrines of the criminal law. They therefore emphasized the importance of *due process* safeguards. In short, while the court in the Crouse case viewed the houses of refuge in a very rosy light, praising it uncritically, the court in the O'Connell case viewed the refuge in a much more negative light, addressing its cruelty and harshness of treatment (Bernard, 1992: 70–72; *People v. Turner*, 1974).

The O'Connell decision was to have far-reaching effects in the development of the movement to establish the juvenile court in Chicago in 1899. The founders of the juvenile court established this institution in part as a method of getting around the argument in the O'Connell case. In the 1905 case of Frank Fisher (ironically, another Pennsylvania case), the court returned once again to the logic of the Crouse case (*Commonwealth v. Fisher*, 1905). In time, this case would be overturned in 1967 in the *Gault* case.

Mid-Nineteenth–Century Reforms

America in the mid-nineteenth century was a nation constantly moving west. The settlements in newly conquered territories were in need of labor. Farm laborers, helpers in retail stores, washerwomen, and kitchen girls were among the kinds of work needed as capitalism spread its tentacles across the land.

Simultaneously, the eastern cities—New York, Boston, Philadelphia—were overpopulated with immigrants from all over Europe. Fleeing economic ruin, political repression, starvation, and religious persecution, they came by the millions. The capitalist class promised jobs for everyone, along with freedom and the "good life." But for most, the reality was quite different. The immigrants in overcrowded tenements and slums soon became the *dangerous classes*, a term applied to them by those in power.

Especially troublesome for those in power were the very young—the "street urchins," the "abandoned waifs," the children of the urban poor. Along with their adult counterparts, they needed to be controlled in some way. The newly emerging justice system—both adult and juvenile—would provide this function, along with schools and other institutions and programs. One such program was the "placing-out" system introduced by the New York Children's Aid Society, to be discussed later.

About the same time, many began to complain about the conditions of the houses of refuge. Not satisfied that these institutions were doing an adequate job of reformation, new methods were recommended. In Massachusetts, for instance, the first compulsory school law was passed in 1836, thereby creating a new category of delinquent, the *truant,* and a new method of controlling youths. New York passed a similar law in 1853. The objective of these laws was that of controlling rather than educating the children of the poor. As Bremner stated (speaking of the New York law): "This legislation was an instrument for placing abandoned and neglected children [of the poor] in institutions." In New York, the Association for Improving the Conditions of the Poor established the New York Juvenile Asylum in 1853. The primary aim of this association was to create a "suitable House of Detention" for "beggars, truants, waifs," and other "morally exposed children and youth." It would remove them from "dangerous and corrupting associates and place them in such circumstances as will be favorable to reform, and tend to make them industrious, virtuous, and useful members of society" (Bremner, 1970: 456, 739, 820). Such promises should now sound familiar.

The connection among compulsory schooling, the new factory system, and various forms of punishment in penal institutions is apparent. As Postman noted, "with the growth of large industrial cities and the need for factory and mine workers, the special nature of children was subordinated to their utility as a source of cheap labor." Although writing about England, historian Lawrence Stone's comments are relevant for America, as he notes that one of the effects of industrial capitalism was "to add support for the penal and disciplinary aspects of school, which were seen by some largely as a system to break the will and to condition the child to routinized labour in the factory" (Stone, 1969: 92, quoted in Postman, 1994: 53).

Public school reforms would continue to have a close connection to juvenile justice reforms. In his book, *Education and the Rise of the Corporate State,* Joel Spring writes that:

> The more general concern of industrialists was that schools produce an individual who was cooperative, knew how to work well with others, and was physically and mentally equipped to do his job efficiently. A cooperative and unselfish individual not only worked well with his fellows in the organization *but was more easily managed.* (Spring, 1972: 43, emphasis added)

William H. Tolman, cofounder of the American Institute of Social Service, commented in 1900 on the importance of the kindergarten program, saying that: "The lessons of order and neatness, the discipline of regulated play . . . are acquisitions, making the child of greater value to himself and, if he can follow up the good start which has been made for him, tending to make him of greater wage-earning capacity. . . ." Tolman further stated that children would be coming into the shops of the employers "in a few years;

how much better for you [the employers] that their bodies have been some-what strengthened by exercise, and their minds disciplined by regulated play" (Spring, 1972: 36–37).

Such innovations in public schooling as kindergarten, extracurricular activities, homeroom, and organized playgrounds combined to teach chil-dren the benefits of cooperative work, discipline, and respect for authority, not to mention submission to the needs of the group. (Individual initiative was apparently not encouraged.) It was not by accident that many of these programs were also established to prevent and control delinquency.

Representatives of the business world began an all-out campaign to support new forms of education that would train the future workers of America (Bowles, 1975). At first, they began with their own educational pro-grams along the lines of improving employee morale and relations between management and the worker. For instance, corporations established such programs as the "social secretary" (to "maintain constant personal contact with the workers"), employee associations and clubs, periodic employee-benefit gatherings, Sunday School programs, company magazines, and even their own public schools (including day-nurseries and kindergartens). The establishment of nurseries and kindergartens functioned to free "both par-ents for work either in the factory or home." The Plymoth Cordage Com-pany used such a system because "the company believed that by removing the children from the house for part of the day, the mother could give her undivided attention to housework." The rationale given by this company was that the husband would function better at work coming from a clean home with hot meals. Another function of kindergartens was to promote the role of women as the "natural caretakers" of children, as they enabled teach-ers to get into the homes of workers and thus interest mothers in children's work (Spring, 1972: 36).

Eventually, corporations began to put pressure on local communities to have the public school system perform some of these functions. Obviously, to do so would save business a great deal of money. As Spring concludes:

> These industrial programs for the management of workers became models for the type of activities adopted by the public school. . . . In some cases, actual programs, like home economics, were transferred from factory education ac-tivities to the public schools to produce workers with the correct social atti-tudes and skills. (Spring, 1972: 22)

In short, the school system evolved "to meet the needs of capitalist em-ployers for a disciplined labor force, and to provide a mechanism for social control. . . ." (Bowles, 1975: 219).

Rather than eliminate inequality and increase upward social mobility, the school system had the function of maintaining class differences. One method adopted was what is now known as the "tracking" system. There was pressure placed on schools to change the curriculum to one of a multi-plicity of course offerings that would correspond to the major strata of the occupational world. A report by the National Education Association in 1910 stated that: "The differences among children as to aptitudes, interests, economic resources, and prospective careers furnish the basis for a rational as opposed to merely a formal distinction between elementary, secondary, and high education" (Cohen and Lazeron, 1972: 186). Ellwood Cubberly, an educational reformer, wrote in 1909 that:

> Our city schools will soon be forced to give up the exceedingly democratic idea that all are equal, and our society devoid of classes . . . and to begin specialization of educational effort along many lines in an attempt to adapt the school to the needs of these many classes. . . . (Cohen and Lazeron, 1972: 187)

Reforms in public schooling were closely related to the problem of juvenile delinquency, as stated previously.[6] For example, in 1916, the Alfred Binet Intelligence Test was established. Henry Goddard, one of the leaders in the development of this test, believed that intelligence-testing was the key to reducing delinquency and claimed that the public schools could be used as "clearinghouses" to pick out "potential delinquents," especially the category he called the low intelligent, "defective delinquent" (Mennel, 1973: 96–99). Thus, the public schools became agencies of social control and a crucial element in the prevention and control of delinquency. Teachers, guidance counselors, truant officers, school social workers, and school psychologists became part of this vast network of social control within the school system. Actually, the desire to use the schools for this purpose was recognized long before, as Charles Loring Brace stated in 1880 that "in the interests of public order, of liberty, of property, for the sake of our own safety and the endurance of free institutions," what is needed is a "strict and careful law, which shall compel every minor to learn to read and write, under severe penalties in the case of disobedience" (quoted in Platt, 1974: 370).

While it can certainly be argued that the school system ultimately meant upward mobility for some (usually those already from privileged classes), for the majority, however, it meant remaining in their original class position. For African Americans and other minorities, the situation was worse. This was especially the case in the public schools of the South, which were patterned after a social order based on caste and class and "separate but equal" (Shelden, 1976).

Some reformers, such as Brace, believed that a family-type setting, preferably in the country, would offset the often brutalizing and impersonal setting of houses of refuge. Actually, such a move had begun in Boston as early as the 1830s, when prominent citizens felt the need to establish a reform school for boys who had not yet been convicted of a crime but nevertheless still roamed the streets and were "in need of discipline." What was needed, they said, was an institution that stood somewhere between the houses of refuge and the public school system. The result was the Massachusetts State Reform School for Boys, opened in 1849. A similar school was opened for girls in Lancaster in 1855, the first of many such institutions based on the "family system" (Brenzel, 1975). The first family system for boys was the Ohio State Reform Farm, opened in 1857 (Bremner, 1970: 705).

In the meantime, a "placing-out" system had emerged in the New York area, the most famous of which was the one operated by the New York Children's Aid Society. What this group did was place children "out West" (to use their phrase) in family-type institutions (e.g., the Ohio school), in actual residences (similar to foster homes today), or on farms. Millions of children came West in what were commonly referred to as "orphan trains" (Holt, 1992). The following comment by Brace, founder of the Children's Aid Society, indicates that economic factors played an important role and that many of these children provided landowners a cheap source of labor:

> The United States has the enormous advantage over all other countries, in the treatment of difficult questions of pauperism and reform, in that is possesses a practically unlimited area of arable land. The demand for labor on this land is beyond any present supply. . . . It is of the utmost importance to them [the farmers] to train up children who shall aid in their work [referring to children whom the Children's Aid Society placed]. (Abbott, 1938: 138)

It is interesting to note one of the methods used by the Children's Aid Society. The Society divided New York City into sections and assigned to each section a "visitor." (This was part of the "Friendly Visitor" program, one that was popular throughout the nation; such a role would eventually evolve into that of social worker.) Hawes describes what the visitors did:

> The visitors would go from house to house, trying to persuade the families to send their children to the public schools or to the industrial schools of the Children's Aid Society. When a visitor found a homeless or neglected child, he took him to the central office of the society, where, after securing the parent's consent—if they could be found—it prepared to send him to a farmer's home in the West. (Hawes, 1971: 101)

Usually the parents could not be found because they were away during the day (when the visitors called), either working or seeking work. One might understandably wonder what happened if the parents refused to cooperate with such a practice. While the records of what those on the bottom of the social order thought of things are typically incomplete, if known at all, a few notable cases suggest that these parents, and their children as well, did not always passively succumb to the "benevolences" of the reformers.[7]

For example, the Baltimore House of Refuge had a case in which a mother attempted to get her daughter from a home where she had been placed by the Refuge. The officials reported:

> After we had found a home for the little girl, the mother made an application for her, which we refused. She succeeded in finding where the child was, and demanded it. The man with whom we had placed her was quite firm, and refused to surrender her, but told the mother that if she conducted herself well, the mother might visit her. She threatened legal proceedings, but our power over the child was superior to hers and thus the injudicious interference of the parents was prevented. (Bremner, 1970: 693–94)

Other incidents of parents trying to maintain their rights over the power of the state are reported by Rendleman. He notes that during the last half of the nineteenth century, the number of court cases challenging the state's power over children increased. In reviewing these cases, he concludes that most commitments were for either poverty or "poverty plus" (e.g., begging, poverty, destitution, neglect, and dependency) and, in some cases, says Rendleman, it is difficult to tell why children were being taken away from their parents in the first place. Court decisions give evidence that children were not committed to institutions because of any violation of the law or because of failings by parents, "but simply because the parents were poor and behaved as poor people always have." There was "an unspoken assumption that the state had an equal if not superior interest in the children and the burden was on the parents to show to the contrary" (Rendleman, 1974: 104–106).

The Fate of Mid-Nineteenth–Century Reforms

Toward the end of the nineteenth century, it was clear to many that earlier reforms and the existing institutions were doing little toward the reformation of delinquents and the reduction of crime. However, as Rothman noted, the asylums constructed during the early and middle nineteenth century failed yet persisted because the original intention to reform gave way to custody. The primary reason for this was a pragmatic one: Once perceived as a threat to all, the dangerous classes could no longer be banished or merely whipped as they were during the colonial period. They had to be controlled physically, for to banish them might result in their being a danger to another community (Rothman, 1971: 240).

While it is certainly true that custody became the order of the day, some reformers never gave up and soon began to agitate for more effective reformation. Upset with the ruling in the O'Connell case, they sought ways of getting around it. They began to argue for an extension of the current system to include a special court for hearing children's cases. But in believing that reformation was not working, reformers were saying, in effect, that *control* was ineffective. Hence, additional "reforms" were merely new measures to control and regulate the deviants, potential deviants, and the poor in general (Piven and Cloward, 1972).

Part of the new upswing in reform activities was a result of the changes occurring in American society during the last half of the nineteenth century: greater industrialization and urbanization, a new wave of immigrants, general unrest and revolt by workers, periodic economic crises in the capitalist system, and other problems. Chicago, the main site of the "child-saving" movement, had grown from a small town of around five thousand in 1840 to a huge city of a million and a half, mostly accounted for by immigrants (Bernard, 1992: 84).

There was also a noteworthy change in the labor-market structure, especially as it affected youth. In the 1880s, with the growth of factories came the movement of both journeymen and apprentices into the ranks of the industrial proletariat, and where teenage helpers posed a constant threat to the wage-earning abilities of young adult journeymen. Skilled crafts began to exclude teenage youth, who were forced to take factory jobs, most of which were dead-end jobs. Thus, between 1865 and 1900, "the ranks of unemployed veterans who flooded into New York, Philadelphia, Chicago, and other great cities after Appomattox were swelled in hordes of young tramp laborers who drifted from place to place and job to job" (Kett, 1977: 147). Many of these youths became what the Schwendigers have called *redundant workers* or what Marx referred to as the *relative surplus population* (Schwendinger and Schwendinger, 1976: 13). Little wonder they behaved in "delinquent" ways.

New theories of crime and delinquency had emerged by this time, heavily influenced by the positivist school of criminology. This school of thought popularized the so-called medical model of deviance. The Progressive Era ushered in a new series of reforms commonly known as the child-saving movement, and resulted in the establishment of new institutions to "care for," "control," and "protect" errant and wayward youth. One such institution was the juvenile court.

The Child-Saving Movement
and the Juvenile Court

Like their earlier nineteenth-century counterparts, the *child-savers* were a group of upper-middle- and upper-class whites with business and professional backgrounds. Also, they were threatened by the deleterious social conditions in the slums of Chicago and other cities. Surveys by noted reformers Z.R. Brockway and Enoch Wines found that children were still being kept in jails and prisons with adult offenders. The child-savers dedicated themselves to saving these children and diverting them from the adult criminal justice system.

The result of their efforts was the establishment of the juvenile court. The new legislation of the period (first in Chicago and Denver in 1899, then elsewhere) created new categories of offenses and extended the state's power over the lives of children and youth. Because of the O'Connell case, only children who had committed felonies could be sent to reform schools. A method of "nipping the problem in the bud" was needed. The logic the reformers used was to define the new juvenile court as a sort of "chancery court," upon which the doctrine of *parens patriae* was based. Only in such a court, argued the child-savers, could "the best interests of the child" be served. The 1899 Illinois Juvenile Court Act simply removed from the jurisdiction of the criminal courts all cases involving juveniles (at first the upper age was sixteen, later it was raised to seventeen), and then formally establish the juvenile court. Thus, the "problem" arising out of the O'Connell case was immediately solved (Bernard, 1992: 88–89).

The new laws that defined delinquency and pre-delinquent behavior were broad in scope and quite vague: (1) the laws covered the usual violations of laws also applicable to adults; (2) the laws covered violations of local ordinances; (3) the laws included such catch-alls as "vicious or immoral behavior, incorrigibility, truancy, profane or indecent behavior, growing up in idleness, living with any vicious or disreputable person," and many more. These would eventually be known as *status offenses* (Platt, 1977: 138).

Prior to the passage of the Juvenile Court Act in Chicago in 1899, several states already had laws defining these status offenses. For instance, in 1895 Tennessee passed an act to provide county reformatories. Under this act, a county could commit "infants under the age of sixteen" if

> . . . by reason of incorrigible or vicious conduct, such infant has rendered his control beyond the power of such parent guardian or next friend, and made it manifestly requisite that from regard to the future welfare of such infant, and for the protection of society he should he placed under the guardianship of the trustees of such reformatory institution. (Shannon, 1896: 1087–1088)

Children could also be committed as "vagrants" or if they were "without a suitable home and adequate means of obtaining an honest living, and who are in danger of being brought up to lead an idle or immoral life" (Shannon, 1896: 1087–1088). Even the Tennessee code copied, almost word-for-word, the original act that created the Philadelphia House of Refuge in 1826 (*Ex Parte Crouse*, 1838).

Influenced by the dominant eclecticism prevailing in the field of criminology, reformers believed that delinquency was the result of a wide variety of social, psychological, and biological factors. They believed that one must look into the life of the child offender in intimate detail to know the "whole truth" about the child. The judge of the juvenile court was to be like a benevolent yet stern father. The proceedings were to be informal without the traditional judicial trappings. There was neither a need for lawyers nor constitutional safeguards because, first of all, the cases were not "criminal" in nature, and second, the court would always act "in the best interests of the child." The court was to be operated like a clinic and the child was to be diagnosed to determine the extent of his condition and to prescribe the correct treatment plan, preferably as early in life as possible.

Even the terminology of the juvenile justice system was, and to some extent still is, different. Children in many parts of the United States are *referred* to the court rather than being arrested; instead of being held in jail pending court action, they are *detained* in a *detention center* or *adjustment center*; rather than being indicted, children are *petitioned* to court; in place of a determination of guilt, there is an *adjudication*; and those found guilty (i.e., adjudicated) are often *committed* to a *training school* or *reform school* rather than being sentenced to a prison.

Envisioned as a benevolent institution that would emphasize treatment rather than punishment, the juvenile court turned out to be a mixture of the two orientations. The confusion can be traced to the mixed legacy of the court that combined a puritanical approach to stubborn children and parental authority with the Progressive Era's belief that children's essential goodness can be corrupted by undesirable elements in their environment. Finckenauer termed the mixture *ambivalent* or even *schizophrenic* (Finckenauer, 1984: 116; Feld, 1999).

The attention of the juvenile court and its supporters was mainly against the children of the poor, especially immigrants. Schlossman suggested that the juvenile court served "as a literal dumping ground." The court provided an arena "where the dependent status of children was verified and reinforced, and where the incapacities of lower-class immigrant parents were, in a sense, certified" (Schlossman, 1977: 92).

The juvenile court system extended the role of probation officer, a role originally introduced in the mid-nineteenth century in Boston.[8] This new role was one of the primary innovations in the twentieth-century juvenile justice system, and the role became one of the most crucial in the entire system. Schlossman wrote that "nothing in a child's home, school, occupation, or peer-group relations was, at least in theory, beyond" the purview of the probation officer. The probation officer "was expected to instruct children and parents in reciprocal obligations, preach moral and religious verities, teach techniques of child care and household management" (Schlossman, 1977: 99). Part of the probation officer's role was likened to that of an exorcist, for he was required to, in a sense, ward off or exorcise the evil temptations of the city. One reformer, Frederic Almy, wrote in 1902: "Loving, patient, personal service" would provide the "antiseptic which will make the *contagion* of daily life harmless" (Schlossman, 1977: 99, emphasis added).

Conceptions of Delinquency: 1860–1920

Social reformers in America accepted a form of "soft determinism" and the "notion that behavior is determined by forces outside the individual actor's control," while operating on the assumption that "if criminal behavior was determined by knowable biological or psychological or social conditions, those conditions could be identified and changed, *at least at the individual level*" (Faust and Brantingham, 1974: 3, emphasis added). However, as implied in this quote, while causal factors were external to the individual (e.g., poverty, bad housing, inequality), the emphasis was and would continue to be on the individual offender.

Most of the reformers tended to accept the version of Social Darwinism known as Reform Darwinism, the view that man was not completely helpless and that man's progress enabled him, through "positive science," to step in and improve his lot. With the help of such writers as Cooley and Henderson, reformers tended to accept the "nature versus nurture" view, with heavy emphasis on the "nurture" side of this dichotomy (Cooley, 1974; Henderson, 1974). However, taken as a whole, the environmental view that combined "bad homes and evil surroundings" dominated the thinking throughout the nineteenth and early twentieth centuries. There is little evidence that the prevailing views have changed very much.

There was also a belief that intervention should be stressed and that "potential criminals and delinquents" could and should be identified and treated at the earliest age possible. Although such a belief had been quite dominant throughout the nineteenth century, the juvenile court was supposed to be one of the chief means through which intervention would be made. The court also enlisted the help of other programs and institutions to carry out such a program. Thus, it is not too surprising to find that public schools, recreation programs, public playgrounds, boys' clubs, YMCAs, and other organizations all helped in dealing with the problem of delinquency, especially in their role of identifying and "containing" so-called "pre-delinquents" (Shelden, 1976; Shelden and Osborne, 1989).

The general images or stereotypes of delinquents and criminals had not changed much since the early nineteenth century. For example, Brace, in commenting on the dangerous classes, said that those who participated in the New York Draft riots of 1863 (protesting being drafted to fight in the Civil War) were "street children grown up." He further commented that this class:

> . . . has not begun to show itself, as it will in eight or ten years, when these boys and girls are mature. Those who were too neglected or too selfish to notice them as children, will be fully aware of them as men. They will vote. They will have the same rights as ourselves, though they have grown up ignorant of moral principle, as any savage or Indian. They will poison society. They will perhaps be embittered at the wealth and the luxuries they never share. Then let society beware, when the outcast, vicious, reckless multitudes of New York boys, swarming now in every foul alley and low street, come to know their power and use it. (Bremner, 1970: 757)

As this quote suggests, the images of delinquents were often contradictory. On the one hand, they were often viewed in a sympathetic light, suggesting they needed help; on the other hand, they were feared and described in some of the most racist and vicious ways.

Many of the child-savers, like their earlier nineteenth-century counterparts, suggested a number of social factors as causal forces of delinquency. But few carried their arguments to the logical conclusion, that changing environmental factors was necessary, at least those social conditions that benefited the privileged. The solution continued to focus on the control, "rehabilitation," or "treatment" of individual offenders or groups of offenders from a particular segment of the population (including those identified as pre-delinquents). The existing social structure was accepted as good and necessary, but there was a need to lead those who went astray back so that they could "fit" into the existing social order and class system. Unfortunately, the only place they were permitted to "fit" was at or near the bottom of that order.[9]

Most of the programs advocated during this period placed primary emphasis on the individual and his or her moral and other personal shortcomings, and received justification from psychological, psychiatric, and psychoanalytic theories of delinquency just beginning to emerge during the late nineteenth century. Such an approach was exemplified in the works of Hall and Healy, both of whom worked closely with the juvenile courts in various cities. These writers advocated a "clinical" approach (using the medical model), one which stressed the need for a "scientific laboratory" to study delinquents. One such laboratory was the juvenile court.

The Fate of the Child-Saving Movement

The child-savers claimed that they had ushered in new innovations in penology, especially with the establishment of industrial and training schools. Actually, the methods used were variations of earlier methods used in houses of refuge and other institutions. Most of the "new" institutions of the twentieth century were placed in rural areas, which was in part a reflection of the belief in "rural purity," a product of the popular anti-urban bias among so many child-savers. It was assumed that the "temptations" of city life would be offset by placement in such a setting. The juvenile court was to be the primary placing agency, thus serving a function similar to that of the Children's Aid Society when it placed children "out West."

The emphasis within these institutions remained relatively unchanged from previous methods. Restraint, control, the teaching of "good work habits" (e.g., cleaning floors, waiting on tables, milking cows, cooking), respect for authority, and a quasi-military model continued to be the hallmark of these institutions.

An example of the kinds of institutions opened during this period was the Shelby County Industrial and Training School, located near Memphis, Tennessee. Opened in 1904 in a farming community, it emphasized farm labor and the development of "habits of industry" through various forms of work and education. One of its founders stated that the *school* (a term often substituted for prison) would be:

> a place where we could educate the youths confined there in the practice, as well as the science, of agriculture; a place where they could be taught to get the best results from the cow in the way of milk, butter, and beef; a place where they could not only raise cotton, but could learn to make it into cloth; a place where they could acquire a knowledge of carpentry, blacksmithing, shoemaking, broommaking, designing, horticulture, floriculture, etc.; in fact, a place where from whence they could go with a technical knowledge which would enable them to take a position in the world as useful citizens.[10]

In a 1912 report, the Board of Directors stated in glowing terms how "successful" this institution had become:

> The boys in the several departments of work and in the school room have shown commendable interest in work and study. All are in school half of every weekday, under the instruction of a thoroughly competent lady school teacher. In the several departments of work, habits of industry have been cultivated which must prove a helpful training for future usefulness. The half-day work and half-day school, which has been in practice in these institutions for years, is now appealing to our public school authorities as a necessary advance in youthful development.
>
> There has been no attempt in the past to indulge in expensive and often impracticable methods. Our work in all departments is necessary, practical, and productive. On the farm and in the garden the actual use of the implement in the hand of the boy, under intelligent supervision, must produce results— and does—which means an abundance of fresh vegetables in their season for our tables and feed for our dairy cows and other stock.
>
> In the bakery and kitchen . . . the boys, under the supervision of a lady teacher of domestic science, are kept exceedingly busy. . . . The laundry force and the boys who do the endless scrubbing, sweeping, and dusting like all being taught the necessity of work. . . . [11]

Thus, even the most menial work was made respectable, so that these youths would fit into their appropriate labor-force position upon release.

This institution was closed in 1935 amid a great deal of controversy, with two grand-jury reports criticizing its methods and lack of results (in terms of a high recidivism rate and overcrowding) (Shelden, 1992).

The "new penology" (as it was called at the time), perhaps best represented by state and county "reformatories," "industrial and training schools," and the like, emphasized menial labor that helped produce profits for both the state and private industry. For instance, the Illinois State Reform School (opened in 1871 at Pontiac) signed contracts with a Chicago shoe company, a company that manufactured brushes, and a company that manufactured cane-seating chairs; this was called the "educational" program at this institution (Platt, 1977: 105). The training in such institutions was supposed to, in the words of the famous penal reformer Frederick Wines, "correspond to the mode of life of working people," and should "be characterized by the greatest simplicity in diet, dress, and surroundings, and *above all by labor* (Platt, 1977: 50, emphasis added). In many of these institutions (e.g., the one in Memphis), emphasis was placed on agricultural training, despite the fact that America was fast moving toward an industrial society. The reformatory regime aimed to teach middle-class values but lower-class skills. "Bookishness" was expressed as something undesirable, while menial labor was described as an "educational" experience. Waiting on tables, cleaning, cooking, and the like were to be taught to the "colored boys" in these institutions, according to the National Conference of Charities and Correction. Reformers aimed to "get the idea out of the heads of city boys that farm life is menial and low. . . " (Platt, 1977: 59–60).

The juvenile court system rapidly spread throughout the country following the lead of Chicago and Denver (both opened in 1899). Juvenile institutions, such as industrial and training schools and reform schools, continued to develop and expand.

Twentieth-Century Developments in Juvenile Justice

During the period roughly between 1920 and the 1960s, there were relatively few structural changes within the juvenile justice system. In Illinois, beginning around 1909, the juvenile court began experimenting with the intensive psychological study and treatment of youthful deviance. The Juvenile Protective League, under the leadership of such notables as Julia Lathrop (head of the U.S. Children's Bureau), Jane Addams (famous reformer and founder of Hull House; see Addams, 1960), Julian Mack (judge of the Boston juvenile court), and William Healy (famous psychologist), established a child guidance clinic, in which the medical model of delinquency was epitomized, Thus, under the direction of Healy, child-guidance clinics focused their attention and energies on the individual delinquent, one who was generally viewed as "maladjusted" to his or her social environment. By 1931, there were more than two hundred such clinics around the country (Krisberg and Austin, 1993: 32–35).

During the 1920s and 1930s, the profession of social work grew to prominence (Lubove, 1965). This field began to dominate the treatment of individual delinquents and interpreted delinquency as stemming from conflicts within the family. Even today, social-work methodology has a strong influence within the juvenile justice system.

Another development, the Chicago Area Project, which had its theoretical thrust from the famous Chicago School of Sociology and the works of Clifford Shaw, focused on community organization to prevent delinquency, From this perspective, delinquency stemmed from the "social disorganization" of slum communities rather than from the exploitation inherent in the capitalist system. Hence, the solution would be found in "fostering local community organizations to attack problems related to delinquency," such as poverty, inadequate housing, and unemployment (Krisberg and Austin, 1993: 35–42). Much of the effort focused on reducing gang delinquency that was so prevalent in Chicago and other large cities (Liazos, 1974: 12; Thrasher, 1927). But such programs did little to alter the social reality of economic deprivation and other structural sources of delinquency. Krisberg and Austin comment that:

> . . . Chicago at that time was caught in the most serious economic depression in the nation's history. Tens of thousands of people were unemployed, especially immigrants and blacks. During this period, a growing radicalization among impoverished groups resulted in urban riots. The primary response by those in positions of power was an expansion and centralization of charity and welfare systems. In addition, there was considerable experimentation with new methods of delivering relief services to the needy [e.g., Hull House]. No doubt, Chicago's wealthy looked favorably upon programs like the Area Project, which promised to alleviate some of the problems of the poor without requiring a redistribution of wealth and power. (Krisberg and Austin, 1978: 33)

The decade of the 1960s brought about some hope for significant changes, but such hope lasted barely into the 1970s. At least two developments stand out during this period. One development was the intrusion into the business of juvenile justice by the United States Supreme Court. Famous court cases such as *In re Gault* (1967),[12] *Kent v. United States* (383 U.S. 541, 1966), *In re Winship* (397 U.S. 358, 1970) promised significant reforms. Sadly, most of the promise was never realized, especially with regard to institutionalizing youth.

The second development, which had some major impact, came on the heels of the efforts of Jerome Miller in the state of Massachusetts, who managed to close most of the reform schools opened in the nineteenth century (Miller, 1998). Despite the success of the closure of most of their institutions and the development of workable alternatives throughout the country, the recent "get-tough" policies do not signal hopeful signs. Krisberg and Austin observed that "Most jurisdictions still rely on placement in institutions, with conditions reminiscent of reform schools one hundred years ago. Children continue to be warehoused in large correctional facilities, receiving little care or attention" (Krisberg and Austin, 1992: 49). The "get-tough" policy has especially targeted minorities, as more institutions have become dominated especially by urban African Americans (Pope and Feyerherm, 1990; Miller, 1996). Moreover, young women continue to be subject to a "double standard," as minor offenses too often result in some form of incarceration (Chesney-Lind and Shelden, 1997). Also, many institutional systems have become huge bureaucracies with a vested interest in keeping a certain percentage of youth incarcerated. One of the best examples is the California Youth Authority, which itself has been subject to considerable controversy (Lerner, 1986).

Looking at the current situation, the juvenile justice system is still focusing almost exclusively on controlling minorities and the poor. Sadly, this is even truer today than it was almost two hundred years ago.

Still Controlling Minorities and the Poor: Current Juvenile Justice Practices

In 1998, the police made about 1.6 million arrests of those under eighteen years of age (Federal Bureau of Investigation, 1998). Just over one fourth (28 percent) of these arrests were for "index crimes," with property offenses accounting for the vast majority of all arrests in this category (70 percent of these were larceny-theft, mostly shoplifting). However, these figures represent a rather small percentage of all youths under the age of eighteen who committed acts that could be considered delinquent. The majority of all youth commit some offense that could theoretically result in a referral to the juvenile court, yet few end up with an arrest.

As shown in Table 5.1, race figures prominently in juvenile-arrest statistics. As noted here, while African American youths comprise about 12 percent of the juvenile population, in 1995 their rate of arrests for all crimes was double what is was for white youths. More dramatic differences are seen for violent crimes, where the arrest rate for African American youths was around five times greater than for white youths, which was actually not as great as what it was in 1972 and in 1982. For drug offenses, however, the differences are even more dramatic. Thus, whereas in 1972 white youths had a *higher* rate than African Americans, by the early 1980s (at roughly the beginning of the "war on drugs"), the difference was reversed. By 1995, the change was incredible: the arrest rate for African Americans was almost three times greater than for whites. Elsewhere in Table 5.1, the percentage changes over these years. What is noteworthy is the more than 400 percent increase in arrest rates for African American youths on drug charges. It is easy to conclude that the war on drugs has been a war on African Americans.

A more detailed look at arrest patterns comes from a study of California cases in 1989 (Krisberg and Austin, 1993: 126–127). This study found that African American youths constituted about 8.7 percent of the total population, they were about 20 percent of those arrested, and their arrest *rate* was double the rate for whites. It is at this stage that a sort of *cumulative racial bias* begins to set in. Thus, as we go farther into the system, African Americans youths are far more likely to begin to receive the most severe disposition.; Evidence of racial bias is clear, as the rate of detention for African Americans is more than four times greater than for whites. This relationship holds even when considering other factors.

As numerous studies have shown, the race, class, and demeanor of a youth often plays a crucial role in police decision-making, especially when there are no complainants and for misdemeanor offenses (Pope and Feyerherm, 1990). A study by Bishop and Frazier is instructive because they followed a cohort of more than 54,000 youths from arrest to adjudication in the juvenile court. While holding constant factors such as seriousness of offense,

TABLE 5.1 *Arrest Rates (Per 100,000 Aged 5–17), for Selected Offenses, by Race, 1972–95.*

	1972		1982		1995	
	White	*Black*	*White*	*Black*	*White*	*Black*
Index Crimes						
Violent	46	497	87	580	146	762
Property	816	2,191	1,032	2,404	1,011	2,050
Total	862	2,888	1,119	2,984	1,157	2,812
Drugs	187	133	153	201	244	682
Total, All Offenses	2,835	5,870	3,296	6,727	3,749	7,760
Percent Change:	**1972–82**		**1982–95**		**1972–1995**	
Total Index						
White	+29.8		+3.4		+34.2	
Black	+3.3		-5.8		-2.6	
Violent						
White	+89.1		+67.8		+217.4	
Black	+16.7		+31.4		+53.3	
Property						
White	+26.5		-2.1		+23.9	
Black	+9.7		-14.7		-6.4	
Drugs						
White	-18.2		+59.5		+30.3	
Black	+51.1		+239.3		+412.8	
All Offenses						
White	+16.3		+13.7		+32.2	
Black	+14.6		+15.4		+32.2	

Sources: Federal Bureau of Investigation, 1973: 130, 132; 1997: 227; McGarrell and Flanagan, 1985: 479–481

prior record, and the like, they concluded that "race is a far more pervasive influence in processing than much previous literature has indicated" (Bishop and Frazier, 1988: 258).

Race may actually play an indirect role in that it relates to offense, which in turn affects the police decision to arrest. Race may also relate to the *visibility* of the offense, which is especially the case with regard to drugs. There is abundant evidence that the war on drugs has, in effect, resulted in a targeting of African Americans on a scale that is unprecedented in American history. As the research by Miller has shown, young African American males received the brunt of law enforcement efforts to "crack down on drugs." He notes that in Baltimore, for example, African Americans were being arrested at a rate six times that of whites, and more than 90 percent were for possession (Miller, 1996: 8; see also Currie, 1993; Tonry, 1995; Mann, 1995; Chambliss, 1995; Lockwood, Pottieger, and Inciardi, 1995).

Another study found that "black youths are more often charged with the felony when [the] offense could be considered a misdemeanor. . . ." Also, those cases referred to court "are judged as in need of formal processing more often when minority youths are involved." When white youths received placements, such placements were more often than not "group home settings or drug treatment, while placements for minorities more typically are public residential facilities, including those in the state which provide the most restrictive confinement" (Kempf, 1992, quoted in Miller, 1996: 257). A study by McGarrell found evidence of substantial increases in minority youths being referred to juvenile court, thus increasing the likelihood of being detained. But cases of the detention, petition, and placement of minorities nevertheless exceeded what would have been expected given the increases in referrals. There has been an increase in the formal handling of drug cases, which has become a disadvantage to minorities. "Given the proactive nature of drug enforcement, these findings raise fundamental questions about the targets of investigation and apprehension under the recent war on drugs" (McGarrell, 1993, quoted in Miller, 1996: 258). As noted in a study of Georgia's crackdown on drugs, the higher arrest rate for African Americans was attributed to one single factor: "it is easier to make drug arrests in low-income neighborhoods. . . . Most drug arrests in Georgia are of lower-level dealers and buyers and occur in low-income minority areas. Retail drug sales in these neighborhoods frequently occur on the streets and between sellers and buyers who do not know each other. Most of these sellers are black. In contrast, white drug sellers tend to sell indoors, in bars and clubs and within private homes, and to more affluent purchasers, also primarily white" (Fellner, 1996: 11).

Some studies have suggested that social class, rather than race per se, best predicted police decisions. For instance, research by Sampson found that the overall socioeconomic status of a *community* was more important than other variables, although race figured prominently. In general, the lower the socioeconomic standing of the community as a whole, the greater will be the tendency for the police to formally process youth they encounter (Sampson, 1986). Of course, minorities, especially African Americans, are far more likely than whites to be found within the lower class and living in poverty.

Demeanor has always played a significant role in police decision-making, especially when it comes to juveniles. Youths who "smart off" or otherwise do not display the "proper" deference are usually the most likely to be formally processed because, in police parlance, they "flunked the attitude test." This is especially the case with minor offenses and even when there is little or no evidence that a crime has been committed (Bartollas and Miller, 1998: 144). As with social class, race will figure into this equation because so many African American youths are angry at the white establishment, especially their representatives like the police, and will express such anger during their contacts with the police. Many display a sort of "defiant air" that challenge the police (Jankowski, 1990).

Regardless of whether race, class, or demeanor are statistically more relevant, one fact remains: growing numbers of African American youths are finding themselves within the juvenile justice system. They are more likely to be detained, to have their cases petitioned to go before a judge, to be waived to the adult system, and to be institutionalized than their white counterparts (Walker, Spohn, and DeLone, 1996: 144). While some of this relates to the nature of the offense, as we have shown, the likelihood of one race being associated with a particular offense, especially drugs, cannot be denied.

More than this, however, race once again enters the picture when it comes to the decision to detain. As noted in several studies, African American youths are more likely to be detained than white youths. Nationally, just over one fourth of nonwhites charged with delinquent offenses were detained in 1991, compared to only 17 percent of whites (the breakdown by specific races is not given in this source). Much larger differences are found when considering the offense charged. For example, for those charged with drug offenses, almost half of the nonwhites (48 percent) but only 25 percent of the whites were detained (Austin, et al., 1995: 44).

More detailed data presented in the California study referred to previously break down race in more detail. For example, almost half (48.5 percent) of the African America youths referred to juvenile court were detained, compared to only 30.6 percent of white youths. Their overall rate of detention was three times that for whites. In fact, no matter what the offense, African American youths were more likely to be detained than white youths; this was especially the case for those charged with drug offenses, as 72 percent of African American youths charged with felony drug offenses were detained compared to only 43 percent of white youths; *more dramatically, of those charged with misdemeanor drug offenses, less than 1 percent of the whites were de-*

tained, compared to almost 30 percent of the African Americans. Even when considering probation status, sex, age, and number of offenses, African Americans were more likely to be detained (Krisberg and Austin, 1993: 126–127).

Class and race have been found to be at least indirectly related to decision-making at the intake stage. Many studies beginning in the 1950s demonstrated the influence of class and race. A review of the evidence by Krisberg and Austin led to the conclusion that "nonwhite youth experience significantly higher rates of detention, petition-filing, and placements than do white youth" (Krisberg and Austin, 1993:101). In 1989, for example, national figures revealed that nonwhite youths were twice as likely as whites to be placed in secure detention (25 percent versus 12 percent), they were almost twice as likely to be petitioned to court (38 versus 20 percent), and twice as likely to be placed in some form of institution upon adjudication (10 versus 5 percent). Figures for 1990 show similar results, except for the proportion petitioned to court. During that year, almost 30 percent of African American youths were detained, compared to about 20 percent of white youths (no mention of other races). Interestingly, white youths were slightly more likely to be adjudicated (58 versus 55 percent), although African American youths were twice as likely to be waived to adult court (4 versus 2 percent). Finally, of the adjudicated cases, 36 percent of African Americans were placed in some sort of institution, compared to 30 percent of whites (Walker, Spohn, and DeLone, 1996: 144). As already mentioned, a study in Florida by Bishop and Frazier found that race was more important than offense and other variables in the processing of cases through the juvenile court.

As many studies have shown, the youth's prior record, instant offense, and previous sentences are among the most important factors in determining the final disposition (Bortner, 1982; Cohen, 1975; Thornberry, 1973, 1979). On the other hand, several studies have noted the importance of race and other social factors in determining the final disposition (Peterson, 1988). It has already been noted that minorities, especially African Americans, do not fare well throughout the court process. Even if the effects of race may disappear by the time the final disposition is made, race has already shaped previous processing decisions, such as the decision on what offense to charge and the decision to detain. Regardless, the effects are the same: African American youths are far more likely than whites to be placed in some form of institution. National figures show that in 1990, 36 percent of the adjudicated African American youths were placed in some form of institution, compared to 30 percent of white youths; not a large difference, but noteworthy. The Florida study by Bishop and Frazier found that 30 percent of African American youths were either incarcerated or transferred to the adult system, compared to about 20 percent of the white youths (Bishop and Frazier, 1988). Krisberg and Austin's study in California found that the rate of commitment to a private facility was 467 for African Americans, compared to only 153 for whites; the rate of commitment to secure county facilities was 1,114 for African Americans compared to only 294 for whites; the rate of commitment to the California Youth Authority (CYA), the most secure institutions in the state (tantamount to "junior prisons"), was 529, compared to only 47 for whites. The figures on commitments to the CYA reveal that even when considering the nature of the offense, current probation status, sex, age, and the number of offenses, African Americans were far more likely than whites to be committed. Like the figures for detention, sentences for drug offenses were dramatic: for felony drug offenses, African Americans were *seven times more likely than whites to be committed* (Krisberg and Austin, 1993: 126–128). Krisberg and Austin have recently observed that:

> Our analysis paints a discouraging picture. Juvenile laws are vaguely worded and inconsistently applied, permitting extensive abuses in the handling of children by social-control agencies whose discretion is largely unchecked. Instead of protecting children from injustices and unwarranted state intervention, the opposite effect frequently occurs. The practices and procedures of juvenile justice mirror our society's class and racial prejudices and fall disproportionately on African American, Latino, and poor people. (1993: 109)

Miller, reflecting on his own thirty-plus years of working with youthful offenders, notes that one of the problems within the modern juvenile justice system is the method of diagnosing youth and recommending appropriate dispositions. He suggests that the "treatment options" that the diagnostician has in mind helps to determine the actual diagnosis of the youth, rather than the other way around, as we generally assume. In reality, he notes, "the theory-diagnosis-treatment flow runs backward. The diagnostician looks first to the means available for handling the client, then labels the client, and finally justifies the label with psychiatric or sociological theory. Diagnosis virtually never determines treatment; treatment dictates diagnosis" (Miller, 1998: 232).

Increasingly, the juvenile courts, perhaps giving in to the "law and order" rhetoric of the past two decades, have begun to rely on one of the most extreme dispositions within the juvenile justice system, namely certifying a youth as an adult. It is as if they have said: "We give up! We have done everything we can think of to help you." Yet, those that the court has "given up on" are disporportionately African American youths. They are, in effect, disposable children.[13]

Giving Up on Delinquent Youth: Transfer to Adult Court

One of the fastest-growing changes within the juvenile justice system is what is commonly known as *waiver* or *certification*. What this term means is that if a juvenile court believes that an offender is too "dangerous" or is "not amenable to treatment," then the court transfers its jurisdiction (i.e., waives) to the adult system by, legally speaking, making the youth an adult.[14] Generally speaking, juvenile courts either lower the age of jurisdiction or exclude certain offenses (in most jurisdictions, homicide), known respectively as *judicial waiver* and *legislative waiver*.

One of the first Supreme Court rulings on judicial waiver was the 1966 case of *Kent v. United States* (383 U.S. 541, 1966). This decision began with a Washington, DC, case in which a youth's case was transferred to an adult court without procedural safeguards (he had no counsel and no hearing was given). The court ruled that when a case is to be transferred from the juvenile court to an adult court, the youth has a right to counsel and a right to have a hearing, and that counsel must be given access to the youth's social history file. In this case, the court ruled that a juvenile must be given a hearing, a juvenile is entitled to counsel, the court must provide a written statement giving the reasons for the waiver, and the defense counsel must be given access to all records and reports used in reaching the decision to waive. It was in this famous case that Justice Abe Fortas issued one of the strongest indictments of the juvenile court ever, writing that: "There is evidence, in fact, that there may be grounds for concern that the child receives the worst of both worlds; that he gets neither the protection accorded to adults nor the solicitous care and regenerative treatment postulated for children" (Bartollas, 1997: 426).

Every state currently has some provisions for transferring offenders to adult courts. In some states, only the age-only provisions are used, with growing numbers making the age lower and lower (e.g., in Vermont it is age ten, in Montana it is twelve, and in Georgia, Illinois, and Mississippi it is thirteen). Most states, however, do not go below fourteen (Bartollas, 1997: 441–442).[15]

There are several important issues surrounding certification. First, although the proportion of those transferred is small (currently around 5 percent), the numbers are increasing. One study found that in four Southern states between 1980 and 1988, the number increased by more than 100 percent (Champion, 1989). Second, contrary to popular opinion, the majority of those transferred to the adult system are not violent offenders, but rather they are property offenders; in some cases, public-order cases such as drunkenness and other minor cases. Third, in many cases, youths who are transferred are not treated any more harshly than they would be in juvenile court, with the majority granted probation. Specifically, in 1992, almost half (45 percent) of all waiver cases involved youths who had committed property offenses, while about one third were those who committed violent crimes, while 12 percent had committed drug offenses. Speaking of drug offenses, the largest increase in certification cases during the period 1987–1991 was for drug offenses, increasing by 152 percent (Donziger, 1996: 135–136).

This suggests that the movement to transfer youth is more a political issue than a public-safety issue. Many local politicians are gaining votes for their "get-tough" stance on juvenile crime, using mostly anecdotal evidence to support their cause (Bortner, 1986); in other cases, it is merely an attempt to get rid of troublesome cases (Bartollas and Miller, 1998: 214–215). In fact, transferring of juveniles to adult court *does not result in a reduction of crime and may even contribute to at least a short-term increase in crime* (Bishop et al., 1996). An even more sinister problem is that of racism. The disturbing fact, typically ignored in the debate, is the fact that the majority of those transferred to the adult court are African American youths.

Within the juvenile justice system, one of the most severe dispositional alternatives has always been and continues to be that of commitment to some form of secure facility, commonly known as juvenile institutions. A commitment to a juvenile correctional institution often represents the "end of the line" for some youthful offenders. As already observed, these institutions, starting with Houses of Refuge, have not had a positive history. Conditions in so-called "training schools" (the direct heirs of Houses of Refuge) have not improved that much over the years; any treatment in these institutions is a rare event.

As of 1991, there were 93,732 juveniles in juvenile correctional institutions: 57,542 in public facilities and 36,190 in private institutions (Austin et al., 1995: 31). Public institutions are becoming reserved for minority youth as they constitute over one half of the inmates, while private institutions appear to be reserved for white youth, as they constitute 56 percent in these institutions. There is an obvious discrepancy in the *rates* of incarceration between whites and African Americans, with the latter having a rate more than three times greater than the former. State-supported institutions are more secure and have little access to the community than is the case with private institutions. They also have the least amount of decent rehabilitation and are typically places where violence is the norm.

Thus, incarceration is a fate that awaits many minority youths. The percentage of incarcerated youth who are racial minorities has risen steadily over the years. National figures show that in 1950 only 23 percent of those in training schools were minorities; in 1960, this figure was 32 percent; in 1970, it was up to 40 percent; and as of 1991, minorities constituted more than 60 percent of those in public training schools (U.S. Department of Commerce, 1975: 419; Walker, Spohn, and DeLone, 1996: 223; Austin et al., 1993: 31). It is interesting to note that the majority of youths confined in *private* facilities are white. This is no doubt because most of the costs are paid for by family members, usually through their insurance.

As for the racial composition of all juvenile institutions, the latest figures show that of a total of 49,956 taken into custody in 1992, 38 percent were white, 43 percent were African American, and the remainder were other races. When considering the *rate* of incarceration, the racial differences are significant; the rate for African Americans was *more than five times that for whites*. Admissions for whites in 1992 were 101 per 100,000 population, compared to 524 for African Americans and 144 for Hispanics. Not surprisingly, drugs accounted for much of this difference. For instance, for males, the rate for drug offenses among whites was only five per 100,000, compared to a phenomenal 151 for African Americans. A one-day sample of a count taken in 1991 showed that for both public and private facilities combined, the incarceration rate for African Americans was more than three times greater than for whites (985 versus 276), and for public facilities, the rate was more than four times as great (675 versus 155). The differences were not as great for private facilities (310 for African Americans and 121 for whites) (Austin et al., 1993: 11, 15, 31).

As noted previously, in the state of California, minorities constitute a numerical majority confined within the CYA, a vast institutional complex with facilities throughout the state. In 1989, a total of 3,435 juveniles were committed to the CYA; 40 percent were African American and 35 percent were Latino. Their rates (per 100,000 population) of confinement were 529 and 117, respectively, compared to a rate of only forty seven for whites. In contrast, during the same year, of those placed in private facilities, 44 percent were white, 25 percent were African American, and 27 percent were Latino. Another form of placement for youths were local county facilities, considerably different in terms of security and overall conditions than the CYA. During 1989, 30 percent of the placements in these facilities were white, 43 percent were Latino, and only 21 percent were African American (Krisberg and Austin, 1993: 126). Clearly, in this state, an old phrase from the civil-rights days comes to mind: "If you're white, you're all right; if you're brown, stick around; if you're black, stay back." As already noted, the "war on drugs" (translation: "war on African Americans") seems to be the driving force.

Notes

1. For more detail on the history of juvenile justice, see the following: Pickett, 1969; Platt, 1977 and 1974; Hawes, 1971; Mennel, 1973; Liazos, 1974; Rendleman, 1974; Schlossman, 1977; and Bernard, 1992.

2. The age of seven has traditionally been viewed, legally, as the age at which children can distinguish between right and wrong and hence theoretically be subject to adult-like punishments. Why seven? This age of demarcation apparently originated in the Middle Ages for the reason that it was the age when children had developed some command over speech, where they could "say and understand what adults can say and understand." It was the Catholic Church that originally designated this age as the "age of reason." In fact, throughout the Middle Ages, a "young male" could be men aged thirty or forty or even fifty, since there were no words for young males between the ages of seven and sixteen (Postman, 1994: 13–14). Postman does not mention anything about girls and women here, probably a reflection of a subtle form of sexism or perhaps a reflection that back in the Middle Ages, as now, females were largely invisible.

3. Thus, informal systems of control have always been reserved for the more privileged youths, while the less privileged have been subjected to formal systems of control. However, if we examine history closely, with few exceptions, it has almost always been the case that minority youth have been much more likely to be viewed not as "juvenile delinquents" (i.e., "malleable" and thus "redeemable"), but as "hardened criminals" not redeemable (since by definition, "adults" are more fixed in their ways and less redeemable). Little wonder that such a great proportion of those certified or waived to adult court in recent years (i.e., viewed as "unredeemable" adult criminals) have been minorities.

4. Although Platt was writing about the later nineteenth century "child-savers," his comments summarize the prevailing view throughout this century: "If, as the child-savers believed, criminals are conditioned by biological heritage and brutish living conditions, then *prophylactic* measures must be taken early in life." Famous prison reformer Enoch Wines commented that "They are born to it, brought up for it. They must be saved" (Platt, 1977: 45, emphasis added; see also Platt's comments on the term *pre-delinquent* and how such youth needed to be "immunized" against the disease of "delinquency" on p. 107).

5. The wording used here is taken *verbatim* from the law, passed in Pennsylvania in 1826, which authorized the House of Refuge, "at their discretion, to receive into their care and guardianship, infants, *males under the age of twenty-one years, and females under the age of eighteen years*, committed to their custody. . . " (emphasis added). Note the obvious distinction based on gender. This exact same statute was reproduced in numerous state laws throughout the nineteenth century. I found an example in my own study of Memphis, Tennessee (Shelden, 1976).

6. For a fuller discussion of this topic from the perspective of an active reformer of the period, see Addams (1909).

7. In my own study of the origins of the juvenile justice system in Memphis, I found several instances where commitments to the county training school were challenged in court, some successfully (Shelden, 1976, 1992, 1993).

8. The origins of probation can be traced to the efforts of a man named John Augustus, a Boston shoemaker who, during the 1840s, volunteered to take on the responsibility of supervising offenders in the community as a substitute to sending them to prison or jail. Since then this rather unique idea has become highly bureaucratized with the average probation officer supervising between fifty and one hundred offenders. The spirit of volunteerism and the offering of a helping hand in the name of true benevolence toward one's human being has turned into a job as a career bureaucrat. Many who engage in this line of work are overwhelmed by the responsibilities and often care little about the persons they supervise. In fact, the "supervision" is often little more than surveillance, which usually consists of a few phone calls. In many instances, probation office follow the motto found on the wall of a California probation office which reads: "Trail 'em, Surveil 'em, Nail 'em, and Jail 'em" (Miller, 1996: 131).

9. An editorial appearing in the Memphis *Commercial Appeal* sums up the prevailing philosophy of those heading up the child-saving movement in Memphis (November 29, 1911):

> "Juvenile court records of the country are convincing the authorities that a great majority of youthful offenders receive their education on the streets. The facts presented should serve as a warning to parents. They should be productive of more improved future conditions.
>
> Children are not naturally evil-minded. They may be mischievously inclined. They may be bad, but not morally bad. It must he remembered, though, that children are in the formative age . . . children must he surrounded with the best and most improved influences. Their early lives should be lived in environments of good, not evil, and little good can be found on the streets. Keep the children at home as much as possible, or in their own neighborhoods. Do not

permit them to roam about uptown streets at night by themselves. . .

If the juvenile courts are confronting a rapid increase in juvenile crime, it is the parent's fault, not the child's.

It has been proven beyond all possibility of contradiction that the greatest percentage of boys and girls who are brought before the courts for delinquency owe their waywardness to the education they have received on the streets at night . . .

The remedy must be keeping children off the streets at night or to make the streets fit places for children. It is almost impossible to do the latter. It is possible to do the former. . . .

Thus, the problem of delinquency was considered a problem of the individual offender or the family, rather than an environment that should be made "fit places for children"(Shelden, 1976).

10. *Memphis Commercial Appeal,* July 21, 1903.

11. *Memphis Commercial Appeal,* July 16, 1912.

12. The case of *In re Gault* involved a fifteen year-old Arizona boy named Gerald Gault, who was adjudicated as a "delinquent" in juvenile court and committed to the Arizona Industrial School for the "period of his majority" (twenty-one years old) because he and some friends made an "obscene" phone call to a neighbor. The U.S. Supreme Court ruled that Gault had been denied certain fundamental rights (like the Illinois court did in Danny O'Connell's case), such as the right to counsel. Writing for the majority, Justice Abe Fortas stated that "Under our Constitution, the condition of being a boy does not justify a kangaroo court." For the full text of this case (and many others, including the O'Connell case), see Faust and Brantingham, 1974. See also Platt, 1977: 161–163.

13. See Renny Golden's (1997) insightful account of the more general problem of how children are treated within the modern welfare system, a system designed, along with the justice system, to control the dangerous classes. It is interesting to note that ironically as the government, in the last years of the twentieth century, has been "ending welfare as we know it" (to use a popular political "sound byte"), we are in the process of increasing the use of the prison system (on both the juvenile and adult levels) to serve basically the same general purpose.

14. One obvious problem that immediately arises, but is rarely discussed, is that if, say, a fifteen-year-old youth is certified as an adult, does that mean he or she can vote, drop out of school, purchase alcohol, leave home, or do anything an adult can do? In actual fact, they cannot, *even if they are placed on probation by the adult court and are still under eighteen.*

15. There was a case in Michigan where a thirteen year-old African American boy was on trial in an adult court for allegedly committing a murder when he was eleven years old. The prosecution is arguing that the child set out to kill someone with the statement "I'm going to shoot somebody." The prosecutor stated that: "A clearer intent was never spoken." The defense claims that the rifle used was a "piece of junk" and was defective, arguing that "even a marksman" would have missed at that distance (about 60 to 100 yards away). The bullet bounced off a tree and struck an eighteen year-old in the head (Associated Press, October 30, 1999). He was eventually convicted and sentenced to a juvenile facility until the age of 21.

6

Perpetuating Patriarchy

Keeping Women in Their Place

Women and the Law

Patriarchy and Images of Women

Several stereotypical images of women have helped shape not only the law, but also the definitions of what behaviors and what kinds of persons are considered "criminal." Among some of the most popular of these images include the following: (1) woman as the pawn of biology (i.e., controlled by biological forces, such as the menstrual cycle, beyond her control); (2) woman as passive and weak; (3) "woman as impulsive and nonanalytic" (i.e., she acts illogically and therefore needs the guidance from the more analytical man); (4) woman as impressionable and in need of protection (i.e., she is childlike and gullible and therefore needs more protection from men); (5) the active woman as masculine (i.e., whenever she breaks away from the traditional roles, it is deemed unnatural or even masculine); (6) the criminal woman as purely evil (i.e., when a woman "falls from grace," she must really be evil, because she is so inherently pure to begin with); and (7) the madonna-whore duality (a woman is either a virtuous person or the paragon of evil or the seductress) (Rafter and Stanko, 1982: 2–4; Pollock, 1996: 4).

Given these images, it is not surprising to find that there has been a tradition in law, going back as far as ancient Rome and Greece, that holds that women are perpetual children and the only adults are men. In Ancient Greece, for instance, only men could be citizens in the political arena and most of the slaves were women (women in general were treated as slaves). In Rome, the status of both women and slaves was improved somewhat as they were incorporated into the family under the rule of *Patria protestas* ("Power of the Father"). This term implied not so much a family relationship but rather a *property relationship*. The woman had to turn over any income she received to the head of the household and had no rights to her own children, no rights to divorce, or for that matter, no rights to life outside the family. According to Roman law, unlike slaves, women could not be emancipated. A woman's relationship to her husband was designated by the concept of *manus*, or hand. From this is derived the modern practice to ask a woman's father for "her hand in marriage" (Eisenstein, 1988: 58–59; Terkel, 1996: 6–7).

The attitudes that shaped these practices are revealed in several different sources, from the Bible to statements by Aristotle. Aristotle said that it is only "natural" that the man is superior and the woman inferior, and equally "naturally," it follows that one governs and the other is governed. In the Bible there are numerous references to this natural state of affairs. In Corinthians (I, 11:3,9), it is written that "The head of every man is Christ; and the head of the woman is the man. . . . Neither was the man created for the woman; but the woman for the man." Timothy (2:11–12) says: "Let women learn in silence with all subjection. But I suffer not a woman to teach, nor to usurp authority over the man" (quoted in Parenti, 1994: 143).

Such control of women is consistent with the system known as *patriarchy*. In her excellent treatment of this subject, Lerner defines patriarchy as "the manifestation and institutionalization of male dominance over women and children in the family and the extension of male dominance over women in society in general. It implies that men hold power in all the important institutions of society and that women are deprived of access to such power" (Lerner, 1986: 239). The legal institution is one among these various institutions mentioned by Lerner that are ultimately controlled by men and by extension is used to control women. Lerner describes it best by an analogy with a stage in a theater:

> Men and women live on a stage, on which they act out their assigned roles, equal in importance. The play cannot go on without both kinds of performers. Neither of them "contributes" more or less to the whole; neither is marginal or dispensable. But the stage set is conceived, painted, defined by men. Men have written the play, have directed the show, interpreted the meanings of the action. They have assigned themselves the most interesting, most heroic parts, giving women the supporting roles. (Lerner, 1986: 12)

Continuing the analogy, Lerner notes that as women become more aware of this inequality, they begin to protest, asking for more roles, more equality in determining what is assigned. At times they may "upstage the men" and at other times they may "pinch-hit" for a male performer. Yet even when they win equal access to desired roles, they must first qualify according to terms set by the men, who are the judges of whether women measure up. Preference is given to women who are docile; those who act differently are punished—by ridicule, ostracism, exclusion. In time, women realize that getting equal parts does not translate into "equality," as long as the script, stage setting, and props are controlled by men (Lerner, 1986: 12–13).

While women's subordinate status existed before capitalism emerged as a dominant mode of production, contrary to the strictly Marxist interpretation,[1] it is nevertheless true that capitalism has made things worse. This is because "capitalism rewards the impulses of exploitation, accumulation, competitiveness, ruthless self-interest, individualized aggrandizement, scarcity psychology, and indifference to the sufferings of the disadvantaged." Capitalism also "relies on sexism as a diversionary force" by focusing on issues other than class inequality, such as abortion and sexual morality, rather than a "critical examination of who gets what, when, and how." Further, under capitalism, "wealth is accumulated by expropriating the labor power of the worker," and both sexism and racism make this that much easier. Women, moreover, are often blamed by conservatives for what ails the society; they are convenient scapegoats (e.g., charges that too many are in the workforce demanding equal pay, or too many are "welfare queens") (Parenti, 1994: 149–150).[2]

Perhaps more importantly, women are viewed as "commodities." Parenti describes the process of *commodification* as "the process of objectifying and transforming the female appearance and body to fit marketable (i.e., marriageable) standards." Women have gone through hundreds of different procedures over the years (e.g., stretching lips and necks, flattened breasts during certain times and expanded them at other times, painted nails and lips), mainly to "gain the attention and approval of men, to persuade men to 'buy' them either as wives or workers" (Parenti, 1994: 150).

Punishing and Controlling Women

What has happened when women have not conformed to these images or in some way acted "out of place" or did not fit the image of a commodified female? Throughout world history, women "offenders" have been subjected to differential forms of punishment that reflect their subservient position. In the Middle Ages, a pregnant woman might receive lenient punishment if she were to "plead her belly," yet could be burned at the stake for the crime of adultery or for murdering her spouse (the latter of which still receives harsher punishment than men murdering their wives). Prior to the rise of imprisonment in the nineteenth century, daughters and wives who were unwanted were often forced into convents and similar institutions, along with political prisoners, the mentally defective, and other outcasts (Dobash, Dobash, and Gutteridge, 1986; Lorde, 1988).

Much of Roman law was eventually incorporated into the English common law, which in turn was copied (with few significant changes) in America. For several years, the only law book used was Blackstone's famous *Commentaries on the Laws in England,* originally published in 1765. American family law incorporated Blackstone's famous dictum that the husband and wife are as one and that one is the husband (Eisenstein, 1998: 58–59).

Not surprisingly, in early American law, the wife could not sue, execute a deed, or engage in any other similar practices without consent of her husband. Women were denied the vote until 1921; in general, laws that were "designed to protect the interests of 'persons' simply did not apply to women." In fact, the Supreme Court ruled in 1867 that a woman who had completed law school and had passed the bar in Illinois nevertheless had no right to practice law! Using the prevailing logic of the time, the court stated in their ruling that the "natural and proper timidity and delicacy which belongs to the female sex evidently unfits it for many of the occupations in civil life . . . " and that the "destiny and mission of women are to fulfill the noble and benign offices of wife and mother" (Chambliss and Courtless, 1992: 31).

Throughout colonial America, women had no identity, other than their relation with their father or later with their husband. The husband had rights over his wife that resembled in many ways the rights of masters over their slaves. Even if a man killed his wife, he would be treated under the law with far more leniency than if his wife killed him. In fact, a man killing his wife was treated almost the same as if he had killed an animal or a servant. Colonial law was often very specific about women, and some crimes were, in effect, "women's crimes" and were severely punished. For instance, the crime of being a "common scold" was applied "to a woman who berated her husband or was too vocal in public settings." The most appropriate punishment for scolding was the "ducking stool" and "branks." The former was placing the female offender in a chair and ducking her in a pool of water several times, for the purpose of drowning her. The latter was a type of metal headgear placed over the head of a woman who was accused of scolding. If the woman tried to move her tongue to speak, sharp spikes would dig into her.

In colonial America, several women were singled out for committing various crimes that were religiously based (see Chapter 1). Anne Hutchinson was persecuted for expressing alternative religious views and eventually banished from Massachusetts in the 1630s. Perhaps the most famous case was that of Mary Dyer, who sympathized with the emerging Quaker movement (a religion strongly resisted by the Puritans). She visited several Quakers who were in jail in Boston; she even gave Anne Hutchinson a show of support by visiting her in jail. Dyer was convicted and banished in 1659. A few months later, she defiantly returned to Boston. For this crime, she was hanged in June of that year (McHenry, 1983; Tolles, 1971; Knappman, 1991; Semmes, 1970). Two centuries later, the state of Massachusetts constructed a statue of her, which currently stands in front of the state capitol of Boston— ironically, across the street from the famous "Commons" where about one hundred years after her death, American "patriots" gathered for drill to fight for "freedom." The inscription on her statue reads "Witness for Religious Freedom." (A photograph is at the beginning of this chapter.)

Then there were the infamous witch hunts, in both Europe and the Americas colonies. These witch hunts stand as classic examples of the use of the legal system to punish women who dared challenge the male power structure. In New England during the 1600s, at least thirty-six women were executed for the crime of being a witch. The crime of witchcraft was among many religious-based laws on the books during colonial times. This was clearly an effort to exert almost complete control by Puritan leaders. Women who were unattached—as wives, sisters, and daughters of men—received the most severe treatment. Most of the so-called witches were merely women who were outspoken in their views or had a great deal of informal power as either healers or community leaders (Pollock, 1996: 7–90). Such "odd" behavior was labeled by those in power as a form of mental illness or just plain "crazy" behavior. One study noted that much of the witchcraft craze stemmed from anxiety over inheritance, a system that would keep property—and hence, power—in the hands of men. Not surprisingly, many accused as witches stood to inherit property because there were no male heirs. Incidentally, many were beyond their childbearing years and there-fore "unneeded" by the male hierarchy (Karlsen, 1987).

Although women played an active role in efforts to pass three key "Civil War amendments" to the Constitution (i.e., thirteenth, fourteenth, and fifteenth amendments), these amendments, which ironically extended equal protection to all persons, ignored women. In other words, these "equal rights amendments to the Constitution simply did not apply to women" (Terkel, 1996: 177–178). It was not until the case of *Reed v. Reed* (1971) that the court said that under the U.S. Constitution, women were "persons."

The Feminist Movement of the nineteenth century led to several sig-nificant changes in the legal status of women. The Married Women's Prop-erty Acts gave women certain property rights that heretofore had been denied, and the issue of domestic violence led to the passage of laws in some parts of the county, because for the first time it was considered a crime. In the first part of the twentieth century, women made some gains in the work-place. Yet despite these new laws, women's gains were often only illusory. The law and legal system remained male-dominated and women continued to be treated as second-class citizens (Terkel, 1996: 177–178; see also Faludi, 1991; MacKinnon, 1989; Sokoloff and Price, 1995: 23–25).

The unequal treatment of women by the law is perhaps nowhere bet-ter demonstrated than their treatment by the criminal justice system and the use of imprisonment as a method of control. In the next section, the histori-cal development of women's prisons is reviewed. This rather sordid history not only illustrates the brutal treatment of women as a group but also the class and racial dimensions of such treatment.

The Ultimate Punishment: A History of Women's Prisons

Prior to the nineteenth century, women offenders were generally housed within the same quarters as men, although kept separate. Reports of early jails and workhouses note the often deplorable conditions in which men, women, and children were all thrown together, along with the mentally ill and both petty and serious offenders. In colonial America, few women of-fenders were incarcerated, which is not surprising because few were incar-cerated in general. Of those who were arrested, most were charged with violations of rather minor religious-type laws (e.g., violation of the Sabbath, adultery), and these were white women only. When they were arrested, they were held in local jails for trial, and the normal punishment was often some sort of "public" reprimand, such as whipping or the "stocks and the pillory" (Collins, 1997: 5).

For African American women, the situation was obviously quite different, because the majority were legally slaves and those who were not were indentured servants (Sellin, 1976). Most violations of laws were handled informally within the plantation, but occasionally the slave owners had to rely on the local criminal justice system. In such cases, they often used what were called "Negro Courts," which were set up specifically for slaves who violated laws that were applicable to slaves but not whites. The "crimes" (often considered felonies) they were charged with included "striking the master three times" (punishable by death). Incidentally, death and even incarceration was rarely taken against slaves because such action was not profitable for the owners (unlike today; prisons are quite profitable). It was not until after the Civil War that African Americans began to appear in penal institutions in large numbers, largely as a result of various "Jim Crow" laws and the infamous "Black Codes" (Shelden, 1979). Many were subjected to the infamous "convict-lease" system (see Chapter 4).

As previously discussed, the early American jails were often mere extensions of the workhouses and almshouses. The Newgate Prison (New York), opened in 1797, was the first institution for felons only, and women offenders were housed in an area separate from men (Collins, 1997; Rafter, 1990: 4–5). By 1835, there were several institutions with separate quarters for women offenders, notably in Maryland and New York (Collins, 1997).

Treatment of prisoners, both male and female, changed dramatically around the 1820s with the founding of the Auburn State Prison, originally housing both men and women, although in separate quarters. Overcrowding soon set in (a condition that would plague prisons up to the present date), and there was little interest in the women offenders, who at that time were viewed with particular distaste. In fact, conditions were so bad that the prison chaplain once remarked that it was bad enough for male prisoners, "but to be a female convict, for any protracted period, would be worse than death" (Freedman, 1981: 16). When Newgate Prison was closed in the 1820s, the men were all eventually transferred to Auburn State Prison, but the women were sent to Bellevue Penitentiary in New York City. However, conditions were so horrible at Bellevue, that a women's annex was built at Mount Pleasant, New York, on the grounds of Sing Sing Prison, and opened in 1839 (Watterson, 1996: 196; Rafter, 1990: 6). Around the same time, a women's annex was built on the grounds of the Ohio Penitentiary and opened in 1837. During this period, it was widely believed that women offenders should be treated more harshly than their male counterparts. This belief was justified by the argument that the female offender was more depraved than her male counterpart since, having been born pure, they had "fallen" farther from grace than their male counterparts—in fact, she was often blamed for the crimes of men (Freedman, 1981: 17–18).

Most of the activities female prisoners performed in these early prisons (still performed today) were designed to "fit them for the duties of domestic life." At first there was little or no separation of male and female prisoners. Several noted reformers, such as Elizabeth Fry, a famous Quaker reformer (1780–1845), along with notables such as Dorothea Dix (1802–1887), Clara Barton (1821–1912), and Josephine Shaw Lowell (1843–1905), began to advocate separate facilities and other reforms. One of the first results of reform activities was the hiring of female matrons, beginning in Maryland after the Civil War. It is interesting to note that the majority of ninteenth- and early twentieth-century prison reformers were not only women but also members of the upper class. As Freedman's study of these nineteenth-century reformers shows, the roster reads like a Who's Who of the American elite—not an uncommon occurrence, because most reforms were carried out by members of the elite (Platt, 1977).

Only a small number of women were imprisoned in the early nineteenth century, and when they were they were confined in separate quarters or wings of male prisons. Not surprisingly, the conditions of their confinement were horrible—filth, overcrowding, and a great deal of sexual abuse by the all-male guards. Typical of such conditions were those found at the Auburn Penitentiary in upstate New York, where at one time there were seventy women inmates housed together in a one-room attic. In 1826, a woman named Rachel Welch became pregnant while in solitary confinement and died shortly after childbirth from the flogging by a prison guard (Rafter, 1990). Sexual abuse was so accepted that in the Indiana State Prison, a prostitution service was set up for the male inmates, using the female prisoners (Freedman, 1981: 15).

It was after the Civil War when the imprisonment of women began to increase, as it did for men. This is not too surprising because the end of this war signaled, in a sense, the triumph of Northern capitalism over the agricultural South (Genovese, 1965). As noted in Chapter 4, the increase in imprisonment rates was particularly noteworthy for African Americans, especially in the South; this was the case for women as well as men. The rate of convictions for women increased enough to justify the building of more prisons.

Separate facilities for women gradually began to emerge following the 1870 meeting of the National Congress on Penitentiary and Reformatory Discipline in Cincinnati. At this time, women and children were often housed in the same prisons as men. One of the resolutions of this conference was that the goal of prisons should be *rehabilitation* rather than punishment. In 1873, the first prison for women was opened, the Indiana Women's Prison. Watterson notes that:

> It embraced the revolutionary notion that women criminals should be *rehabilitated* rather than punished. Young girls from the age of sixteen who "habitu-

ally associate with dissolute persons" and other uneducated and indigent women were ushered into the model prison apart from men and isolated from the "corruption and chaos" of the outside world. The essential ingredient of their rehabilitative treatment would be to bring discipline and regularity into their lives. Obedience and systematic religious education would, it was felt, help the women form orderly habits and moral values. (Watterson, 1996: 198)

Several other women's prisons were opened over the next forty years, including the Massachusetts Prison at Framingham (1877), the New York Reformatory for Women at Westfield Farm (1901), the District of Columbia Reformatory for Women (1910), and the New Jersey Reformatory for Women at Clinton (1913). These institutions would be "separate, home-like institutions" where women "would have an opportunity to mend their criminal ways" and "learn to be good housewives, helpmates, and mothers" (Watterson, 1996: 198).

There was a flurry of women's prison reform activities between 1870 and 1900. Freedman suggests that four major factors contributed to the rise of the women's prison movement during this time: (1) an apparent increase in female crime after the war and an increase in women prisoners; (2) the women's Civil War social-service movement; (3) the emergence of charity and prison-reform movements in general, many of them emphasizing the problem of crime and the notion of rehabilitation; and (4) the beginnings of a feminist movement that emphasized a separatist approach and a reinterpretation of the notion of the "fallen woman" (Freedman, 1981: 14).

The alleged "crime wave" among women following the war primarily involved the wives and daughters of men who had died in the war. The large number of deaths during the war created a class of poor women who began to be arrested on mostly "public order" offenses and offenses against morality (Freedman, 1981: 14).

Several reformers placed the blame of the rise of female criminality on the attitudes and sexist practices of men. One noted reformer, Josephine Shaw Lowell, complained that many women "from early girlhood have been tossed from poorhouse to jail, and from jail to poorhouse, until the last trace of womanhood in them has been destroyed." She condemned law officers who regarded women "as objects of derision and sport" and who "wantonly assaulted and degraded numerous young women prisoners." Many specifically blamed the "double standard" whereby men condemned female sexual activity while condoning their own and, moreover, arrested and imprisoned prostitutes but not the men who enjoyed their services. Finally, reformers complained of male guards in prisons where women were confined. Investigations found that women "may be forced to minister to the lust of the officials or if they refused, submit to the inflection of the lash until they do" (Freedman, 1981: 59–60).

Reformers argued that women prisoners would be treated more fairly and would stand a better chance of being reformed if they were confined in separate institutions controlled by women. Reformers countered male resistance by arguing that "the shield of a pure woman's presence" would enable them "to govern the depraved and desperate of her own sex." The *reformatory* would be the institution that would provide the needed "reform" (Freedman, 1981: 61).

The Emergence of Women's Reformatories

Rafter's historical account of the rise of women's prisons noted that two major types of prisons emerged during the nineteenth century. One type was the *custodial prison;* as its name implies, these institutions emphasized custody and security as the main goals. The custodial prison resembled the classic penitentiary originally designed for male prisoners, and their purpose was as the name suggests, to warehouse (or in modern vernacular, to "incapacitate"). There were three main types of custodial prisons for women: (1) those that were either within or attached to male prisons; (2) prison farms in the South; and (3) totally independent prisons; the first type was the most common (Rafter, 1990: 83). The second type was the *reformatory* (discussed in Chapter 4), which, in contrast, were supposed to be more "treatment"-oriented.

The first reformatories relied on domestic routines and, upon release, women were placed in suitable private homes as housekeepers. These institutions, and most to follow, were all designed according to the *cottage plan* whereby separate housing facilities would be as nearly as possible like an average family home that would teach these women to become good homemakers. While the women reformers often claimed to be staunch feminists, the organization of prison life they created was perfectly suited to keep women in their traditional place. In fact, the design won the approval of many skeptical men, one of whom commented that "girls and women should be trained to adorn homes with the virtues which make their lives noble and ennobling. *It is only in this province that they may most fittingly fill their mission*" (Freedman, 1981: 62, emphasis added by Freedman). The end result, of course, would perpetuate women's traditional roles of dependency as housewives and maids. Even a cursory look at women's prisons today reveals that little has changed, especially the treatment of women as children and training them to continue their domestic roles.

Freedman suggests that although reformers "claimed that their goal for each inmate, as for each prison, was female self-sufficiency, they trained women inmates for dependency in domestic employment and in other ways treated them as juveniles, referring even to elderly prisoners as 'girls' and setting up cottage households with the inmates in the role of children." Even a cursory look at women's prisons today reveals that little has changed, especially the treatment of women as children and training them to continue their domestic roles (Freedman, 1981: 61).

The Role of Racism

Not surprisingly, most of the women in custodial institutions were African American, whereas most in reformatories were white. Thus, the energies of prison reformers like Elizabeth Fry and Dorothea Dix were directed toward *white* women prisoners. For African American women prisoners, the custodial prisons where most of them were housed represented merely a continuation of their slave status prior to the Emancipation Proclamation (Rafter, 1990).

This was especially the case in the South, where a form of penal servitude served as a replacement for the old slave plantations. African American women prisoners, like their male counterparts, often were leased out to local businesses such as farms, mines, and railroads to work on various kinds of chain gangs. According to the 1880 census, in Alabama, Louisiana, Mississippi, North Carolina, Tennessee, and Texas, more than one third of the 220 African American female prisoners were leased out, compared to only one white woman prisoner in a total population of forty (Rafter, 1990).

The proportion of African American women prisoners was even higher than their male counterparts in some states. In New York, for instance, 44 percent of the women inmates were African American, compared to only 20 percent for African American men. In Tennessee, in 1868, *every female inmate was African American,* compared to around 60 percent of the male prisoners (Rafter, 1990).

The overrepresentation of African Americans varied widely by region. In 1880, the percentage of women prisoners who were African American ranged from 7 percent in the Northeast to 85.8 percent in the South. By 1904, the proportion of African American women in Northern prisons had increased to around 18 percent, while in the South it was 90 percent. By 1923, both percentages had decreased somewhat to 15.4 and 79.6, respectively. This latter decrease may be attributed to the rise of reformatories during the interim period, which were much more likely to house white inmates. Indeed, in 1923 almost two thirds (64.5 percent) of the women inmates in custodial prisons were African American, compared to only 11.9 percent in reformatory institutions. Ranges by specific institutions were marked. Between 1860 and 1934, fully four fifths of the inmates at the Tennessee Penitentiary for Women were African American, in contrast to only 3 percent at the Albion State Prison in New York (Rafter, 1990: 142–146). Not surprisingly, the early prison system reflected the segregation in the general society, as African American women were housed in prisons where there was little or no hope of any sort of rehabilitation (i.e., "custodial" prisons), while white women were most likely to be sentenced to "reformatories" where there was at least a formal commitment to rehabilitation (Rafter, 1990; Collins, 1997).

The federal prison system for women developed much later than the state prison system. Women convicted of federal crimes were generally sentenced to state prisons, but as the number of female inmates grew after the Civil War, efforts were made to open the federal system to women. The first of the federal prisons for women only was in Alderson, West Virginia, which opened in 1927, and housed fifty women in fourteen cottages. By 1929, there were more than 250 inmates, most of whom had violated various drug laws (the Harrison Act of 1914 outlawed several kinds of drugs) and the Volstead Act of 1919 (Prohibition). Largely in response to the rise of organized crime (a direct result of Prohibition), legislation passed in 1930 that created the Federal Bureau of Prisons, which authorized the construction of several new prisons (Collins, 1997: 21).

The proportion of women in prison who are African American has continued to increase over the years. Historically, African American women have been most likely to be incarcerated in Southern prisons. For instance, in 1880, African American women constituted 86 percent of the female inmates in the South, compared to only 7 percent in the Northeast, 29 percent in the Midwest, and 20 percent in the West. In 1904, these percentages had increased in every region, with the South leading at 90 percent, the Midwest catching up with 48 percent. By 1978, African American women constituted half of the total female prison population (Rafter, 1990: 142). As noted later in the chapter, in all sections of the country, African Americans were imprisoned in numbers vastly disproportionate to the percentage in the general population. Their percentages declined somewhat by the end of the 1980s and early 1990s, largely as a result of an increase in Hispanics but also as a result of more white women being sentenced on drug charges.

Controlling Women's Bodies and Sexuality

Although the number of prisons and prisoners increased significantly after the Civil War, the number of prisons for women and the rate of imprisonment soared after the turn of the century. Part of this increase was no doubt a reflection of the class conflicts of the period, as more immigrants came to America and labor continued to challenge capitalist rule. Nativism and racism was rampant. As Rafter noted, there was a "social purity" movement during this period as the behaviors of many immigrants shocked the moral sensibilities of the upper classes. In response, those in power attempted to control these classes through the use of formal methods of social control, especially the selective enforcement of various "morals offenses" (Rafter, 1988). The Women's Prison Association of New York issued the following statement in 1906:

> . . . If promiscuous immigration is to continue, it devolves upon the enlightened, industrious, and moral citizens, from selfish as well as from philanthropic motives, to instruct the morally defective to conform to our ways and

exact from them our own high standard of morality and legitimate industry. (Rafter, 1990: 93–94)

Continuing, this writer asked rhetorically, "Do you want immoral women to walk our streets, pollute society, endanger your households, menace the morals of your sons and daughters? Do you think the women here described are fit to become mothers of American citizens? Shall foreign powers generate criminals and dump them on our shores?" (Rafter, 1990: 93–94).

Throughout the late nineteenth and early twentieth centuries, reformers constantly focused on women's sexuality because there was a widespread belief that promiscuity and venereal disease were the latest scourges in society. By housing these wicked and immoral women in newly constructed reformatories, it was believed that they could be treated and cleansed of their diseases and thus rendered capable of serving men upon their release. Most of this effort was directed toward promiscuous girls, as discussed later in this chapter.

Clearly, to those in power, there was an obvious threat and serious steps needed to be taken. This was part of a much larger campaign to stamp out the growing labor movement that had begun during the last half of the nineteenth century. These were not just ordinary "criminals," but rather were "social scum" threatening the very foundation of the social order.

Proof that the criminal justice system focused on morals offenses rather than the usual violent and property crimes can be seen in the commitment offenses of many women offenders that ended up in the reformatories. Women sent to reformatories were convicted mostly of "public-order" offenses. In the Albion Reformatory (New York), for instance, more than 80 percent (81.4 percent) were convicted of public order offenses, the most common of which was "disorderly conduct," followed by sex-related offenses. Similarly, in the Ohio Reformatory, just over half (53 percent) were convicted of public-order offenses, including a variety of what can be called morals offenses, such as lewd and lascivious carriage, stubbornness, idle and disorderly conduct, fornication, serial premarital pregnancies, keeping bad company, adultery, and even venereal disease. One woman was sent to Albion Reformatory for five years on the charge of having had "unlawful sexual intercourse with young men and remaining at hotels with young men all night." Another woman had quit school, had a brief affair with a soldier, contracted a venereal disease, and was hospitalized and subsequently sent to the reformatory. Another woman was raped by her father (who made her pregnant) and was subsequently sentenced for "running around" with men while she was seven months pregnant (Rafter, 1990: 107–119, 161).

The reformatory was clearly an attempt to control not just women offenders but also a particular *class* of women—in this case, lower and working-class *immigrant* women. Part of this was a backlash against the thousands of immigrant women who entered the labor force and began to lead relatively independent lives. This was what disturbed the ruling classes: young women *on their own and doing what they please.* Indeed, young women by the thousands were leaving home and, instead of getting married right away (as was their "innate duty"), they enjoyed the life of single, independent women. They began to smoke, drink, go to "dance halls" (precursors of modern night clubs), and engage in premarital sexual relationships. The reformatory would certainly do its best to try to "cure" this problem. In so doing, the reformatory was one among many attempts to extend the power of the state over the lives of the lower and working classes, especially immigrants.

Custodial institutions, such as Tennessee State Prison, Auburn State Prison, and New York and Ohio penitentiaries housed women convicted primarily of property offenses (mostly larceny). There was also a clear racial difference in the two types of institutions: in custodial prisons, the majority were African Americans, the reformatory institutions housed mostly whites (Rafter, 1990: 146). While many were convicted of violent offenses, the context within which these "violent" crimes occurred paralleled most of those of today among women offenders: the killing of a spouse or lover after years of abuse. Cases cited by Rafter are illustrative of this context. In one case, heard by the Tennessee Supreme Court, the defendant was only eighteen or nineteen and her husband was fifty and he had abused her severely. In one instance she "was seriously injured by a blow to the ovaries"; on another occasion, "he had hit her on the head with a poker" and, in general, "treated his wife cruelly and inhumanly, frequently whipped, cursed, and abused her" (Rafter, 1990: 110).

The control of women by the criminal justice system has not been confined to adults. Indeed, these developments paralleled similar if not identical efforts to control young women and girls.

Young Women and the Juvenile Justice System[3]

Keeping Girls in Their Place: The Development of Institutions for Girls

As discussed in the previous chapter, the *parens patriae* doctrine was first challenged in the case of *Ex Parte Crouse* (1938). It is noteworthy that the case involved a young girl, Mary Ann Crouse, for it raises the question of how the juvenile justice system responded to girls and young women. The *Crouse* case raised questions about the role of the state as a "parent." When asked to review the care of juveniles, judges in the nineteenth century were reluctant to examine too closely state intervention into minors' lives if it was justified in familial terms. Ironically, such reviews were not undertaken even if a parent so requested (as in the Crouse case). The remainder of the nineteenth century witnessed intensification of the notion of the state as parent, which posed a significant threat to the everyday lives and rights of girls.

The Child-Saving Movement and the Juvenile Court

The Progressive Era (1890–1920) ushered in another shift and codification of attitudes toward youths in American society. While social activists of the era used some of the language of the stubborn-child law, their initiatives ushered in unprecedented government involvement in family life and more specifically into the lives of adolescents (Teitelbaum and Harris, 1977). The shift culminated in the creation of an entirely separate system of justice: the juvenile court. The child-saving movement had a special meaning for girls.

The child-saving movement made much rhetorical use of the value of such traditional institutions as the family and education: "The child-savers elevated the nuclear family, especially women as stalwarts of the family, and defended the family's right to supervise the socialization of youth" (Platt, 1977: 98). But while the child-savers were exalting the family, they were crafting a governmental system that would have authority to intervene in familial areas and, more specifically, in the lives of young people in unprecedented ways.

Based on an assumption of the "natural dependence of youth," the juvenile court was charged with determining the guilt or innocence of accused underage persons and with acting for or in place of defendants' parents. The concern of the child-savers went far beyond removing the adolescent criminal from the adult justice system. Many of their reforms were actually aimed at "imposing sanctions on conduct unbecoming youth and disqualifying youth from the benefit of adult privileges" (Platt, 1977: 199). Other students of the court's history have expanded on this point; they assert that the pervasive state intervention into the life of the family was grounded in colonial laws regarding "stubborn" and "neglected" children. Those laws incorporated the thinking of their time, that "parents were godly and children wicked," yet most child-savers actually held an opposite opinion, that children were innocent and either the parents or the environment was morally suspect (Teitelbaum and Harris, 1977: 34). Although the two views are incompatible, they have nevertheless coexisted in the juvenile court system since its inception. At various times, one view or the other has predominated, but both bode ill for young women.

One of the unique features of the new juvenile, or family, courts was that they focused to a great extent on monitoring and responding to youthful behaviors that were "indicative" of future problems in addition to being violations of the law. For instance, part of the Tennessee juvenile code included the phrase "who are in danger of being brought up to lead an idle or immoral life" (Shelden, 1981: 432). Thus, girls and their moral behavior were of specific concern to the child-savers. Scientific and popular literature on female delinquency expanded enormously during this period, as did institutions specifically devoted to the reformation of girls (Schlossman and Wallach, 1978; Odem, 1995; Messerschmidt, 1987).

The child-savers were keenly concerned about prostitution and such other "social evils" as white slavery (Schlossman and Wallach, 1978; Odem, 1995; Rafter, 1988: 54). Ironically, while child-saving was a celebration of women's domesticity, the movement was not without female leaders. In a sense, privileged women found in the moral purity crusades and the establishment of family courts a safe outlet for their energies. As the legitimate guardians of the moral sphere, upper-middle-class women were seen as uniquely suited to patrol the normative boundaries of the social order. Embracing rather than challenging these stereotypes, women managed to carve out for themselves a role in the policing of women and girls. Many early activities of the child-savers revolved around monitoring the behavior of young girls, particularly immigrant girls, to prevent their "straying from the path" of "correct and lady-like" behavior (Feinman, 1980; Freedman, 1981; Messerschmidt, 1987; Gordon, 1988; Odem, 1995).

Just exactly how women, many of them highly educated, became involved in patrolling the boundaries of working-class girls' sexuality is a depressing but important story. Initially, upper-middle-class women reformers were focused on regulating and controlling male not female sexuality. Involved in the social-purity movement, these reformers had a Victorian view of women's sexuality and saw girls as inherently chaste and sexually passive. If a girl lost "the most precious jewel in the crown of her womanhood," to their way of thinking, it was men who had forced them into sexual activity (Odem, 1995: 25).

The protection and saving of girls, then, led these women to wage an aggressive social movement aimed at raising the age of consent (which in many parts of the country hovered at ten or twelve years of age) to sixteen or older. The pursuit of claims of statutory rape against men was another component of this effort, and such charges were brought in a number of cases despite evidence that in about three quarters of the cases Odem reviewed in Los Angeles, the girls entered into sexual relationships with young men willingly. Led largely by upper- and upper-middle-class women volunteers, many of whom were prominent in the temperance movement (e.g., Frances Willard), this campaign (not unlike the Mothers Against Drunk Driving campaign of later decades) drew an impressive and enthusiastic following, particularly among white citizens (Odem, 1995).

African American women participated in other aspects of progressive reform, but they were less than aggressive on the pursuit of statutory-rape complaints. They suspected that any aggressive enforcement of these statutes was likely to fall most heavily on young African American men (while doing little to protect girls of color), and this is precisely what occurred. Of the very small number of cases where stiff penalties were imposed, African American men were not infrequently sent to prison to reform their "supposedly lax and immoral habits," while white men were either not prosecuted or given probation (Odem, 1995).

Efforts to vigorously pursue statutory-rape complaints ran headlong into the predictable staunch judicial resistance, particularly when many (but not all) cases involved young, working-class women who had chosen to be sexually active. Eventually, as Odem's work documents, reformers (many of them now professional social workers) began to shift the focus of their activities. Now it was the "delinquent girl" who was the focus of reform and "moral campaigns to control teenage female sexuality" began to appear. Reformers during this later period (1910–1925) assumed that they had the authority to define what was appropriate conduct for young working-class women and girls, which of course was based on middle-class ideals of female sexual propriety. Girls who did not conform to these ideals were labeled as "wayward" and thus "in need of control" by the state in the form of juvenile courts, reformatories, and training schools (Odem, 1995: 4–5).

Perhaps the clearest example of the ironies of this sort of child-saving is Alice Stebbins Wells, a social worker who became the first policewoman in the United States. In 1910, she was hired by Los Angeles because she argued that she could not serve her clients (young women) without police powers. Her work, and the work of five other female police officers hired during the next five years, was chiefly "to monitor 'dance halls, cafes, picture shows, and other public amusement places' and to escort girls who were 'in danger of becoming delinquent to their homes and to make reports to their parents with a proper warning'" (Odem and Schlossman, 1991: 90).

Women reformers played a key role in the founding of the first juvenile court in Los Angeles in 1903 and vigorously advocated the appointment of women court workers to deal with the "special" problems of girls. This court was the first in the country to appoint women "referees," who were invested with nearly all the powers of judges in girls' cases. Women were also hired to run the juvenile detention facility in 1911. The logic for this was quite clear: "in view of the number of girls and the type of girls detained there . . . it is utterly unfeasible to have a man at the head of the institution," declared Cora Lewis, chairman of the Probation Committee, which established the Juvenile Hall. The civic leaders and newly hired female court workers "advocated special measures to contain sexual behavior among working-class girls, to bring them to safety by placing them in custody, and to attend to their distinctive needs as young, vulnerable females" (Odem and Schlossman, 1991: 190).

The evolution of what might be called the "girl-saving" effort was then the direct consequence of a disturbing coalition between some feminists and other Progressive Era movements. Concerned about female victimization and distrustful of male (and to some degree female) sexuality, prominent women leaders, including Susan B. Anthony, found common cause with the more conservative social-purity movement around such issues as the regulation of prostitution and raising the age of consent. Eventually, in the face of stiff judicial and political resistance, the concern about male sexuality more or less disappeared from sight, and the delinquent girl herself became the problem. The solution: a harsh "maternal justice" meted out by professional women (Odem, 1995: 128).

Girls were the losers in this reform effort. Studies of early family-court activity reveal that almost all of the girls who appeared in these courts were charged with immorality or waywardness (Chesney-Lind, 1973; Schlossman and Wallach, 1978; Shelden, 1981). The sanctions for such misbehavior were extremely severe. For example, the Chicago family court sent half the girl delinquents but only a fifth of the boy delinquents to reformatories between 1899 and 1909. In Milwaukee, twice as many girls as boys were committed to training schools (Schlossman and Wallach, 1978: 72). In Memphis, females were twice as likely as males to be committed to training schools (Shelden, 1981: 70).

In Honolulu during 1929–1930, more than half the girls referred to juvenile court were charged with "immorality," which meant there was evidence of sexual intercourse; 30 percent were charged with "waywardness." Evidence of immorality was vigorously pursued by both arresting officers and social workers through lengthy questioning of the girls and, if possible, males with whom they were suspected of having sex. Other evidence of "exposure" was provided by gynecological examinations that were routinely ordered in most girls' cases. Doctors, who understood the purpose of such examinations, would routinely note the condition of the hymen. Girls were twice as likely as males to be detained for their offenses and spent five times as long in detention on average as their male counterparts. They were also nearly three times more likely to be sentenced to the training school. Indeed, half of those committed to training schools in Honolulu well into the 1950s were girls (Chesney-Lind, 1973).

Not surprisingly, large numbers of girls' reformatories and training schools were established during the Progressive Era, in addition to places of "rescue and reform." For example, Schlossman and Wallach note that twenty-three facilities for girls were opened during the 1910–1920 decade (in contrast to the 1850–1910 period, when the average was five reformatories a decade), and they did much to set the tone of official response to female delinquency. These institutions were obsessed with precocious female sexuality and were determined to instruct girls in their proper place (Schlossman and Wallach, 1978: 70).

According to Pisciotta, there was a slight modification of the *parens patriae* doctrine during this period. The "training" of girls was shaped by the image of the ideal woman that had evolved during the early part of the nineteenth century. According to this ideal, which was informed by what some have called the "separate-spheres" notion, a woman belonged in the "private sphere," performing such tasks as rearing children, keeping house, caring for a husband, and serving as the moral guardian of the home. In this capacity, she was to exhibit qualities like obedience, modesty, and dependence. Her husband's domain was the "public sphere"; that is, the workplace, politics, and the law. He was also, by virtue of his public power, the final arbiter of public morality and culture (Pisciotta, 1983: 264–268; see also Daly and Chesney-Lind, 1988). This white middle-class "cult of domesticity" was, of course, very distant from the lives of many working- and lower-class women who, by necessity, were in the labor force. Borrowing from Rothman (1978), Pisciotta notes that the ideal woman was like a "Protestant nun." A statement by the Ladies Committee of the New York House of Refuge summed up the attributes early court advocates sought to instill:

> The Ladies wish to call attention to the great change which takes place in every girl who has spent one year in the Refuge; she enters a rude, careless, untrained child, caring nothing for cleanliness and order; when she leaves the House, she can sew, mend, darn, wash, iron, arrange a table neatly, and cook a healthy meal. (Pisciotta, 1983: 265)

The institutions established for girls set about to isolate them from all contact with males while training them in feminine skills and housing them in bucolic settings. The intention was to hold the girls until marriageable age, and to occupy them in domestic pursuits during their sometimes lengthy incarceration. The child-savers had little hesitation about such extreme intervention in the lives of girls. They believed "delinquency" to be the result of a variety of social, psychological, and biological factors, and they were optimistic about the juvenile court's ability to remove girls from influences that were producing delinquent behavior. As noted in Chapter 5, the juvenile court was established to function in a way totally unlike other courts (e.g., the juvenile court judge as a benevolent yet stern father, informal procedures).

Nowhere has the confusion and irony of the juvenile court been more clearly demonstrated than in its treatment of girls labeled delinquent. Many of these girls were incarcerated for noncriminal behavior during the early years of the court.

"The Best Place to Conquer Girls"

Brenzel's history of the first reform school for girls, the State Industrial School for Girls in Lancaster, Massachusetts, established in 1856, and other studies of early training schools are vivid accounts of the girls and the institutions. The Lancaster school was intended "to be a school for girls—for the gentler sex . . . with all the details relating to employment, instruction, and amusement, and, indeed, to every branch of domestic economy" (Brenzel, 1975: 41). Such rhetoric would eventually find its way into the other training schools for girls. In Memphis, the Home of the Good Shepherd, established in 1875, was designed for the "reformation of fallen . . . women and a home or house of refuge for abandoned and vicious girls." Moreover, because the girls had "fallen from grace," they needed to be saved for the "preservation of the State's young manhood . . . " (Shelden, 1981: 58). Lancaster's first superintendent, Bradford K. Peirce, echoed this sentiment: "It is sublime to work to save a woman, for in her bosom, generations are embodied, and in her hands, if perverted, the fate of innumerable men is held" (Brenzel, 1983: 4).

Lancaster, a model for all juvenile training schools, was to save children from "perversion through conversion." "Loving care" and confinement in an atmosphere free from the sins and temptations of city life would redirect girls' lives. What sorts of crimes had the girls committed? More than two thirds had been accused of "moral" rather than criminal offenses: vagrancy, beggary, stubbornness, deceitfulness, idle and vicious behavior, wanton and lewd conduct, and running away (Brenzel, 1983: 81). Of the first ninety-nine inmates at Lancaster, only slightly over half (53 percent) were American-born. Significantly, at least half of the girls had been brought to Lancaster because of the actions of parents and relatives. Similarly, many girls in the Home of the Good Shepherd in Memphis had been brought into the juvenile court because of running away, incorrigibility, or various charges labeled by the court as "immorality," including sexual relations that ranged from sexual intercourse to "kissing and holding hands in the park" (Shelden, 1981: 63). In a study of juvenile court records in four cities around the turn of the century, Schlossman and Wallach arrived at the same conclusion: "immorality" seems to have been the most common charge against females. Included under the rubric were coming home late at night, masturbating, using obscene language, riding at night in automobiles without a chaperon, and strutting about in a lascivious manner (Schlossman and Wallach, 1978: 72).

Clearly, early training schools were deeply concerned with female respectability and, therefore, worked to control the sexuality of lower- and working-class adolescent girls. As Rafter noted, such control within the institutional regime was supposed to train so-called loose young women "to accept a standard of propriety that dictated chastity until marriage and fidelity thereafter" (Rafter, 1990: 159).

These institutions for girls strove for a family-like atmosphere from which, after having been taught domestic skills, girls would be released to the care of other families as domestic workers. Gradually, however, vocational training in appropriate manual skills (sewing and the cutting of garments), age-group classification, and punishment characterized the institutional regime. By the late 1880s, Lancaster had devolved into a "middle place between the care of that Board [Health, Lunacy and Charity] and a Reformatory Prison." Lancaster's original goal of establishing a "loving family circle" had been supplanted by "harsh judgment, rudimentary job training, and punitive custody" (Brenzel, 1983: 153, 160).

The Juvenile Court and the Double Standard of Juvenile Justice

The offenses that bring girls into the juvenile justice system reflect the system's dual concerns: adolescent criminality and moral conduct. Historically, they have also reflected a unique and intense preoccupation with girls' sexuality and their obedience to parental authority. What happened to the girls once they arrived in the system?

Relatively early in the juvenile justice system's history, a few astute observers became concerned about the abandonment of minors' rights in the name of treatment, saving, and protection. One of the most insightful of these critical works is Tappan's *Delinquent Girls in Court* (1947). Tappan evaluated several hundred cases in the Wayward Minor Court in New York City during the late 1930s and early 1940s, and concluded that there were serious problems with a statute that brought young women into court simply for disobedience of parental commands or because they were in "danger of becoming morally depraved." He was particularly concerned that "the need to interpret the 'danger of becoming morally depraved' imposes upon the court a legislative function of a moralizing character." Noting that many young women were being charged simply with sexual activity, he asked, "What is sexual misbehavior—in a legal sense—of the nonprostitute of sixteen, or eighteen, or of twenty when fornication is no offense under criminal law?" (Tappan, 1947: 33).

Tappan believed that the structure of the Wayward Minor Court "entrusted unlimited discretion to the judge, reformer, or clinician and his personal views of expedience," and cautioned that, consequently, "the fate of the defendant, the interest of society, the social objectives themselves, must hang by the tenuous thread of the wisdom and personality of the particular administrator." The arrangement was deeply disturbing to Tappan: "The implications of judicial totalitarianism are written in history" (Tappan, 1947: 33).

A more recent study, of the Los Angeles Juvenile Court during the first half of the twentieth century, supplies additional evidence of the juvenile justice system's historical preoccupation with girls' sexual morality, a preoccupation that clearly colored the Los Angeles court's activity into the 1950s. As Brenzel and others found, the majority of these girls were from immigrant families and/or the lower and working classes.

Odem and Schlossman reviewed the characteristics of the girls who entered the court in 1920 and in 1950. In 1920, 93 percent of the girls accused of delinquency were charged with status offenses; of these, 65 percent were

charged with immoral sexual activity (athough the vast majority—56 percent—had engaged in sex with only one partner, usually a boyfriend). The
researchers found that 51 percent of the referrals had come from the girls'
parents, a situation they explained as working-class parents' fears about
their daughters' exposure to the "omnipresent temptations to which
working-class daughters in particular were exposed to in the modern ecol-
ogy of urban work and leisure." The working-class girls had been encouraged by their families to work (in fact, 52 percent were working or had been
working within the past year), but their parents were extremely ambivalent
about changing community morals and some were not hesitant about involving the court in their arguments with problem daughters (Odem and
Schlossman, 1991: 196).

Odem and Schlossman also found that the Los Angeles Juvenile Court
did not shirk from its perceived duty. Seventy-seven percent of the girls
were detained before their hearings. Both pre- and post-hearing detention
were common and clearly linked to the presence of venereal disease. Thirty-
five percent of all delinquent girls and more than half being held for sex offenses had gonorrhea, syphilis, or other venereal infections. The researchers
noted that the presence of venereal disease and the desire to impose treatment (which in those times was lengthy and painful) accounted for the large
numbers of girls in detention centers. Analysis of court actions revealed that
although probation was the most common court response (61 percent were
accorded probation), only 27 percent were released on probation immediately following the hearing. Many girls, it appears, were held for weeks or
months after initial hearings. Girls not given probation were often placed in
private homes as domestics or in a wide range of private institutions, such
as the Convent of the Good Shepherd or homes for unmarried mothers. Ultimately, according to Odem and Schlossman, about 33 percent of the "problem girls" during this period were sentenced to institutional confinement
(Odem and Schlossman, 1991: 198–199).

In a more detailed analysis, Odem demonstrated that in the Los Angeles Juvenile Court, women court officials acted as "maternal guardians" as
they attempted to instill in these working-class girls a middle-class standard
of respectability by "dispensing the maternal guidance and discipline supposedly lacking in the girls' own homes. Referees and probation officers
scolded their charges for wearing too much makeup and dressing in a
provocative manner." Odem quotes one juvenile court referee who commented that: "Any girl who will go before the public with her hair and eye-
lashes beaded and paint on her face is going to attract attention . . . [and] is
surely inviting trouble." Girls were also chastised for visiting "amusement
resorts" that the court thought "inappropriate and dangerous for adolescents" and that sex before marriage was simply wrong (Odem, 1995: 142).

It is obvious these court officials were quite obsessed with the sexuality of these young women. Odem notes that after a girl was arrested, "pro-

bation officers questioned her relatives, neighbors, employers, and school officials to gather details about her sexual misconduct and, in the process, alerted them that she was a delinquent in trouble with the law." Following this, a girl was usually detained in juvenile hall and further questioned about her sexual behavior, asking her to give a complete sexual history, starting with her first act of intercourse, while pressuring her to reveal the names of all her partners, the exact times and locations of sexual activities, and the number of times she had sex. Further court discipline was leveled to those who did not give complete information (Odem, 1995: 143–144). Not surprisingly, no such obsessive concern was evident when it came to the sexual behavior of boys.

Between 1920 and 1950, the makeup of the court's female clientele changed little: "the group was still predominantly white" (69 and 73.5 percent)—although the number of African American girls rose from 5 to 9 percent—working class, and from disrupted families. However, girls were more likely to be in school and less likely to be working in 1950.

Girls referred to the Los Angeles court in 1950 were overwhelmingly referred for status offenses (78 percent), although the charges had changed slightly from 1920 charges. Thirty-one percent of the girls were charged with running away from home, truancy, curfew, or "general unruliness at home." Nearly half of the status offenders were charged with sexual misconduct, although again, this was "usually with a single partner; few had engaged in prostitution." The rate of venereal disease had plummeted; only 4.5 percent of all girls tested positive. Despite this, the concern for female sexual conduct "remained determinative in shaping social policy" in the 1950s (Odem and Schlossman, 1991: 200).

Referral sources changed within the intervening decades, as did sanctions. Parents referred 26 percent of the girls at mid-century; school officials, about the same percentage in 1950 as 1920 (21 and 27 percent), and police officers, a greater number (54 percent compared with 29 percent in 1920). Sanctions shifted somewhat, with fewer girls detained before their hearings in 1950 (56 percent compared with 77 percent in 1920), but the Los Angeles court placed about the same proportion of girls in custodial institutions (26 percent in 1950, 33 percent in 1920).

Studies continue to pick up on problems with the vagueness of contemporary status-offense categories, which are essentially "buffer charges" for suspected sexuality. Consider Vedder and Somerville's observation in the 1960s that although girls in their study were incarcerated in training schools for the "big five" (i.e., running away from home, incorrigibility, sexual offenses, probation violation, and truancy), "the underlying vein in many of these cases is sexual misconduct by the girl delinquent" (Vedder and Sommerville, 1970: 147). Such attitudes were also present in other parts of the world. Naffine wrote that in Australia, official reports noted that "most of those charged [with status offenses] were girls who had acquired habits of immorality and freely admitted sexual intercourse with a number of boys" (Naffine, 1987: 13).

Another study, conducted in the early 1970s in a New Jersey training school, revealed large numbers of girls incarcerated "for their own protection." When asked about this pattern, one judge explained, "Why most of the girls I commit are for status offenses. I figure if a girl is about to get pregnant, we'll keep her until she's sixteen and then ADC [Aid to Dependent Children] will pick her up" (Rogers, 1972: 223–246).

Andrews and Cohn reviewed the handling of cases of ungovernability in New York in 1972 and concluded that judges were acting "upon personal feelings and predilections in making decisions." Included among their evidence were statements made by judges, for example: She thinks she's a pretty hot number; I'd be worried about leaving my kid with her in a room alone. She needs to get her mind off boys" (Andrews and Cohn, 1974: 1383–1409).

Similar concern about premature female sexuality and the proper parental response is evident throughout the comments. One judge remarked that at the age of fourteen, some girls "get some crazy ideas. They want to fool around with men, and that's sure as hell trouble." Another admonished a girl, "I want you to promise me to obey your mother, to have perfect school attendance, to give up these people who are trying to lead you to do wrong, not to hang out in candy stores or tobacco shops or street corners where these people are, and to be in when your mother says" (Andrews and Cohn, 1974: 1404).

Empirical studies of the processing of girls' and boys' cases between 1950 and the early 1970s documented the impact of these sorts of judicial attitudes. That is, girls charged with status offenses were often more harshly treated than their male or female counterparts charged with crimes. Gibbons and Griswold, for example, found in a study of court dispositions in Washington State between 1953 and 1955 that girls were far less likely than boys to be charged with criminal offenses, but more than twice as likely to be committed to institutions (Gibbons and Griswold, 1957: 109). Some years later, a study of a juvenile court in Delaware discovered that first-time female status offenders were more harshly sanctioned (as measured by institutionalization) than males charged with felonies. For repeat status offenders, the pattern was even starker: female status offenders were six times more likely than male status offenders to be institutionalized (Datesman and Scarpitti, 1977: 70).

The double standard of juvenile justice also appeared in countries other than the United States. Linda Hancock found in Australia that females (most of whom were appearing in court for uncontrollability and other status offenses) were more likely than males to receive probation or institutional supervision. In addition, females charged with criminal offenses received lesser penalties than males and females brought to court under "protection applications" (Hancock, 1981: 8). Another study found that females in England were less often fined and more often placed on supervision or sent to an institution than males (May, 1977). In another English study, Smart reported that 64 percent of females and 5 percent of males were institutionalized for noncriminal offenses (Smart, 1976: 134). In Portugal in 1984, 41 percent of the girls were charged with status offenses, but only 16.8 percent of the boys were placed in institutions. Likewise, a study of a juvenile court in Madrid revealed that of youths found guilty of status offenses, 22.2 percent of the girls but only 6.4 percent of the boys were incarcerated (Cain, 1989: 222–225).

In short, numerous studies of the juvenile courts during the past few decades suggest that court personnel participated directly in the judicial enforcement of the sexual double standard. Such activity was most pronounced in the system's early years, but there is evidence that the pattern continues, in part because status offenses can still serve as buffer charges for sexual misconduct. Some of the problem with status offenses, although they are discriminatory, is understandable. They are not like criminal cases, regarding which judges have relatively clear guidelines. Standards of evidence are delineated, elements of the crime are laid out in the statutes, and civil rights are, at least to some extent, protected by law.

In status-offense cases, judges have few legal guidelines. Many judges apparently fall back on one of the orientations built into the juvenile justice system: the Puritan stance supportive of parental demands, more or less without question; or the progressive stance, whereby they take on the parental roles. These orientations were severely tested during the 1970s, when critics mounted a major drive to deinstitutionalize status offenders and divert them from formal court jurisdiction. (For more detailed information about the deinstitutionalization movement, see Chesney-Lind and Shelden, 1998: 187–190.)

Women and Criminal Justice Today

One thing that cannot be overlooked in any analysis of women, crime, and criminal justice is the interrelationship between class and race. Indeed, the vast majority of female offenders, especially those who end up in prison, are drawn from the lower class and are racial minorities (Daly, 1992; Miller, 1986; Chesney-Lind, 1997).

Women's crime cannot be separate from the overall social context within which it occurs. In recent years, the plight of women has not improved a great deal. While women have entered into the labor force in increased numbers in recent years (to around 60 percent versus less than 40 percent in the 1950s), their employment is found largely in traditional female occupations, especially in retail trade and service occupations. Women still constitute more than 80 percent of all nurses, 75 percent of all teachers (except in colleges and universities), almost 80 percent of all secretarial and administrative-support positions (e.g., clerical work, cashiers), and about 80 percent of all the hairdressers and other "personal service occupations." Furthermore, while gains have been made, women still earn less than men—and their "gains" have come largely because so many men have been eliminated from the labor force. In fact, while in 1960, 89 percent of all married men and 32 percent of married women were in the labor force, by 1994 the male percentage had decreased to 77 percent and the female percentage had increased to 61 percent. Also, a far greater proportion of women are working part-time: as of 1993, almost half (47 percent) of women workers worked part-time, compared to 32 percent of the men (U.S. Department of Commerce, 1995: 405, 435; Folbre, 1995).

More importantly, increasing numbers of households are being maintained by women with children. While in 1960 only 6 percent of all families with one or more children was headed by a woman, by 1993 this figure had jumped to 18 percent. Not surprisingly, race plays a role here, for 41.5 percent of African American families were headed by a woman in 1993, compared to only 14.3 percent of white families (U.S. Department of Commerce, 1995: 434). More importantly, however, is the fact that in 1993 more than one fourth of all children lived with only one parent, 88 percent of whom lived with their mother. Moreover, about 44 percent of all African American children and 42 percent of Hispanic children live in poverty, compared to only 17 percent of white children (Eitzen and Zinn, 1998: 270).

Women in these situations are far more likely to be living in poverty: whereas in 1959, only 20 percent of all poor families were headed by women, by 1992, more than half (52 percent) were (Folbre, 1995). As of 1995, about two thirds of *all* people living in poverty were women (Eitzen and Zinn, 1998: 269). This latter fact is what is sometimes known as the *feminization of poverty*, which may be somewhat misleading, suggesting that this problem is racially neutral. In fact, however, poverty hits racial minorities (especially minority women) far more than whites: as of 1995, 29.3 percent of all African American families and 30 percent of Hispanic families lived in poverty, compared to only 8.5 percent of white families (Eitzen and Zinn, 1998: 268).

One specific example of the role of class and race is demonstrated in a detailed and sophisticated study by Daly of a sample of women offenders in a court system in New Haven, Connecticut. From a larger sample of 397 cases, this study focused in depth on a smaller sample of forty men and forty women who were sentenced to prison (i.e., they went through all stages of the criminal justice process). Of the forty women, twenty-four (60 percent) were African American, five (12 percent) were Puerto Rican, and the remainder (28 percent) were white. Half of the women were raised in single-parent families, and only two of the women were described as growing up in "middle-class households." Most of these women were described by Daly as having grown up in families "whose economic circumstances were precarious," while in about two thirds of the cases, their biological fathers were "out of the picture" while they were growing up. Only one third completed high school or the equivalent General Education Diploma (GED). Two thirds "had either a sporadic or no paid employment record" and more than 80 percent were unemployed at the time of their most recent arrest (Daly, 1992:23–24).

Not surprisingly, the same kind of profile has been given by a nationwide survey conducted by the American Correctional Association (1990); a detailed study by Miller on a group of women offenders in Milwaukee (1986); and studies of women prisoners by Rafter (1990); Freedman (1981), and Pollock-Byrne (1990); along with studies of female juvenile offenders (Chesney-Lind and Shelden, 1998).

Perhaps the most outrageous form of judicial sexism comes from the attempt to criminalize pregnant women addicted to drugs, especially crack cocaine. A 1997 study by Siegel, appropriately called "The Pregnancy Police Fight the War on Drugs," reveals one of the most repressive sides of the war on drugs. It was during the height of the war on drugs, in the late 1980s, that "crack babies" began to make the headlines. More than two hundred prosecutions were directed toward women as overzealous prosecutors misused the law (stretching the limits of legal reasoning) against women. Siegel cites the racial bias in such a crackdown by observing that in Florida in 1989, more than seven hundred pregnant women in public and private clinics were tested for drugs. There was virtually no difference by race in the percentage of who tested positive (15.4 percent of the white women tested positive versus 14.1 percent of the African American women), yet African American women were almost *ten times more likely* to be reported to the authorities for drug abuse (Siegel, 1997: 251).

One woman in North Carolina was charged with "assault with a deadly weapon" (that weapon being crack cocaine) with the "intent to kill her fetus"; she was sentenced to twenty years in prison. In another case, a woman was charged with "felony child neglect" when her child tested positive for cocaine. Fortunately, most women charged were spared the maximum punishments by sympathetic judges, although some did not.

One woman who did not escape punishment was a Florida woman who was convicted (her first conviction ever) of "drug-trafficking" for "delivering drugs to her infant through the umbilical cord." This woman had sought treatment for her cocaine addiction but could find no program that would accept her. After giving birth, with no complications, the attending nurses and doctors said the baby looked and acted perfectly normal. Routine tests revealed cocaine in her system, and the hospital notified authorities, whereupon she was arrested, eventually convicted, and sentenced to one year in jail and fourteen years of probation. In South Carolina, a total of eighteen women were charged with "criminal neglect" of their fetuses (Siegel, 1997).

According to Siegel, hundreds more women were subjected to civil proceedings seeking to deny them custody of their children. Not surprisingly, African American and poor women have been the most likely targets of such actions. Part of this reason stems directly from the fact that good prenatal care is simply not available to poor women and women of color. Studies have shown that in most hospitals, poor women are summarily denied drug treatment if they are pregnant; this is part of the "blame the user" mentality of the "drug czar" William Bennett who took over the war on drugs during the 1980s. As usual, it became easier to avoid looking at such relevant problems as poverty and racism (Siegel, 1997: 255). During all of the "drug scare" propaganda during the 1980s, the so-called "crack baby" became a very convenient symbol. In time, careful research showed that this was more hype and exaggeration than fact. For instance, one research study found that less than 2 percent of all newborns were exposed to cocaine and that such exposure rarely had any effect on the baby's health. So-called "crack babies" are really "poverty babies." Siegel concluded that "Mothers who use crack were convenient scapegoats for conservative administrations to blame in order to divert the public's attention away from the declining social and economic conditions affecting increasing numbers of Americans" (Siegel, 1997: 257).

Chivalry, however, is largely a racist and classist concept in that such lenient treatment is typically reserved for white women from the higher social classes. Moreover, any "lenient" treatment granted to women is due largely to the fact that their crimes are so minor compared to men and the criminal careers are not nearly as lengthy as men, two variables that are highly predictive of treatment in the criminal justice system (Moyer, 1992). Field observations of police officers confirm the suspicion that "demeanor" also plays a significant role (Piliavan and Briar, 1964). Visher's detailed analysis of field observations of more than five thousand police/citizen encounters in twenty-four cities led her to conclude that while offense type is important, age, race, and demeanor all played important roles. Significantly, she discovered that female offenders who were young, African American, or hostile did not receive any preferential treatment, while white women who displayed a calm and deferential attitude received lenient treatment by the police (Visher, 1983). Additional support for the argument that African American female offenders are treated more harshly came from a study in California of a sample of all felony cases in 1980, where it was found that the odds of women being arrested ranged from a high of one in forty-two for African American females in their twenties to a low of one in 667 for white females seventy years or older (Wilbanks, 1986).

The most dramatic illustrations of the lack of chivalry toward African American and other minority women come from examining who gets sentenced to prison; this has been in recent years a direct result of the war on drugs. This "war" has had a dramatic impact on the criminal justice system and women, especially the dramatic growth in the prison population.

Sentencing Patterns, the War on Drugs, and Women

As discussed in previous chapters, there is no way to separate the phenomenal growth in prison populations from the war on drugs, a war that has targeted huge numbers of African Americans. While there is little relationship between race and illicit drug use, African Americans are far more likely to be arrested and sent to prison. For women, the poor in general and African Americans in particular have been singled out. As of 1991, about one third of women offenders had been sentenced on drug offenses, compared to around one in ten in 1979. Further, more than one third of the women doing time in prison on drug charges had been convicted of drug *possession.*

If this is not bad enough, a large percentage of women sentenced to prison on parole violations have not committed any new crimes, but rather were returned for not passing their urine tests. Moreover, sentences to federal prisons have zoomed upward because of drug offenses. In 1989, 44.5 percent of women in federal prison were in for drugs, and this figure went up to 68 percent in just two years. About twenty years ago, about two thirds of women convicted of felonies in federal court were given probation; in 1991, only 28 percent were. Further, the average time served for women on drug offenses went from twenty-seven months in 1984 to sixty-seven months in 1990 (Chesney-Lind, 1997: 147–148). Overall, the proportion of women offenders in prison because of drug offenses went from 12 percent in 1986 to 32.8 percent in 1991. In fact, the percentage increase in women sentenced to prison for drugs has been much greater than for men sentenced for drugs. For instance, between 1987 and 1989 in the state of New York, the number of women sentenced for drugs increased by 211 percent, compared to only an 82 percent increase for men. In Florida, during the 1980s, admissions to prison for drugs increased by a whopping 1,825 percent; however, for female offenders, this increase was an astounding 3,103 percent (Donziger, 1996: 151).

Much of the increase in women prisoners comes from the impact of *mandatory sentencing* laws, passed during the 1980s crackdown on crime. Under many of these laws, mitigating circumstances (e.g., having children, few or no prior offenses, nonviolent offenses) are rarely allowed. One recent survey found that just over half (51 percent) of women in state prisons had no or only one prior offense, compared to 39 percent of the male prisoners (Donziger, 1996: 152).

Thus, this society's recent efforts to "get tough" on crime has had a most negative impact on female offenders, as more are finding their way into the nation's prison system. In fact, largely because of the war on drugs, the number of new women's prisons has dramatically increased in recent years. Whereas between 1940 and the end of the 1960s only twelve new women's prisons were built, in the 1970s a total of seventeen were built, and thirty-four new prisons were built in the 1980s. The women in these prisons are less likely to be there because of a violent crime (Donziger, 1996: 148).

Women in Today's Prisons

While women constitute around 20 percent of all those arrested and only about 6 percent of those in prison, their numbers and their rate of incarceration have been dramatically increasing during the past twenty years. As of December 31, 1996, there was a total of 74,730 (compared to only 8,850 in 1976) women in federal and state prisons, constituting 6.3 percent (versus 3.6 percent in 1976) of all prisoners (Shelden, 1982: 347; Maguire and Pastore, 1996). These latest figures represent an incredible numerical increase of 744 percent and their proportion increased by 75 percent during the past twenty years. Moreover, as indicated in Table 6.1, the incarceration *rate* of women went from eight per 100,000 in 1975 to forty-five per 100,000 in 1994, for an increase of 463 percent.

These increases do not match the increases in women's crime as measured by arrests, except if the impact of the war on drugs is considered, along with greater attention to domestic violence. During this period, there has been a dramatic change in the criminal justice system's response to female drug use, as it has for all illegal drug use, as well as domestic violence. In the latter case, such increased attention to domestic violence has led to an increase in arrests of women for both aggravated assault and "other assaults" (Chesney-Lind, 1997).

A Profile of Women in Prison

This war on crime and war on drugs has really been, in effect, a war on women and minorities. As are male prisoners, most women in prison are poor and uneducated, but more women than men prisoners are minorities. Also, about 80 percent of women prisoners have children, which presents problems peculiar to women. Table 6.2 shows background characteristics of women in prison, according to a survey by the American Correctional Association (American Correctional Association, 1990). As indicated, most of the women are racial minorities with little education, one third of whom

TABLE 6.1   Incarceration Rates of Men and Women, State and Federal Institutions, 1925–1994.

Year	Total	Male	Female	Ratio
1925	79	149	6	24.8:1
1935	113	217	8	27.1:1
1945	98	193	9	21.4:1
1955	112	217	8	27.1:1
1965	108	213	8	26.6:1
1975	111	220	8	27.5:1
1985	202	397	17	23.4:1
1994	389	753	45	16.7:1
% increase				
(1975–85)	82.0	80.5	112.5	
(1985–94)	92.6	89.7	164.7	

Source: Maguire and Pastore, 1996: 556

had less than a high school education. The occupational histories show that virtually every inmate had worked at some time, mostly in low-skill, low-wage jobs in the service and retail trade industries. The profile further reveals that most of these women were not "career criminals," as about 60 percent had fewer than five previous arrests, while about one fourth (26.3 percent) had been arrested only once. For almost half (45.8 percent), this was the first time they had ever been incarcerated. The most common of the offenses on their current sentence was, not surprisingly, a drug offense (20.7 percent), with murder second (15 percent) and larceny-theft third (12 percent).

These data also reveal that while most had been married at some time, the majority were now either divorced or separated. Indicative of the low social status of many women inmates is the fact that around 30 percent never had a driver's license nor a checking account, while 60 percent had received welfare assistance at one time. As already noted, most had at least one child and about 30 percent had three or more. It is also significant that 42 percent had their first child when they were under eighteen, and another 26 percent when they were eighteen or nineteen years of age. Research suggests that having children as a teenager puts one at high risk for greater involvement in criminal behavior (Dryfoos, 1990). Further, such a situation places the children at risk as well. Note that in almost every case, someone other than the child's father has custody of the child, usually grandparents or the mother's siblings.

What is also of interest is the personal background of these women. Almost half had another family member who had been in prison, which is an-

TABLE 6.2   *A Profile of Women Prisoners (1990).*

Characteristic	Percent
Race	
White	43.4
African American	41.5
Hispanic	9.8
Other	5.3
Age	
Under 19	2.9
20–24	2.9
25–29	28.1
30–34	23.2
35–39	12.9
40 or more	15.0
Marital Status	
Never Married	36.5
Married	21.6
Separate or Divorced	33.8
Percent never had a driver's license	28.3
Percent never had a checking account	32.8
Percent with at least one child	79.1
Percent under eighteen when had first child	42.0
Of those with children, percent in which someone other than father has custody	92.4
Percent with other family member ever in prison	48.4
Percent ever run away from home	46.5
Percent ever physically abused	53.0
Percent ever sexually abused	35.6
Percent used alcohol daily or once/twice a week	41.1
Percent used heroin daily or once/twice a week	24.7
Percent used cocaine daily or once/twice a week	32.4
Percent used marijuana daily or once/twice a week	33.3
Percent high school grad or more	42.8
Work Experience	
Service occupations	45.0
Sales/clerical occupations	34.3
Percent ever received welfare	60.1
Most common offense, first arrest	
Larceny-theft	19.2
Drug-abuse violations	16.2
Fraud/forgery/embezzlement	13.4

TABLE 6.2 (Continued).

Characteristic	Percent
Drug abuse violations	20.7
Murder/manslaughter	15.0
Fraud/forgery/embezzlement	13.2
Larceny-theft	11.9
Prior Arrests	
One	26.3
2–4	35.0
5 or more	38.7
Times incarcerated, including current	
Once	45.8
Twice	39.8

Source: American Correctional Association, 1990

other strong predictor of criminality (Dryfoos, 1990). Indicative of a negative family life is the fact that so many had run away and were abused. In fact, the percentage who were abused is a somewhat low number, given what other researchers have found through other data (Chesney-Lind, 1997). In fact, the American Correctional Association survey, on which these data are based, also surveyed a sample of incarcerated juvenile females, and these data reveal a far greater pattern of abuse. For instance, among the juveniles, an astounding 80 percent had run away at least once; 39 percent reported that they had run away ten or more times. Also, more than half (54 percent) had attempted suicide at least once. A greater proportion of the juveniles had been physically abused (62 percent) and sexually abused (54 percent) than was the case for the adults.

As for substance abuse, the figures show a pattern of rather extensive abuse. Alcohol abuse was common for these women, as 41 percent used it either daily or once or twice a week. However, for juveniles, such abuse was even greater, as 60 percent had used alcohol either daily or once or twice a week. One fourth of the adult women used heroin frequently, while around one third used cocaine and marijuana. Among the juveniles, while the abuse of heroin was minimal and their use of cocaine was approximately the same as adults, marijuana use was far more prevalent, as almost half (47 percent) used it daily and another 17 percent used it once or twice a week.

Finally, it is interesting that for the adult women, the majority were not *career criminals* (if this term is based on the usual proof of such a status; namely, five or more arrests) and almost half (45.8 percent) had any prior prison sentences (i.e., they were *first-timers*). This is probably indicative of the war on drugs and its effect on women drug users: it has, in effect, criminalized those who in previous years would never have been sent to prison but would have instead been placed on probation, if they were arrested at all (Chesney-Lind, 1997).

Some Concluding Thoughts

More women are finding themselves completely left out of the recent economic upturn American society has experienced. Like earlier generations, minority women have suffered the most, as they find themselves mired in poverty with the sole responsibility of child-rearing. Even among women who are working, times are getting harder. In fact, between 1970 and 1990, there was a 500 percent increase in the number of women who held more than one job. Most of these jobs have been in the lowest paying sectors of society: service and retail trade. Women suffer the most as a result of a divorce: while men realize an average increase in income of 43 percent, women's income drops by an average of 73 percent. Only one of six divorced women receive alimony, and only 13 percent with preschool children receive child support. The majority of single-parent households are run by women, and most are living at or near the poverty level (Parenti, 1994: 146–148).

Given the continuous war on drugs along with efforts to "end welfare as we know it," women—especially minority women—are going to continue to experience being processed by the criminal justice system.

Notes

1. For the classic statement on this position, see Engles (1972); a good critique of this thesis is provided by Lerner (1986: Chapter 1).

2. For a discussion of how and why capitalism promotes selfishness, greed, the need for power and control, etc., see Heilbroner (1985: especially Chapters 2 and 3).

3. Portions of the following section are taken from Chesney-Lind and Shelden (1998).

7

A Look Ahead in the New Millennium

The Crime-Control Industry—Still Controlling the Dangerous Classes

As we begin the new millennium, we are witnessing a most serious development, one that poses a significant threat to the country. The threat consists of what can be called the "crime control industry." It is an industry run amok. It is awash with cash and profits beyond anyone's imagination. It needs crime. It needs victims. It needs the blood of citizens, like a vampire does. As the news industry saying goes, "If it bleeds, it leads."

Crime today, as always, is often front-page news. It dominates the local nightly newscasts, complete with film footage of the victims and the perpetrators. Prime-time television is often similarly dominated by crime—from full-length movies to so-called "live" broadcasts of police in action catching criminals. Millions flock to the movie theaters every week to see the latest episodes of crime and violence. Crime also becomes a hot item during every election year, with opposing candidates typically trying to see who can be the toughest. Crime also becomes the subject of hundreds of books, both popular fiction and non-fiction, as well as academic discourses.

What is not often realized is that "fighting crime" has become a booming business, with literally hundreds of companies, large and small, itching for a slice of a growing pie of profits. Employment in this industry offers careers for thousands of young men and women, many with college degrees in criminal justice programs at more than three thousand colleges and universities. The criminal justice system alone provides a steady supply of career possibilities, as police officers, prison guards, probation officers, and many more. Most of these jobs offer not only good starting pay but also excellent benefits and a promise of future wage increases and job security. Many have formed unions, some of which have become stronger than any union heretofore. A multitude of businesses, ranging from small "mom and pop" security businesses to huge corporations listed on the New York Stock Exchange, have found it profitable to "invest in crime."

We have witnessed in the twentieth century the emergence of a "criminal justice industrial complex" (one part of the crime-control industry) that has recently taken over where the "military industrial complex" left off. The police, the courts, and the prison system (or what some have called the "prison industrial complex") have become huge, self-serving, and self-perpetuating bureaucracies with a vested interest in keeping crime at a certain level. They need victims, they need criminals—even if they have to invent them, as they have throughout the war on drugs and war on gangs.[1] In short, it is good that we have crime, otherwise billions of dollars in profits would be lost and hundreds of thousands of people would be out of work (including this author). Fighting crime has become, in effect, a Keynesian stimulus to the economy.[2]

While elected officials and many others talk about the need to "turn the corner" on the crime problem, to "make the streets safe" for potential victims, what is ignored is that there is no way crime will be reduced by any significant amount (e.g., a 50 percent reduction) because it would have such a negative impact on our economy. Simply put, we cannot afford to really put a large dent in the crime problem. Actually, to be more specific, various special interests (except the average citizen) cannot afford to reduce crime. In fact, the traditional reasons for putting people in prison—incapacitation, retribution, rehabilitation—may be giving way to another reason: increasing the profits of big business and providing economic uplift in rural communities. (In effect, taxpayers are subsidizing private industry in that tax dollars pay for prisons and jails, which in turn contract with businesses for various supplies.)

Despite the fact that the official crime rate has been in decline through most of the 1990s, the public's *fear* of crime has not diminished. For instance, a Time/CNN poll in 1995 found that an overwhelming majority (89 percent) believes that crime is rising and just over half (55 percent) is concerned about being a crime victim (Blakely and Snyder, 1997: 151).

In words that were written more than one hundred years ago, Karl Marx commented sarcastically about some of the "positive functions" of crime and criminal justice when he wrote:

> The criminal produces not only crime but also the criminal law; he produces the professor who delivers lectures on this criminal law; and even the inevitable text-book in which the professor presents his lectures as a commodity for sale in the market. . . . Further, the criminal produces the whole apparatus of the police and criminal justice, detectives, judges, executioners, juries, etc. . . . Crime takes off the labour market a portion of the excess population, diminishes competition among workers, and to a certain extent stops wages from falling below the minimum, while the war against crime absorbs another part of the same population. The criminal therefore appears as one of those natural "equilibrating forces" which establish a just balance and open up a whole perspective of "useful" occupations. (Marx, 1893: 52–53)

We have now entered into a new century and the new millennium offers us many challenges, but at the same time presents some rather pessimistic predictions. What has occurred during the last one third of the twentieth century is that crime and its control has become one of the fastest-growing businesses in world history. As the manufacturing base of America has declined, we have seen in its place the rise of a fast-growing service industry. Within this industry is found what can be called the "crime-control industry."

The Crime-Control Industry

The recognition of the existence of a crime-control industry is not of recent origins. One of the first to recognize this as a problem was Quinney in his book, *Class, State, and Crime*, first published in 1977. In this book, he wrote that there is what he termed a *social-industrial complex,* of which a *criminal justice industrial complex* is a part. This much larger complex is "an involvement of industry in the planning, production, and operation of state programs. These state-financed programs (concentrating on education, welfare, and criminal justice), as social expenses necessary for maintaining social order, are furnished by monopolistic industries" (Quinney, 1980: 133). Large corporations, Quinney suggested, have found a new source of profits in this industry, with the criminal justice industry leading the way. Private industry, in short, has found that there is much profit to be made as a result of the existence of crime.

Part of the reason for the growth of the crime-control industry is that our society has decided that a *technocratic* solution to the crime problem is the best course to take. This perspective, which is almost identical to the perspective taken toward the Vietnam War, suggests that the solution to crime requires a combination of science and technology. Such a position was stated well by the President's Crime Commission in 1967:

> More than 200,000 scientists and engineers have applied themselves to solving military problems and hundreds of thousands more to innovation in other areas of modern life, but only a handful are working to control the crimes that injure or frighten millions of Americans each year. Yet the two communities have much to offer each other: Science and technology is a valuable source of knowledge and techniques for combating crime; the criminal justice system represents a vast area of challenging problems (President's Commission, 1967a: 1).

It is obvious that the government took up the challenge, for since this time the crime-control industry has become enormous. It is so huge that it is almost impossible to estimate the amount of money spent and the profits made.

One can clearly see the size of this complex by first noting the annual expenditures of the three main components of the criminal justice industrial complex: law enforcement, courts, and corrections. During the 1980s and early 1990s, total expenditures increased by almost 200 percent, with the largest increase for corrections, which went up by more than 250 percent. The most recent estimates indicate that the total expenditures stood at around $97 billion in 1993; Donziger estimates that as of 1995, these sums exceeded $100 billion annually (Maguire and Pastore, 1998: 3–4; Donziger, 1996: 85). A recent estimate is that by 2005, annual expenditures will be more than $200 billion (Chambliss, 1999: 5).

Employment within the crime-control industry is growing rapidly, providing many career opportunities for both college and high-school graduates. The most recent data show that in fiscal year 1993 there were just over

1.8 million employed within this system, a 65 percent increase from 1982. The largest component is within the corrections category, with just over 1.4 million, representing an increase of more than 90 percent from 1982. The U.S. Census reports that the hiring and training of correctional officers is the "fastest-growing function" of all government functions. As of 1992, there were more people working in corrections than all people employed in any Fortune 500 company except General Motors, according to a *USA Today* article.[3] Given that the corrections industry is such an important and perhaps the most lucrative part of the crime-control industry, a separate section is devoted to this.

Chapter 4 presented evidence of the huge increases in the prison population during recent years. What needs to be underscored here is that the mere *size* of the correctional complex is truly incredible. The most recent data show that as of the middle of 1998, there were more than 1.8 million people behind bars. The overall incarceration rate was about 660 per 100,000 population, which ranks the United States as number one in the world. (It is growing more every day so that by the time you read these lines, this rate will be even higher, perhaps moving past the 700 mark.) To give the reader some comparison, consider that the United States is way ahead of other industrial democracies, whose incarceration rates tend to cluster in a range from around 55 to 120 per 100,000 population, with some well below that figure, such as Japan's rate of 36. The average incarceration rate for *all countries of the world* is around 80; thus, America's incarceration rate is almost eight times greater than the average country (Currie, 1998: 15). For the period between 1985 and 1996, the total number of inmates increased by 121 percent, with the largest increases noted in the federal and state prison system (up 132 percent). The overall imprisonment rate went up by 96 percent during this period. While these increases were noteworthy during the later 1980s, they were most pronounced during the first half of the 1990s (Proband, 1997, 1998b; Coight, 1998).

As noted in Chapter 4, the actual *number* of prisons has increased, along with, in some cases, the *capacity* within the prison (e.g., "megaprisons"). Prison construction varied widely by state and region, with the largest increases occurring in the South (adding ninety-five prisons for an increase of 18 percent), with the state of Texas leading the way—adding forty-nine new prisons for an increase of 114 percent. Oklahoma added seventeen new prisons for an increase of 74 percent. As of 1995, California had the most prisons, with 102, followed by Florida at ninety-eight, North Carolina with ninety-three, and Texas with ninety-two (Mays and Winfree, 1998: 171).

The fastest-rising component of the entire criminal justice system is the *correctional-industrial complex*. It is within this specific industry that the profits from crime appear to be the greatest.

The Correctional-Industrial Complex: Cashing in on Crime

Many writers have focused on only one aspect of the crime-control industry, specifically the correctional-industrial complex or prison-industrial complex (Donziger, 1996: 85–98; see also Lilly and Knepper, 1993; Schlosser, 1998). While not taking the place of the military-industrial complex, the growth of the correctional-industrial complex has had similar causes. One cause is that because we no longer have many external enemies, we must now have internal enemies. The new internal enemy is crime, especially and incidentally crimes committed by minorities. Donziger has noted that during the past twenty years, expenditures on crime control have increased twice as fast as military spending. This complex has resulted from "a confluence of special interests that has given prison construction in the United States a seemingly unstoppable momentum" (Schlosser, 1998: 54).

The study by Lilly and Knepper focused on what they have called the *correctional-commercial complex*, which they describe as a sort of "subgovernmental policy-making" system consisting of an alliance between government and private enterprise. As already suggested, Lilly and Knepper note that this system is quite similar to the military-industrial complex, because it consists of patterns of interrelationships known variously as policy networks, subgovernment, or the iron triangle. Lilly and Knepper prefer the term *subgovernment* and proceed to argue that such a system may not be legally a form of government, but that nevertheless may exert greater influence than more formal structures of the government. In comparing this system to the military equivalent, they note that within the military subgovernment there is an "iron triangle" of the Pentagon, private defense contractors, and various members of Congressional committees (e.g., armed services committees, defense appropriations committees). They note further that the decision-making within any given policy arena "rests within a closed circle or elite of government bureaucrats, agency heads, interest groups, and private interests that gain from the allocation of public resources" (Lilly and Knepper, 1993: 152).

Aside from firms who build and operate correctional systems, there are several types of businesses that benefit directly from the imprisonment of offenders. These are firms that provide several different kinds of services, such as food, vocational training, medical services, drug detecting, personnel management, architecture and facilities design, and transportation, etc.[4] There are also companies that sell a variety of products, such as protective vests for guards, fencing, furniture, linen, locks, and many more.

Among the federal agencies cited by Lilly and Knepper are the Law Enforcement Assistance Administration (LEAA), established in 1968 as a result of the passage of the Omnibus Crime Control and Safe Streets Act. During the 1970s, LEAA gave more than $8 billion to state and local agencies, mostly for crime-control-hardware (e.g., riot gear, tanks, police helicopters). In 1982, the Office of Justice Programs was created, with five branches: Bureau of Justice Assistance, Bureau of Justice Statistics, Office of Juvenile Justice and Delinquency Prevention, Office for the Victims of Crime, and the National Institute of Justice. Then there is, of course, the FBI and the Department of Justice itself (Lilly and Knepper, 1993: 155–156).[5]

Finally, Lilly and Knepper note that there are several professional organizations that they say comprise the third portion of the corrections-commercial triangle, including the American Bar Association (ABA) and the American Correctional Association (ACA). The ACA has become an active lobbyist for the correctional system, sort of analogous to what the American Medical Association does for the medical profession.

Lilly and Knepper note that there is a "pattern of interaction among the participants in the correctional-commercial complex." They do this in the following specific ways: (1) each shares a close relationship with a constant flow of information, money, and influence; (2) there is an "overlap of interests," including a "flow of influence and personnel" (e.g., "heads of private firms are often former government officials or corrections administrators who have left public service for private interest"); (3) it operates without public scrutiny and exerts tremendous influence over policies; and (4) it is becoming a permanent fixture in national policies and they define their activities as "in the public interest" (Lilly and Knepper, 1993: 157–163).

The money involved in this system is huge, exceeding $25 billion in 1990, with more than a half million people employed. Private-business interests are constantly on guard for opportunities to make a profit. Lilly and Knepper cite one interesting example: in 1987, the Texas legislature passed a bill to add two thousand more prison beds; during the hearings, "salesmen wearing strange polyester suits and funky perfume descended on the state capital to hawk corrections products." Another example comes from a company that supplies health care, Prison Health Services Incorporated, which has become a multimillion-dollar enterprise. Also, prison food services is a billion-dollar enterprise that is growing between 10 and 15 percent per year. Even the Campbell Soup Company is getting in on the action, noting that the prison system is the fastest-growing market in food service. The list does not include leasing companies, brokerage houses, and banking firms, such as E.F. Hutton and Merrill Lynch, which will be discussed later (Lilly and Knepper, 1993: 158).

A good illustration of how companies are "cashing in" on the boom in corrections is found in the amount of advertising done in journals related to this industry. One example comes from two major journals serving the correctional industry, *Corrections Today* and *The American Jail*, plus the ACA's annual *Directory*.[6] (*Corrections Today* is the leading prison trade magazine and the amount of advertising in this magazine tripled in the

1980s.) In a sampling of a few issues of these two journals, advertisements were found everywhere, including the following companies and their products:

> Prison Health Services, Inc., a company that has, since 1978, "delivered complete, customized health-care programs to correctional facilities only. The first company in the United States to specialize in this area, we can deliver your program the fastest, and back it up with services that are simply the best"; Southwest Microwave, Inc., manufactures fence security, with its latest invention known as "Micronet 750," which is "more than a sensor improvement," it is "a whole new paradigm in fence detection technology"; Acorn Engineering, Inc., with their stainless-steel fixtures known as "Penal-Ware" (e.g., lavatories, toilets, showers) and "Master-Trol" electronic valve system; Rotondo Precast, Inc., boasting "over 21,000 cells . . . and growing"; Nicholson's BesTea with "tea for two or . . . two thousand" . . . "Now mass-feeding takes a giant stride forward . . ."; Northwest Woolen Mills, manufacturing blankets with the slogan "We've got you covered"; and "Prison on Wheels" from Motor Coach Industries, with their "Inmate Security Transportation Vehicle." (*Corrections Today*, August 1996)

More than two hundred different companies are listed in these sources; however, this is a mere sampling, for there is now a website on the Internet.[7]

A report by the Center on Juvenile and Criminal Justice notes that in the California budget for fiscal year 1994, for the first time ever showed that just as much money would be spent on the state correctional system as on the state's university system. The report also notes that between 1984 and 1994, the state constructed nineteen prisons but only one new state university. It is not surprising that the number of employees within this vast correctional system increase by 169 percent between 1984 and 1992, while there was an 8.7 percent *decrease* in the number of employees in higher education. The report also notes that working for the prison system is rewarding because prison guards earn about 58 percent more than the average guard nationally. It is estimated that by the year 2000, there will be roughly an equal number of prisoners as undergraduate students within the California state university system (Baum and Bedrick, 1994). A report by Schiraldi notes that the California Correctional Peace Officer's Association (the union representing prison guards) has become a potent political force in that state. In 1992 alone, this group was the second largest contributor to Political Action Committees, contributing just over $1 million to various candidates. In 1990, they gave almost $1 million to Pete Wilson's successful campaign for governor. The total contributions given in 1990 were ten times that given by the California Teachers' Association (Schiraldi, 1994).

The Privatization of Prisons: More Profits for Private Industry

A recent development in the criminal justice field, related specifically to the prison system, is the trend toward what is known as *privatization*, in which a private corporation takes over the operation of a jail or prison. Several years ago, Spitzer and Scull warned about the tremendous growth in privatization in general, especially within the private police industry. They quoted one source that called this phenomenon "creeping capitalism" or the transfer of "services and responsibilities that were once monopolized by the state to profit-making agencies and organizations" (Spitzer and Scull, 1977: 18). Privatization is a trend that includes more than the criminal justice system. As noted by Laursen, *contracting out*, as it is often termed, involves a number of services formerly provided by state and local governments, such as public education, health care, waste collection, and many more. Laursen points out that "at least eighteen categories of government services" saw an increase in private-sector involvement between 1987 and 1995 (Laursen, 1996).

The extent of privatization is not known, nor do we have any estimates of the amount of money involved. However, a copy of the 1995 annual report of one such corporation, *Corrections Corporation of America (CCA)*, was made available to this author. In this report the reader is told, first, that CCA is the "leading private-sector provider of detention and corrections services to federal, state, and local governments." There is also a subsidiary, CCA International, which provides similar services in foreign countries. Still another subsidiary is TransCor America, which "is the nation's largest and most experienced prisoner extradition company." CCA is a big corporation, with its stock trading on the New York Stock Exchange. As of 1995, CCA operated forty-six correctional facilities, including one in England, two in Australia, and two in Puerto Rico. It is a growth corporation, indicating an obvious vested interest in a relatively high rate of incarceration. Revenues went from $13 million in 1986 to $207 million in 1995 (an increase of 1,492 percent), while assets increased from $8 million to almost $47 million (an increase of 488 percent), and stockholders equity has gone from $24 million to $96 million (up 300 percent).[8]

An interesting update on CCA was provided in a recent issue of *The Nation*. First, it is noted that for the first nine months of 1998 CCA's net income rose by 63 percent over 1997 ($63 million). Second, it was revealed that in 1998, CCA purchased one of its leading competitors, U.S. Corrections Corporation. Third, and perhaps most interesting, was that CCA currently exists only as a "brand name" because it "merged" with a special real estate trust they had formed, known as Prison Realty Corporation. This trust "essentially operates as a tax shelter, enabling the company to evade paying any corporate income taxes." This clever scheme saves the trust around $50 million per year in taxes (Bates, 1999).

A number of serious problems have occurred with respect to the privatization of prisons and jails. A study by Brayson addressed some of these issues (Brayson, 1996). Perhaps the most serious issue raised by Brayson is the fact that private profit is the driving force in the privatization of the correctional system. Brayson quotes a report by Equitable Securities in March 1996 called "Crime Can Pay," in which it issued a "strong buy" advice to investors. The report concluded: "We consider the industry very attractive. There is substantial room for continued private-prison growth." The potential for profits has not escaped Wall Street. Ted Goins, of Branch, Cabell and Co., of Richmond, Virginia, compiled a list of "theme stocks" for the 1990s. His highest recommendation was for CCA. A Prudential Securities vice president, who is part of a "prison-financing team," is quoted as saying that "We try to keep a close eye on all the crime bills" (Thomas, 1994). Wall Street is indeed eager to back the growth in "crime-control stocks," with such companies as Merrill Lynch, Prudential Securities, Smith Barney Shearson, and Goldman Sachs among the leaders in support of privatization. As Brayson notes: "Between 1982 and 1990, California voters approved bonds for prison construction totaling $2.4 billion. After interest is paid to lenders, the total cost will be $4.1 billion. Now the big investors are bullish on private prisons." The firm of Raucher, Pierce and Refsnes of Dallas, Texas, is the underwriter and investment banker for Wackenhut Corrections. This company is reportedly doing about $5–7 million worth of business each year, mostly "buying bonds and securities from the private-prison companies or the state entities that issue them and resell them to investors. That securities market is now a $2–3 billion industry, up from nothing eight years ago. . . . " So enthralled about the profits, such securities firms have already launched the next phase of such development, which will have private companies financing their own construction with help from securities firms (Brayson, 1996: 34). Such an industry obviously depends on a steady supply of prisoners, and they just as obviously do not have a vested interest in reducing crime and protecting victims. After all, profits must keep rising.

Wackenhut Corporation, another leader in this industry, has had a suspect history. It was founded in 1954 by former FBI agent George Wackenhut. Board members have included several top people in the intelligence industry, including many former CIA figures, such as Frank Carlucci (National Security Advisor for Reagan), William Raborn (former CIA head), and Bobby Ray Inman (former CIA Deputy Director). Even former CIA head William Casey was once Wackenhut's outside counsel. The current head of Wackenhut, George Canosa, was once part of the right-wing Cuban-American Foundation (Brayson, 1996).

Wackenhut was at one time heavily involved in security checks for many corporations during the height of the Cold War. During the 1960s, it had files on as many as 2.5 million "suspected dissidents" and, through its publication *Security Review* regularly attacked the anti-war movement. One investigation by *The Nation* found that several employees of Wackenhut in El Salvador were involved in an unsuccessful plot, with ultra right-wing members of the Salvadoran Militia, to kidnap U.S. Ambassador Pat Cannon. Wackenhut denies the charge, but admits it still has employees in El Salvador. Wackenhut was named in a 1991 lawsuit alleging involvement in the manufacturing and selling of weapons and explosives to the Contras of Nicaragua. Also, a Congressional Committee recently found that the company may have broken some laws in its surveillance work for oil companies on the Alaskan pipeline (Brayson, 1996: 30).

As noted in a *Wall Street Journal* story, some of the same companies that produced the technology used in the Vietnam War are manufacturing and selling high-tech weaponry to fight the war on crime. A new iron triangle (consisting of politicians, small communities, and businesses) similar to the one used in fighting the Vietnam War has been forged, and businesses—large and small—are lining up to reap the enormous profits. Wall Street financial giants such as Goldman Sachs, Merrill Lynch, and Prudential are competing to underwrite prison construction with private, tax-exempt bonds that require no voter approval. Such defense industries as Westinghouse Electric Corp., Minnesota Mining and Manufacturing Co., and GDE Systems, Inc. (a division of the former General Dynamics) are among those competing for a piece of the action. Such lesser-known companies are also cashing in; among them are Esmore Correctional Services, which is the largest U.S. maker of police electronics—it cashed in on a contract to build and manage a one thousand-bed prison in Eloy, Arizona. Eloy is a town with a population of 7,200 located between Phoenix and Tucson, which will no doubt reap many benefits of having a prison located there (Thomas, 1994).

Like the Cold War, the war on crime requires huge amounts of technical research and (as Quinney noted over twenty years ago) researchers, especially those seeking grants from the Department of Justice, are eager to reap the financial benefits of such state-supported research. Dozens of private corporations are also eager to cash in on the technology needed to fight the "domestic enemy" of crime (Thomas, 1994).

During its annual meeting, the American Jail Association advertised many new products. (The annual meeting of the ACA has an even greater display of advertisers.) Advertising included such lines as "Tap into the Sixty-Five Billion Local Jails Market" and "Jails are BIG BUSINESS" (Donziger, 1996: 93). A company called Correctional Medical Services provides medical care to around 150,000 inmates, three times as many as they served in 1987, as reported in a *USA Today* article appropriately titled "Prison Business Is a Blockbuster" (Meddis and Sharp, 1994).

A boom in prison construction in rural areas has resulted in one interesting fact: 5 percent of the population increase in rural areas during the 1980s was accounted for by the growth in inmates. In those rural counties that built a prison or jail, the new inmate population accounted for almost half of the population growth in the 1980s. Incidentally, a total of 213 new rural prisons were built in the 1980s, up from only forty in the 1970s; in fact, between 1900 and 1980, only 146 new rural prisons were built in the entire country. Many rural towns have begun to solicit state governments to build a prison nearby. In Texas, some towns "bombarded the [Texas Department of Prisons] with incentives that range from country-club memberships for wardens to longhorn cattle for the prison grounds" (Donziger, 1996: 94).

Politicians often seek assistance from private enterprise when it comes to building prisons. Faced with severe overcrowding in the 1980s, liberal New York Governor Mario Cuomo found that real estate prices were far too high near the City of New York, where the majority of inmates are from. So he received help from a Republican state senator from the northern part of New York, who in turn arranged for low prices on land for prisons. The result? While twenty-five years ago this area had only two prisons, today it has eighteen, with one under construction. One prison now occupies land formerly used for the Olympic Village at Lake Placid, while others have been opened in abandoned factories and sanatoriums. This recent prison boom "has provided a huge infusion of state money to an economically depressed region." These prisons bring in about $425 million in annual payroll and operating expenses—in effect, an annual "subsidy" of more than $1,000 for each person in the area. The annual salary is around $36,000 for a correctional officer in this area, more than 50 percent higher than the average salary for the state as a whole (Schlosser, 1998: 57–58). Indeed, prisons are good for business and for job creation. One downside, however, is the fact that hundreds of families of inmates have to make the long bus ride to visit their relatives. Ironically, this fact has created yet another business, begun in 1973 by an ex-convict, who founded Operation Prison Gap, which operates a bus service for these families. They now have thirty-five buses and vans traveling on weekends and holidays (Schlosser, 1998: 58).

The construction industry is also experiencing a boom from the crime problem. An article appearing in the weekly construction industry bulletin, *ENR News*, is instructive (Ichniowski, 1994). It was noted that the Federal Crime Bill, signed into law by President Clinton in 1994, was a $30 billion package, which included $8.3 billion in grants to the states for prison construction. About $6.5 billion would be financed from a Violent Crime Reduction Fund (which is ironic, because there is no evidence that building more prisons reduces violence—in fact, just the opposite is true). This money would come from a reduction of the federal payroll by 235,000 people. Commenting on the bill, Thomas G. Pinkerton, national director for prison builder Hansen Lind Meyer of Iowa City, Iowa, said, "I think the challenge is to be sure that the facilities that are built are as efficient to operate as possible." He noted that operations account for 90 percent of a prison's thirty-year costs. Jack Rizzo, of Perini Corp., noted that the states have held back on prison construction in recent years, but "we're now starting to see that market segment come back." Spending on state prisons increased four times faster than spending on education during the 1980s. In many states it is now one of the largest budget items (Dumaine, 1991). During the previous ten years, states have spent $30 billion on prison construction. Following Medicare, corrections is the fastest-growing item in most state budgets (Cronin, 1992). While the inmate population now exceeds 1 million, experts estimate than this will double in the near future, with the cost of around $40 billion for more cells. Currently, operating and capital expenses for prisons and jails exceeds $1 billion each year (Nadel, 1995).

These private corporations, like CCA and Wackenhut, can usually operate a prison for around 10 to 15 percent lower than state and local agencies, and construction times are often halved. It is within the state system that private corporations can find the most business because, after all, the majority of criminal offenses are violations of state rather than federal law. Further, states now spend about $20 billion per year on corrections-related expenses, which represents an average of 6 percent of their total budgets; this figure was less than 2 percent in 1980. California seems to be the leader, with total annual expenditures of $3.6 billion (Cronin, 1992; Nadel, 1995).

Another method of "cashing in on crime" is through court fees and charges leveled against inmates. For example, in 1995 the state of Virginia collected $36 million in court fees just for trials alone. In 1994, Michigan collected $400,000 for inmates' bank accounts and pensions. Each year the Michigan Department of Corrections collects as much as $1 million in rent from inmates of halfway houses and prison work camps. That state passed a law in 1994 that will charge inmates up to $60 per day and prisoners will begin to pay for doctor visits. A new Missouri law will make failure to pay incarceration-related debts a violation of parole; this will no doubt increase the recidivism rate. A county in Kentucky began to charge inmates for doctors' visits and monthly visits dropped from 1,125 to 225. A similar program in Mobile, Alabama, reported similar results. Nevada collects between $800,000 and $1 million per year in room and board (Parenti, 1996).

A variation of this general theme is found in so-called "joint ventures" between private companies and the state prison system, which have made millions in profits through prison labor. Many private companies are taking advantage of cheap inmate labor and the tax breaks provided by California's Joint Venture Program. With the passage of Proposition 139 in 1990, private companies were allowed to use inmates to make products to be sold on the open market. One company employs eighteen inmates at San Quentin to do data-entry work for firms such as Chevron, Bank of America, and Macy's. Inmates in Ventura make phone reservations for TWA at $5 an hour; on the outside with unionized labor, this job would pay $18 per hour. Low wages are common. In Arizona, 10 percent of the inmates work for private companies and make less than the minimum wage. Many benefits accrue to private companies, including the fact that they don't have to pay benefits. In Oregon, $4.5 million worth of "Prison Blues," a line of jeans, was sold (Parenti, 1995).

Among the more recent developments in the prison industry has been the entrance of long-distance phone companies. Such industry giants as AT&T, Bell South, and MCI have found prisons to be an excellent market for long-distance business. Indeed, this makes sense because inmates all over the country spend countless hours on the telephone talking with relatives. Of course, this requires a collect call, which brings these companies into prison for the huge profits to be made. AT&T has an ad that reads: "HOW HE GOT IN IS YOUR BUSINESS. HOW HE GETS OUT IS OURS." MCI, not wanting to miss out, went so far as installing, for free, pay phones through-out the California prison system. They levy a $3 surcharge for each phone call made, the cost of which is paid for by the inmate's relative. MCI offered the Department of Corrections 32 percent of the profits (Schlosser, 1998: 63).

Finally, there are people known as *bed brokers*. These individuals act like travel agents, only in this case, they help locate jail and prison beds rather than hotel rooms. An example is a company known as Dominion Management, of Edmond, Oklahoma. They will search for a correctional facility with an empty bed for a fee, a sort of "rent-a-cell" program. Areas suffering from overcrowding are often in desperate need for additional space, the cost of which can run between $25 to $60 per "man-day." These bed brokers will earn a commission of around $2.50 to $5.50 per man-day (Schlosser, 1998: 65–66).

Taking advantage of prison inmates for profits is nothing new in the history of prisons. As noted in Chapter 4, throughout the nineteenth and well into the twentieth century, several forms of inmate labor was practiced, including the notorious convict-lease system and the chain gang, the latter of which is making a comeback in certain areas.

Private-Security: Crime Is Good for Business

Another part of this complex is the private-security business, which is perhaps one of the fastest-growing industries in the nation. The total amount of expenditures within this industry came to $52 billion in 1990. In 1990, the private-security industry employed more than 1.5 million people, outnumbering police officers by a 2:1 margin. In that year, more than 2.6 percent of the workforce was employed in the private-security industry, double the percentage it was in 1970 (Farnham, 1992). The latest figures show that this ratio is about 3:1, with more than $100 billion, dwarfing law-enforcement expenditures of around $40 billion. This increase occurred despite an over-all drop in reported serious crime during the same period. The key, say industry analysts, is that the public still does not feel safe (Buss, 1996).

Owners of businesses are concerned over liability for crimes committed on their premises, which could cost them a great deal even if one preventable incident occurred. Also, overall costs of most security devices have been declining. One company that is benefiting from the public's fear of crime is Security World, a chain of eight stores owned by Winner Corporation of Sharon, Pennsylvania. This is the company that made The Club (i.e., auto theft protector) popular. Another big seller is central alarm systems, which accounts for about $3 billion per year in sales (Buss, 1996).

These businesses have a lot to worry about. A study of 197 lawsuits filed against businesses by crime victims found that, of the cases that went to a jury, the awards averaged from $2.2 million for wrongful deaths to $700,000 for robberies. Juries awarded such damages when it was determined that the business lacked adequate security. Insurance companies are encouraging businesses to purchase extra "crime insurance," warning businesses, "Don't risk a lot for a little" (Buss, 1996).

Private-security products for the home are another example of the "cashing in on crime" frenzy. According to *Common Cause,* the American public spent $65 billion on private-security products in 1993. It is estimated that this should increase to $104 billion by 2000. Obviously, this is fueled by the public's *fear* of crime rather the *reality* of crime. From 1988 to 1992, the sales of home-security products increased by 32 percent. *Common Cause* estimated that by 1997, one of every five American homes was wired with some private-security device. This worries law enforcement because about 95 percent of all home-alarm calls received by the police turn out to be false. Thus, it is not surprising that the police rarely place such alarm calls on their priority list (Common Cause, 1995).

The residential security market is estimated to be about a $5 billion with sales estimated to increase by as much as 30 to 50 percent during the 1990s. Sales of new home-security devices increased by 30 percent in 1993 alone. Costs range from Radio Shack's simple $9.95 personal alarm to more than $10,000 (Fitzgerald, 1994). Honeywell, ADT Security Systems, and AT&T are leading the pack. Sales in these alarms went from $4 billion in 1986 to $6 billion in 1993, an increase of 50 percent. Revenues from automobile security devices increased by 15 percent in 1993 to $540 million. The market for nonlethal weapons, such as mace, is estimated to be around $300 million (Server, 1994). Another company cashing in on crime is Counter Technology, Inc., of Bethesda, Maryland, a company that provides a wide range of services for its clients. The company grew from a mere $88,000 in revenues in 1987 to $14 million in 1994, a jump of more than 1,500 percent (Litvan, 1995).

Private-security police, or "rent-a-cop," is another booming industry. During the 1980s, this industry grew at twice the rate of public law-enforcement agencies and received 70 percent more funds. Pinkerton's is among the leaders with revenues exceeding $600 million. There are more than 57,000 private-security firms in the country. Currently there are two security guards for every federal, state, and local police officer (Carlson, 1995).

Wackenhut Corporation is the leader in security guard services with contracts with the U.S. Department of Energy, the State Department, and NASA. Revenues in 1990 exceeded $500 million with profits of almost $7 million ($1.80 a share for stockholders). An international firm, it operates prisons and jails in more than forty countries (Millman, 1991).

Westec Security is a private patrol service, which patrols, for a fee, exclusive neighborhoods. These guards drive around neighborhoods twenty-four hours a day. The cost per home is $85 per month. Borg-Warner Security has a contract to patrol certain sections of Washington, D.C.'s, Georgetown neighborhood with foot patrols. Protection One, based in Culver City, California, earned $22 million in sales last year. The Justice Department estimates that the private-protection business does $52 billion worth of business and is growing at about 8 percent per year. The industry employs about 1.5 million people, about two and a half times public law enforcement (Munk, 1994).

Suburban crime went up a reported 30 percent between 1985 and 1991, according to the FBI. Sales of home alarms went up 80 percent between 1986 and 1991. Some are calling mace the "new Christmas stocking stuffer," and many are being displayed in a "candy-cane motif." At one shop, a "fresh display of thirty-six canisters sold out in three days" (Farnham, 1992).

Paralleling the growth in the private-security industry has been the emergence of so-called "gated communities." This has been perhaps most apparent in Southern California where, beginning in the late 1960s, literally millions of affluent whites "fled" to outlying regions, such as Simi Valley to the northwest (site of the first Rodney King trial) and Orange County to the southeast. As the excellent study by Davis shows, what has occurred in this area is the development of "fortress cities" that are divided between the "fortified cells" of the affluent suburbs and "places of terror" in the inner cities (and even the once mostly white, relatively quiet San Fernando Valley) "where the police battle the criminalized poor" (Davis, 1992: 224). A recent study of the national growth of these communities found that the number of gated communities went from fewer than five thousand in the early 1970s to more than twenty thousand as of 1996. And they are growing rapidly—a leading national real estate developer estimates that about 80 percent of new urban housing projects will be gated. In 1988 alone, one third of the 140 housing developments in the well-to-do Orange County, California (next to Los Angeles County) were gated, twice the amount five years earlier. With such developments, little wonder the title of this study is *Fortress America* (Blakely and Snyder, 1997: 7).

Other Components of the Crime-Control Industry

There are other components of the crime-control industry, including the educational system, especially the thousands of criminal justice programs within colleges and universities. There are currently about three thousand such programs in this country. Nationwide, the average budget of each department or program offering degrees in criminal justice varies considerably, and no firm estimates are available. However, using $500,000 (which is about the annual budget for the department where this author works), the total annual expenditures come to around $1.5 billion. Additional expenditures have come in the form of grants from various government agencies (e.g., National Institute of Justice). Total funding for research on the problem of crime in fiscal year 1993 came to $997,023, an increase of almost 700 percent since 1983 (Maguire and Pastore, 1998).

Other components of this industry that might be included are the following: (1) the profits made by hospitals and insurance companies (e.g., hospital emergency-room visits, doctors' fees, insurance premiums on automobiles, and other insurances covering crime) and the salaries of those who deal with victims (e.g., doctors, nurses, paramedics, insurance adjusters); (2) the profits from the sale of books (e.g., college textbooks, trade books), magazine and journal articles, newspaper coverage (and the advertisers who profit from crime stories), television crime shows (and their advertisers), and movies about crime (with the enormous salaries paid to actors and actresses who star in them); (3) the money collected by courts through various fines (especially traffic tickets), special courses defendants can enroll in as a condition of (or in lieu of) their sentence (e.g., traffic schools, petty larceny programs); and (4) the money collected by bailbondsmen. One could no doubt think of other categories; the point is that the existence of a crime problem is extremely profitable for millions of people, a few private corporations, and the government.

It is difficult to provide completely accurate dollar estimates of the money involved and the profits made by businesses in this industry, but from these reported figures, a conservative estimate comes to between $250 billion and $300 billion per year (roughly the equivalent to the Pentagon budget).

The Social Context: Growing Inequality

Under most forms of capitalism in today's world, the relations of production are marked by an almost total separation of the workers (i.e., producers) from the means of production. One class—usually referred to as the *capitalist class* or *ruling class*—owns most of the means of production; that is to say, a small group (around 2 percent of the total population) owns most of the factories, land, buildings, wealth, income, and other assets, which in turn translates into an enormous amount of power in society. What is important to note is the fact that wealth itself in its current form is not an end in itself, but rather it is a *"means for gathering more wealth,"* which in turn serves "to augment the power of a dominant class" (Heilbroner, 1985: 35).

Inherent in this power relationship is the fact that the typical worker has no choice but—as Marxists always put it—"to sell their labor power" to the capitalist. What is especially important is the fact that possessing "capital" in all of its forms and owning the means of production leads directly to the most important ingredient in the relations of production, namely *domination.* Unlike other forms of domination in history (e.g., the domination of the army, church), this form involves the power *to refuse to sell commodities or buy labor power* (Heilbroner, 1985: 39–40). One recent example is the power that large corporations have in moving their factories to low-wage foreign countries.

One crucial difference between the capitalist system and other systems is the *drive for profit,* which can be almost an obsession. As Heilbroner so aptly puts it, one uniqueness about capitalism is "the restless and insatiable drive to accumulate capital." Heilbroner suggests that this can be explained in part by the desire to obtain prestige and distinction among one's fellow human beings, something that was pointed out by Adam Smith. More than any other measure of prestige and distinction, the possession of capital "confers on its owners the ability to direct and mobilize the activities of society. . . ." In short, it is *capital* that "calls the tune" and that control over the access to capital "invests their owner with an attribute that goes beyond prestige and preeminence." "This," says Heilbroner, "is power." Moreover, wealth itself becomes *"a social category inseparable from power,"* and "wealth can only come into existence when the right of access of all members of society to an independent livelihood no longer prevails, so that control over this access becomes of life-giving importance." Quoting Adam Smith, Heilbroner gets to the essence of capitalist society, especially in modern American society; namely, that "Wherever there is great property, there is great inequality. For one rich man, there must be at least five hundred poor, and the affluence of the rich supposes the indigence of the many" (Heilbroner, 1985: 42–46, quoting from Smith's famous *The Wealth of Nations,* 1976: 709–710).

Within a capitalist system, power and control seem to be the most distinctive characteristics. The desire to have power and control over others tends to permeate throughout the society, whether we are talking about owners of large multinational corporations or leaders of drug gangs trying to maintain power and control over their local drug markets. It is essentially the same phenomenon, although on much different scales. Within a capitalist society, there tends to be an insatiable desire to continue "converting money into commodities and commodities into money." Everything, it seems, is turned into a "commodity"—from the simplest products (e.g., paper and pencil) to human beings (e.g., women's bodies, slaves) and crime. More importantly, the size of one's wealth has no bounds. Indeed, "daily life is scanned for possibilities that can be brought within the circuit of accumulation," because any aspect of society that can produce a profit will be exploited, including the misery and suffering of people who have been victimized by crime (Heilbroner, 1985: 60). Life itself has been "commodified."[9]

The accumulation of capital—and hence great wealth and inequality—would not be possible without the assistance of the state. Instead of Smith's "invisible hand of the market" (what is often erroneously called a "free market"), there are profits secured with the assistance of the government, both state and local, in the form of tax loopholes, subsidies, and other forms of what is essentially taxpayer assistance. Some call this "corporate welfare."[10] In fact, the entire idea of "free-market capitalism" is a myth. As a matter of fact, big business could not exist (and has never existed) without strong support from the government—and hence taxpayers. A recent study by two economists in Holland found that *every one of the top one hundred transnational corporations in the world* (*Fortune* magazine's list) has benefited in some way from their host government; in fact, at least twenty would have folded if they were not given large subsidies from their governments when they faced serious trouble. True capitalism has never really existed in this country.[11]

The key point that needs to be made is that capitalism, while bringing about a virtual cornucopia of goods and a standard of living that is the envy of the world, has its negative effects, which is that it produces a tremendous amount of inequality. Within a capitalist system, especially that which exists in American society, *such inequality is inevitable and a natural by-product of the system itself.* And despite the so-called "economic boom" in recent years, inequality has worsened.

We are currently in the midst of an important era in history, the last stage of the Industrial Revolution (Eitzen and Zinn, 1998: 188–192). Like previous transformations (e.g., from agriculture to manufacturing), several forces are operating to produce this change: (1) technological, (2) the globalization of the economy, (3) the movement of capital, and (4) the overall shift of the economy away from manufacturing to information and services.

Among the most important technological changes is the computer chip, which has led to the replacement of many workers by computers and robots. This has, in turn, resulted in a loss of millions of unskilled and semi-skilled jobs. The second force is the globalization of the economy. Currently, the U.S. economy is part of a much more competitive world economy. To increase their profits in this competitive economy, U.S. corporations have had to cut costs, usually by laying off workers or closing plants. The decline in manufacturing has been especially pronounced.

The third force involves the movement of capital or "capital flight," which is a process whereby companies have invested overseas, relocated plants within the United States, or engaged in mergers with other corporations. All of these efforts have had the effect of eliminating the jobs of many workers. In fact, multinational corporations based in the United States have huge investments in foreign countries, and many pay few if any income taxes.[12] More U.S. corporations are finding it profitable to move most of their manufacturing to Third World countries, where labor is cheap, and there are no unions, no restrictions on child labor (most of this labor is reminiscent of "sweatshops" in the nineteenth century), and no restrictions on worker safety. More than 1,100 American factories (e.g., Ford, General Motors, RCA) are in Northern Mexico (Eitzen and Zinn, 1998: 190).

As previously noted, the movement from manufacturing to service has been significant. Whereas in 1960, 31 percent of the labor force was employed in manufacturing industries, by 1994 this percentage had shrunk by half to a mere 15.9. In contrast, the percentage employed in service-producing industries (e.g., transportation, public utilities, retail trade, services) went from 62 to almost 80 percent, with the specific category of services accounting for the largest increase (from 13.6 to 28 percent).[13] From 1973 to 1989, about 35 million jobs were created and most of these were in the service sector; approximately one half of these involved few skills and were low-paying (some of the highest-paying jobs are within the criminal justice system). Between 1988 and 1993, 1.7 million high-wage, mostly blue-collar manufacturing jobs were lost, while about a million were created in the lowest-paid service sectors. Today the United States could be described as a "low-wage society." The average weekly earnings of workers (in 1997 dollars) went from $494 in 1973 to $424 in 1997 (Sklar, 1998). As of 1990, an estimated 18 percent of full-time workers are classified as living under the official poverty line, compared to 12 percent in 1979 (Eitzen and Zinn, 1998: 200).

The average wage in constant dollars for full-time workers declined in the late 1970s following a steady increase from the early 1950s. Since the late 1970s, wages have leveled off. In short, in terms of what the dollar can purchase, the wages of the typical worker have not changed in twenty years. The effects on the typical *male* worker has been especially negative. The median earnings of males have decreased while wages for females have increased, which is partly explained by the rise in low-wage workers from 7.4 percent of the labor force in the mid-1970s to 13.9 percent in 1990. In fact, many male workers have in effect *disappeared* from the labor force (many of them are in prison). While in the early 1950s, almost 90 percent of the men in America were "in the labor force" (meaning they were either working or actively seeking work), by the mid-1990s this percentage had shrunk to about 75 percent. During this same time, the percentage of women in the labor force went from just over 30 percent to about 60 percent. A portion of the gains for women may be accounted for by the incredible increase in the proportion of workers employed as *temporary* workers. In fact, the number of temporary workers increased by 211 percent between 1970 and 1990. A report from the National Association of Temporary and Staffing Services (the mere existence of this organization is itself most significant) reveals that in the last quarter of 1998 there were 2.94 million temporary workers, up from 1.17 million in 1990. Three fourths of these workers are employed in two major categories: clerical (40.5 percent) and industrial (34.5 percent). Manpower, Inc., and Kelly Temporary Services are among the leading employers in America today, with profits in recent years increasing much faster than most other companies (Folbre et al., 1995: Tables 2.4 and 2.5; Gilbert, 1998: Chapter 3; Cleeland, 1999).

Another way of describing this process is what Bluestone and Harrison have called *deindustrialization,* which is the reduction in our nation's rank in the world economy (Bluestone and Harrison, 1982). A specific example of this occurred in New York City. Between 1970 and 1984 approximately 500,000 jobs, which were in industries that *did not require a high school diploma,* were lost. These were mostly unskilled and semiskilled jobs typically filled by minorities and young people. During this same period, the city gained about 240,000 jobs in industries that *required more than a high school diploma* (Schorr, 1989: 301).

As noted in the introductory chapter of this book, the degree of inequality in this society has increased significantly during the last twenty years or so of the twentieth century. There is little doubt that this has contributed to the growth of those considered part of the dangerous classes.

In recent years there has been an attempt by the American government to build up a global economy dominated by big business (Chomsky, 1994, 1996a, 1998). The principle behind this is what is known as "economic freedom"—meaning that big business is "free" to invest, sell, and keep all the profits. To do this, it needs a "favorable business climate" and a stable local environment (meaning free of political turmoil, such as citizens trying to seek some form of democracy).

Getting support from American citizens has been of vital importance. To do this, the state has used the threat of an external enemy—for about forty years it was "Communism" and the Soviet Union via the "Cold War." With external enemies diminishing, the state has been forced to invent new, internal threats, such as crime or, more specifically, gangs and especially drugs. Just as anti-Communism helped mobilize the American people to support the massive war expenditures to guarantee a "stable business climate" overseas, the anticrime, antigang, and antidrug hysteria has helped mobilize a frightened public to support massive, almost military-like expenditures for the war on crime. Creating fear among the public—fear of the usual scapegoats (e.g., gangs, foreigners, drug dealers)—helps sell the "need" for more hardware in this internal "war" (Glassner, 1999). The main targets for this war continue to be those groups deemed "superfluous" to the creation of wealth and profit as we move from a manufacturing to a service/information economy—that is, the dangerous classes. As Marx noted, capitalism creates a surplus labor force and the state in turn has to figure out ways to control this population.

As big business continues to reap enormous profits, and as more people are inevitably relegated to the surplus population (especially inner-city minorities), the potential for the disruption of "normal business activities" increases, whether through radical democratic grassroots activities or through criminal activity. As long as such potential exists, so will the potential for the increase in the crime-control industry.

Where Do We Go From Here?

The previous chapters on the history of the American criminal justice system demonstrate to the reader the built-in, systemic class, racial, and gender bias. As the modern crime control-industry continues to grow, and as the economy continues to "boom" for a small segment of the population (while almost completely ignoring the majority), the criminal justice system will continue to target those deemed "dangerous," "superfluous," and "unneeded." Fighting crime has indeed become a big business with a vested interest in processing more citizens through the criminal justice system, even if certain crimes are invented (e.g., through drug legislation).

In reviewing the history of criminal justice, what we are actually reviewing is the continuous attempt to *control* crime; in so doing, this has been in effect if not in design an attempt to engage in the *control of the dangerous classes*, however this group has been defined over the years. Because crime is still very much with us, perhaps in the new millennium we should be looking elsewhere for our answers.

In recent years, I have found myself searching in other directions for answers to these and other problems. One direction has been in the area of philosophy and various Eastern religions, such as Buddhism, and some of the views of Native Americans. I have returned to many of the writings of Quinney, arguably one of the foremost criminologists and critical thinkers of the twentieth century, whose latest works point us in the direction of "peacemaking" by seeking peace within ourselves and various nonviolent and noncoercive alternatives (Quinney, 1991, 1998; Quinney and Wildeman, 1991). We can certainly see a trend in recent years, one that is likely to continue for some time, toward a searching for something that has been missing from our lives, and this is a sort of spiritual awareness. Indeed, a cursory look in any bookstore reveals numerous books in the self-help and religious sections. It is probably no accident that among the biggest selling books in recent years are those like *The Celestine Prophecy* by James Redfield (1993) and the books of Depak Chopra, such as *The Seven Spiritual Laws of Success* (1995).

Although I do not claim to have all the answers, after more than twenty-five years of studying and teaching about the subject of crime and delinquency, I am convinced that some fundamental changes need to be made in the way we live and think before we see any significant decrease in these problems. I have previously published these ideas when I was referring to confronting youth crime, but this can also apply to crime in general (Shelden, 1998). One of the key ideas that I was attempting to convey was this: we are always talking about the "problem of delinquency" or the "problem of youth" or that youths in trouble need to change their attitudes, their behaviors, their lifestyles, their methods of thinking. It seems that it is always *they* who have to change. What is invariably included in this line of thinking is the use of labels to describe these youth (and adult offenders). The labels keep changing, along with changing times. As Miller noted (1998: 234), we began with "possessed" youths in the seventeenth century, moved to the "rabble" or "dangerous classes" in the eighteenth and late nineteenth centuries, the "moral imbeciles" and the "constitutional psychopathic inferiors" of the early twentieth century. We continued in the twentieth century with the "psychopath" of the 1940s to the "sociopath" of the 1950s, and finally to more recent labels like "compulsive delinquent," the "learning disabled," the "unsocialized aggressive," even the "socialized aggressive," and finally the "bored" delinquent. "With the growth of professionalism, the number of labels has multiplied exponentially." Miller continues by suggesting that the problem with these labels is that it seems to be a way "whereby we bolster the maintenance of the existing order against threats that might arise from its own internal contradictions." And it reassures us "that the fault lies in the warped offender and takes everyone else off the hook. Moreover, it enables the professional diagnostician to enter the scene or withdraw at will, wearing success like a halo and placing failure around the neck of the client like a noose" (Miller, 1998: 234). More importantly, we continue to believe that harsh punishment works, especially the kind of punishment that includes some form of incarceration, so that the offender is placed out of sight and, not coincidentally, out of mind.

But there is a problem here. As noted in this book, throughout the eighteenth and nineteenth centuries, we have continued to succumb to the "edifice complex." We love to build these edifices, no matter what they are called (e.g., a new courthouse, a new prison, a new correctional center, a new police station). Perhaps it is because politicians like to have some kind of permanent structure to leave behind as a legacy so they can tell the people who voted for them to look at this or that building as "proof" they have done something about crime. Or perhaps it is because they are so profitable and are part of the huge crime-control industry.

I believe otherwise. I believe that we need to quit looking solely at the "troubled youth" or "criminals" as the main source of the problem, or even their "troubled families" and "troubled communities." It is time that those of us among the more privileged sectors of society consider that we are just as much a part of the problem; perhaps more so.

In short, if anyone wants to know where the answers lie and where to begin to look for solutions, I think it prudent that all of us begin by simply looking in the mirror. We should begin by asking ourselves: Is there anything that *I* can do differently? Is there something wrong with *my* attitudes, *my* beliefs, *my* actions that may contribute to the problem? If we want some answers, begin by searching *within ourselves.* This is the message from many who espouse some of the philosophies of the East. Let me quote from one such source, a book written by a Vietnamese Zen Master and poet Thich Nhat Hanh in his book, *Peace Is Every Step:*

> When you plant lettuce, if it does not grow well, you don't blame the lettuce. You look into the reasons it is not doing well. It may need fertilizer, or more water, or less sun. You never blame the lettuce. Yet if we have problems with our friends or our family, we blame the other person. But if we know how to take care of them, they will grow well, like lettuce. Blaming has no positive effect at all, nor does trying to persuade using reason and arguments. That is my experience. No blame, no reasoning, no argument, just understanding. If you understand, and you show that you understand, you can love, and the situation will change. (Hanh, 1991: 78)

Later in his book, he describes young prostitutes in Manila as follows:

> In the city of Manila there are many young prostitutes; some are only fourteen or fifteen years old. They are very unhappy. They did not want to be prostitutes, but their families are poor and these young girls went to the city to look for some kind of job, like street vendor, to make money to send back to their families. Of course, this is true not only in Manila, but in Ho Chi Minh City in Vietnam, in New York City, and in Paris also. After only a few weeks in the city, a vulnerable girl can be persuaded by a clever person to work for him and earn perhaps one hundred times more money than she could as a street vendor. Because she is so young and does not know much about life, she accepts and becomes a prostitute. Since that time, she has carried the feeling of being impure, defiled, and this causes her great suffering. When she looks at other young girls, dressed beautifully, belonging to good families, a wretched feeling wells up in her, a feeling of defilement that becomes her hell.
>
> But if she could look deeply at herself and at the whole situation, she would see that she is the way she is because other people are the way they are . . . . No one among us has clean hands. No one of us can claim that it is not our responsibility. The girl in Manila is that way because of the way we are. Looking into the life of that young prostitute, we see the lives of all the "non-prostitutes." And looking at the non-prostitutes and the way we live our lives,

we see the prostitute. Each thing helps to create the other . . . the truth is that everything contains everything else. We cannot be, we only inter-be. We are responsible for every thing that happens around us (Hanh, 1991: 97–98).

The thrust of Hanh's book is that before we can achieve peace on earth, which includes a world without crime and suffering, we have to develop peace within ourselves. How else can we make the world a better place, unless we make our own lives better? How can we tell the "criminals" in our midst how to live their lives if we do not set good examples? As Quinney has recently written: "If human actions are not rooted in compassion, these actions will not contribute to a compassionate and peaceful world. If we ourselves cannot know peace, be peaceful, how will our acts disarm hatred and violence?" (Quinney, 1995: 10). Without such hatred and violence, there will be no need to even have, much less need to control, the dangerous classes.

Notes

1. For a detailed analysis of the phoniness of the war on drugs, see Baum (1997) and Gordon (1994); for a discussion of the war on gangs, see Shelden et al. (1997) and Klein (1995).

2. John Maynard Keynes, an early twentieth-century economist, was most popular for his theory about how government expenditures could "stimulate" a stagnating economy. In this particular case, expenditures on prisons, jails, courtrooms, police cars, and the like stimulate the economy, creating thousands of jobs in the process.

3. At least 70 percent of a typical prison's operating budget goes to salaries and benefits (Mergenbagen, 1996).

4. Examples Lilly and Knepper cite include Hopeman Correctional Systems, Bevles Correctional Food Service Equipment, and Szabo Correctional Services.

5. For a more detailed description of federal "crime-control bureaucracies" like LEAA, especially their origins and functions in preserving the capitalist order, see Quinney (1974, Chapter 3).

6. This annual publication is fascinating in itself and illustrates how big this portion of the industry is. The most recent publication I have is the 1997 edition. Numbering more than seven hundred pages, it lists hundreds of prisons and juvenile correctional facilities in both the United States and Canada, along with the federal system. In this issue there are almost one hundred different companies whose ads appear within.

7. The site is called "corrections yellow pages" (http://www.correctionsyellow-pages.com); see also http://www.corrections.com. There are at least one thousand different ads at this site!

8. Information taken from the 1995 stockholders report of Corrections Corporation of America.

9. A fascinating slant on this process is described as the "McDonaldization" of American society. This has been defined as "the process by which the principles of the fast-food restaurant are coming to dominate more and more sectors of American society, as well as of the rest of the world." See Ritzer (1996: 1).

10. A great deal has been written lately about "corporate welfare." See, for instance, Zepezauer and Naiman (1996), Albeda et al. (1996: 20–21) and Derber (1998, Chapter 8).

11.   The Holland study was done by Ruigrok and van Tulder (1995). Reference to this study was made in Chomsky (1998). For documentation of the claim that there has never been a truly free market capitalism in this country, see Zinn (1995) and Chomsky (1993).

12   Of all American-based multinationals with assets over $100 million, more than one third (37 percent) paid *no* federal taxes in 1991, while the average tax for those who did pay was around 1 percent (Zepezauer and Naiman, 1996: 70).

13.   (U.S. Department of Commerce, 1995: 424.) On page 415 of this report, it is noted that one of the fastest-rising service occupations has been that of "corrections officer," with a projected increase by 2005 of between 60 and 80 percent.

References

Abbott, G. 1938. *The Child and the State.* Chicago: University of Chicago Press.

Adamson, C. R. 1984a. "Toward a Marxian Penology: Criminal Populations as Economic Threats and Resources." *Social Problems* 31: 435–458.

———. 1984b. "Hard Labor and Solitary Confinement: Effects of Business Cycle and Labor Supply on Prison Discipline in the United States, 1790–1835." *Research in Law, Deviance and Social Control* 6: 19–56.

———. 1999. "Punishment after Slavery: Southern State Penal Systems, 1865–1890." In R. P. Weiss (ed.), *Social History of Crime, Policing and Punishment.* Brookfield, VT: Ashgate.

Addams, J. 1909. *Spirit of Youth and the City Streets.* New York: Macmillan.

———. 1910. *Twenty Years at Hull-House.* New York: Macmillan.

Adler, J. S. 1986. "Vagging the Demons and Scoundrels: Vagrancy and the Growth of St. Louis, 1830–1861." *Journal of Urban History* 13: 3–30.

———. 1989a. "A Historical Analysis of the Law of Vagrancy." *Criminology* 27: 209–229.

———. 1989b. "Rejoinder to Chambliss." *Criminology* 27: 239–250.

Agee, P. 1975. *Inside the Company: CIA Diary.* New York: Bantam Books.

Albeda, R., N. Folbre, and the Center for Popular Economics. 1996. *The War on the Poor.* New York: The New Press.

Allen, H. E., and C. E. Simonsen. 1998. *Corrections in America* (8th ed.). Upper Saddle River, NJ: Prentice-Hall.

American Correctional Association. 1990. *The Female Offender.* College Park, MD: American Correctional Association.

———. 1997. *1997 Directory.* Lanham, MD: American Correctional Association.

Amsterdam, A. 1988. "Race and the Death Penalty." *Criminal Justice Ethics* 7: 84–86.

Anderson, D. 1995. *Crime and the Politics of Hysteria.* New York: Times Books.

Andrews, R. H., and A. H. Cohn. 1974. "Ungovernability: The Unjustifiable Jurisdiction." *Yale Law Journal* (June): 1383–1409.

Ares, C. E., A. Rankin, and H. Sturz. 1963. "The Manhattan Bail Project: An Interim Report on the Use of Pre-Trial Parole." *New York University Law Review* 38: 71–92.

Ariès, P. 1962. *Centuries of Childhood.* New York: Knopf.

Bacon, S. 1939. "The Early Development of American Municipal Police," unpublished Ph.D. dissertation, Yale University.

Balbus, I. 1973. *The Dialectics of Legal Repression.* New Brunswick, NJ: Transaction.

Baldus, D. C., G. Woodworth, and C. A. Pulaski. 1990. *Equal Justice and the Death Penalty: A Legal and Empirical Analysis.* Boston: Northeastern University Press.

Barak, G. 1975. "In Defense of the Rich; The Emergency of the Public Defender." *Crime and Social Justice* 3: 2–14.

———. (ed.). 1991. *Crimes by the Capitalist State.* Albany, NY: SUNY Press.

Barkan, S. E. 1977. "Political Trials and the Pro Se Defendant in the Adversary System." *Social Problems* 24: 324–336.

Barnes, H. E. 1972. *The Story of Punishment.* Montclair, NJ: Patterson Smith (originally published in 1930).

————. and N. K. Teeters. 1951. *New Horizons in Criminology*. Englewood Cliffs, N.J.: Prentice-Hall.

Bartlett, D. L., and J. B. Steele. 1992. *America: What Went Wrong?* Kansas City: Andrews and McMeel.

Bartollas, C. 1997. *Juvenile Deliquency* (5th ed.). Boston: Allyn and Bacon.

Bartollas, C. and S. J. Miller. 1998. *Juvenile Justice in America* (3rd ed.). Upper Saddle River, NJ: Prentice-Hall.

Bates, E. 1999. "CCA, the Sequel." *The Nation*, June 7: 22–23.

Baum, D. 1997. *Smoke and Mirrors: The War on Drugs and the Politics of Failure*. Boston: Little, Brown/Back Bay Books.

Baum, N., and B. Bedrick. 1994. *Trading Books for Bars: The Lopsided Funding Battle Between Prisons and Universities*. San Francisco: Center on Juvenile and Criminal Justice.

Baumer, E. 1994. "Poverty, Crack, and Crime: A Cross City Analysis." *Journal of Research in Crime and Delinquency*, 31: 311–327.

Beard, C. 1935. *An Economic Interpretation of the Constitution*. New York: Macmillan.

Beccaria, C. 1963. *On Crimes and Punishment*. New York: Bobbs-Merrill.

Beck, A. J., and P. M. Brien. 1995. "Trends in the U. S. Correctional Populations: Recent Findings from the Bureau of Justice Statistics." In K. C. Haas and G. P. Alpert (eds). *The Dilemmas of Corrections* (3rd ed.). Project Heights, IL: Waveland Press.

Becker, H. S. 1963. *Outsiders: Studies in the Sociology of Deviance*. New York: Free Press.

Bedau, H. (ed.) 1964. *The Death Penalty in America*. Garden City, NY: Doubleday.

Belenko, S. R. 1993. *Crack and the Evolution of the Anti-Drug Policy*. Gulfport, CT: Greenwood Press.

Belknap, J. 1996. *The Invisible Woman: Gender, Crime, and Justice*. Belmont, CA: Wadsworth.

Benekos, P., and A. V. Merlo. 1995. "Three Strikes and You're Out!: The Political Sentencing Game." *Federal Probation* 59: 3–9.

Benner, L. A., B. Neary, and R. M. Gutman. 1973. *The Other Face of Justice: A Report of the National Defender Survey*. Chicago: National Legal Aid and Defender Association.

Bennett, W. L. 1994. *Inside the System: Culture, Institutions, and Power in American Politics*. New York: Harcourt Brace.

Bernard, T. J. 1992. *The Cycle of Juvenile Justice*. New York: Oxford University Press.

Berrigan, P. 1970. *Prison Journals of a Priest Revolutionary*. New York: Holt, Rinebart & Winston.

Blackstock, N. 1975. *COINTELPRO: The FBI's Secret War on Political Freedom*. New York: Vintage Books.

Blakely, E. J., and M. G. Snyder. 1997. *Fortress America: Gated Communities in the United States*. Washington, DC: Brookings Institution Press.

Blauner, R. 1972. *Racial Oppression in America*. New York: Harper & Row.

Bluestone, B., and B. Harrison. 1982. *The Deindustrialization of America*. New York: Basic Books.

Bonczar, T. P. and A. J. Beck. 1997. *Lifetime Likelihood of Going to State or Federal Prison*. Washington, DC: U.S. Department of Justice.

Bordua, D. (ed.). 1967. *The Police: Six Sociological Essays*. New York: John Wiley.

Borosage, R., and J. Marks. 1976. *The CIA File*. New York: Grossman.

Bortner, M. A. 1982 *Inside a Juvenile Court: The Tarnished Idea of Individualized Justice*. New York: New York University Press, 1982.

Bottomore, T., L. Harris, V.G. Kiernan, and R. Miliband (eds.). 1983. *A Dictionary of*

Marxist Thought. Cambridge, MA: Harvard University Press.

Bowers, W. J. 1974. *Executions in America.* Lexington, MA: D.C. Heath.

Bowles, S. 1975. "Unequal Education and the Reproduction of the Social Division of Labor." In M. Carnoy (ed.). *Schooling in a Corporate Society.* New York: David McKay.

Boyle, J., and A. Gonzales. 1989. "Using Proactive Programs to Impact Gangs and Drugs." *Law and Order* 37: 62–64.

Brace, C. L. 1872. *The Dangerous Classes of New York.* New York: Wynkoop and Hallenbeck.

Brayson, C. 1996. "Crime Pays for Those in the Prison Business." *The National Times* (September): 28–35.

Breggin, P. R., and G. R. Breggin. 1998. *The War Against Children of Color.* Monroe, ME: Common Courage Press.

Bremner, R. H. (ed.). 1970. *Children and Youth in America.* Cambridge: Harvard University Press.

Brenzel, B. 1975. "Lancaster Industrial School for Girls: A Social Portrait of a Nineteenth Century Reform School for Girls." *Feminist Studies* 3: 40–53.

———. 1983. *Daughters of the State.* Cambridge: MIT Press.

Brown, D. 1971. *Bury My Heart at Wounded Knee.* New York: Holt, Rinehart, and Winston.

Brownstein, H. H. 1991. "The Media and the Construction of Random Drug Violence." *Social Justice.* 18: 85–103.

Burns, H. 1974. "Racism and American Law." In R. Quinney (ed.). *Criminal Justice in America.* Boston: Little, Brown.

———. 1990. "Law and Race in Early America." In D. Kairys (ed.). *The Politics of Law* (rev. ed.). New York: Pantheon Books.

Buss, D. 1996. "The Brave New World of Business Security." *Nation's Business,* May.

Bynum, T. 1982. "Release on Recognizance: Substantive or Superficial Reform?" *Criminology* 20: 67–82.

Cable, G. 1962. *The Silent South.* Montclair, NJ: Patterson Smith (originally published in 1888).

Cain, M. (ed.). 1989. *Growing Up Good: Policing the Behavior of Girls in Europe.* London: Sage.

Calavita, K., and H.N. Pontell. 1994. "The State and White Collar Crime: Saving the Savings and Loans." *Law and Society Review* 28: 297–324.

Campaign for an Effective Crime Policy. 1998. *"Three Strikes": Five Years Later.* Washington, DC: The Sentencing Project.

Carey, A. 1995. *Taking the Risk Out of Democracy.* Chicago: University of Illinois Press.

Carlson, T. 1995. "Safety Inc.: Private Cops Are There When You Need Them." *Policy Review* 73 (Summer): 66–72.

Center for Research on Criminal Justice. 1977. *The Iron Fist and the Velvet Glove* (2nd ed.). Berkeley: Center for Research on Criminal Justice.

Chambliss, W. J. (ed). 1969. *Crime and the Legal Process.* New York: McGraw-Hill.

———. 1975a. "The Law of Vagrancy." In W. S. Chambliss (ed.), *Criminal Law in Action.* New York: John Wiley.

———. 1975b. "Vice, Corruption, Bureaucracy, and Power." In Chambliss, *Criminal Law in Action.*

———. 1976. "Functional and Conflict Theories of Crime: the Heritage of Emile Durkheim and Karl Marx." In W. J. Chambliss and M. Mankoff (eds.). *Whose Law, What Order?* New York: John Wiley.

———. 1977. "Markets, Profits, Labor, and Smack." *Contemporary Crises* 1: 53–76.

————. 1989. "On Trashing Marxist Criminology." *Criminology* 27: 231–238.

————. 1993. "On Lawmaking" and "The Creation of American Law and Crime Control in Britain and America." In W. J. Chambliss and M. S. Zatz (eds.). *Making Law: The State The Law, and Structural Contradictions.* Bloomington, IN: Indiana University Press.

————. 1995. "Crime Control and Ethnic Minorities: Legitimizing Racial Oppression by Creating Moral Panics." In D. F. Hawkins (ed.), *Ethnicity, Race, and Crime.* Albany, NY: Suny Press.

————. 1999. *Power, Politics, and Crime.* Boulder, CO: Westview.

————. and T. E. Ryther. 1975. *Sociology: The Discipline and Its Direction.* New York: McGraw-Hill.

————. and R. Seidman. 1982. *Law, Order, and Power* (2nd ed.). Reading, MA: Addison-Wesley.

————. and T. F. Courtless. 1992. *Criminal Law, Criminology, and Criminal Justice.* Belmont, CA: Wadsworth.

Champion, D. 1989. "Teenage Felons and Waiver Hearings: Some Recent Trends, 1980–1988," *Crime and Delinquency* 33.

Chapin, B. 1983. *Criminal Justice in Colonial America: 1600–1660.* Athens, GA: University of Georgia Press.

————. 1996. *Provincial America: 1600–1763.* New York: Free Press.

Chesney-Lind, M. 1973. "Judicial Enforcement of the Female Sex Role: The Family, Court and the Female Delinquent." *Issues in Criminology* (Fall): 51–59.

————. 1997. *The Female Offender.* Thousand Oaks, CA: Sage.

————. and R. G. Shelden. 1998. *Girls, Delinquency, and Juvenile Justice* (2nd ed.). Belmont, CA: Wadsworth.

Cheyney, E. P. 1913. *An Introduction to the Industrial and Social History of England.* New York: Macmillan.

Chomsky, N. 1987. "On the Responsibility of Intellectuals." In E. Peck (ed.), *The Chomsky Reader.* New York: Pantheon Books.

————. 1988. *The Culture of Terrorism.* Boston: South End Press.

————. 1989. *Necessary Illusions: Thought Control in Democratic Societies.* Boston: South End Press.

. 1992. *Deterring Democracy.* New York: Hill and Wang.

————. 1993. *Year 501: The Conquest Continues.* Boston: South End Press.

————. 1994. *Keeping the Rabble in Line.* Monroe, ME: Common Courage Press.

————. 1996a. *Powers and Prospects.* Boston: South End Press.

————. 1996b. *Class Warfare.* Monroe, ME: Common Courage Press.

————. 1996c. " 'Consent Without Consent': Reflections on the Theory and Practice of Democracy." *Cleveland State Law Review* 44: 415–437.

————. 1998. *The Common Good.* Monroe, ME: Odonian Press/Common Courage Press.

————. 1999a. *Profit over People.* New York: Seven Stories Press.

————. 1999b. "Domestic Terrorism: Notes on the State System of Oppression." *New Political Science* 21: 303–324.

————. and E. S. Herman. 1979. *The Political Economy of Human Rights, Vol. I: The Washington Connection and Third World Fascism.* Boston: South End Press.

Chopra, D. 1994. *The Seven Spiritual Laws of Success.* San Rafael, CA: Amber-Allen.

Christie, N. 1993. *Crime Control as Industry: Toward Gulags, Western Style?* London: Routledge.

Churchill, W., and J. Vander Wall. 1988. *Agents of Repression.* Boston: South End Press.

————. 1990. *COINTELPRO Papers.* Boston: South End Press.

Clark, L. D. 1975. *The Grand Jury: The Use and Abuse of Political Power.* New York: Quadrangle.

Clarke, S. H. and G. G. Koch. 1976. "The Influence of Income and Other Factors on Whether Criminal Defendants Go to Prison." *Law and Society Review* 11: 57–92.

Cleeland, N. 1999. "Temps Become Full-Time Factor in Industry." *Los Angeles Times* (May 29, A1, A12).

Clinard, M. B., R. Quinney, and J. Wildeman. 1994. *Criminal Behavior Systems.* (3rd ed.) Cincinnati: Anderson.

Cohen, S. 1972. *Folk Devils and Moral Panics: The Creation of the Mods and Rockets.* London: MacGibbon and Kee.

Cohen, D. K., and M. Lazeron. 1972. "Education and the Corporate Order." In R. C. Edwards, M. Reich, and T. E. Weisskopf (eds.). *The Capitalist System.* Englewood Cliffs, NJ: Prentice Hall.

Cohen, L. E. 1975. *Delinquency Dispositions: An Empirical Analysis of Processing Decisions in Three Juvenile Courts.* Washington, DC: U.S. Department of Justice.

Coight, C. C. 1998. "5.7 Million under Correctional Supervision." *Overcrowded Times* 9 (October).

Cole, D. 1999. *No Equal Justice: Race and Class in the American Criminal Justice System.* New York: The New Press.

Collins, C. F. 1997. *The Imprisonment of African-American Women.* Jefferson, NC: McFarland.

Collins, C., and J. L. Askin-Steve. 1996. "The Islamic Gulag: Slavery Makes a Comeback in Sudan." *Utne Reader* (March–April).

Common Cause. 1995. "The Anti-Crime Business." *Common Cause Magazine.* Spring.

Conquest, R. 1995. "Playing Down the Gulag." *Times Literary Supplement* (February 24).

Cook, F. 1974. "Setting Up the Vets." In S. Weissman (ed.), *Big Brother and Holding Company: The World Behind Watergate.* Palo Alto, CA: Ramparts Press.

Cooley, C. H. 1974. "Nature v. Nurture in the Making of Social Careers." In F. Faust and B. Brantingham (eds.). *Juvenile Justice Philosophy.* St. Paul, MN: West.

Critchley, T. A. 1972. *A History of Police in England and Wales.* Montclair, NJ: Patterson Smith.

———. 1975. "The New Police in London, 1750–1830." In J. Skolnick and T. Gray (eds.), *Police in America.* Boston: Little, Brown.

Cronin, M. 1992. "Guilded Cages." *Time.* May 25.

Currie, E. 1993 *Reckoning: Drugs, the Cities, and the American Future.* New York: Hill and Wang.

———. 1998. *Crime and Punishment in America.* New York: Metropolitan Books.

Dailey, B. R. 1991. "Ann Hutchison." In E. Forner and J. A. Garraty (eds.). *A Reader's Companion to American History.* Boston: Houghton Mifflin.

Daly, K., and M. Chesney-Lind. 1988. "Feminism and Criminology." *Justice Quarterly* 5: 497–538.

Datesman, S., and F. Scarpitti. 1977. "Unequal Protection for Males and Females in the Juvenile Court." In T. N. Ferdinand (ed.). *Juvenile Delinquency: Little Brother Grows Up.* Newbury Park, CA: Sage.

Davis, M. 1992. *City of Quartz.* New York: Vintage.

deBeaumont, G., and A. de Tocqueville. 1964. *On the Penitentiary System in the United States and Its Application in France.* Carbondale, IL: Southern Illinois University Press (originally published 1833).

de Mause, L. (ed.). 1974. *The History of Childhood.* New York: Psychohistory Press.

de Tocqueville, A. 1961. *Democracy in America.* New York: Schoken.

Deloria, V. 1969. *Custer Died for Your Sins.* New York: Macmillan.

Derber, C. 1998. *Corporation Nation.* New York: St. Martins's Press.

Diamond, S. 1974. "The Rule of Law Versus the Order of Custom." In R. Quinney (ed.). *Criminal Justice in America: A Critical Understanding.* Boston: Little, Brown.

Dinnerstein, L., and D. M. Reimers. 1975. *Ethnic Americans: A History of Immigration and Assimilation.* New York: Harper & Row.

Ditton, J. 1977. "Perks, Pilferage, and the Fiddle: The Historical Structure of Invisible Wages." *Theory and Society* 4: 39–71.

Dobash, R. E., and R. Dobash. 1979. *Violence Against Wives.* New York: Free Press.

———, and S. Gutteridge. 1986. *The Imprisonment of Women.*New York: Basil and Blackwell.

Domhoff, G. W. 1979. *The Powers That Be.* New York: Random House.

———. 1990. *The Power Elite and the State.* New York: Aldine De Gruyter.

———. 1998. *Who Rules America? Power and Politics in the Year 2000.* Mountain View, CA: Mayfield.

Donner, F. J. 1980. *The Age of Surveillance.* New York: Knopf.

Donziger, S. 1996. *The Real War on Crime.* New York: Harper/Collins.

Dumaine, B. 1991. "New Weapons in the Crime War." *Fortune* 123 (11): 180–185.

Durkheim, E. 1947. *The Division of Labor in Society.* Glencoe, IL: The Free Press.

Duster, T. 1970. *The Legislation of Morality.* New York: Free Press.

Eastman, M. (translator and editor). 1959. *Capital, The Communist Manifesto and Other Writings.* New York: The Modern Library.

Eisenstein, Z. R. 1998. *The Female Body and the Law.* Berkeley: University of California Press.

Eitzen, D. S., and M. B. Zinn. 1998. *In Conflict and Order* (8th ed.) Boston: Allyn and Bacon.

Ekirch, A. R. 1987. *Bound for America.* New York: Oxford University Press.

Empey, L. T. 1982. *American Delinquency.* Homewood, IL: Dorsey Press.

Engles, F. 1972. *The Origin of the Family, Private Property, and the State.* New York: International Publishers.

Erickson, K. T. 1966. *Wayward Puritans.* New York: John Wiley.

Evans, S. M. 1989. *Born for Liberty: A History of Women in America.* New York: Free Press.

Ewen, S. 1976. *Captains of Consciousness: Advertising and the Social Roots of Consumer Culture.* New York: McGraw-Hill.

Faludi, S. 1991. *Backlash: The Undeclared War Against American Women.* New York: Anchor Books.

Farnham, A. 1992. "U.S. Suburbs Are Under Siege." *Fortune* 126 (14): 42–44.

Farrell, R. A., and V. L. Swigert. 1978. "Prior Offense Record as a Self-Fulfilling Prophecy." *Law and Society Review* 12: 437–453.

———. 1988. *Social Deviance* (3rd ed.). Belmont, CA: Wadsworth.

Feagin, J. R., and H. Vera. 1995. *White Racism.* New York: Routledge.

Federal Bureau of Investigation (FBI). 1998. *Uniform Crime Reports.* Washington, DC: U.S. Government Printing Office.

Feinman, C. 1980. *Women in the Criminal Justice System.* New York: Praeger.

Feld, B. 1999. "A Funny Thing Happened on the Way to the Centenary." *Punishment and Society* 1: 187–214.

Fellner, J. 1996. "Stark Racial Disparities Found in Georgia Drug Law Enforcement." *Overcrowded Times* 7, 5 (October).

Ferdinand, T. N. 1967. "The Criminal Patterns of Boston Since 1849." *American Journal of Sociology* 73: 84–99.

Finckenauer, J. O. 1984. *Juvenile Delinquency and Corrections.* New York: Academic Press.

Finder, A. 1999. "Jailed Until Found Not Guilty." *The New York Times,* June 6: 33–34.

Fitzgerald, K. 1994. "Gizmos Turn Home Protection into a Boom." *Advertising Age* 64: 51–52.

Flaherty, D. H. 1972. *Privacy in Colonial New England.* Charlottesville: University

Press of Virginia.

———. 1984. "Criminal Practice in Provincial Massachusetts." In D. R. Coquilette (ed.). *Law in Colonial Massachusetts, 1630–1800*. Boston: The Colonial Society of Massachusetts, distributed by the University Press of Virginia.

Folbre, N., and The Center for Popular Economics. 1995. *The New Field Guide to the U.S. Economy*. New York: The New Press.

Foote, C. 1954. "Compelling Appearance in Court: Administration of Bail in Philadelphia." *University of Pennsylvania Law Review* 102: 1031–1079.

Foucault, M. 1979. *Discipline and Punish: The Birth of the Prison*. New York: Vintage.

Freedman, E. B. 1981. *Their Sisters' Keepers: Women's Prison Reform in America, 1830–1930*. Ann Arbor, MI: University of Michigan Press.

Friedman, L. J. 1970. *The White Savage: Racial Fantasies in the Postbellum South*. Englewood Cliffs, NJ: Prentice Hall.

Friedman, L. M. 1973. *A History of American Law*. New York: Simon and Schuster.

———. 1993. *Crime and Punishment in American History*. New York: Basic Books.

Friedrichs, D. O. 1996. *Trusted Criminals: White Collar Crime in Contemporary Society*. Belmont, CA: Wadsworth.

Galliher, J. F., and J. L. McCartney (eds.). 1977. *Criminology: Power, Crime, and Criminal Law*. Homewood, IL: Dorsey Press.

Galliher, J. F., and B. E. Baum. 1977. "Nebraska's Marijuana Law: A Case of Unexpected Legislative Innovation." In Galliher and McCartney. *Criminology: Power, Crime, and Criminal Law*.

Gardiner, J. 1969. "Wincanton: The Politics of Corruption." In Chambliss, *Crime and the Legal Process*.

Garfinkel, H. 1949. "Research Note on Inter- and Intra-Racial Homicides." *Social Forces* 27: 369–381.

Garland, D. 1990. *Punishment and Modern Society: A Study in Social Theory*. Chicago: University of Chicago Press.

Garrow, D. J. 1981. *The FBI and Martin Luther King, Jr*. New York: Penguin Books.

Geis, G. 1964. "Sociology and Jurisprudence: Admixture of Lore and Law." *Kentucky Law Journal* 52: 267–293

———. 1996. "A Base on Balls for White Collar Criminals." In D. Shichor and D. K. Sechrest (eds.) *Three Strikes and You're Out: Vengeance as Public Policy*. Thousand Oaks, CA: Sage.

Genovese, E. 1976. *Roll, Jordan, Roll: The World the Slaves Made*. New York: Vintage Books.

Gibbons, D., and M. J. Griswold. 1957. "Sex Differences among Juvenile Court Referrals." *Sociology and Social Research* 42: 106–110.

Giddens, A. 1971. *Capitalism and Modern Social Theory*. New York: Cambridge University Press.

Gilbert, D. 1998. *The American Class Structure* (5th ed.). Belmont, CA: Wadsworth.

Gilliard, D. K. 1999. *Prison and Jail Inmates at Midyear 1998*. Washington, DC: Bureau of Justice Statistics.

———. and A. J. Beck. 1996. *Prison and Jail Inmates, 1995*. Washington, DC: Bureau of Justice Statistics.

Glassner, B. 1999. *The Culture of Fear*. New York: Basic Books.

Glick, H. R. 1983. *Courts, Politics, and Justice*. New York: McGraw-Hill.

Goffman, I. 1961. *Asylums*. New York: Doubleday.

Golden, R. 1997. *Disposable Youth: America's Child Welfare System*. Belmont, CA: Wadsworth.

Goldfarb, R. 1965. *Ransom: A Critique of the American Bail System*. New York: Harper and Row.

———. 1975. *Jails: The Ultimate Ghetto of the Criminal Justice System*. New York:

Doubleday.

Goldstein, H. 1990. *Problem-Oriented Policing*. New York: McGraw-Hill.

Goldstein, P. J., H. H. Brownstein, P. J. Ryan, and P. A. Bellucci. 1997. "Crack and Homicide in New York City: A Case Study in the Epidemiology of Violence." In C. Reinarman and H. G. Levine (eds.), *Crack in America: Demon Drugs and Social Justice*. Berkeley, CA: University of California Press.

Goode, E., and N. Ben-Yehuda. 1994. *Moral Panics: The Social Construction of Deviance*. Cambridge, MA: Blackwell

Gordon, D. 1994. *The Return of the Dangerous Classes: Drug Prohibition and Policy Politics*. New York: W. W. Norton.

Gordon, L. 1988. *Heroes in Their Own Lives*. New York: Viking.

Graham, J. M. 1977. "Amphetamine Politics on Capitol Hill." In Galliher and McCartney, *Criminology: Power, Crime, and Criminal Law*.

Greenberg, D. (ed.) 1993. *Crime and Capitalism* (2nd ed.). Philadelphia: Temple University Press.

Greenberg, D. 1974. *Crime and Law Enforcement in the Colony of New York, 1691–1776*. Ithaca: Cornell University Press.

Gross, S. R., and R. Mauro. 1989. *Death and Discrimination: Racial Disparities in Capital Sentencing*. Boston: Northeastern University Press.

Haber, S. 1964. *Efficiency and Uplift: Scientific Management in the Progressive Era, 1890–1920*. Chicago: University of Chicago Press.

Hall, J. 1969. "The Law of Theft: The Carrier's Case." In W. J. Chambliss (ed.), *Crime and the Legal Process*. New York: McGraw-Hill.

Hancock, L. 1981. "The Myth That Females Are Treated More Leniently Than Males in the Juvenile Justice System." *Australian and New Zealand Journal of Sociology* 16: 4–14.

Hanh, T. N. 1991. *Peace Is Every Step*. New York: Bantam Books.

Hanson, R., and J. Chapper. 1991. *Indigent Defense Systems: Report to the State Justice Institute*. Williamsburg, VA: National Center for State Courts.

Harring, S. 1976. "The Development of the Police Institution in the U.S." *Crime and Social Justice* 5: 54–59.

———. 1977. "Class Conflict and the Suppression of Tramps in Buffalo, 1892–1894." *Law and Society Review* 11, 5 (Summer).

———. 1978. "The 'Most Orderly City in America'; Class Conflict and the Development of the Police Institution in Milwaukee, 1880–1914." Paper presented at the American Sociological Association annual meeting. September.

———, and L. McMullen. 1975. "The Buffalo Police: Labor Unrest, Political Power, and the Creation of the Police Institution." *Crime and Social Justice* 4: 5–14.

Harris, J. R. 1997. "The Growth of the Gulag: Forced Labor in the Urals Region, 1929–1931." *The Russian Review* 56: 265–281.

Harris, M. 1978. *Cows, Pigs, Wars, and Witches: The Riddles of Culture*. New York: Vintage Books.

Haskins, G. L. 1960. *Law and Authority in Early Massachusetts*. New York: Macmillan.

———. 1969. "A Rule to Walk By." In R. Quinney (ed.), *Crime and Justice in Society*. Boston: Little, Brown.

Hawes, J. 1971. *Children in Urban Society*. New York: Oxford University Press.

Hawkins, D. F. (ed.). 1995. *Ethnicity, Race, and Crime*. New York: SUNY Press.

Hay, D. 1975. "Property, Authority, and the Criminal Law." In D. Hay, P. Linebaugh, J. G. Rule, E.P. Thompson, and C. Wilslow (eds.), *Albion's Fatal Tree: Crime and Society in Eighteenth-Century England*. New York: Pantheon.

Hays, S. P. 1959. *The Response to Industrialism, 1885–1914*. Chicago: University of Chicago Press.

Heilbroner, R. L. 1985. *The Nature and Logic of Capitalism*. New York: W.W. Norton.

Helmer, J. 1975. *Drugs and Minority Oppression.* New York: Seabury Press.

Henderson, C. R. 1974. "Relation of Philanthropy to Social Order and Progress." In Faust and Brantingham (eds.), *Juvenile Justice Philosophy.*

Hepburn, J. 1977. "Social Control and the Legal Order: Legitimate Repression in a Capitalist State." *Contemporary Crises* 1.

Herman, E., and N. Chomsky. 1988. *Manufacturing Consent.* New York: Pantheon.

Higginbotham, 1996. *Shades of Freedom: Racial Politics and Presumptions of American Legal Process.* New York: Oxford University Press.

Hindus, M. S. 1980. *Prison and Plantation: Crime, Justice, and Authority in Massachusetts and South Carolina, 1767–1878.* Chapel Hill, NC: University of North Carolina Press.

Hobbes, T. 1947. *Leviathan.* New York: Oxford University Press.

Hoebel, E. A. 1973. *The Law of Primitive Man.* New York: Atheneum Press.

Hofstadter, R. 1955. *Social Darwinism in American Thought.* Boston: Beacon Press.

Hogg, R. 1979. "Imprisonment and Society under Early British Capitalism." *Crime and Social Justice* 12.

Holmes, S. A. 1994. "Ranks of Inmates Reach One Million in a Two-Decade Rise." *New York Times,* October 28, p. A1.

Holt, M. I. 1992. *The Orphan Trains.* Lincoln, NE: University of Nebraska Press.

Huberman, L. 1963. *Man's Worldly Goods.* New York: Monthly Review Press.

Humphries, D., and D. Greenberg. 1993. "The Dialectics of Crime Control." In D.Greenberg *Crime and Capitalism* (rev. ed.). Philadelphia: Temple University Press.

Ichniowski, T. 1994. "Construction Industry Finds Crime Does Pay." *ENR News: McGraw-Hill Construction Weekly,* August 8.

Ignatieff, M. 1978. *A Just Measure of Pain.* New York: Pantheon.

Inciardi, J. A. 1975. *Careers in Crime.* Chicago: Rand McNally.

Irwin, J. 1980. *Prisons in Turmoil.* Boston: Little, Brown.

———. 1985. *The Jail: Managing the Underclass in American Society.* Berkeley: University of California Press.

Irwin, J., and J. Austin. 1997. *It's About Time: America's Imprisonment Binge* (2nd ed.). Belmont, CA: Wadsworth.

Ives, G. 1914. *History of Penal Methods.* London: Stanley Paul.

Jablon, R. 2000. "L.A. Prepares for Worst as Police Scandal Grows." *Associated Press,* February 19.

Jackson, B. (ed.) 1984. *Law and Order: Criminal Justice in America.* Chicago: University of Illinois Press.

Jackson, P. 1992. "Minority Group Threat, Social Context, and Policing." In A. E. Liska (ed.), *Social Threat and Social Control.* Albany, NY: State University of New York Press.

Jankowski, M. S. 1991. *Islands in the Street: Gangs and American Urban Society.* Berkeley, CA: University of California Press.

Jeffery, C. R. 1969. "The Development of Crime in Early English Society." In W. J. Chambliss (ed.), *Crime and the Legal Process.* New York: McGraw-Hill.

Jenkins, P. 1994. " 'The Ice Age,' the Social Construction of a Drug Panic." *Justice Quarterly,* 11: 7–31.,

Johnson, B. D., A. Golub, and J. Fagan. 1995. "Careers in Crack, Drug Use, Drug Distribution, and Non-Drug Criminality." *Crime and Delinquency* 41: 275–295.

Johnson, C. S. 1930. *The Negro in American Civilization.* New York: Henry Holt.

Johnson, E. H. 1957. "Selective Factors in Capital Punishment." *Social Forces* 36: 165–169.

Johnson, G. B. 1941. "The Negro and Crime." *The Annals* 217: 93–104.

Johnson, H. A., and N. T. Wolfe. 1996. *History of Criminal Justice* (2nd ed.). Cincinnati, OH: Anderson Publishing.

Josephson, M. 1962. *The Robber Barons.* New York: Harcourt Brace Jovanovich.

Kalmanoff, A. 1976. *Criminal Justice: Enforcement and Administration.* Boston: Little, Brown.

Karlsen, C. F. 1987. *The Devil in the Shape of a Woman.* New York: W. W. Norton.

Kelly, M. 1975. "The First Urban Policeman." In G. F. Killinger and P. Cromwell (eds.), *Issues in Law Enforcement.* Boston: Holbrook Press.

Kelly, R. M. 1976. "Increasing Community Influence over the Police." In A. W. Cohn and E. C. Viano (eds.), *Police Community Relations.* Philadelphia: Lippincott.

Kempf, K. 1992. *The Role of Race in Juvenile Justice Processing in Pennsylvania.* Harrisburg, PA: Pennsylvania Commission on Crime and Delinquency.

Kennedy, R. 1997. *Race, Crime, and the Law.* New York: Vintage.

Kett, J. F. 1977. *Rites of Passage: Adolescence in America, 1790 to the Present.* New York: Basic Books.

Killinger, G. F., and P. Cromwell (eds.). 1973. *Penology.* St. Paul, MN: West.

————.(eds.). 1975. *Issues in Law Enforcement.* Boston: Holbrook Press.

Klein, M. 1995. *The American Street Gang.* New York: Oxford University Press.

————, C. Maxson, and L. Cunningham. 1991. "Crack, Street Gangs, and Violence." *Criminology* 29: 623–650.

Knapp Commission. 1975. "Police Corruption in New York." In Skolnick and Gray, *Police in America.*

Knappman, E. W. 1994. *Great American Trials: From Salem Witchcraft to Rodney King.* Detroit, MI: Visible Ink Press.

Kolko, G. 1963. *The Triumph of Conservatism: A Reinterpretation of American History, 1900–1916.* New York: Free Press.

Krisberg, B., and J. Austin. 1978. *The Children of Ishmael: Critical Perspectives on Juvenile Justice.* Palo Alto, CA: Mayfield.

————. 1993. *Reinventing Juvenile Justice.* Newbury Park, CA: Sage.

Lane, R. 1967. *Policing the City: Boston, 1822–1885.* Cambridge: Harvard University Press.

Langbein, J. H. 1983. "Albion's Fatal Flaws." *Past and Present* 98: 96–120.

Lasswell, H. 1930. "Propaganda." *Encyclopedia of the Social Sciences.* New York: Macmillian.

Laursen, E. 1996. "A Tale of Two Communities." *Z Magazine* (October): 45–50.

Leong, A. 1998. "From Bruce Lee to Vincent Chin: Stereotyping in Anti-Asian Violence." Paper presented at the Northeastern Association of Criminal Justice. Newport, RI. June.

Lerner, G. 1986. *The Creation of Patriarchy.* New York: Oxford University Press.

Lerner, S. 1986. *Bodily Harm: The Pattern of Fear and Violence at the California Youth Authority.* Bolinas, CA: Common Knowledge Press.

Leslie, R. J. 1977. "The Alliances of the CIA to Political and Underworld Figures." Seminar paper, Department of Sociology-Anthropology, SUNY-Cortland.

Levinthal, C. 1996. *Drugs, Behavior, and Modern Society.* Boston: Allyn & Bacon.

Lewis, A. 1964. *Gideon's Trumpet.* New York: Harper & Row.

Liazos, A. 1974. "Class Oppression: The Functions of Juvenile Justice." *Insurgent Sociologist* (Fall).

Lilly, J. 1993. "Great Leader's Gulag: Siberian Timber Camps Are Relics of the Cold War." *Far Eastern Economic Review* (September 9): 21–22.

Lilly, J. R., and P. Knepper. 1993. "The Correctional-Commercial Complex." *Crime and Delinquency* 39: 150–166.

Lindesmith, A. R. 1965. *The Addict and the Law.* New York: Vintage Books.

Linebaugh, P. 1975. "The Tyburn Riot Against the Surgeons." In D. Hay et al. (eds.), *Albion's Fatal Tree.*

———. 1976. "Karl Marx , the Theft of Wood, and Working Class Composition: A Contribution to the Current Debate." *Crime and Social Justice* 6: 5–16.

———. 1985. "(Marxist) Social History and (Conservative) Legal History: A Reply to Professor Langbein." *New York University Law Review* 60: 212–243.

Link, A. 1967. *American Epoch: A History of the U.S. Since the 1890s* (3rd ed.). New York: Alfred A. Knopf.

Lipsitz, G. 1982. *Class and Culture in Cold War America.* South Hadley, MA: J. F. Bergin.

Litvan, L. M. 1995. "Security for Success." *Nation's Business* 83 (6), June, p. 15.

Lockwood, D., A. E. Pottieger, and J. A. Inciardi. 1995. "Crack Use, Crime by Crack Users, and Ethnicity." In D. F. Hawkins (ed.), *Ethnicity, Race, and Crime.* Albany, NY: SUNY Press.

Lorde, A. 1988. "Age, Race, Class, and Sex: Women Redefining Difference." In P. S. Rothenberg (ed.), *Racism and Sexism: An Integrated Study.* New York: St. Martin's Press.

Los Angeles Times. 1984. "South Central Sales Explode into $25 'Rocks.'" November 25.

———. 2000. "Outside Probe Sought in LAPD Scandal." February 11.

Lubove, R. 1965. *The Professional Altruist: The Emergence of Social Work as a Career, 1880–1930.* Cambridge. MA: Harvard University Press.

Lyman, J. L. 1975. "The Metropolitan Police Act of 1829." In Killinger and Cromwell.

Lynch, M. J., and W. B. Groves. 1989. *A Primer on Radical Criminology* (2nd ed.). Albany, NY: Harrow and Heston.

Maas, P. 1975. "Serpico: The Cop Who Defied the System." In Skolnick and Gray, *Police in America.*

Mackey, P. E. 1982. *Hanging in the Balance: The Anti-Capital Punishment Movement in New York State, 1776–1861.* New York: Garland Press.

MacKinnon, C. 1989. *Toward a Feminist Theory of the State.* Cambridge: Harvard University Press.

Madison, J. 1961. "No. 10: Madison." In A. Hamilton, J. Madison, and J. Jay (eds.), *The Federalist Papers.* New York: Mentor.

Maguire, K., and A. L. Pastore (eds). 1995. *Sourcebook on Criminal Justice Statistics—1994.* Washington, DC: Department of Justice, Bureau of Justice Statistics.

———. 1996. *Sourcebook on Criminal Justice Statistics—1995.* Washington, DC: Department of Justice, Bureau of Justice Statistics.

———. 1997. *Sourcebook on Criminal Justice Statistics—1996.* Washington, DC: Department of Justice, Bureau of Justice Statistics.

———. 1998. *Sourcebook of Criminal Justice Statistics— 1997.* Washington, DC: U.S. Department of Justice.

———. 1999. *Sourcebook of Criminal Justice Statistics—1998.* Washington DC: U.S. Department of Justice.

Mancini, M. J. 1978. "Race, Economics, and the Abandonment of Convict Leasing." *Journal of Negro History* 63.

Mann, A. (ed.). 1963. *The Progressive Era: Renaissance or Liberal Failure.* New York: Holt, Rinehart and Winston.

Mann, C. R. 1995. *Unequal Justice: A Question of Color.* Bloomington, IN: Indiana University Press.

Marchetti, V., and J. D. Marks. 1974. *The CIA and the Cult of Intelligence.* New York: Dell.

Marx, K. 1975. "Debates on the Law of the Theft of Wood." In Marx and Engles, *Collected Works.*

———. 1977. *Capital* (Vol. 1). 1977. New York: Vintage Books.

———. 1988. *The Economic and Philosophic Manuscripts of 1844.* Buffalo, NY:

Prometheus Books.

———. 1993. "The Usefulness of Crime." In Greenberg, David (ed.), *Crime and Capitalism* (rev. ed.). Philadelphia: Temple University Press.

———, and F. Engels. 1955. *The Communist Manifesto.* Arlington Heights, IL: Crofts Classics.

———. 1975. *Collected Works* (Vol. 1). New York: International Publishers.

Massey, D. S., and N. A. Denton. 1963. *American Apartheid: Segregation and the Making of the Underclass.* Cambridge: Harvard University Press.

Mauer, M. 1994. *Americans Behind Bars: The International Use of Incarceration, 1992–1993.* Washington, DC: The Sentencing Project.

———. 1995. *Young Black Americans and the Criminal Justice System: Five Years Later.* Washington, DC: the Sentencing Project.

———. 1997. "Racial Disparities in Prison Getting Worse in the 1990s." *Overcrowded Times* 8, 1 (February).

May, D. 1977. "Delinquent Girls Before the Court." *Medical Science Law Review* 17: 203–210.

Mays, G. L., and L. T. Winfree, Jr. 1998. *Contemporary Corrections.* Belmont, CA: Wadsworth.

McConville, S. 1998. "Local Justice: The Jail." In N. Morris and D. J. Rothman (eds.), *The Oxford History of the Prison.* New York: Oxford University Press..

McCoy, A. W. 1973. *The Politics of Heroin in Southeast Asia.* New York: Harper & Row.

McDonald, W. F. (ed.) 1979. *The Prosecutor.* Beverly Hills, CA: Sage.

McGarrell, E. F., and T. J. Flanagan (eds.). 1986. *Sourcebook of Criminal Justice Statistics–1985.* Washington, DC: U.S. Department of Justice.

McGarrell, E. 1993. "Trends in Racial Disproportionality in Juvenile Court Processing: 1985–1989." *Crime and Delinquency* 39: 29–48.

McHenry, R. (ed.). 1983. *Famous American Women: A Biographical Dictionary from Colonial Times to the Present.* New York: Dover Publications.

McKelvey, B. 1968. *American Prisons.* Montclair, NJ: Patterson Smith (originally published 1936).

McKirdy, C. R.. 1984. "Massachusetts Lawyers on the Eve of the American Revolution: The State of the Profession." In D. R. Coquilette (ed.), *Law in Colonial Massachusetts, 1630–1800.* Boston: The Colonial Society of Massachusetts, distributed by the University Press of Virginia.

Meddis, S. V., and D. Sharp. 1994. "Prison Business Is a Blockbuster." *USA Today,* December 13: 10A.

Meier, A., and E. Rudwick. 1970. *From Plantation to Ghetto.* New York: Hill & Wang.

Melossi, D. 1978. Review of *Punishment and Social Structure.* By G. Rusche and O. Kirchheimer. *Crime and Social Justice* 9.

———, and M. Lettiere. 1998. "Punishment in the American Democracy: The Paradoxes of Good Intentions." In R. P. Weiss and N. South (eds.), *Comparing Prison Systems: Toward a Comparative and International Penology.* Australia: Gordon and Breach.

Mennel, R. 1973. *Thorns and Thistles: Juvenile Delinquents in the U.S., 1820–1940.* Hanover, NH: University Press of New England.

Mergenbagen, P. 1996. "The Prison Population Bomb." *American Demographics* 18: 6–42.

Merry, S. E. 1990. *Getting Justice and Getting Even: Legal Consciousness among Working Class Americans.* Chicago: University of Chicago Press.

Messerschmidt, J. W. 1987. "Feminism, Criminology, and the Rise of the Female Sex Delinquent, 1880–1930." *Contemporary Crises* 11: 243–263.

———. 1997. *Crime as Structured Action: Gender, Race, Class, and Crime in the Making.* Thousand Oaks, CA: Sage.

Michalowksi, R. 1985. *Order, Law, and Crime.* New York: Macmillan.

Miliband, R. 1969. *The State in Capitalist Society.* New York: Basic Books.

Miller, E. 1986. *Street Woman.* Philadelphia: Temple University Press.

Miller, J. G. 1996. *Search and Destroy: African-American Males in the Criminal Justice System.* New York: Cambridge University Press.

———. 1998. *Last One over the Wall* (2nd ed.). Columbus: Ohio State University Press.

Miller, M. B. 1974. "At Hard Labor: Rediscovering the 19th-Century Prison." *Issues in Criminology* 9: 91–114.

Millman, J. 1991. "Captive Market." *Forbes* 148, 6, p. 190.

Mills, C. W. 1959. *The Sociological Imagination.* New York: Oxford University Press.

Milovanovic, D. 1994. *A Primer in the Sociology of Law.* New York: Harrow and Heston.

Miringoff, M., and M. Miringoff. 1999. *The Social Health of the Nation.* New York: Oxford University Press.

Mokhiber, R. 1996. "Corporate Crime: Underworld U.S.A." In K. Danaher (ed.), *Corporations are Gonna Get Your Mama: Globalization and the Downsizing of the American Dream.* Monroe, ME: Common Courage Press.

Monkkonen, E. 1975. *The Dangerous Class: Crime and Poverty in Columbus, Ohio, 1860–1885.* Columbus: Ohio State University Press.

Moore, J. 1991. *Going Down to the Barrio.* Philadelphia: Temple University Press.

Morash, M. A., and E. A. Anderson. 1978. "Liberal Thinking on Rehabilitation: A Workable Solution to Crime." *Social Problems* 25: 556–563.

Morgan, E. S. 1958. *The Puritan Dilemma: The Story of John Winthrop.* Boston: Little, Brown and Company.

Morris, N., and D. J. Rothman (eds.) 1995. *The Oxford History of the Prison.* New York: Oxford University Press.

Moyer, I. L. 1992. "Police/Citizen Encounters: Issues of Chivalry, Gender, and Race." In I. L. Moyer (ed.), *The Changing Roles of Women in the Criminal Justice System* (2nd ed.). Prospect Heights, IL: Waveland Press.

Munk, N. 1994. "Rent-A-Cops." *Forbes* 154 (8): 104–105.

Murray, C. 1994. *Losing Ground: American Social Policy, 1950–1980.* New York: Basic Books.

Murray, J. B. 1986. "An Overview of Cocaine Use and Abuse." *Psychological Reports:* 243–264.

Murton, T., and J. Hyams. 1969. *Accomplices to the Crime: The Arkansas Prison Scandal.* New York: Grove Press.

Musto, D. F. 1973. *The American Disease: Origins of Narcotic Control.* New Haven, CT: Yale University Press.

Myers, M. A., and J. L. Massey. 1999. "Race, Labor, and Punishment in Postbellum Georgia." In Weiss, *Social History of Crime, Policing, and Punishment.*

Nadel, B. 1995. "Putting a Lock on Prison Costs." *American City and County* 110 (1).

Naffine, N. 1987. *Female Crime: The Construction of Women in Criminology.* Sydney, Australia: Allen and Unwin.

National Commission on Law Observance and Enforcement. 1931. *Lawlessness in Law Enforcement.* Washington, DC: U. S. Government Printing Office.

Nelson, W. E. 1974. "Emerging Nations of Modern Criminal Law in the Revolutionary Era: An Historical Perspective." In R. Quinney (ed), *Criminal Justice in America: A Critical Understanding.* Boston: Little, Brown.

———. 1975. *The Americanization of Common Law.* Cambridge, MA: Harvard University Press.

Neubauer, D. W. 1996. *America's Courts and the Criminal Justice System* (5th ed.). Belmont, CA: Wadsworth Publishing Company.

Newsweek. 1988. "Crack, the Drug Crisis: Hour by Hour Crack." November 28.

New York Times. 1989a. "Crack—A Disaster of Historic Dimensions." May 28, p. E14.

New York Times. 1989b. "The Spreading Web of Crack." October 2, p. 2.

New York Times. 1989c. "Crack, Bane of Inner City Is Now Gripping Suburbs." October 1, p. A1.

Nohn, H. 1976. "The Hughes, Nixon, Lansky Connection." *Rolling Stone,* May 20.

Nye, R. 1951. *Midwestern Progressive Politics.* East Lansing: Michigan State University Press.

O'Connor, J. 1973. *The Fiscal Crisis of the State.* New York: St. Martin's Press.

Odem, M. 1995. *Delinquent Daughters: Protecting and Policing Adolescent Female Sexuality in the United States, 1885–1920.* Chapel Hill: University of North Carolina Press.

———, and S. Schlossman. 1991. "Guardians of Virtue: The Juvenile Court and Female Delinquency in Early 20th-Century Los Angeles." *Crime and Delinquency* 37: 186–203.

Osgood, R. K. 1984. "John Clark, Esq., Justice of the Peace, 1667–1728." In Coquillette, *Law in Colonial Massachusetts.*

Parenti, C. 1995. "Inside Jobs: Use of Prison Labor in the U.S." *New Statesman and Society* 8: 20–21.

———. 1996. "Pay Now, Pay Later: States Impose Prison Peonage." *The Progressive* 60 (7): 26–29.

Parenti, M. 1993. *Against Empire.* San Francisco: City Light Books.

———. 1994. *Land of Idols: Political Mythology in America.* New York: St. Martin's Press.

Parks, E. L. 1977. "From Constabulary to Police Society: Implications for Social Control." In Galliher and McCartney, *Criminology: Power, Crime, and Criminal Law.*

Pasqualini, J. 1993. "Glimpses Inside China's Gulag." *The China Quarterly* 134: 352–358.

Patterson, E. B., and M. J. Lynch. 1991. "Biases in Formalized Bail Procedures." In M. J. Lynch and E. B. Patterson (eds.), *Race and Criminal Justice.* New York: Harrow and Heston.

"People v. Turner." 1974. In Faust and Brantingham, *Juvenile Justice Philosophy.*

Peterson, R. D. 1988. "Youthful Offender Designations and Sentencing in the New York Criminal Courts." *Social Problems* 35.

Pfohl, S. 1994. *Images of Deviance and Social Control: A Sociological History.* New York: McGraw-Hill.

Phillips, K. 1990. *The Politics of the Rich and the Poor.* New York: Random House.

Pickett, R. 1969. *House of Refuge.* Syracuse: Syracuse University Press.

Piliavin, I., and S. Briar. "Police Encounters with Juveniles." *American Journal of Sociology* 70: 206–214.

Pisciotta, A. 1982. "Saving the Children: The Promise and Practice of *Parens Patriae,* 1838–98." *Crime and Delinquency* 28: 410–425.

———. 1983. "Race, Sex, and Rehabilitation: A Study of Differential Treatment in the Juvenile Reformatory, 1825–1900." *Crime and Delinquency* 29: 254–268.

———. 1994. *Benevolent Repression: Social Control and the American Reformatory-Prison Movement.* New York: New York University Press.

Piven, F. F., and R. Cloward. 1972. *Regulating the Poor: The Functions of Social Welfare.* New York: Vintage Books.

Platt, A. 1974. "The Triumph of Benevolence: Origins of Juvenile Justice in the U.S." In R. Quinney (ed.), *Criminal Justice in America: A Critical Understanding.* Boston: Little, Brown.

————. 1977. *The Child Savers* (rev. ed.). Chicago: University of Chicago Press.

Poggi, G. 1978. *The Development of the Modern State.* Palo Alto, CA: Stanford University Press.

Pollock, J. M. 1996. "Gender, Justice, and Social Control: A Historical Perspective." In A. V. Merlo and J. M. Pollock (eds.), *Women, Law, and Social Control.* New York: Allyn and Bacon.

Pope, C., and W. Feyerherm. 1990. "Minority Status and Juvenile Justice Processing: An Assessment of the Research Literature." (Parts I and II). *Criminal Justice Abstracts* 22 (2, 3).

Postman, N. 1994. *The Disappearance of Childhood.* New York: Vintage.

Pound, R. 1922. *An Introduction to the Philosophy of Law.* New Haven: Yale University Press

————. 1942. *Social Control through Law.* New Haven: Yale University Press.

Poveda, T.G. 1994. *Rethinking White Collar Crime.* Westport, CT: Praeger.

Powell, J. C. 1891. *The American Siberia.* Chicago: H.J. Smith.

Powers, E. 1966. *Crime and Punishment in Early Massachusetts.* Boston: Beacon Press.

President's Commission on Law Enforcement and Administration of Justice. 1967a. *Task Force Report: Science and Technology.* Washington, DC: U.S. Government Printing Office.

————. 1967b. *Task Force Report: The Police.* Washington, DC: U.S. Government Printing Office.

Proband, S. C. 1997a. "Black Men Face 29 Percent Lifetime Chance of Prison." *Overcrowded Times* 8, 1.

————. 1997b. "Jail and Prison Populations Continue to Grow in 1996." *Overcrowded Times* 8, 4.

————. 1998a. "Corrections Populations Near 6 Million." *Overcrowded Times* 9 (June).

————. 1998b. "Prison Populations Up 5.2 Percent in U.S. in 1997." *Overcrowded Times* 9, 4.

Quinney, R. (ed.) 1969. *Crime and Justice in Society.* Boston: Little, Brown.

————. 1970. *The Social Reality of Crime.* Boston: Little, Brown.

————. 1974. *Critique of Legal Order: Crime Control in Capitalist Society.* Boston: Little, Brown.

————. 1979. *Criminology.* Boston: Little, Brown.

————. 1980. *Class, State, and Crime* (2nd ed.). New York: Longman.

————. 1995. "Socialist Humanism and the Problem of Crime: Thinking About Erich Fromm in the Development of Critical/Peacemaking Criminology." Unpublished manuscript, Northern Illinois University.

————. 1998. *For the Time Being.* New York. SUNY Press.

Quinney, R., and J. Wildeman. 1991. *The Problem of Crime: A Peace and Social Justice Perspective* (3rd ed.). Mountain View, CA: Mayfield.

Radelet, L. A. 1977. *The Police and the Community,* 2nd ed. Beverly Hills, CA: Glencoe Press.

Radelet, M. L. 1981. "Racial Characteristics and the Imposition of the Death Penalty." *American Sociological Review* 46: 918–927.

————, H. A. Bedau, and C. E. Putnam. 1992. *In Spite of Innocence.* Boston: Northeastern University Press.

Rafter, N. H. (ed.). 1988. *White Trash: The Eugenic Family Studies, 1899–1919.* Boston: Northeastern University Press.

————. 1990. *Partial Justice: Women, Prisons, and Social Control.* (2nd ed.). New Brunswick, NJ: Transaction Books.

————. 1997. *Creating Born Criminals.* Chicago: University of Illinois Press.

————, and E. A. Stanko (eds.). 1982. *Judge, Lawyer, Victim, Thief: Women, Gender*

Roles, and Criminal Justice. Boston: Northeastern University Press.

Rawson, R.A. 1990. "Cut the Crack: The Policymaker's Guide to Cocaine Treatment." *Policy Review* 11 (Winter).

Reaves, B. A. 1998. *Felony Defendants in Large Urban Counties, 1994.* Washington, DC: U.S. Department of Justice, Bureau of Justice Statistics.

Redfield, J. 1993. *The Celestine Prophecy.* New York: Warner Books.

Reiman, J. H. 1998. *The Rich Get Richer and the Poor Get Prison* (5th ed.). Boston: Allyn and Bacon.

Reinarman, C., and H. G. Levine. 1997a. "Crack in Context." In Reinarman and Levine, *Crack in America.*

———. 1997b. "The Crack Attack: Politics and Media in America's Latest Drug Scare." In Reinarman and Levine, *Crack in America.*

Reith, C. 1975. *The Blind Eye of History: A Study of the Origins of the Present Police Era.* Montclair, NJ: Patterson Smith (originally published in 1952).

Rendleman, D. 1974. "Parens Patriae: From Chancery to Juvenile Court." In F. Faust and P. Brantingham (eds.), *Juvenile Justice Philosophy.* St. Paul, MN: West.

Richards, S. 1990. "Commentary: Sociological Penetration of the American Gulag." *Wisconsin Sociologist* 27: 18–28.

Richardson, J. F. 1974. *Urban Police in the U.S.* Port Washington, NY: Kennikat Press.

———. 1975. "The Early Years of the New York Police Department." In J. Skolnick and T. Gray (eds.). *Police in America.* Boston: Little, Brown.

Ritzer, G. 1996. *The McDonalization of Society* (revised ed.). Thousand Oaks, CA: Pine Forge Press.

Rogers, K. 1972. " 'For Her Own Protection': Conditions of Incarceration for Female Juvenile Offenders in the State of Connecticut." *Law and Society Review:* 223–246.

Rossides, D. W. 1997. *Social Stratification: The Interplay of Class, Race, and Gender* (2nd ed.). Upper Saddle River, NJ: Prentice-Hall.

Rothman, D. 1971. *The Discovery of the Asylum.* Boston: Little, Brown.

———. 1980. *Conscience and Convenience: The Asylum and Its Alternatives in Progressive America.* Boston: Little, Brown.

———. 1998. "Perfecting the Prison." In Morris and Rothman, *The Oxford History of the Prison.*

Rothman, R. 1998. *Social Inequality* (2nd ed.). Upper Saddle River, NJ: Prentice-Hall.

Rothman, S. 1978. *Woman's Proper Place: A History of Changing Ideals and Practices, 1870 to the Present.* New York: Basic Books.

Rotman, E. 1998. "The Failure of Reform: United States, 1865–1965." In Morris and Rothman, *The Oxford History of the Prison.*

Ruigrok, W., and R. van Tulder. 1995. *The Logic of International Restructuring.* London: Rutledge.

Rusche, G., and O. Kirchheimer. 1968. *Punishment and Social Structure.* New York: Russell and Russell (originally published in 1938).

Rush, G. E. 1994. *The Dictionary of Criminal Justice.* The Duskin Publishing Group.

Rush, G. E. 1997. *Inside American Prison and Jails.* Incline Village, NV: Copperhouse Publishing.

Sabol, W. J. 1989. "Racially Disproportionate Prison Population in the United States." *Contemporary Crises* 13: 405–432.

Samaha, J. 1999. *Criminal Procedure* (4th ed.). Belmont, CA: Wadsworth.

Sampson, R. J. 1986. "SES and Official Reaction to Delinquency." *American Sociological Review* 51: 876–885.

Schiraldi, V. 1994. *The Undue Influence of California's Prison Guards' Union: California's*

Correctional-Industrial Complex. Center on Juvenile and Criminal Justice.

———, and J. Zeidenberg. 1999. *The Punishing Decade: Prison and Jail Estimates at the Millennium.* Washington, DC: Justice Policy Institute.

Schlosser, E. 1998. "The Prison-Industrial Complex." *The Atlantic Monthly* (December).

Schlossman, S. 1977. *Love and the American Delinquent: The Theory and Practice of "Progressive" Juvenile Justice, 1825–1920.* Chicago: University of Chicago Press.

———, and S. Wallach. 1978. "The Crime of Precocious Sexuality: Female Delinquency in the Progressive Era." *Harvard Educational Review* 8: 65–94.

Schmidhauser, J. R. 1960. *The Supreme Court: Its Politics, Personalities and Procedures.* New York: Holt, Rinehart and Winston.

Schorr, L. 1989. *Within Our Reach: Breaking the Cycle of Disadvantage.* New York: Anchor.

Schwartz, B. 1993. *A History of the Supreme Court.* New York: Oxford University Press.

Schwendinger, H., and J. Schwendinger. 1976. "Delinquency and the Collective Varieties of Youth." *Crime and Social Justice* 5 (Spring–Summer).

Seagal, D. 1993. "Tales from the Cutting-Room Floor: The Reality of 'Reality-Based' Television." *Harper's Magazine,* November.

Sellin, J. T. 1944. *Pioneering in Penology: The Amsterdam Houses of Correction in the Sixteenth and Seventeenth Centuries.* Philadelphia: University of Pennsylvania Press.

———. (ed.) 1967. *Capital Punishment.* New York: Harper and Row.

———. 1976. *Slavery and the Penal System.* New York: Elsevier.

Semmes, R. 1970.*Crime and Punishment in Early Maryland.* Montclair, NJ: Patterson Smith.

Server, A. 1994. "Crime Stoppers Making a Killing." *Fortune* 129 (7): 109–111.

Shank, G. 1978. Review of "Pioneering in Penology" and "Slavery and the Penal System" by J. T. Sellin. *Crime and Social Justice* 10: 36–52.

Shannon, R. T. (ed). 1896. *Code of Tennessee.* Nashville: Marshall and Bruce.

Shapiro, I., and R. Greenstein. 1997. "Trends in the Distribution of After-Tax Income: An Analysis of Congressional Budget Office Data." Center on Budget and Policy Priorities, Washington, DC, August 14.

Shaw, A. G. L. 1966. *Convicts and the Colonies.* London: Faber and Faber.

Shearing, C. D., and P. C. Stenning. 1987. "Reframing Policing." In C. D. Shearing and P. C. Stenning (eds.), *Private Policing.* Newbury Park, CA: Sage.

Shelden, R. G. 1976. "Rescued from Evil; Origins of the Juvenile Justice System in Memphis, Tennessee, 1900–1917." Ph.D. dissertation, Southern Illinois University, Carbondale.

———. 1980. "From Slave to Caste Society: Penal Changes in Tennessee, 1840–1915." *Tennessee Historical Quarterly* 38: 462–478.

———. 1981. "Sex Discrimination in the Juvenile Justice System: Memphis, Tennessee, 1900–1917." In M. Q. Warren (ed.), *Comparing Male and Female Offenders.* Newbury Park, CA: Sage.

———. 1982. *Criminal Justice in America: A Sociological Approach.* Boston: Little, Brown.

———. 1992. "A History of the Shelby County Industrial and Training School." *Tennessee Historical Quarterly* (Summer): 96–106.

———. 1993a. "Origins of the Memphis Juvenile Court." *Tennessee Historical Quarterly* 52:33–43.

———. 1993b. "Convict Leasing." In Greenberg, *Crime and Capitalism.*

———. 1998. "Confronting the Ghost of Mary Ann Crouse: Gender Bias in the Juvenile Justice System." *Juvenile and Family Court Journal* 49: 11–26.

———, and W. Brown. 1997. "The Crime Control Industry and the Management of the Surplus Population." Paper presented at the Western Society of Criminology annual meeting, February.

———, and L. T. Osborne. 1989. "'For Their Own Good': Class Interests and the Child-Saving Movement in Memphis, Tennessee, 1900–1917." *Criminology* 27: 801–821.

———, S. Tracy, and W. Brown. 1997. *Youth Gangs in American Society*. Belmont, CA: Wadsworth.

Sherman, L. W., L. Steele, D. Lauferweiler, N. Hoffer, and S. A. Julian. 1989. "Stray Bullets and Mushrooms, Random Shooting of Bystanders in Four Cities, 1987–1988." *Journal of Quantitative Criminology* 5: 297–316.

Shichor, D., and D. K. Sechrest (eds.). 1996 *Three Strikes and You're Out: Vengeance as Public Policy*. Thousand Oaks, CA: Sage.

Sidel, R. 1992. *Keeping Women and Children Last*. New York: Penguin.

Siegel, L. 1997. "The Pregnancy Police Fight the War on Drugs." In Reinarman and Levine, *Crack in America*.

Silver, A. 1967. "The Demand for Order in Civil Society." In D. Bordua (ed.), *The Police: Six Sociological Essays*. New York: John Wiley.

Simon, J. 1993. *Poor Discipline: Parole and the Social Control of the Underclass, 1890–1990*. Chicago: University of Chicago Press.

Sklar, H. 1998. "Let Them Eat Cake." *Z Magazine* (November).

———. 1999. "For CEOs, a Minimum Wage in the Millions." *Z Magazine* (July/August).

Skolnick, J. 1994. *Justice Without Trial* (3rd ed.). New York: Macmillan.

———, and T. Gray (eds.). 1975. *Police in America*. Boston: Little, Brown.

———, and D. H. Bayley. 1986. *The New Blue Line: Police Innovation in Six American Cities*. New York: Free Press.

Smart, C. 1976. *Women, Crime, and Criminology: A Feminist Critique*. London: Routledge and Kegan Paul.

Smelser, N. J. 1973. *Karl Marx on Society and Social Change*. Chicago: University of Chicago Press.

Smith, A. 1976. *The Wealth of Nations*. Oxford: Clarendon Press.

Sokoloff, N. J., and B. R. Price (eds.). 1995. *The Criminal Justice System and Women* (2nd ed.). New York: McGraw-Hill

Solzhenitsyn, A. 1970. *The Gulag Archipelago*. New York: Bantam Books.

Spitzer, S. 1975. "Toward a Marxian Theory of Deviance." *Social Problems* 22: 638–651.

———. 1993. "The Political Economy of Policing." In Greenberg, *Crime and Capitalism*.

———, and A. T. Scull. 1977. "Privatization and Capitalist Development: The Case of Private Police." *Social Problems* 25.

Spring, J. 1972. *Education and the Rise of the Corporate State*. Boston: Little, Brown.

Stabile, C. A. 1995. "Feminism without Guarantees: The Misalliances and Missed Alliances of Postmodernist Social Theory." In A. Callari, S. Cullenberg, and C. Biewener (eds.), *Marxism in the Postmodern Age*. New York: Gulliford Press.

Staples, W. G. 1997. *The Culture of Surveillance: Discipline and Social Control in the United States*. New York: St. Martin's Press.

Starkey, M. L. 1949. *The Devil in Massachusetts: A Modern Inquiry into the Salem Witch Trials*. Garden City, NJ: Doubleday and Company.

State Task Force on Youth Gang Violence. 1986. *Final Report*. Sacramento, CA: California Council on Criminal Justice.

Sternberg, D. 1974. "The New Radical-Criminal Trials: A Step Toward a Class-for-Itself in the American Proletariat." In Quinney (ed.), *Criminal Justice in America*.

Stoddard, E. R. 1975. "The Informal 'Code' of Police Deviancy." In Skolnick and

Gray, *Police in America.*

Stone, L. 1969. "Literacy and Education in England, 1640–1900." *Past and Present* 42 (February).

Sudnow, D. 1965. "Normal Crimes: Sociological Features of the Penal Code in a Public Defender Office." *Social Problems* 12: 255–276.

Sutton, J. R. 1988. *Stubborn Children: Controlling Delinquency in the United States, 1640–1981.* Berkeley: University of California Press.

Swisher, K., C. Wekesser, and W. Barbour (eds). 1994. *Violence Against Women.* San Diego, CA: Greenhaven Press.

Tabb, W. 1970. *The Political Economy of the Black Ghetto.* New York: W.W. Norton.

Takagi, P. 1975. "The Walnut Street Jail: A Penal Reform to Centralize the Powers of the State." *Federal Probation* (December): 18–26.

Tannenbaum, F. 1933. *Osborne of Sing Sing.* Chapel, NC: University of North Carolina Press.

Tappan, P. 1947. *Delinquent Girls in Court.* New York: Columbia University Press.

Taylor, C. S. 1990. *Dangerous Society.* East Lansing, MI: Michigan State University Press.

Taylor, A. A. 1941. *The Negro in Tennessee, 1865–1880.* Washington, DC: Associated Publishers.

Teitelbaum, L. E., and L. J. Harris. 1977. "Some Historical Perspectives on Governmental Regulation of Children and Parents." In *Beyond Control: Status Offenders in the Juvenile Court,* edited by L. E. Teitelbaum and A. R. Gough. Cambridge, MA: Ballinger.

Tennessee Board of Prison Commissioners, *Report to the Governor* (annual and biennial reports). Nashville, 1896–1914.

Terkel, G. 1996. *Law and Society: Critical Approaches.* Boston: Allyn and Bacon.

Thomas, P. 1994. "Making Crime Pay: Triangle of Interests Creates Infrastructure to Fight Lawlessness." *Wall Street Journal,* May 12: A1, A6.

Thornberry, T. P. 1973 "Race, Socioeconomic Status and Sentencing in the Juvenile Justice System." *Journal of Criminal Law and Criminology* 64: 90–98.

Thrasher, F. 1927. *The Gang.* Chicago: University of Chicago Press.

Tigar, M. E., and M. R. Levy. 1977. *Law and the Rise of Capitalism.* New York: Monthly Review Press.

Time. 1988. "Where the War is Being Lost." March 14.

Tipple, J. 1970. *The Capitalist Revolution.* New York: Pegasus.

Tolles, F. B. 1971. "Mary Dyer." in E. T., James, J. W. James, and P. S. Boyer (eds.), *Notable American Women, 1906–1950.* Cambridge, MA: Belknap Press of Harvard University Press.

Tonry, M. 1995. *Malign Neglect: Race, Crime, and Punishment in America.* New York: Oxford University Press.

———. 1998. "Crime and Punishment in America, 1971–1996." *Overcrowded Times* 9, 2 (April).

Trueblood, D. 1999. "Crack as Moral Panic: The Racial Implications Inherent to Crack and Powder Cocaine Sentencing." Masters thesis, Department of Criminal Justice, UNLV.

U.S. Census Bureau. 1918. *Prisoners and Juvenile Delinquents in the U.S., 1910.* Washington, DC: U.S. Government Printing Office.

U.S. Department of Commerce, Bureau of the Census. 1995. *Statistical Abstract of the United States, 1995.* Washington, DC: U.S. Government Printing Office.

U.S. Sentencing Commission. 1995. *Cocaine and Federal Sentencing Policy, Special Report to Congress.* Washington, DC: U. S. Government Printing Office.

Vago, S. 1997. *Law and Society* (5th ed.). Upper Saddle River, NJ: Prentice Hall.

Vedder, C. B., and D. B. Sommerville. 1970. *The Delinquent Girl.* Springfield, IL: Charles C. Thomas.

Visher, C. A. 1983. "Gender, Police Arrest Decisions, and Notions of Chivalry." *Criminology* 21:5–28.

Walker, S. 1980. *Popular Justice: A History of American Criminal Justice.* New York: Oxford University Press.

———. 1994. *Sense and Nonsense about Crime and Drugs* (4th ed.). Belmont, CA: Wadsworth.

———. 1998. *Popular Justice: A History of American Criminal Justice* (2nd ed.). New York: Oxford University Press.

———, C. Spohn, and M. DeLone. 1996. *The Color of Justice: Race, Ethnicity, and Crime in America.* Belmont, CA: Wadsworth.

———, C. Spohn, and M. DeLone. 2000. *The Color of Justice: Race, Ethnicity, and Crime in America* (2nd ed.). Belmont, CA: Wadsworth.

Wambaugh, J. 1972. *The Blue Knight.* New York: Dell.

Washington Post. 1989. "Drug Buy Setup for Bush Speech: DEA Lured Seller to Lafayette Park." September 22, p. A1.

———. 2000. "LAPD Corruption Case Keeps Growing." February 13.

Watterson, K. 1996. *Women in Prison: Inside the Concrete Womb.* Boston: Northeastern University Press.

Weber, M. 1946. *From Max Weber: Essays in Sociology* (translated by H. H. Gerth and C. W. Mills). New York: Oxford University Press.

Webb, G. 1998. *Dark Alliance.* New York: Seven Stories Press.

Weinberg, D. H. 1996. "A Brief Look at Postwar U.S. Income Inequality." *Current Population Reports: Household Economic Studies, U.S. Census Bureau* (P60–191, June)

Weiss, R. P. 1978. "The Emergence and Transformation of Private Detective Industrial Policing in the United States, 1850–1940." *Crime and Social Justice* 9: 35–48.

———. 1983. "Radical Criminology: A Recent Development." In E. H. Johnson (ed.). *International Handbook of Contemporary Developments in Criminology,* Vol. 1. Westport, CT: Guilford Press.

———. 1987a. "Humanitarianism, Labour Exploitation, or Social Control? A Critical Survey of Theory and Research on the Origin and Development of Prisons." *Social History* 12: 331–350.

———. 1987b. "From 'Slugging Detectives' to 'Labor Relations': Policing Labor at Ford, 1930–1947." In Shearing and Stenning, *Private Policing.*

———. (ed.). 1999a. *Social History of Crime, Policing, and Punishment.* Brookfield, VT: Ashgate.

———. 1999b. "Conclusion: Imprisonment at the Millennium 2000—Its Variety and Patterns Throughout the World." In R. P. Weiss and N. South (eds.), *Comparing Prison Systems: Toward a Comparative and International Penology.* Amsterdam: Gordon and Breach.

Whitt, J. A. 1993. "Toward a Class-Dialectical Model of Power: An Empirical Assessment of Three Competing Models of Political Power." In Chambliss and Zatz, *Making Law.*

Wice, P. B. 1985. *Chaos in the Courthouuse: The Inner Workings of the Urban Criminal Courts.* New York: Praeger.

Wiebe, R. 1967. *The Search for Order, 1877–1920.* New York: Hill and Wang.

Wienstein, J. 1968. *The Corporate Ideal in the Liberal State, 1900–1918.* Boston: Little, Brown.

Wilbanks, W. 1986. "Are Female Felons Treated More Leniently by the Criminal Justice System?" *Justice Quarterly* 3: 517–529.

Williams, W. A. 1988. *The Contours of American History*. New York: W. W. Norton.

Wilson, J. Q., and G. L. Kelling. 1989. "Making Neighborhoods Safe." *Atlantic Monthly* (February): 46–52.

Wilson, V., Jr. 1974. *The Book of the Founding Fathers*. Brookeville, MD: American Historical Research Associates.

Wilson, W. J. 1987. *The Truly Disadvantaged*. Chicago: University of Chicago Press.

Wines, E. C., and T. Dwight. 1973. *Report on the Prisons and Reformatories of the United States and Canada*. New York: AMS Press (originally published in 1867).

Wolff, E. 1994. "Trends in Household Wealth in the United States, 1962–83 and 1983–98." *Review of Income and Wealth* (Series 40, No. 2), June.

———. 1995. *Top Heavy: A Study of Increasing Inequality of Wealth in America*. New York: The Twentieth Century Fund Press.

Wolfgang, M., and M. Riedel. 1975. "Race, Judicial Discretion, and the Death Penalty." In W. J. Chambliss (ed.), *Criminal Law in Action*. New York: John Wiley.

———, A. Kelly, and H. C. Nolde. 1962. "Comparisons of the Executed and the Commuted Among Admissions to Death Row." In M. E. Wolfgang, L. Savitz, and N. Johnston (eds.), *The Sociology of Punishment and Correction*. New York: John Wiley.

Woodward, C. V. 1955. *The Strange Career of Jim Crow*. New York: Oxford University Press.

———. 1969. *Origins of the New South, 1877–1913*. Baton Rouge: Louisiana State University Press.

Worden, A. P. 1991. "Privatizing Due Process: Issues in the Comparison of Assigned Counsel, Public Defender, and Conracted Indigent Defense System." *Justice System Journal* 14: 390–419.

———. 1993. "Counsel for the Poor: An Evaluation of Contracting for Indigent Criminal Defense." *Justice Quarterly* 10: 613–637.

Wright, E. O. 1998. *Class Counts*. New York: Cambridge University Press.

Wu, C. (ed.). 1972. *Chink: Anti-Chinese Prejudice in America*. New York: World.

Wu, H. 1996. "The Need to Restrain China." *Journal of International Affairs* 49: 355–360.

Zalman, M., and L. Siegel. 1994. *Cases and Comments on Criminal Procedure*. St. Paul: West.

Zepezauer, M. 1994. *The CIA's Greatest Hits*. Tuscon, AZ: Odonian Press.

Zimring, F. E., and G. Hawkins. 1991. "What Kind of Drug War?" *Social Justice* 18: 104–121.

Zinn, H. 1990. *The Politics of History* (2nd ed.). Urbana, IL: University of Illinois Press.

———. 1994. *You Can't Be Neutral on a Moving Train: A Personal History of Our Times*. Boston: Beacon Press.

———. 1995. *A People's History of the United States* (2nd ed.). New York: Harper Collins.

———. 1997. *The Zinn Reader: Writings on Disobedience and Democracy*. New York: Seven Stories Press.

Name Index

Subject Index